"With the need for mental health services, at an all-time high, this book comes at the right time. This is not only a book for school counselors, but also for administrators as they develop their team to better envelope the whole child. Administrative Leaders and School Counselors: Building on Theory, Standards, and Experiences for Optimal Mental Health Collaboration is a must read for future school counselors and those that lead them."

Dr. Don Beck, *Ed.D., Superintendent Marion ISD*

"Administrative Leaders and School Counselors: Building on Theory, Standards, and Experiences for Optimal Mental Health Collaboration provides an exceptional roadmap filled with evidenced-based resources, relevant information from experts in the field and equips administrative leaders and counselors with the tools necessary to create a system that embraces the plate on which all education rests, student mental wellness. As a former Director of Student Services, professional school counselor and licensed clinician, I highly recommend this book as go-to resource for both administrative leaders and school counselors."

Dr. Jennifer Roberts, *Ed.D., LPC-S, CSC, Regional Director for HOPE Squad*

Administrative Leaders and School Counselors

This practice-based text offers a roadmap to optimal collaboration for all school leaders – including counselors, superintendents, principals, and university faculty – to provide the best mental health outcomes for students.

Administrative Leaders and School Counselors is a timely publication that creatively and cohesively authenticates the relationship between administrative leaders and school counselors. In order to systemically promote mental health consciousness and considerations for school counselors as practitioners and in training, collaboration among school leaders is essential for comprehensive school counseling programs, practices, funding, partnerships, and services designed for students. The first to feature perspectives from a diverse set of leadership positions in schools, the book provides individuals with exposure to educational leadership models and decisions that impact the roles of school counselors.

The book will appeal to faculty who are teaching and training those who are or will ultimately be working as professional school counselors, counseling psychologists, or educational leaders such as principals, directors, department chairs, and superintendents.

Lisa A. Wines, Ph.D., LPC-S, CSC, is a professor at Prairie View A & M University and CEO of L & A Professional Services, LLC in Texas.

Judy A. Nelson, Ph.D., LPC-S, CSC, is the sole proprietor of Nelson Consulting in Tucson, Arizona.

Natalie Fikac, Ed.D., CSC, SMART, CTDLF, is the owner, CEO, and lead consultant at Wellness First Consulting in Texas.

Administrative Leaders and School Counselors
Building on Theories, Standards, and Experiences for Optimal Mental Health Collaboration

Edited by Lisa A. Wines, Judy A. Nelson, and Natalie Fikac

NEW YORK AND LONDON

Cover image: © Getty Images

First published 2024
by Routledge
605 Third Avenue, New York, NY 10158

and by Routledge
4 Park Square, Milton Park, Abingdon, Oxon, OX14 4RN

Routledge is an imprint of the Taylor & Francis Group, an informa business

© 2024 selection and editorial matter, Lisa A. Wines, Judy A. Nelson and Natalie Fikac; individual chapters, the contributors

The right of Lisa A. Wines, Judy A. Nelson and Natalie Fikac to be identified as the authors of the editorial material, and of the authors for their individual chapters, has been asserted in accordance with sections 77 and 78 of the Copyright, Designs and Patents Act 1988.

All rights reserved. No part of this book may be reprinted or reproduced or utilized in any form or by any electronic, mechanical, or other means, now known or hereafter invented, including photocopying and recording, or in any information storage or retrieval system, without permission in writing from the publishers.

Trademark notice: Product or corporate names may be trademarks or registered trademarks, and are used only for identification and explanation without intent to infringe.

Library of Congress Cataloguing-in-Publication Data
Names: Wines, Lisa A., editor. | Nelson, Judy A., editor. | Fikac, Natalie, editor.
Title: Administrative leaders and school counselors : building on theory, standards, and experiences for optimal mental health collaboration / edited by Lisa A. Wines, Ph.D., LPC-S, CSC, Judy A. Nelson, Ph.D., LPC-S, CSC, and Natalie Fikac, Ed.D., CSC, SMART, CDTLF.
Description: First edition. | New York : Routledge, 2024. | Includes bibliographical references and index. |
Identifiers: LCCN 2023014236 (print) | LCCN 2023014237 (ebook) | ISBN 9781032113999 (hbk) | ISBN 9781032114019 (pbk) | ISBN 9781003219750 (ebk)
Subjects: LCSH: Educational leadership--United States--Psychological aspects. | Students--Mental health--United States. | School psychologists--In-service training--United States. | Student counselors--In-service training--United States. | Group work in education--United States.
Classification: LCC LB2806 .A295 2024 (print) | LCC LB2806 (ebook) | DDC 371.2/0110973--dc23/eng/20230714
LC record available at https://lccn.loc.gov/2023014236
LC ebook record available at https://lccn.loc.gov/2023014237

ISBN: 978-1-032-11399-9 (hbk)
ISBN: 978-1-032-11401-9 (pbk)
ISBN: 978-1-003-21975-0 (ebk)

DOI: 10.4324/9781003219750

Typeset in Times New Roman
by MPS Limited, Dehradun

Access the Support Material: www.routledge.com/9781032113999

This book is a culmination of the resounding need for all contributors to combine our personal, professional, and technical brilliance, which are orchestrated by GOD, who is present in all things, everywhere! As a result of a purposeful path and plan made for me (Jeremiah 29:11), I can thank many along the way who are deserving, but in no way do I think they were placed there by accident. Mom, it is so good to have a best friend who, at the same time, parented me. Dad, there is much you have shared with me about life, and those teachings are peppered-in throughout this text. Son, I am proud that you are *so humane*. Just know that all references made in this book safely transfers to any field of study you are called within to serve. To my past and present administrative leaders, along with mentors (Hi Judy), thank you for the intended and unintended lessons that fire this publication. To the school district leaders who I know and with whom I network, collaborate, and consult, thank you for the trust and choice to operate with me under an unspoken code-of-honour. To the school-aged students, graduate students, and interns to whom I have been assigned over the years, there is no this (the book) without that (you). TOGETHER, let us keep reconfiguring our educational systems to meet the mental health needs of all – on both a personal (vertical) and systemic level (horizontal)!

Lisa A. Wines

My personal dedication goes to my parents, Kathryn (1928–2020) and Edwin (1926–2022) Goss, who shaped me into the woman and leader that I am today. They exposed me to the world through travel, to rich ideas through literature, to intellectual challenges through education, to a spiritual life through church, and to fun and intimacy through family activities. My parents never lectured me on what I should do or how to behave. I simply watched them and saw what they did and how they behaved. I watched their work ethic, their commitment to their communities, their generosity of time and talent, and the satisfaction they gleaned from leading a good life. Thank you, Mom and Dad!

Judy A. Nelson

My personal dedication goes to every professional school counselor (PSC) and PSC leader that I have been honored to support and walk alongside in my educational journey. Professional school counselors serve and support our most vulnerable, and work tirelessly to do what is best for all students in their school communities. I have worked with and learned from the best of the best. PSCs are both the heartbeat and the glue of the campus, and the leaders who support PSCs are the champions of the behind the scenes work that allow PSCs to be seen and heard. A special heartfelt hug to each and every HADoG (Houston Area Director of Guidance and Counseling) for ALL that you do! Love and hugs to you all!

Natalie K. Fikac

Contents

List of Figures and Tables	*xii*
About the Editors	*xiv*
List of Contributors	*xvi*
Foreword	*xxii*
Preface	*xxiv*
Acknowledgements	*xxvi*

SECTION I
Incorporating a Foundation of Mental Health in School Counseling — 1

1 Mental and Behavioral Health in Schools — 3
JUDY A. NELSON, LISA A. WINES, AND NATALIE FIKAC

2 School Counselors' Perspective of Mental Health in Schools — 16
CHENDA T. MOORE

3 Promoting Positive Mental Health in Changing Times — 31
LORRY ROYAL

4 Restorative Practices that Support Student Mental Health Concerns — 46
CHRISTINA SHAW

SECTION II
Integrating Mental Health in the Development and Training of School Counselors — 57

5 Leadership Models for School Counselors to Promote Mental Health — 59
SANDY BENAVIDEZ AND NATALIE FIKAC

6 Training School Counselors in Graduate Programs to be Mental Health Conscious — 70
JUDY A. NELSON AND LISA A. WINES

7 Student Development and Performance in Academics, Intrapersonal, and Dispositions for School Counselors-in-Training to Address Mental Health Needs 85
LISA A. WINES

8 Dynamic School Counselor Professional Development Focusing on Continuous Mental Health Education 121
NATALIE FIKAC

9 Site Supervision and Mentorship: Practices that Influence Positive Mental Health in Schools 134
SANDY BENAVIDEZ AND KIMBERLY MCGOUGH

SECTION III
Examining Mental Health Expertise in the Hiring and Retention of Highly Qualified School Counselors 143

10 Character and Disposition as Necessary Measures of Success for School Counselors as Mental Health Professionals 145
JENI JANEK

11 What Directors Need to Know about the Comprehensive School Counseling Programs that Support Student Mental Health 153
JENNIFER AKINS

12 Interviewing and Placement of School Counselors to Include Mental Health Practices 169
AMY CMAIDALKA, LAURIE RODRIGUEZ, AND CARLA VOELKEL

13 Creating and Maintaining the Best School Counseling Team for Mental Health and Wellness 183
MONYA CROW AND JILL ADAMS

SECTION IV
Developing, Designing, Implementing, and Evaluating Comprehensive School Counseling Programs Utilizing a Mental Health Perspective 193

14 Managing Programs that Support Mental Health 195
TISHA KOLEK

15 Mental Health Considerations for District and School Level Crisis Prevention, Intervention, and Postvention Plans 205
BENNY MALONE

16 Data Collection and Analysis Supporting Systemic Approaches to Mental Health 230
ERNEST COX

17	Accountability Measures for Positive Mental Health LOREE MUNRO	254
18	Utilizing Budgets, Grants, Donations, and Financial Audits to Support Mental Health SERETHA J. AUGUSTINE AND JUDY A. NELSON	264
19	Partnerships that Streamline Mental Health Services in Schools CARLETE METOYER	274

SECTION V
Professional Advocacy to Ensure Mental Health Services for All Students — 285

20	School Counselors Advocating for Mental Health Practices LESLEY CASAREZ	287
21	Administrative Leaders and School Counselors Advocating for Supporting Mental Health in Their Programs SUMMER MARTIN	302

Index — *328*

Figures and Tables

Figures

1.1	Administrator Leadership Model Infused with Counselor Attributes	8
2.1	Five Steps to Promote and Support Mental Health Needs of Students	20
3.1	Solutions to Ethical Problems in Schools (STEPS)	38
7.1	Essential Governing Values, Staples, and Principles of Student Development	91
7.2	Plagiarism Process/Chart	98
7.3	Stage Review for School Counselor Kokoro Development	103
16.1	Pyramid for Comprehensive School Counseling Services	240
16.2	Time on Task	245
16.3	Monthly Time Analysis and Data Check-In	246
16.4	Services Provided by Elementary PSCs	250
19.1	Addressing Ethical Issues	282
19.2	Partnership Timelines	284

Tables

1.1	Typical and Preferred Models	4
1.2	Administrator and Counselor Roles	6
4.1	The Seven Critical Cs	50
7.1	School Counseling Student Infraction or Incident Types	92
7.2	Written Format Sanctions	94
7.3	Participatory-Format Sanctions	95
7.4	Technological-Format Sanctions	96
7.5	Literary-Format Sanctions	96
7.6	Culminating-Format Sanctions	97
8.1	Criteria for Award-Winning School Counseling Programs	122
8.2	Counseling Awareness Events or Topics	128
15.1	Large Scale Disasters and Crisis Events with Potential Impact on US Schools 2001 to 2020	206
15.2	Counselor Knowledge of Risk Factors for Suicide in Students	216
15.3	Percentage of Valid Child Abuse Reports by Type of Abuse	218
15.4	Inclusion of Certain National Standards in School Crisis Plans for Students and Staff: Comparison by District Size	222
16.1	Historic and Developmental Data	231

16.2	Examples of Appropriate Activities for School Counselors (ASCA, 2012)	236
16.3	Examples of Inappropriate Activities for School Counselors (ASCA, 2012)	237
17.1	Crosswalk of School Accountability Measures and ASCA Standards and Competencies	256
18.1	Example Local Allocations	265
19.1	Impact of Partnerships	276
20.1	Advocacy Calendar	294
21.1	Shared School Leadership Advocacy Standards and Skills among Superintendents, Principals, and School Counselors	306

About the Editors

Lisa A. Wines, Ph.D., LPC-S, CSC, is a tenured, Full Professor at Prairie View A & M University. She has served as lecturer/adjunct faculty for the University of Houston in the Psychological Learning Sciences Department and Sam Houston State University Counselor Education Department. She has worked in university settings since 2003 and has studied abroad in both undergraduate and doctoral-level programming (Mexico and Costa Rica). She developed a study-abroad program for counselors-in-training at Texas A & M University, Corpus Christi, along with having taught and worked with school counselors abroad in Saint Lucia, located in the Caribbean. Dr. Wines holds credentials as a Licensed Professional Counselor Supervisor and a Certified School Counselor for the state of Texas. As a Certified Yoga Teacher, she often infuses holistic practices and whole body awareness in teaching, therapy, and training services. She was recently accepted into an Ayurvedic Health Counselor program, with emphasis on mind–body–spirit connections. She is the founder and Chief Executive Officer for L & A Professional Services, LLC, The Center for Healing, Therapy, and Wellness, located in the Montgomery County area. She has developed and administered multiple expressive alternative therapy treatment protocols, in addition to utilizing other holistic practitioners to whom patients are referred, whereas applications of transformational and functional medicine are applied. In her practice, she often engages in the supervision, training, professional speaking, and the development of graduate students and licensed professional counselor associates in her Hands-of-Grace Intern Program.

Judy A. Nelson, Ph.D., LPC-S, CSC, is a retired teacher, professional school counselor, counselor educator, and therapist in private practice. Currently she is a licensed professional counselor and supervisor in the state of Arizona and the sole proprietor of Nelson Consulting located in Tucson, Arizona. Through her company, she presents workshops and training in school districts and at universities, provides outside evaluations for grants, organizes assessments and surveys for school districts and other entities, and consults with organizations that are interested in systemic change. Throughout her career in the field of counseling, Dr. Nelson was honored by her peers in a variety of ways. She was the president of the Texas Counseling Association, the secretary of that organization, and a Board member. She was the recipient of the following awards: the *Counseling Outcomes, Research, and Evaluation* Visibility Article of the Year Award, the Texas Counseling Association

Service Award over several years, the Texas Counseling Association Research Award, the Sam Houston State University College of Education Research Award and Service Award, the International Association of Addiction and Offender Counselors (IAAOC) Outstanding Professional Award, the Briggs-Pine *Association of Spiritual, Ethical, and Religious Values in Counseling* Award, and she was the Texas School Counselor of the Year. Dr. Nelson is the co-editor of 2 other books published by Routledge: *School Counselors as Practitioners: Building on Theory, Standards, and Experience for Optimal Performance* and *Responding to Critical Cases in School Counseling: Building on Theory, Standards, and Experience for Optimal Interventions.*

Natalie Fikac, Ed.D., CSC, SMART, CDTLF, is a passionate leader who has served the field of education for over 27 years as a teacher, reading interventionist, professional school counselor at both the elementary and secondary level, and campus and district level administrator. She holds a master's degree in school counseling and administration and a doctorate in educational leadership. In her most recent LEA experience, she served as the Director of Guidance & Counseling, supporting 85 professional school counselors and leading the district crisis team. Dr. Fikac has also served at the Texas Education Agency on the mental and behavioral health team and has supported school mental health at the regional level at the South Southwest MHTTC at the University of Texas Austin. She currently adjuncts in the School Counseling Program at Liberty University and Angelo State University and lives by the motto "You can't pour from an empty cup" aspiring to promote self-presentation and self-compassion in all areas of her life. She is passionate about growing leaders and learners hoping to be able to educate and advocate at a variety of levels on behalf of students and families in the areas of leadership, mental and behavioral health, social-emotional needs, and overall wellness and resiliency. Over the past 26 years, she has presented at numerous conferences and workshops at the local, state, and national levels, delivering training to professional school counselors, counselors, and administrators. She is also a Mindful Self-Compassion teacher and a Certified Dare to Lead™ Facilitator trained by Dr. Brené Brown and has trained over 800 leaders across the globe.

List of Contributors

Jill Adams, M.Ed., has served in the educational field for over 20 years. She started her career as a classroom teacher and completed her master's degree in counseling in 2006. For the past 17 years, she has served as a middle school and high school counselor and most recently as the Director of Counseling and Social work for Lewisville ISD. She has been a presenter at several state conferences and is currently the President Elect of Texas School Counselor Association, has served on the board for the past 5 years and is a Trust Based Relational Intervention (TBRI©) practitioner. Jill also serves as an educational and leadership consultant with Monya Crow through Power of the Pair LLC which provides consulting services to school districts across the nation.

Jennifer Akins, M.Ed., is a Certified School Counselor (CSC) and a Licensed Professional Counselor (LPC). Akins holds a M.Ed. in school counseling from Dallas Baptist University, as well as bachelor's degrees in neuroscience and in psychology from the University of Texas at Dallas. Akins currently serves as the Senior Director of Guidance and Counseling in McKinney ISD, a district of approximately 24,000 students in Texas. Akins also has a small private practice where she provides CBT for individuals, couples, and families.

Seretha J. Augustine, Ed.D., earned her doctorate degree in ethical leadership from University of St. Thomas-Houston, a master's degree in counseling from Prairie View A & M University, and a bachelor's degree in accounting from University of Houston-Downtown. She holds additional certifications from the Texas Education Board in Mathematics, Counseling, and Principal Leadership. She is currently the Senior Director for Student Support Services in Galena Park Independent School District. She is charged with supervising and supporting all district counselors and high school registrars. She has been an educator for 26 years and enjoys serving her current counseling team. She is passionate about the field of counseling which shows in her dedication to help and support her district counselors to be equipped with the resources and tools needed to be successful for their students.

Sandy Benavidez, Ed.D., CSC, works as the Director of Guidance and Counseling for Keller ISD. She is responsible for serving 35,000 students in the district. Before moving to Keller ISD, Dr. Benavidez worked at Region 10 and 11 Education Service Center and was responsible for massive programming efforts in the areas of mental health, school counseling, and school safety. In this capacity she served 1.4 million students across 300 school districts. Dr. Benavidez is an executive board member at the All Things Made New (ATMN) non-profit organization, where she oversees all mental health initiatives.

Lesley Casarez, Ph.D., CSC, is the Education Specialist for Counseling and Mental Health at Education Service Center Region 15. Her accomplishments include numerous scholarly presentations and several publications. Prior to coming to her current position, she was on the faculty at Angelo State University and worked as a public school counselor and teacher. Dr. Casarez completed her Ph.D. in Educational Psychology at Texas Tech University and holds degrees from Sul Ross State University, Texas State University, and the University of Texas at Austin.

Amy Cmaidalka, M.Ed., PSC, has been in education for 18 years. Amy has been a kindergarten teacher, a professional school counselor, and is currently a social emotional learning specialist. Prior to her current position, Amy was the lead counselor for elementary through middle school and the lead section 504 coordinator for the district. Amy earned her master's and bachelor's degrees from the University of Houston-Clear Lake. Amy is implementing a Gator Wellness Initiative for Dickinson ISD. This initiative is a social emotional learning model that focuses on early childhood, students, staff, and the community. She is passionate about advocating for professional school counselors, mental health, trauma informed practices, and self-wellness.

Ernest Cox Jr, Ph.D., NCC, CSC, is a School Counselor Consultant and Director of Counseling and Wellness. He has 20 years of experience in public, private, independent, and higher education serving in multiple capacities including counselor educator and supervisor, director of counseling, and professional school counselor (all levels). He has served as a task force member who rewrote *Texas Model for Comprehensive School Counseling Programs*, 5th edition, and a co-chair for the *Texas Evaluation for Professional School Counselors*, 3rd edition, Task Force. He has served the profession on the Texas School Counselor Association and Texas Association for Counselor Education and Supervision boards as President, Past-President, Director of Guidance and Counseling at Large, and Vice-President of Counselor Education and Supervision. He is the recipient of the TARCA Public Relations Award (2015), the TCA Dr. Jamesanna Kirven Outstanding Counselor Award (2015), the Texas School Counselor Association Presidential Award for work on the *Texas Model for Comprehensive School Counseling Programs*, 5th edition (2018), the Texas Counseling Association Professional Writing Award (2019), and the Texas School Counselor Association School Counseling Educator of the Year Award (2020).

Monya Crow, M.Ed., LPC-S, has been in the counseling and educational field for 25 years. She began as a classroom teacher serving students in the Special Education program through a Behavior Intervention Classroom. Upon earning a master's degree in counseling, Monya served as a crisis and intervention counselor for students in grades K–12. Concurrently, she opened a private practice where she specialized in working with adults in couples counseling, adult women in life transitions, and adolescents. For the last 5 years, Monya has served in the role of Executive Director of Counseling and Social Work for Lewisville ISD in addition to serving on the board of the Texas School Counseling Association and is a Trust Based Relational Intervention (TBRI©) practitioner.

Jenipher (Jeni) Janek, LPC has over 20 years of experience in public education. Relative to student safety, Jeni has served as a school safety contact at ESC Region 12 in Texas for the past 8 years as well as the School Crisis Response Team Leader, serving 86 school districts and charter schools in the 12 counties covered by ESC Region 12. She has forged strong relationships with law enforcement and community partners both in the private sector and with mental health providers and works at this time with local mental health liaisons to ensure intervention for high-risk situations regarding students who pose a threat to harming themselves or others.

Tisha Kolek, M.Ed., is the Director of SEL & Health Services in Dripping Springs ISD. In this role, she supports the school counselors, nurses, as well as the Social Emotional Learning of K–12 Students. Prior to this new role, which she began in August of 2021, she served as the Coordinator of Counseling Services at Region 13 Education Service Center in Austin. She has also worked as a Director of School Counseling in a school district for 5 years. She has experience as a professional school counselor at the elementary, middle, alternative, and high school levels, as well as classroom teaching experience at each campus level. Her professional passion is supporting educators in all capacities to help ensure that students have equitable access to opportunities regardless of their stories.

Benny Malone, MSW, CSC, LPC-S, is an author, speaker, and mental health advocate and holds a master's degree in social work from the University of Houston. She has completed more than a hundred hours of post-graduate training in professional counseling, special education, and educational leadership. Benny has served on the board of directors and various committees of the Texas Counseling Association and co-authored several articles on school counseling best practices and mental health. She is also the author of *Psychotic Rage! A True Story of Mental Illness, Murder, and Reconciliation*, which details her son's long journey with serious mental illness. In her professional career of over 30 years, Benny has worked as an educational administrator, school counselor, special education teacher, state agency social worker, and consultant. Benny is a trained volunteer educator for the National Alliance on Mental Illness (NAMI).

Summer Martin, Ph.D., is the Director of Counseling Services in Richardson ISD, located in Richardson, Texas. She has been in education for 21 years and has served as a high school counselor for 13 years before coming to Richardson to serve as the Director. She is also an adjunct professor at Dallas Baptist University, teaching graduate level school counseling courses. Dr. Martin has served on the Lone Star State School Counselor Association Board of Directors since 2016 in various positions including Director of Communications/Technology, VP of Counselor Educators, President-Elect, President, and currently serves as Past-President. Dr. Martin studied counseling at Texas Christian University and received her Ph.D. in Educational Psychology at University of North Texas and continues to focus on counseling supervision and best practices, counselor leadership, and resiliency in schools.

Kimberly McGough, Ph.D., LPC-S, CSC, is an assistant professor at Lamar University and the Professional School Counseling Program Coordinator. Before working at Lamar, Dr. McGough worked as a school counselor for 13 years at the secondary level. Her counseling specialty includes working with adolescents and their families within the school system and in private practice. Her research interests include but are not limited to: phenomena surrounding at-risk behavior in adolescence and the development of grit across various student populations in online university settings.

Carlete Metoyer, LPC, Consultant, is a Licensed Professional Counselor, Professional School Counselor, and Certified Compassion Fatigue Professional. Carlete is the owner of

List of Contributors xix

CSM Counseling Solutions, where she focuses on reducing the stigma associated with seeking mental health services while helping clients achieve wholeness in their lives.

Chenda T. Moore, LPC, has been an educator for over 26 years. She has been a teacher, professional school counselor, district administrator, adjunct college professor, and licensed professional counselor. She is a Youth Mental Health First Aid instructor and ASK About Suicide facilitator. Dr. Moore is the owner of Chenda's Hope, LLC. Dr. Moore provides training and motivational presentations to organizations on a variety of topics.

Loree Munro, M.Ed., has served in public education for 32 years. Ms. Munro earned her degree in school counseling at Sam Houston State University 2007. Loree has been a school counselor at the middle and high school levels in several districts. She began her employment with New Caney ISD in 2011 and has served as a high school lead counselor, Academic Dean, Director of Advanced Academics & Counseling, and Executive Director of Instructional Programs where she provides leadership to the Directors of Career & Technical Education, Counseling, Fine Arts, Special Education, and Special Programs. Loree is a Licensed Professional Counselor Supervisor (LPC-S) and enjoys keeping her counseling skills sharp in the private practice arena. In 2019, Loree was awarded a Demonstration Project grant from the Center for School Behavioral Health and a BridgeUp Magic grant from the Menninger Clinic.

Laurie Goforth Rodriguez, M.Ed., LLSP, is a proud Oklahoma State graduate and began teaching in 1992, first as a general education social studies teacher and then as a special education teacher. She became a diagnostician in 2000 before moving into special education district leadership in 2003. Laurie's leadership mantra is "whatever the student needs is our job description" and "mental health matters First" and her goal and focus is on making sure the professionals in her department have access to the leadership training, pedagogical and counseling skills they need to meet students' needs. Laurie lived in a children's home in high school and would likely have been an unfortunate statistic, but she credits her high school career counselor with starting her on the pathway to success because he helped her fill out (and pay for) her college applications. She believes school counselors have an incredible opportunity to influence children's lives.

Lorry Royal, Ph.D., LPC, NCC, CSC, is an Assistant Professor in the Department of Counseling at Texas A & M University @ Commerce. Lorry attended East Texas State University in Commerce, Texas, where she majored in Elementary Education and received a bachelor's degree. She continued her education and earned a master's degree in counseling, with a certification in School Counseling, from Texas A & M University-Commerce. Lorry has worked as a school counselor, working with grade levels Pre-K through 12th for over 20 years in small, rural school districts. She completed her doctoral degree in counselor education and supervision in December 2020. She is a Licensed Professional Counselor in the state of Texas and is also a certified equine therapist through the Equine Assisted Growth and Learning Association. Lorry has also been working in private practice providing counseling services to individuals, families, children, and adolescents as well as continuing to work in the rural school system as a school counselor.

Christina Shaw, Ed.D., PSC, LPC-Associate, has 17 years of experience in education, with 10 years teaching elementary school, and 7 years as a Professional School Counselor. After 13 years as an elementary educator, she ventured to junior high to be a Student Support Counselor.

She is a certified trainer for Youth Mental Health First Aid, Ask About Suicide (ASK+), and Restorative Practices. Also, she is a certified yoga teacher completed with Breathe for Change. Dr. Shaw is a Certified Trauma and Resilience Practitioner-Educator (CTRP-E) through STARR Commonwealth. She is most passionate about Restorative Practices, trauma-informed school, mindfulness, and relationships within a school setting. In June 2021, Christina Shaw received her educational doctoral degree at Concordia University-Texas in Austin.

Carla Voelkel, M.Ed., is a public-school educator who has served in a variety of roles during her 42 years of experience. This has included high school teacher, elementary school assistant principal, middle school principal, director and executive director positions which included coordinating elementary and secondary counselors, assistant superintendent, and deputy superintendent. Currently, she is the proud superintendent of Dickinson ISD, and she has served in this capacity since 2018. Her mission is to ensure students and staff have the tools, experiences, and support necessary to learn and make continuous growth, and she believes comprehensive guidance with leadership from skilled, well-trained, and compassionate counselors is essential for student success.

Online Companion Contributors

Jacqueline Jenkins Booker has a master's degree in counseling from Prairie View A & M University. She has an undergraduate degree in business administration from University of Texas at Arlington. She is a certified school counselor, licensed professional counselor, LCDC intern and has a MYS certification. She worked as a school counselor for 15 years. Additionally, she has worked in a psychiatric hospital, residential adolescent group homes, and private practice providing therapy to clients from adolescents to adults. Jacqueline currently works in her own private practice in the Katy-Houston area.

Aleister Lonnie Gamble is a graduate of the Master of Education in clinical mental health counseling program at the University of Houston looking forward to becoming a Licensed Professional Counselor in the state of Texas. Aleister graduated from University of North Carolina-Greensboro with a bachelor's degree in psychology and a bachelor's degree in sociology in 2013. They have contributed to research involving sexual orientation and relational styles of college students.

Estrella Godinez is a Licensed Professional Counselor-Associate (LPC-A) in the state of Texas. She graduated from Sam Houston State University in December 2021 with a master's degree in clinical mental health counseling. Ms. Godinez has contributed to research publications pertaining to the mental health of immigrated youth in schools and to the studies of psychopathology in adolescents with borderline personality disorder. Most recently, she wrote *A Yearning Desire* (Un Deseo Anhelante), a short story in English and Spanish, in the title *Serving Refugee Children*.

Lindsay King graduated from the University of Houston, main campus in 2019 with a bachelor's degree in psychology. She continued her education at the university from fall 2019 to Spring 2022, earning her Master of Education in counseling. Mrs. King plans on continuing her education and expanding her knowledge to help people with their mental and behavioral health.

Jeanette Oviedo graduated from the University of Houston with a bachelor's degree in psychology and a minor in Human Development and Family Studies. Mrs. Oviedo contributed to a research study about women's menstrual cycles and sleeping patterns. She is a second-year graduate student at Sam Houston State University in the Clinical Mental Health Counseling field. She plans to continue to pursue her interests in counseling by serving diverse populations and expanding her knowledge in multicultural counseling.

Ana Paula Quiroz graduated from Texas A & M University in May 2021 with a bachelor's degree in psychology and earned an Associate of Arts degree from Lone Star College in the Honors College. During her last 2 years of college she joined the SKY Campus Happiness program in which she served as a meditation mediator and service leader for college students. Ana Paula plans to pursue a master's degree in clinical mental health counseling in hopes of building a healthier and stronger community.

James Vidrine is a second-year graduate student pursuing a career in clinical mental health counseling at The University of Houston. He graduated from Texas A & M University with a bachelor's degree in psychology in 2020 and is interested in doing research on anxiety and depression in adolescents, addictions, and couples counseling. He strives to help put an end to the stigmas surrounding mental health and practice in underserved communities.

Foreword

Act as if what you do makes a difference. It does.

William James

My leadership journey in school counseling began many years ago. In fact, it actually started when I was a student, since my family moved frequently due to my father's military service. Often the first time I heard my name spoken at a new school was through the greeting of a school counselor. The reassuring smiles and friendly hands to hold as I walked to the latest new classroom stand out in my memory to this very day.

School counselors occupy a unique and highly impactful space in schools. Not only do comprehensive school counseling programs make a measurable difference in student outcomes and learning experiences, but they also create a ripple effect on the health and wellbeing of the entire community.

Yet, despite the significance of the role, most schools and districts have only a handful of individuals to fill them. Too often the depth and breadth of the counselor's skills are only partially utilized. Indeed, it's not uncommon for school counselors to function as a "jack of all trades" for administrative and clerical duties rather than as a highly trained and uniquely qualified specialist providing direct services to students and families. Fortunately, school counselors, and other professional allies, are starting to change that paradigm through leadership and advocacy both at the legislative and individual district and campus levels.

This book was created to assist school counselors, and others that may support and supervise school counselors, in uncovering and growing their knowledge and confidence in designing, implementing, and evaluating comprehensive school counseling programs that are rooted in data and embraced by the school community.

St. Francis of Assisi once wrote, "Start by doing what is necessary, then what is possible, and suddenly you are doing the impossible." This quote really resonated with me as a young school counselor. It has stayed with me throughout my journey into leadership. This book captures many of those necessary practices, procedures, and skills to ensure success. In its pages you will find the collected wisdom of practitioners who believe in all that is truly possible for the comprehensive school counseling model. The strategies and resources shared will launch you well into the "impossible."

Thank you for the energy you pour into your work. Thank you for choosing a service profession that makes such a profound impact on both our young people and our communities. Through this study, through your dedication and talents, and through your connections with your fellow professionals, your own journey is now underway. Good luck and always remember that you WILL make a difference.

Jennifer Akins
President, Texas School Counselor Association 2022–2023

Preface

As we, the editors of this book, discussed chapter titles and content areas to prepare our book proposal, we were particularly cognizant of the challenges of public education in the 21st century. Our priority was to address the mental health of students, not only because historically and presently there was stigma associated with these services, but additionally due to the negative impact driven by certain messages on social media, a pandemic that placed many students in online schooling for at least a year or more, along with the surge of negative attitudes and beliefs about educators in general. These challenges might very well impede the healthy development of the children of our nation including mental health, physical well-being, and academic attainment.

Lately, we read news articles and hear television and radio news accusing teachers and other school professionals of having an agenda to take away parent rights and to expose children to information that is inappropriate. We are all parents ourselves and believe strongly in parents' rights to know what their children are learning and how it is being presented. However, we also know that children go to school to socialize, to learn, and to develop into citizens of the world. Teachers, administrators, school counselors, and other school personnel work tirelessly to help students achieve academic excellence, social and emotional stability and regulation, and paths to interesting careers through post-secondary choices. They honestly do not have time to promote their own political or social views to students. They are too busy planning lessons for a diverse group of students, assessing student needs, ensuring benchmarks are met, and developing relationships with students that encourage trust and the ability to learn. Educators are smart people who understand that manipulating children is ethically inappropriate.

Administrators and counselor leaders know that students come from diverse backgrounds, some with immense opportunities and others from families suffering from abuse, poverty, substance use, mental illness, or violence. Whatever privilege or distress students live under, recently they have all experienced the COVID-19 pandemic and its repercussions. Schools have been shuttered for a year or more, mask mandates have been on again and off again leaving everyone confused, and counseling services have been more difficult to provide in an online format. According to the Centers for Disease Control and Prevention (2022), many children who were required to stay home from school to stop the spread of COVID-19 were exposed to abuse and neglect from a parent or other adult in the home. Additionally, students have observed or possibly been a part of a great deal of confusion surrounding not only COVID-19, but also political strife which might even be within their own families. It is our belief that leaders in schools and communities have the capacity to meet today's challenges, particularly if they collaborate, plan for healthy school environments, and put children first.

School leaders provide equitable, safe, and excellent educational programs for the benefit of student development. How do they do this?

We strongly support the concept of distributed leadership in school settings. Distributed leadership provides leadership opportunities to everyone on a campus and expects and encourages autonomy, capacity, and accountability. In this model, everyone is a leader, thus ensuring confidence, competence, and excellent mental health among the staff which means that the best educational skills are being passed on to students. A good fit with distributed leadership is the transformational leadership model or theory. Transformational leaders do not reward and punish staff members to gain compliance and to achieve goals; rather, they work to transform their teachers and other school personnel to create positive change in members as well as in the values that lead to effective teaching and learning. Transformational leaders embrace the idea of shared responsibility and accountability and inspire their followers to commit to shared goals and values.

For school counselors, distributed and transformational leadership pair well together and create opportunities for working collaboratively with administrators for the benefit of career satisfaction and positive mental health of everyone on the campus. Additionally, students will be engaged with adults who have a shared value system and goals that are consistent with positive student mental health and academic success. It is no secret that school counselors' training and expertise has often been sidetracked for convenience and misunderstanding of the role. Unfortunately using school counselors for clerical work, substitute teaching, discipline, and other non-counseling duties leads to burnout for the counselors and a lack of mental health support for the youth in our schools.

We offer this textbook as a blueprint for collaboration, value sharing, and positive mental health among stakeholders for the benefit of the future of all students. The reader will encounter the terms school counselors, counselor leaders, directors of counseling, administrators, and principals; however, our aim is to highlight the necessity of partnerships among counselors and other school leaders for the purpose of working in concert to improve the mental health of students leading to their academic success. These alliances, particularly among counselors and administrators, improve the potential for healthy student relationships with staff, other students, and their own family members. Additionally, students will improve the most important relationship of all, and that is the relationship they have with themselves. When students have positive mental health, they are more likely to be able to identify their strengths and talents and to use these to achieve their academic and career goals.

Each chapter in our book provides guidance on leadership standards, values, and practices, as well as ethical, multicultural, and strategic considerations around topics essential to excellent school counseling. These topics include mental health in schools, restorative practices, training, professional development, supervision, evaluation, partnerships, crisis prevention, and intervention, budgetsand advocacy. This comprehensive look at the relationship among administrators and counselors sets the stage for collaboration that will support student mental health as well as healthy development in general. Administrators who embrace the leadership and mental health skills of school counselors have found that their school communities have benefitted overwhelmingly, and they are sharing their experiences and expertise with you in his valuable book.

Judy A. Nelson

Acknowledgements

We would like to acknowledge the fine leaders in schools and universities that we have had the privilege with whom to work. The goodwill, creativity, and integrity with which they have provided leadership has been an inspiration to us and has taught us more than we could ever have gleaned from a book. Thank you, strong leaders! We captured their wisdom, hard work, and exceptional leadership in this text.

We would also like to acknowledge the graduate students who spent substantial time and effort working on the online component of this book. Their biographies can be found in the list of contributors.

Section I

Incorporating a Foundation of Mental Health in School Counseling

The importance of mental health as a focus for services in schools is addressed in Section I. Professional school counselors are trained to identify students who need mental health support, assess the specific needs of these students, provide evidenced-based strategies to assist in stabilizing students in crisis, and refer students to outside agencies and therapists when necessary. This section addresses ways school counselors and their administrative leaders need to incorporate mental and behavioral health in schools, including school counselors' perspective, ways to promote mental health in these unpredictable times, and how to bring restorative practices while addressing mental health in schools.

> School counselors and administrative leaders should no longer believe that fostering educational growth and curriculum strands supersede addressing the composites to wellness, inevitably increasing mental health status – not only in our students, but in each adult, who has a daily responsibility for each student served.
>
> Lisa A. Wines

> The foundation of any school counseling program should focus on the mental health needs of students, staff, and families. School counselors are uniquely positioned and qualified to be leaders in the field of mental health counseling. Administrators who ensure that the expertise of school counselors is fully recognized and utilized, will ensure that all students benefit.
>
> Judy Nelson

> School communities are in great need of leaders who advocate on behalf of supporting the mental health needs of students, staff, and families. Professional school counselors and administrative leaders lead from important influential spaces where organizational, district wide, and campus wide programming and supports can address these needs.
>
> Natalie Fikac

DOI: 10.4324/9781003219750-1

Section I

Incorporating a Foundation of Mental Health in School Counseling

1 Mental and Behavioral Health in Schools

Judy A. Nelson, Lisa A. Wines, and Natalie Fikac

> **Leadership Quote**
>
> Together school counselors and district administrators establish reciprocal feedback loops that help recognize, identify, plan, intervene, and support the mental health needs of students in our schools, because without it, the stage is only set for triaging.
>
> Lisa A. Wines

> **Aspirational Statements**
>
> - Mental health treatment in schools should not be ancillary in nature, but rather primary and in conjunction with educational curricula.
> - When schools address the mental health needs of students, the academic needs as well as the post-secondary needs, they are addressing the whole child.
> - School counselors are credentialed professionals, who should be regarded as front-line interventionists, qualified to stabilize, mitigate, and remediate the mental health conditions of students in our schools.

Introduction and Background

The mental health needs of students have significantly increased over the past decade. Schools have become the de facto mental health providers for students across the country. According to the United States Department of Health and Human Services, one in five children and adolescents experience a mental health concern during their school years. These mental health concerns range from stress, depression, and substance use and abuse to self-injurious behaviors and suicidal ideation (SAMHSA, 2019). Other less prominently identified mental health conditions in children, separate from mood and emotional disorders, are eating and personality disorders, medicinal contraindicated disorders, or gender dysphoria/dysmorphia. But what happens when students experience natural disasters or school shootings? These types of events may not only exacerbate current mental health issues, but often, traumatic and crisis situations can create onset disorders, which are situational in nature as opposed to genetic, predisposed, or biological factors.

DOI: 10.4324/9781003219750-2

According to the Youth Behavior Risk Survey Assessment (Underwood et al., 2019), the number of students who have seriously considered attempting suicide or attempted suicide has steadily increased in number from 2009 to 2019. Suicide is the second leading cause of death in these youth ages 14–18. Three out of five of these students do not receive the needed treatment due to access or the stigma associated with mental health. Fortunately, schools are in a unique position to provide these needed services and supports, and school counselors are equipped with training and tools needed to support students.

School counselors and school counselor leaders must advocate for resources and programming on campuses and in school districts that address and support the mental health needs of all students. School counselors have completed coursework, research and training that can aid in providing solution-focused and short-term mental health supports for students. School counselors also have relationships with other mental health supports within schools and in the school community. School counselor leaders are equipped with decision-making powers to assist in creating relationships to provide wraparound support for students. With school counselors and school counselor leaders working collaboratively with school community stakeholders, student mental and behavioral health needs can be met. With the significant increase of mental health needs of students globally due to the COVID-19 pandemic, and recent incidents of school violence, this collaborative partnership is essential.

Leadership Program Values and Standards

Leadership in schools requires school counselors to build comprehensive school counseling programs that, by design, incorporate ways to address the mental health needs of students in schools. This is referred to as program values. Program values are often found in a district's vision and mission statements and may be philosophical in nature. School districts and their administrators have responded to this call to action in multiple ways such as through their school-wide programs, campus improvement plans, and/or prevention and intervention programs.

In light of building a comprehensive program, school counselors are asked to include a vision and mission statement in alignment with their school districts. These vision and mission statements should incorporate leadership program values, making a position statement that not only addresses the educational, career, personal, and social components of the whole child, but more deeply, the mental health needs of students served. However, when this fails to happen, and when school counselors are unsure of how to advocate for their comprehensive program in this way, it unfortunately leaves school counselors, who are already properly trained to address mental health concerns, in roles and delivering services that place their focus elsewhere.

The National School Board Association (NSBA) published an online article titled: 'Preferred Provider School Counseling Model' (Baldassarre, 2019), in which a comparison of a typical school-based counseling model is made to a preferred provider model of school counseling. Within this chart, one item is highlighted and stated as follows:

Table 1.1 Typical and Preferred Models

Typical School-Based Counseling	*Preferred Provider Model*
School employee clinicians participate in scheduled non-counseling related duties such as hall monitoring and lunch supervision pursuant to the collective bargaining agreement.	Preferred Provider clinicians focus only on providing services to students with little to no interruption or interface due to school district collective bargaining

Note: Adapted from Baldassarre (2019). Chart created by N. Fikac, 2022.

There are many implications in the aforementioned chart. To start, a school employee who is a clinician may or may not be a school counselor and was not defined, as such, in the publication. Additionally, if the employee clinician definition fails to incorporate the school counselor, then the question becomes why is the preferred provider clinician not inclusive of the school counselor? More salient is the question, why might it be that typical school-based counseling programs require clinicians to participate in scheduled non-counseling related duties, as opposed to operating within their ability to concentrate on providing services with minimal interruptions?

The Substance Abuse and Mental Health Services Administration (SAMHSA) issued a joint informational bulletin calling on states and district administrators to provide mental health and substance abuse information and services to the public (i.e., students and their families). Included within the bulletin were best-practice models, not infused with leadership values, but with models that promote the use of: multi-tiered systems of support, comprehensive school mental health systems, building mental health literacy, infusing counseling, psychological, and social services coordination, school resource officers, crisis intervention teams, behavioral health aides, and the limitations of rural communities providing these services.

School counselors harness a professional responsibility to demonstrate leadership skills on their campuses through their own words and actions via building programs, rendering services, intervening in crises, and advocacy efforts. School counselors often serve on administrative and grade-level teams, where their skill sets are used to problem-solve and plan co-occurring events. Standards written for school counselors should drive their work, particularly where leadership can take shape.

According to the National Board for Professional Teaching Standards (2016), it was made evident that "accomplished school counselors accept a leadership role as an opportunity to further increase the visibility and impact of the school counseling program" (2016: 50). This document summarizes the school counselor leadership role as:

- communicating a clear and compelling vision;
- understanding the complexities students face while remaining optimistic;
- recommending school-wide programs and instituting improvement teams;
- believing that they should build networks with other professionals who can support, collaborate, and assist;
- articulating their use of data and evidence-based practices;
- using specialized skills, particularly under duress, that includes much optimism and effective communication;
- life-long learning with a niche in emotional intelligence.

(2016: 51)

Leadership in Practice

School counselors understand how to use research and use literature to inform their practices. In fact, it is no surprise that the American School Counseling Association published an article written by Young (2019) generating the question "Does the act of doing, as opposed to leading, create sustainable counseling programs and student outcomes?" This question is a great one, and one response that contributes to sustainability is adopting a leadership model that aligns with the training of administrator leaders who study and practice educational leadership.

There are many leadership models for administrators to follow in leading schools. Some of these leadership models are extremely helpful and are referenced to as transformational leadership, servant leadership, and transactional leadership. Northouse (2021) references these three models in the latest edition of his book, and the authors of this chapter believe that these particular models offer a good fit to the optimal school counselor role and performance.

Transformational Leadership

Transformational leadership (Northouse, 2021), which should be the heart-center or heartbeat in a school district and campus, is when a leader works with a team to identify areas of change and cohesively creates a vision of change using inspiration, and together, executes the change. It requires a committed relationship between the leader and his or her followers. School counselors and their relationships with students are a committed exchange to promote growth and change through a dynamic process of counseling.

There are four types of transformational leadership: a) idealized influence, b) intellectual stimulation, c) individualized consideration, and d) inspirational motivation (Bass, 1985). With school counselors in mind, the notion of idealized influence may suggest that the use of self as a primary vessel in the relationship, combined with ethical practices, core beliefs, and conviction, is how trust is built. Regarding the notion of intellectual stimulation, school counselors are extremely like-minded with educational leaders and administrators, in that they help locate and build autonomy in students without judgment. An obvious purpose for school counselors here is to consider each student individually – with their particular needs and desires in mind. Understanding each student's needs and their motivation for change is definitely an intricate part of the role school counselors play in the lives of students. Finally, inspirational motivation is where school counselors use their premium communication skills coupled with an ability to identify students' strengths, all while peppering in optimism, and is shared among leaders and these professionals.

Table 1.2 outlines these elements in a side-by-side comparison.

Table 1.2 Administrator and Counselor Roles

Administrative Leader	School Counselor
Idealized Influence	
• Role model	• Exhibits positive and replicable behaviors and attitudes
• High moral compass and ethical	• Governed by ethics in the field and ethical decision-making models
Inspirational Motivation	
• Communicates high expectations of followers	• Uses positive communication and goal setting and redefining throughout the counseling relationship
Intellectual Stimulation	
• Challenges follower's beliefs and values	• Appreciates beliefs and values in students and redirects faulty patterns of thought while enhancing the emotional intelligence
Individualized Consideration	
• Supportive environment where leaders listen and followers become self-actualized	• Establishes a therapeutic environment, filled with appropriate listening and empathy so that students become autonomous and self-actualized

Note: Adapted from Bass (1985). Chart created by N. Fikac, 2022.

This is very similar to how school counselors are trained to work with students and families to identify need areas, using themselves as a mechanism and motivation for change (change agent), with a professional collaboration, yet clear plan of execution within a framework of emotional intelligence.

Servant Leadership

Another powerful leadership model that many administrators apply is servant leadership. Via title alone, it seems school leaders and counselors would adopt this model because these leaders are responsible for serving students. A servant leader's primary goal is to serve, using a shared power, placing the needs of employees first. This type of leader is normally concerned with the question: do people grow, and while being catered to, do they become freer, healthier, wiser, and more autonomous? Brown et al. stated that "[a]t the heart of servant leadership is an attitude of compassion and service that serves as the foundation of trust, credibility, and relationships" (2020: 67). There are ten principles of servant leadership: listening, healing, empathy, awareness, persuasion, conceptualization, foresight, stewardship, commitment to growth of people, and building community. All ten principles are necessities to providing counseling services to students and their families.

Transactional Leadership

There are many elements of transactional leadership that have appeal for school counselors to consider. Using the self as an instrument to promote change in students is quite important, and one element to apply. The relationship is reciprocal in nature and promotes continuation. Transactional leadership simply focuses on "transacting work for reward" (Brown et al., 2020: 70), and within it are a few different types: contingent reward leadership, management by exception, and laissez-faire leadership.

In name, it may seem impossible that these types mirror counseling approaches or concepts, but in description, there are many overlapping facets that allow for counselors and school leaders to use similar skills. Contingent reward leadership is fueled by empowerment, in that leaders enable their employees to take control of their tasks responsibly. School counselors do this so often with students, related to their personal lives, academics, extracurricular, and accomplishing goals that have been set. Management by exception, is where leaders help identify and address mistakes, followed by an appropriate course of action. School counselors assist students in just that, without focusing on the negative, but rather focusing on how he or she can address thoughts and feelings behind experiences, along with and transforming the approach, if necessary. The laissez-faire leadership model has elements that are applicable to working with students, whereas counselors harness a belief and trust in the students they are serving and refrain from being too directive, giving advice, or providing too much instruction. Transactional leadership, and many of its components, are applicable to school counselors. Much of the skills, approaches, and strategies are exactly what school counselors use with students, all of which have efficacious outcomes.

Administrator Leadership Model Infused with Counselor Attributes

In closing, all the aforementioned approaches to mitigating and interceding in the mental health and wellness of students, particularly when infused with educational administration leadership theory and school counselor training and credentials, make for quite an integrated approach to student development – in their mental health and in their education.

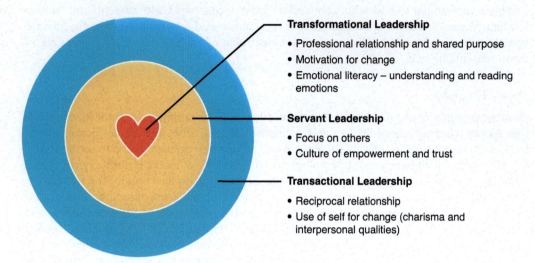

Figure 1.1 Administrator Leadership Model Infused with Counselor Attributes.

Mental and Behavioral Health Considerations

Although this chapter in its entirety addresses the issues of mental and behavioral health considerations, it is worthy to note that systems, as well as people, can be mentally or behaviorally healthy or unhealthy. School systems are particularly vulnerable to unrest, misinformation, emotional rather than rational responses, and so forth. This is because schools must consider students, parents, faculty, administrators, and the community-at-large when making changes or simply conducting the daily business of educating many children. Everyone has an idea about how systems should work, and sometimes these ideas either collide with each other or simply fail.

School counselors can be natural assets to driving school systems toward positive mental health. They can do this in a variety of ways such as preparing the staff through professional development to better relate to their students, keeping administrators informed about potential problems that might be avoided if acted upon before a crisis ensues, advocating for the CSCP so that all students have access to the counseling curriculum and individual planning throughout the academic year, and responding to students in crisis when needed. School counselors are often the first to notice teachers who need help, students who are in crisis, parents who are disruptive and causing problems in the neighborhood, and all manner of other human behaviors that can either become disasters or can be offered the help that will avoid a disaster. When school counselors lead, systems shine, and everyone benefits.

Ethical Considerations

School counselors are obligated to not only adhere to the *ASCA Ethical Standards for School Counselors* (2022) in their day-to-day responsibilities working with students, parents, school staff, and community members, but to use their leadership skills in doing so. Counselors make many decisions each day, and they must weigh their ethical obligations before taking action. Ethical standards are particularly important when these decisions impact the mental health of individuals. In the section of the Standards titled *Responsibility to Students*, the following standards are especially important when dealing with mental health crises or issues.

Supporting Student Development

When school counselors use their leadership skills to support or mitigate mental health issues, in general, they:

> a have a primary obligation to the students, who are to be treated with dignity and respect as unique individuals;
> [...]
> e aim to provide counseling to students in a brief context and support students and families/guardians in obtaining outside services if the student needs long-term clinical counseling;
> f do not diagnose, but remain acutely aware of how a student's diagnosis can potentially affect the student's academic success;
> [...]
> i are knowledgeable of laws, regulations and policies affecting students and families and strive to protect and inform students and families regarding their rights;
> j provide effective, responsive interventions to address student needs;
> k consider the involvement of support networks, wraparound services and educational teams needed to best serve students.

School counselors must place the needs of students as a priority. While there might be competing factors for certain courses of action, the counselor must take into account what is best for the student's mental health. If short-term counseling sessions with the student and his or her family cannot ameliorate the problem, the school counselor should have access to the necessary time and resources for longer-term counseling. The mindset and dated model of school counselor intervention being very short-term (sometimes just a few minutes) should be reconciled, and school counselors should be available to see students week after week when their issues affect their educational, career, personal, and social needs, particularly when necessary and permission is granted by the parent. An outside therapist working with students may not focus on the educational aspects of student development. However, if an outside referral is in order, then collaboration, continuity-of-care, and standard-of-care practices must be in place, leaving the student with an intrinsic development that will remain life changing and self-enhancing.

The counselor must have a bank of referrals to meet the needs of a variety of students. For example, the referral list should include therapists who speak the languages of the student populations, can determine the mental health needs using formal, informal, quantitative and qualitative measures or assessments, and should include agencies or nonprofits that operate on a sliding scale. While school counselors do not diagnose students, they are trained in diagnostic criteria, can provide their impressions to referring agencies or persons, understand how to recognize serious mental health issues, when to alert parents or guardians about concerning behaviors, and when to refer families to support services. School counselors are also knowledgeable regarding the laws, regulations, and policies that protect students and their families. These might include limits of confidentiality, child abuse reporting laws, federal laws regarding parental rights to information about their children, and school district policy that addresses pregnant students or student drug use, to name a few. The following standards are regarding harm to self and others.

Serious and Foreseeable Harm to Self and Others

When school counselors use their leadership skills to support or mitigate mental health issues, related to self-harm and harm to others, they:

a *inform parents/guardians and/or appropriate authorities when a student poses a serious and foreseeable risk of harm to self or others.* When feasible, this is to be done after careful deliberation and consultation with other appropriate professionals. School counselors inform students of the school counselor's legal and ethical obligations to report the concern to the appropriate authorities unless it is appropriate to withhold this information to protect the student (e.g. the student might run away if he/she knows parents are being called). The consequence of the risk of not giving parents/guardians a chance to intervene on behalf of their child is too great. Even if the danger appears relatively remote, parents should be notified.

b *use risk assessments with caution.* If risk assessments are used by the school counselor, an intervention plan should be developed and in place prior to this practice. When reporting risk-assessment results to parents, school counselors do not negate the risk of harm even if the assessment reveals a low risk, as students may minimize risk to avoid further scrutiny and/or parental notification. School counselors report risk assessment results to parents to underscore the need to act on behalf of a child at risk; this is not intended to assure parents their child isn't at risk, which is something a school counselor cannot know with any level of certainty.

c *do not release a student who is a danger to self or others until the student has proper and necessary support.* If parents will not provide proper support, the school counselor takes necessary steps to underscore to parents/guardians the necessity to seek help and at times may include a report to child protective services.

d *report to parents/guardians and/or appropriate authorities when students disclose a perpetrated or a perceived threat to their physical or mental well-being.* This threat may include, but is not limited to, physical abuse, sexual abuse, neglect, dating violence, bullying or sexual harassment. The school counselor follows applicable federal, state, and local laws and school district policy.

Responsibility to Students

School counselors:

> f Respect students' and families' values, beliefs, sexual orientation, gender identification/expression and cultural background and exercise great care to avoid imposing personal beliefs or values rooted in one's religion, culture or ethnicity.

Responsibility to the School

School counselors:

> i advocate for equitable school counseling program policies and practices for all students and stakeholders;

j advocate for the use of vetted, bilingual/multilingual translators to represent languages used by families in the school community and support broader cultural communication and engagement;
k affirm the abilities of and advocate for the learning needs of all students. School counselors support the provision of appropriate accommodations and accessibility;
l provide culturally responsive information to families to increase understanding, improve communication, promote engagement and improve student outcomes;
m promote culturally sustaining practices to help create a safe and inclusive school environment with equitable outcomes for all students;
n adhere to educational/psychological research practices, confidentiality safeguards, security practices and school district policies when conducting research;
o use school and community resources to promote equity and access for all students;
p use inclusive language in all forms of communication and ensure students and stakeholders have access to materials in their preferred languages when possible;
q collaborate as needed to provide optimum services with other school and community professionals with legitimate educational interests (e.g., school nurse, school psychologist, school social worker, speech-language pathologist), following all local, state and federal laws.

Cultural Complexities

Schools are more than ever diverse in the 21st century, and school counselors are trained to be culturally competent in their work with students, parents, school staff, and community members. Some school districts, in large urban areas, report demographics of students speaking more than 200 different languages in one building. The conversation of multiculturalism is insurmountable and cannot be caged to one ideology or way of thinking. Legislation, rules, and policies of white lawmakers and district policy makers are not necessarily equitable or just for all students. And, yet, the charge of public education is to provide services to all students. There are a myriad of complex considerations, and just when you believe you understand, our societal shifts cause us to know that this reality is quite dynamic. For example, immigration issues may change the demographics of a school district considerably requiring district employees to adjust their strategies for educating all students. While it may feel difficult for some to provide culturally appropriate counseling, it is important for school counselors to provide services to all students and their families. Additionally, school counselors must advocate for equity and social justice school district policies that reflect social justice values.

When responding to mental health crises in schools, counselors must take into consideration the cultural differences of the families with which they work. For example, families who identify as Latino/a/x might tend to expect certain behaviors from school counselors and leaders, while families of mixed race might have other types of expectations from the school, based on their home cultures. School counselors who find themselves troubled or conflicted by certain cultural aspects of students and their parents must seek consultation and/or supervision.

The ADDRESSING Model

It is incumbent upon school counselors to address their concerns with other professionals to be able to respond appropriately to their clients. However, it is also important for school counselors to consider the vast continuum of causes of mental health issues such as environment, onset of symptoms, and drug and alcohol use. School counselors are trained to assess behaviors and symptoms that might indicate serious mental health issues. While counselors in schools are not charged with diagnosing mental health disorders, they can supply assessments such as observations and checklists to providers who make such diagnoses.

The ADDRESSING model (Hays, 1996) allows for school counselors to use their counseling skills within the context and complex identities of human diversity. Multiculturalism is more than just something to consider; it is an individual's way of life – their way of being. This model is an acknowledgment of ethnic, cultural, and racial groups, specifically those who are considered as minoritized or disenfranchised. They may be scrutinized as special populations that receive attention to their differences within a dominant society. Transitioning into a deeper expansion of a necessary concept derives terms of diversity, equity, and inclusion. This commitment moves from individual consideration toward attacking the power structures within institutions, policies, and practices that support systemic discrepancies or disparities for some and not for others. Although there may not be models that comprehensively address the individual and system in the field of counseling, our first responsible charge is to begin with the individual, which the ADDRESSING model supports.

The ADDRESSING model (Hays, 1996) has nine cultural influences. They are: a. Age and Generational Influences; b. Developmental or Other Disabilities; c. Religion and Spiritual Orientation; d. Ethnic and e. Racial Identity; f. Socioeconomic Status; g. Sexual Orientation; h. Indigenous Heritage; i. National Origin; and j. Gender. Within these nine areas, there are historically marginalized or non-dominant groups that exhibit one or several of these influences. Therefore one's mental health might be affected in ways that are not generalizable and poignant enough for school counselors to understand the intersectionality between the cultural influences and imbalance in mental health.

Clinical Treatment Teams Applied in Educational Settings

When faced with serious mental health issues that constrict students' ability to achieve academic success, school counselors can form treatment teams to respond to these serious concerns in an ethical and culturally competent manner. Inviting school social workers and psychologists, behavior specialists, and other support personnel to assist with serious concerns takes the burden of decision-making off one person. These teams provide a wide variety of perspectives and expertise and expand the possibility of positive outcomes for students. School districts can improve the treatment team approach by modeling the use of teams in hospital and agency settings so that every professional's expertise is used to the fullest extent. School counselors have a vital voice in that process as they are often the ones with day-to-day contact with students. The following sections from the ASCA Code of Ethics (2022) are relevant to the school counselor's responsibility to respond to and advocate for students' values and beliefs around religion, culture, and ethnicity:

A. RESPONSIBILITY TO STUDENTS

A.1 Supporting Student Development

School counselors:

a Have a primary obligation to the students, who are to be treated with dignity and respect as unique individuals.

> b Foster and affirm all students and their identity and psychosocial development.
> c Support all students and their development by actively working to eliminate systemic barriers or bias impeding student development.
> d Provide culturally responsive instruction and appraisal and advisement to students.
> e Provide culturally responsive counseling to students in a brief context and support students and families/guardians in obtaining outside services if students need long-term clinical/mental health counseling.
> [...]
> h Respect students' and families' values, beliefs and cultural background, as well as students' sexual orientation, gender identity and gender expression, and exercise great care to avoid imposing personal biases, beliefs or values rooted in one's religion, culture or ethnicity.
> j Advocate for equitable, anti-oppressive and anti-bias policies and procedures, systems and practices, and provide effective, evidence-based and culturally sustaining interventions to address student needs.

Strategic Considerations

School counselor leaders must strategically consider the scope of practice of school counselors. School counselors receive coursework and training in supporting students with mental and behavioral health concerns and are positioned to provide solution-focused supports and services to students in need. Best practices suggest that school counselors are an integral part of a Multi-tiered System of Support (MTSS) and referral pathway. Their supporting role includes providing guidance, research-based practices and suggestions as well as interventions to students. School counselor leaders must educate and advocate for school counselors to ensure that campus and district level administrators understand a school counselor's unique role.

Successfully supporting the mental and behavioral health needs of students begins with creating a Comprehensive School Mental Health System (CSMHS) (NCSMH, 2020). Creating this foundation within a school community allows for strategically convening the correct partners to the table to provide wraparound supports for students. The National Center for School Mental Health provides a school mental health curriculum that can aid school counselor leaders in working through this process.

The foundational first step of this process is teaming; ensuring that the correct individuals and partners are at the table to begin strategizing on how to meet the mental and behavioral health needs of students (NCSMH, 2020). This school mental health team functions in a MTSS, and it is important that the school counselor leader leads this process.

The next step in this process includes needs assessment and resource mapping.

A needs assessment can help teams both develop and assess existing mental health services and supports, as well as identify the most pressing mental health concerns.

[...]

A resource map (also referred to as an asset map or environmental scan) can be a map that shows the location and type of available mental and behavioral health services or a directory/guide that lists available services and resources. Because schools often collaborate with multiple agencies (e.g., healthcare, juvenile services, social services, behavioral health) and programs, understanding the services provided by each agency/program reduces duplication and inappropriate use of services.

(NCSMH, 2020)

School counselor leaders are equipped with the knowledge and expertise to both advocate for their school counselors within their scope of practice as well as create partnerships with internal supports and external agencies.

School counselors are also key players in screening students for mental and behavioral health concerns. Once students are screened, school counselors can assist in appropriately referring students to the level of support needed by each student within tiers one, two and three. This should be outlined by the referral pathway after teaming and needs assessment/resource mapping have occurred. School counselors are a part of the referral pathway providing services and supports to students within their scope of practice including solution-focused individual counseling, skill building, or small group counseling.

Putting these first three steps into place for a CSMHS are both foundational and essential. With a CSMHS in place, students are more likely to have their mental and behavioral health needs met in school thus showing improved academic performance and meeting the needs of the whole child. School counselor leaders are positioned to support and advocate on behalf of the school counselors they lead as schools work to build CSMHSs.

Conclusion

In conclusion, school counselors and school counselor leaders are equipped, empowered and poised to serve as subject matter experts, provide training, and put systems and supports in place to ensure that the mental and behavioral health needs of all students are met. School counselors and school counselor leaders must have a voice at the table when policies, procedures, and systems are aligned and developed to support the whole child.

References

American School Counselor Association (2022) *ASCA Ethical Standards for School Counselors*. Alexandria, VA: ASCA.

Baldassarre, M.R. (2019) "Preferred provider school counseling model". Online. Available HTTP: <https://www.nsba.org/ASBJ/2019/April/Preferred-Provider-School-Counseling-Model>

Bass, B. (1985) *Leadership and Performance Beyond Expectations*. New York, NY: Free Press.

Brown, S., Marinan, J., and Partridge, M.A. (2020) "The moderating effect of servant leadership on transformational, transactional, authentic, and charismatic leadership', *Journal of International Business Disciplines*, 15(2): 67–86.

Hays, P.A. (1996) "Addressing the complexities of culture and gender in counseling", *Journal of Counseling & Development*, 74: 332–338.

McCance-Katz, E., and Lynch, C. (2019) "Guidance to states and school systems on addressing mental health and substance use issues in schools", *Joint Informational Bulletin* (July 1). Online. Available HTTP: <https://store.samhsa.gov/sites/default/files/d7/priv/pep19-school-guide.pdf>

National Association of School Psychologists. (2021) "Comprehensive school-based mental and behavioral health services and school psychologists" [handout]. Online. Available HTTP: <https://www.nasponline.org/resources-and-publications/resources-and-podcasts/mental-health/school-psychology-and-mental-health/school-based-mental-health-services>

National Board for Professional Teaching Standards. (2016) *School Counseling Standards.* Online. Available HTTP: <https://www.nbpts.org/wp-content/uploads/2017/07/ECYA-SC.pdf>

National Center for School Mental Health (NCSMH) (2020) *School Mental Health Quality Guide: Teaming*, Baltimore, MD: NCSMH, University of Maryland School of Medicine.

Northouse, P. (2021) *Leadership: Theory & Practice* (9th edn), Thousand Oaks, CA: Sage Publications, Inc.

Substance Abuse and Mental Health Services Administration (SAMHSA) (2019) *Ready, Set, Go, Review: Screening for Behavioral Health Risk in Schools*, Rockville, MD: Office of the Chief Medical Officer, Substance Abuse and Mental Health Services Administration.

Underwood, J.M., Brener, N., Thornton, J., Harris, W.A., Bryan, L.N., Shanklin, S.L., Deputy, N., Roberts, A.M., Queen, B., Chyen, D., et al. (2019) "Overview and methods for the youth risk behavior surveillance system – United States", *Morbidity and Mortality Weekly Report*, Suppl. 2020 Aug 21, 69(1): 1–10. doi: 10.15585/mmwr.su6901a1>

Young, A. (2019) "From doer to leader: school counselors' natural reaction is often to "do" rather than lead. Leaders don't do. Leaders get things done", Online. Available HTTP: <https://www.ascaschoolcounselor-digital.org/ascaschoolcounselor/november_december_2019/MobilePagedArticle.action?articleId=1536790#articleId1536790>

2 School Counselors' Perspective of Mental Health in Schools

Chenda T. Moore

Leadership Quote

School counselors have the training, drive, and capacity to support the mental health of students and staff. Administrators must be trained to understand how school counselors can contribute to the continuous improvement of the school through positive mental health interventions.

Judy A. Nelson

Aspirational Statements

- School counselors are credentialed to provide mental health support to students, not to just focus on academic needs. Emotional and mental health support of students should be the primary focus of services they provide.
- Mental health support of students is paramount in schools, especially with the recent economic and societal effects from the coronavirus and pandemic.

Introduction and Background

The role of professional school counselors has transformed from its initial place of guidance and vocational school counseling. Over time, the emotional and social needs of students have become greater; therefore, priority should be placed on these needs in order to support academic success. Crisis, which is never separated from mental health, can occur at any time. Some examples of mental health crises can include attempted or completed suicide, suicidal ideation, or non-suicidal self-injurious (NSSI) behavior. It should be understood that suicide attempts among young people have continued to rise, yet the stigma associated with mental health continues to exist in our society. Others are accidental, such as the natural death of a family member or staff member. Experiences of crisis have layers to them, because the experience is housed within the individual. For example, a teenage crisis may also include a break-up or loss of a relationship with a friend or boyfriend/girlfriend. When crises occur, school counselors, with the support of their administrative leaders, are expected to provide emotional and mental health support to students, staff, and families.

DOI: 10.4324/9781003219750-3

In responding, professional school counselors usually are the first line of defense, generally having to drop everything in order to properly respond to the crisis.

According to the Center for Disease Control (CDC, 2021), three out of five students who have considered or attempted suicide did not receive mental health treatment due to lack of access or the stigma related to mental illness. In 2019, the National Institute of Mental Health (NIMH) determined that suicide is the second leading cause of death for young people between 10 and 24 years old. These statistics of young people should be a vital impetus for school administrators to allow school counselors to practice their scope of work, versus operationally managing the school or spending an inordinate amount of time on non-counseling duties, in order to focus on the mental health of students.

School counselors have been provided with the mental health training and counseling skills, through their graduate programs, to support students while in school. Unfortunately, some students may need more intensive and long-term therapeutic treatment beyond the school day. The school counselor's scope of care may not be enough to fully support the long-term needs of the student. Additional care may be needed from medical professionals, such as a psychiatrist or pediatrician. Both the collaboration and continuity of care is key to serving and supporting the whole child.

Leadership Values and Program Standards

Leadership as an Agent of Change in the Role of the School Counselor

School counselors are servant leaders, in nature. Meaning, they are servants first in making certain the needs of others are of high priority. Their work is to care for stakeholders such as students, staff, parents, and community. Servant leaders are sharers of power; they are aligned with administrative leaders to accomplish the goals outlined in the campus strategic plan. According to Northouse (2022), transformational leaders work with a team to identify the needed change, create a vision to guide the change, and execute the determined process with the group members to make the change happen. In order to advocate for the needs of students, school counselors should become a transformational leader in addition to their servanthood. This leader inspires and motivates the team to consider the individualized needs of each student – all while contributing to the positive mental health of all involved.

School counselors need to promote their role as a change agent to increase the academic success of students, while teaching mental health components of emotional and social intelligence. School counselors work collaboratively with campus administrative leaders to identify areas of need and collectively work together to create programs that will inspire change and student academic success. In order for more school counselors to truly operate as an agent of change for individuals and systems, the collection, analysis, and sharing of data with stakeholders makes these outcomes hard to refute or ignore. Quantitative and qualitative data (i.e. process, perception, and outcomes) are keys to "selling", promoting, modification, or development of the counseling program to administrators and stakeholders alike. Although obstacles arise, standing firm in place promotes the work needed to appropriately support students. School counselors must view themselves as advocates and change agents, which requires them to have courage and make intentional efforts.

According to the American School Counselor Association (ASCA, 2019), the role of the school counselor includes working with students, parents, school staff, and community members to enhance their mental health and wellness. Their main responsibilities are supporting the overall development of each student. The most current edition of the ASCA National Model (2019) includes four quadrants designed to develop an excellent comprehensive school counseling program (CSCP). The first is *Define* which is to determine the student and professional standards that are important for each individual campus. Secondly, the school counselor is to *Manage* the CSCP by using program focus and program planning. Third, the school counselor will *Deliver* direct and indirect services to students. These services include instruction of the core counseling curriculum, appraising and advising students, counseling individuals, counseling small groups, and collaborating and consulting with students, parents, staff, and the community-at-large. Last, the school counselor will *Assess* the CSCP including program assessment as well as school counselor assessment.

The Texas Model for Comprehensive School Counseling Programs (TEA, 2018), as another optimal example, identifies four service delivery components that school counselors should be using to guide their work in enhancing the educational development of students. These components are explicit to their role: guidance curriculum, responsive services, individual planning, and system support. These four delivery service components are utilized in responding to needs of students and campus when identified.

Guidance curriculum (i.e. *Instruction* in the ASCA Model) is delivered in a classroom or small group setting. This component focuses on requirements from the state, federal, district, or campus level. Child abuse prevention is an example of a required curriculum that must be taught to students. Individual planning (i.e. *Appraisal and Advisement* in the ASCA Model) involves assisting students in the planning of their educational needs and encompasses seeing each student assigned to that school counselor's caseload. Course planning has traditionally served as an example of individual planning in which all students need to participate, but is completed in an individualized manner. But more precisely and appropriate for today's times, what school counselors discuss with students in individual planning should lead back to a mental health agenda without waiver. Responsive services (i.e. *Deliver* direct and indirect services in the ASCA Model) are needed for critical cases (Nelson and Wines, 2021), or specialized circumstances, based on the individual needs of the student. Responding to a crisis is an example of responsive services, which historically have been understood as efforts to stabilize one's mental health status. System support (i.e. *Assess* the program and the school counselor in the ASCA Model) focuses on evaluating or managing the program for continuous improvement. Additionally, the needs of campuses are met through this method of service delivery. Supporting the mental health conditions of staff have increased recently, particularly during the coronavirus pandemic. School counselors have had to provide emotional and mental health support to staff, in addition to the already overloaded work with students. The increased mental health needs of students and staff, responsive services and system supports have become ever-more present.

In delivering these services, school counselors collaborate with administrators, campus staff, and parents to ensure understanding and support for the programs developed. Administrators ensure that school counselors have the resources (time, space, and funds) to appropriately deliver the determined curriculum. Campus staff offer support via understanding the time needed with students and adjusting their schedule accordingly. Parents provide support to school counselors by encouraging their child to utilize services rendered, offering information about medical conditions that affect their educational trajectory, and when necessary, accepting responsibility in their need to know and support strategies and interventions offered by the school at home.

Additional Supports or Partnerships

Partnership with local mental health agencies and collaboration with parents or guardians may provide students with additional therapeutic treatments that are beyond the school counselor's scope-of-practice. Depending on the partnership agreement, the student and therapist may meet at the campus during the school day in person or virtually. Offering the school day option may increase the likelihood of a student receiving the consistent and long-term therapy services they may need. Unfortunately, the stigma of receiving mental health therapy seemingly continues to exist in our society. Without support from the school counselor, some parents may be hesitant to seek therapeutic support for their child, for any number of reasons like lack of insurance, funds, or time due to work schedules.

Grants are available for mental health agencies and school districts to submit an application for mental health services based on recent societal events such as an area-wide natural disaster or a national pandemic. Combined, these two entities working together might increase the opportunity to receive grant funding. In addition to grant funding, offering free therapeutic support to students and families is another way to create needed partnerships. This option opens the doors for students to receive therapeutic support, whereas parents may not have the necessary funds or time.

Procedures and Protocols

It is very important that clear guidelines are established to ensure the safety of students and staff. Procedures would need to be clearly established to make sure all protocols of safety are followed. These guidelines may include vetting the agency therapists and training them on campus procedures. A smooth-working relationship between the school district and community agency requires regular communication about procedures and progress of treatment. It can also include the agency providing the school with recommendations that support the student's plan of treatment.

Traditionally, teachers who work on a master's degree in counseling have been allowed to earn practicum or internship hours when time permits on that same campus. School districts have not traditionally partnered with post-secondary institutions to allow master's students to work with students on campus if they are not currently a staff member on that same campus. To increase the therapeutic support for young people, creating a partnership that permits master's students to complete their internship experience in the district on campuses, with proper supervision and guided support, will directly benefit students. Both entities should keep in mind clear procedures and protocols necessary for service delivery and confidentiality/privacy.

It is true that the role of the school counselor has transformed over the decades to include more emotional, mental, and social support of students. Historically, guidance counselors, an outdated name for professional school counselors, focused on vocational pursuits after high school graduation (ASCA, 2019). Partnerships with community mental health agencies and post-secondary institutions may be necessary to ensure wraparound services are provided based on the needs of individual students and families.

Leadership in Practice

National and local trends sway and impact the work of school counseling professionals. District counselor leaders educate campus and district administrators about the unique role of the school counselor. Advocating for the school counselor to be able to provide services that support the mental health needs of students through individual and group guidance activities is a key leader role. In addition, a district leader encourages school counselors to be transformational leaders. Ensuring school counselors have the tools necessary to

20 *Chenda T. Moore*

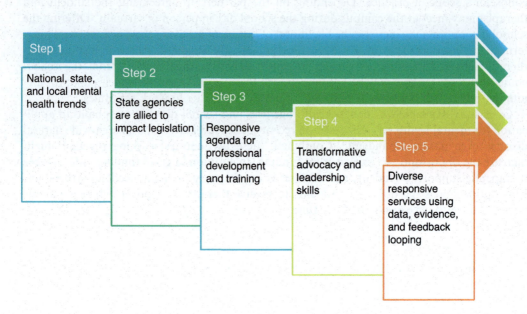

Figure 2.1 Five Steps to Promote and Support Mental Health Needs of Students. Created by J. Nelson.

promote, train, and support mental health needs of students is paramount in building confidence toward advocacy. Figure 2.1 depicts the five steps of this process.

- *Step 1*: This step is reflective of national trends in mental health that affect the profession of school counseling. Here exists a mandate, an obvious calling, to state and local entities to respond – to do something about the influx or national change. Opportunities to create programs, modify counseling approaches, and identify services needed for those served in the school community should not be ignored.
- *Step 2*: At this step, state committees and education agencies gather to develop or change state laws that affect the professional practice of school counselors. This makes the role of the counselor more authenticated, essential, and defines the work of school counselors without misunderstanding and without these decisions being made at the campus level by administrators.
- *Step 3*: This step is significant in that the district directors become charged to identify a professional development agenda, that is responsive to trends, training not only school counselors, but informing other stakeholders or professional groups (i.e. district administrators, special education, social-emotional division, school district board members).
- *Step 4*: Within this step, the role of the school counselor is transformative, and their advocacy and leadership skills are necessary to meet the needs of those served and to aid in maintaining the scope of practice historically and currently necessary to address the mental health stability and educational standing of all students.
- *Step 5*: This step ensures responsive services that are appropriate and diversified, while collecting and analyzing data that supports the implementation of specific programs or services, prior to circling back to the first step, making this process cyclical and never-ending.

District leaders advocate for school counselor tasks that are appropriate to their position on the campus. Advocacy is of utmost importance for school counselors. The ability to determine the needs of students and create a program that will garner support from campus administration is a main role of school counselors. Garnering support requires quantitative and qualitative data, which speaks to the needs of students that will help lead to academic success. School counselors need to be able to review and interpret sets of data allowing administrators full understanding. In addition, sharing the stories of successes about students and families to stakeholders is key to maintaining support. School counselors need to be encouraged to share their successes, rather than staying silent about the work they do every day – this is quite critical.

School counselors should have access to the tools to advocate for their time with students, such as a needs assessment survey, data collection technology, and guidance curriculum training. A campus needs assessment survey can be created using software available within the district such as Office 365 or Google Form. The survey can be created based on what the campus wants to know from students, staff, and parents without identifying personal and Family Educational and Rights Privacy Act (1974) protected information. Once the needs are determined, a good record must be kept of all data and information collected. Best practice would be to regularly review the goals and tweak as needed.

Mental and Behavioral Health Considerations

Infusing Mental and Behavioral Health Considerations into the Comprehensive School Counseling Program

Mental and behavioral health considerations must be taken into account as school counselors develop their comprehensive school counseling programs. Assessing students, staff, and parents about their concerns regarding mental health is a starting point. Alternatively, sometimes a crisis such as a student suicide, a teacher's death, violent acts at school, and other situations that need immediate attention will supercede the need for assessment and drive the school counselor's response to ensure that students' mental health needs are addressed. In any of the above situations, the school counselor should have previously exhibited the necessary competencies for responding to such crises.

Stakeholders

Administrators should rely on the school counselor to be a leader on the school crisis committee and should look to the school counselor for sound professional judgments in serious and complex situations. Providing professional development to teachers and other school staff is one way that school counselors can contribute to being prepared for potential crisis situations. Additionally, school counselors should reach out to community helpers such as law enforcement, firefighters, emergency medical services, and medical and counseling professionals to determine how those entities can help during a crisis. Collaborating with stakeholders throughout the academic year establishes relationships that will be helpful in times of critical need.

School Counselor

School counselors have a responsibility to safeguard their own mental health. This is made clear in the ASCA and ACA codes of ethics as well as most state regulations or statutes. School counselors are pulled in many directions, and much is required of them. They are obligated to know when they are impaired for any reason whether it be personal or professional, and they must seek help to be able to care for others in their charge. The school counselor can be a beacon of positive mental health for the school staff and students encouraging everyone to be cognizant of their own needs and mental health status. Organizing time throughout the year for play and relaxation is one way that school counselors can remind everyone on campus to take care of themselves.

Ethical Considerations

There are ethical considerations when learning about the perspective on mental health in schools. American Counseling Association Code of Ethics (2014) and American School Counselor Ethical Standards (2022) has components of the codes applicable to providing services to students. They range from professional responsibility, obligations, decision-making models, and wellness. Although there may be other ethical considerations not mentioned herein, understanding codes of ethics is a mandate for school counseling professionals, and their administrators should be privy to these mandates, in order to service students, staff, and families ethically to prevent a breach of students' rights.

American Counseling Association Code of Ethics (2014)

> **C.5 Nondiscrimination**
>
> Counselors do not condone or engage in discrimination against prospective or current clients, students, employees, supervisees, or research participants based on age, culture, disability, ethnicity, race, religion/spirituality, gender, gender identity, sexual orientation, marital/partnership status, language preference, socioeconomic status, immigration status, or any basis proscribed by law.

Professional Responsibility

School counselors consider the vulnerabilities of students and remain cognizant of individual needs when it comes to making professional decisions. The American Counseling Association Code of Ethics (2014) expects counselors to advocate for change by helping to remove potential barriers that may prevent appropriate access for all clients. It is the professional responsibility of all counselors, whether within the school or community setting, to have this professional stance. Individual biases, or implicit biases, need to be addressed in order to serve and support the mental health needs of students and prevent services from being affected by inherent biases.

> *C.2.e Consultations on Ethical Obligations*
>
> Counselors take reasonable steps to consult with other counselors, the ACA Ethics and Professional Standards Department, or related professionals when they have questions regarding their ethical obligations or professional practice.

Consultation with other professionals should be a best practice especially when it comes to ethical matters. Various circumstances will arise whereas seeking the professional opinion from others, with similar credentials, better authenticates and substantiates the actions of the school counseling professional. No one professional should practice in a silo. Reasonable steps should be taken and documented to show that sincere efforts were taken to seek input from fellow experts in the profession when helping intercede or mitigate the mental health needs of students, staff, and families.

Professional Wellness

In addition to being aware of the needs of students or clients, school counselors should be aware of their own individual needs. Self-awareness and self-compassion are important to being personally and professionally well. Appropriate steps should be taken to prevent potential burnout in which the counselor may become impaired whereby students or clients are negatively affected.

It is important to note that the ACA Code of Ethics (2014) specifically states within Section C of the introduction that counselors are to "engage in self-care activities to maintain and promote their own emotional, physical, mental, and spiritual well-being to best meet their professional responsibilities" (p. 8). In order to serve and support clients, counselors should maintain their own wellness.

C.2.g Impairment

Counselors monitor themselves for signs of impairment from their own physical, mental, or emotional problems and refrain from offering or providing professional services when impaired. They seek assistance for problems that reach the level of professional impairment, and, if necessary, they limit, suspend, or terminate their professional responsibilities until it is determined that they may safely resume their work. Counselors assist colleagues or supervisors in recognizing their own professional impairment and provide consultation and assistance when warranted with colleagues or supervisors showing signs of impairment and intervene as appropriate to prevent imminent harm to clients.

There are similarities in the code of ethics practiced by certified school counselors and licensed professional counselors. First and foremost, is the idea of doing no harm. As noted in the ACA Code of Ethics (2014), "the primary responsibility of counselors is to respect the dignity and promote the welfare of clients" (p. 4).

A.4 Avoiding Harm and Imposing Values

A.4.a Avoiding Harm

Counselors act to avoid harming their clients, trainees, and research participants and to minimize or to remedy unavoidable or unanticipated harm.

It is the responsibility of the counselor to consult with fellow professionals or supervisors about difficult or uncertain situations.

D.2 Provision of Consultation Services (ACA Code of Ethics, 2014)

D.2.a Consultant Competency

Counselors take reasonable steps to ensure that they have the appropriate resources and competencies when providing consultation services. Counselors provide appropriate referral resources when requested or needed.

D.2.b Informed Consent in Formal Consultation

When providing formal consultation services, counselors have an obligation to review, in writing and verbally, the rights and responsibilities of both counselors and consultees. Counselors use clear and understandable language to inform all parties involved about the purpose of the services to be provided, relevant costs, potential risks and benefits, and the limits of confidentiality.

American School Counselor Association Ethical Standards for School Counselors (2022)

A.1 Supporting Student Development

School counselors:

a Have a primary obligation to the students, who are to be treated with dignity and respect as unique individuals.
b Aim to provide counseling to students in a brief context and support students and families/guardians in obtaining outside services if the student needs long-term clinical counseling.

The aim of school counselors is to provide brief or short-term support to students while in school. When mental health needs are a consideration, one may wonder how brief or short-term support can offer a thorough approach to service delivery. Therefore, providing community resources to families and the importance of partnership with local mental health agencies becomes even more important for long-term support that may be needed for students and families.

The American School Counselor Association (ASCA) Ethical Standard for School Counselors (2022) states the following about professional wellness:

B. RESPONSIBILITIES TO PARENTS/GUARDIANS, SCHOOL AND SELF

B.3 Responsibilities to Self

School counselors:

e Engage in professional development and personal growth throughout their careers. Professional development includes attendance at state and national conferences and reading journal articles. School counselors regularly attend training on school counselors' current legal and ethical responsibilities.
f Monitor their emotional and physical health and practice wellness to ensure optimal professional effectiveness. School counselors seek physical or mental health support when needed to ensure professional competence.
g Monitor personal behaviors and recognize the high standard of care a professional in this critical position of trust must maintain on and off the job. School counselors are cognizant of and refrain from activity that may diminish their effectiveness within the school community.

Responsibility to Students

Professional school counselors who also hold a licensed professional counselor (LPC) credential follow the requirements and protocols of the school district first, no matter if their role is serving as an alpha or grade level counselor or a mental health counselor that is not assigned a student group. A Mental Health Counselor can have different titles in different school districts. Some possible titles include Student Support Counselor or Crisis Counselor. Individuals who serve in this role may be both a certified school counselor (CSC) and licensed professional counselor (LPC) or only the LPC credential. Since the increase in mental health concerns of students, more school districts are financially supporting these positions but are inconsistent in the requirements of certificates and or licenses.

School counselors do not diagnose (ASCA Ethical Standards for School Counselors, 2022) but must be aware of a student's diagnosis and work in tandem with the partnering agency to develop appropriate accommodations or modifications. These accommodations or modifications support academic success. Collaboration and partnership that creates wraparound services and educational teams will best serve the needs of students.

A. RESPONSIBILITY TO STUDENTS

A.1 Supporting Student Development

School counselors:

c Do not diagnose but remain acutely aware of how a student's diagnosis can potentially affect the student's academic success.

The ASCA Ethical Standards for School Counselors (2022) states the following about professional responsibilities related to consultation:

B. RESPONSIBILITIES TO PARENTS/GUARDIANS, SCHOOL AND SELF

B.3 Responsibilities to Self

School counselors:

j Apply an ethical decision-making model and seek consultation and supervision from colleagues and other professionals who are knowledgeable of the profession's practices when ethical questions arise.

The ASCA Ethical Standards for School Counselors (2022) states the following about professional responsibilities related to multicultural considerations:

B. RESPONSIBILITIES TO PARENTS/GUARDIANS, SCHOOL AND SELF

B.3 Responsibilities to Self

School counselors:

i Monitor personal behaviors and recognize the high standard of care a professional in this critical position of trust must maintain on and off the job. School counselors are cognizant of and refrain from activity that may diminish their effectiveness within the school community.

k Honor the diversity and identities of students and seek training/supervision when prejudice or biases interfere with providing comprehensive school counseling services to all pre-K–12 students. School counselors will not refuse services to students based solely on personally held beliefs/values rooted in one's religion, culture or ethnicity. School counselors work toward a school climate that embraces diverse identities and promotes equitable outcomes in academic, career and social/emotional development for all students.

While school counselors follow the ASCA Ethical Standards for School Counselors (2022) to advocate for students' values and beliefs, restrictions from the local education agency (LEA) or district administration should be considered when it comes to following protocols and procedures. While advocating for the individual needs of students is a priority, adhering to district policies may sometimes conflict with the school counselor's personal beliefs. Personal beliefs must be set aside to adhere to written policies while promoting equity and access for all students.

Professional development for all staff related to working with students and families from diverse backgrounds continues to be a necessity. School counselors are in a position to provide these types of training to staff but may be afraid due to societal views or fear of showing vulnerabilities. Research has shown that growth of self and others requires facing vulnerabilities so others could learn to face theirs (Brown, 2013). Courage is needed when discussing uncomfortable or controversial topics.

The ASCA Ethical Standards for School Counselors (2022) states the following about professional responsibilities related to data collection:

A. RESPONSIBILITY TO STUDENTS

A.3 Comprehensive Data-Informed Program

School counselors:

a Provide students with a culturally responsive school counseling program that promotes academic, career and social/emotional development and equitable opportunity and achievement outcomes for all students.
b Collaborate with administration, teachers, staff and stakeholders for equitable school improvement goals.
c Use data-collection tools adhering to standards of confidentiality as expressed in A.2.
d Review and use school and student data to assess and address needs, including but not limited to data on strengths and disparities that may exist related to gender, race, ethnicity, socioeconomic status, disability and/or other relevant classifications.
e Deliver research-based interventions to help close achievement, attainment, information, attendance, discipline, resource and opportunity gaps.
f Collect and analyze participation, ASCA Mindsets & Behaviors and outcome data to determine the progress and effectiveness of the school counseling program.
g Share data outcomes with stakeholders.

Ethical Decision-Making Model

In any therapeutic relationship, whether in the school or community setting, difficult situations may come up daily and without any notice. The American Counseling Association (ACA, 2014) expects counselors to "engage in a carefully considered ethical decision-making process" because of the responsibility to clients in the community setting or in the school setting, students.

The ethical decision-making process requires intentionality in using the five foundational principles: autonomy, justice, beneficence, nonmaleficence, and fidelity (Forester-Miller and Davis, 2016). Honoring these foundational principles can only influence (through the counseling relationship) and support (the student, staff, or family served) to understand how all these principles are directly indicative of positive mental health and wellness.

Autonomy gives individuals the freedom to make appropriate choices within the confines of not impinging on the rights of others. Counselors also determine that these individuals have the mental capacity to make competent choices so harm to self or others is prevented.

Justice is treating individuals based on their needs. Not all clients are the same so consideration is given based on individual needs. Accommodations may be required based on individual needs.

Beneficence requires the counselor to do good, prevent harm when possible, and be proactive in prevention and intervention that is for the good of clients.

Nonmaleficence is not doing harm to individuals. This principle focuses on not doing harm and preventing risk of harm.

Fidelity involves the "notions of loyalty, faithfulness, and honoring commitments.

(Forester-Miller and Davis, 2016: 2)

There are seven steps in the ethical decision-making model that Forester-Miller and Davis (2016) incorporated from various researchers identified in their work. A summary of these steps follows:

1 *Identify the problem* – This step involves gathering information and outlining the facts by asking questions that relate to ethical, legal, professional, or clinical issues. Viewing the problem from different perspectives may prevent over-simplifying the solution.
2 *Apply the ACA Code of Ethics* – Reviewing the ethical codes to determine if the standards could be applied to the problem. If the problem is deemed to be more complex, then the next steps would need to be considered.
3 *Determine the nature and dimensions of the dilemma* – This step examines the foundational principles of autonomy, justice, beneficence, nonmaleficence, and fidelity. Professional judgment needs to be made to prioritize the principles especially when some of the principles may conflict. Professional literature is reviewed to determine the most current professional thinking and diversity issues are addressed. Consultation with another professional or supervisor may be appropriate in this stage to ensure all implications and considerations have been made. In addition, consultation with the state or national professional associations may be helpful.
4 *Generate potential courses of action* – This is the brainstorming phase to consider potential courses of action and possible solutions. There is no judging or eliminating of solutions in this stage.
5 *Consider the potential consequences of all options and determine a course of action* – Potential consequences of all parties involved are evaluated. This stage involves the elimination of options that may cause more problematic consequences. All remaining options are reviewed to determine which ones best address the situation.
6 *Evaluate the selected course of action* – Ethical considerations are once again reviewed in this stage. Three simple tests are applied to determine the best course of action:

   a *Justice*: The counselor assesses their own sense of fairness – whether all individuals would be treated the same in the situation.
   b *Publicity*: The counselor considers if they would want their behavior reported in the media.
   c *Universality*: The counselor assesses whether their recommended course of action could be applied to another counselor in the same situation.

If the course of action taken causes new ethical issues, then the counselor goes back to the beginning and reevaluates each step. If the counselor is satisfied with their response to this step then they can move to the implementation stage.

> 7 *Implement the course of action* – The best practice is to follow up and assess if the actions taken have the anticipated effect and consequences.

When applying the ethical decision-making model, consultation with other professionals is not only a best practice, but essential. Courses of action may be different based on the individual preferences of professionals. The one right answer is rarely found when it comes to complex ethical dilemmas. Following a systematic model can help to explain the course of action chosen and potentially not harm the client.

Cultural Complexities

School counselors serve all students no matter their ethnicity and appropriately address personal biases so clients are not negatively affected or harmed. Equitable services for all students or clients must be considered prior to treatment. If the counselor is not able to set aside personal discomforts then they must seek consultation and or supervision.

Professionals should seek to understand all individuals within their scope of service. Culturally responsive training should be received and open communication or discussion with trusted individuals should be sought to ensure safety for clients. School counselors are committed to providing culturally appropriate services to students. Maintaining a sense of empathy and curiosity while providing support will build and maintain a therapeutic relationship that is authentic and safe.

Strategic Considerations

Principals and district administrators need training on the job responsibilities of school counselors, specifically the scope of their role in supporting the overall needs of students (see Figure 2.1). A collaborative approach is the best method when it comes to determining the best way to support students (ASCA, 2019). School counselors must be willing to put in the effort and time to collect, analyze, and explain the findings to stakeholders.

There must be collective effort to effect change. Goals and objectives must be mapped out and clearly defined to ensure all stakeholders understand. A team approach will increase the program's effectiveness with everyone participating in the planned activities. A strategic and collaborative team will create programs that benefit all stakeholders, especially students.

Conclusion

The work of professional school counselors continues to evolve as the emotional and mental health needs of students and staff increases. The ever-changing landscape of schools, including each educational level, will require school counselors and their district leaders to review job descriptions and plot out how to support campus principals as they navigate the best way to utilize the position. School counseling is no longer just a position or service but a program that is comprehensive in nature in order to support the whole child.

In summary, school counselors must advocate for their time with students by creating a collaborative program that supports the district and campus mission and vision. School counselors must be willing to voice the needs of their students and campus, backed by qualitative and quantitative data, in order to implement a comprehensive school counseling program. Advocacy of the profession, services provided, and programs that support not just the mental health needs of students but the whole child that promotes academic success. School counselors need to become courageous as they take a more active role in advocating for services and programs.

References

American Counseling Association (2014) *ACA Code of Ethics*. Online. Available HTTP: <https://www.counseling.org/Resources/aca-code-of-ethics.pdf>

American School Counselor Association (ASCA) (2019) *Embrace the Past, Welcome the Future: A Brief History of School Counseling*. Adapted from Gysbers, N.C. (2010). Online. Available HTTP: <https://www.schoolcounselor.org/getmedia/52aaab9f-39ae-4fd0-8387-1d9c10b9ccb8/History-of-School-Counseling.pdf>

ASCA (2022) *ASCA Ethical Standards for School Counselors*, Alexandria, VA: Author.

Bray, B. (2016) "The counselor's role in ensuring school safety", *Counseling Today*. Online. Available HTTP: <https://ct.counseling.org/2016/08/counselors-role-ensuring-school-safety/>

Brown, B. (2013) *Daring Greatly: How the Courage to be Vulnerable Transforms The Way We Live, Love, Parent and Lead*, London: Portfolio Penguin.

Center for Disease Control (CDC) (2021). *Suicide Statistics*. Online. Available HTTP: <https://www.cdc.gov/nchs/pressroom/sosmap/suicide-mortality/suicide.htm>

Forester-Miller, H. and Davis, T.E. (2016) *Practitioner's Guide to Ethical Decision Making*. Online. Available HTTP: <https://www.counseling.org/docs/default-source/ethics/practioner-39-s-guide-to-ethical-decision-making.pdf?sfvrsn=f9e5482c_10>

Online Counseling Programs (2017) *Guidance to School Counselor: The Evolution of Professional School Counseling*. Online. Available HTTP: <https://onlinecounselingprograms.com/resources/history-of-school-counseling/>

National Institute of Mental Health (2019) *Suicide Statistics*. Online. Available HTTP: <https://www.nimh.nih.gov/health/statistics/suicide>

Nelson, J.A. and Wines, L.A. (2021) *Responding to Critical Cases in School Counseling: Building on Theory, Standards, and Experience for Optimal Crisis Intervention*, Abingdon: Taylor & Francis.

Northouse, P. (2022) *Leadership: Theory and Practice* (9th edn), Thousand Oaks, CA: Sage Publications, Inc.

Substance Abuse and Mental Health Services Administration (2019) *Ready, Set, Go, Review: Screening for Behavioral Health Risk in Schools*, Rockville, MD: Office of the Chief Medical Officer, Substance Abuse and Mental Health Services Administration.

Texas Education Agency (TEA) (2018) *The Texas Model for Comprehensive School Counseling Programs*, Austin, TX: Author.

U.S. Department of Education (1974) Family Educational Rights and Privacy Act. Online. Available HTTP: <https://www2.ed.gov/policy/gen/guid/fpco/ferpa/index.html>

3 Promoting Positive Mental Health in Changing Times

Lorry Royal

Leadership Quote

Advocating and creating awareness for students, while fostering compassion and empathy, is a continual need both personally and professionally. Providing opportunities for education and training in these areas is integral for school counselors across the board.

Lorry Royal

Aspirational Statements

- Professional school counselors are advocates, leaders, collaborators, and consultants who create systemic change.
- School counselors, working in tandem with school leadership, create and build comprehensive school counseling programs that are designed to meet the needs of all students through advocacy, inclusivity, and equity.

Introduction and Background

In the early spring of 2020, as many educators across the United States were enjoying the last few days of the traditional week-long respite, otherwise known as *spring break*, news began to spread quickly regarding the global coronavirus disease 2019 (COVID-19) (WHO, 2020a) that caused a worldwide pandemic. Due to the contagious nature of the virus, many precautions were put into place, including *social isolation* (Ministry of Health T.R., 2020; WHO, 2020b). With mandated federal and local government orders to *shelter in place*, educational entities were forced to find new and creative ways to connect virtually with students and families through an online platform. For many school counselors, this meant finding innovative ways to create meaningful connections, virtually, with their students, while attempting to navigate the waters of uncertainty.

Working remotely from home took on an entirely new meaning for most school counselors and created additional challenges for meeting the needs, particularly the mental health needs, of both the students, faculty, and school administrators. The American School Counselor

Association National Model (2019) defines the four system components of a comprehensive school counseling program. These components include the program's foundation, delivery, management, and accountability (ASCA, 2019). As noted in the 4th edition of the ASCA National Model, school districts should have a structured crisis plan in place with school counselors and administrators working collaboratively.

Crisis Management

> During times of crisis, the role of the professional counselor is critical. Counselors are expected to provide counseling for students, coordinate all counseling activities, communicate with faculty and parents, seek support from the crisis team, and contact neighboring schools. Counselors provide direct counseling services during the intervention and postvention phases of the crisis. They are expected to serve students and personnel during times of crisis by providing individual and group interventions; to consult with administrators, faculty, parents, and professionals; and to coordinate services with the school and the community.
>
> (Jackson-Cherry and Erford, 2018: 409)

The Role of the School Counselor

Dollarhide and Saginak (2012) noted that school counselors often have variable and undefined roles. In addition to the numerous responsibilities that many school counselors held before the pandemic, spending time researching and creating resources such as "bitmoji" online offices with interactive links and taking on further administrative responsibilities were set as taking precedence in working with students and district administration.

According to Savitz-Romer et al. (2020), many school counselors reported being tasked with providing additional support services to teachers, other faculty members, and administration as well as delivering technology devices and other social services to students and their families. Additionally, many school counselors became responsible for:

- Taking on the role of attendance clerk, which entailed tracking daily and hourly attendance, including contacting parents when students were not present in their online classes.
- Creating online systems to "check-in" with students to create a two-way line of communication for students to have access to the school counselor and help the school counselors stay apprised of how students were coping while working from home.
- Conducting phone calls to parents making sure students had the necessary equipment and Internet access as well as other basic needs such as meals and community resources.
- Creating daily or weekly social-emotional lessons and resources to share with students and families.
- Developing resources and wellness checks for faculty and staff.
- Hosting online hourly and daily individual or group meetings for students, parents, and staff.
- Hosting individual and group counseling sessions while circumnavigating the boundaries of confidentiality.

(ACA, n.d.a)

Leadership Program Values and Standards

One of the core characteristics of a successful school is the emphasis and utilization of the school counselors within the instructional program.

(Benigno, 2017: 175)

The services and support provided through comprehensive school counseling programs can be instrumental in facilitating both the continued growth and development of the students within the school system and the system itself. Through the process of mentorship, interventions, monitoring, and reporting, a continuing system remains in place that can help to ensure that the student's needs are being met. At the same time, the teachers and administration are better able to address those specific academic needs. Individualized attention and evaluation for students across all levels are often required to address developmental and academic needs. Counselors are "often considered to be the fortress of wisdom and knowledge, for all things counseling and education-related, by students, parents, and even many faculty members" (Cotton-Royal, 2020: 10). Through evaluation and interventions, in addition to ongoing collaboration with other stakeholders within the school community, counselors are better able to articulate the needs of their students and prioritize those developmental and academic strategies, in combination with programs and interventions.

Nevertheless, scholarship has theorized that school counselors, "who cultivate academic, personal/social, and college and career supports to students and comprehensive counseling and guidance programs, are fundamental to the success of the students they serve" (Cotton-Royal, 2020: 10). Notwithstanding published documentation of appropriate school counselor roles, these defined functions often remain ambiguous in daily practice (Robertson et al., 2016). "A national survey of school counselors and principals revealed many principals believed appropriate tasks for school counselors include registering and scheduling all students; administering cognitive, achievement, and aptitude tests; and maintaining student records" (Robertson et al., 2016: 2). In their research, Savitz-Romer et al. reported that "school counselors faced a myriad of organizational constraints in fulfilling their professional responsibilities, including an onslaught of administrative duties and a lack of guidance on how to enact their roles remotely" (2020: 2).

School counselors' pre-pandemic work environments were portrayed through research as constrictive, with a loss of efficacy due to lack of funding and support at both the federal and state levels, unmanageable caseloads, inappropriate or poorly defined roles, inadequate accountability systems, and insufficient professional development resources (Savitz-Romer et al., 2020; Warren et al., 2020). Chandler et al. (2018), reported that a predominant emphasis placed on administrative duties, in addition to the issue of role ambiguity (Blake, 2020), creates barriers and impedes students from making the necessary connections with the school counseling team, resulting in the loss of student support. The expectations of school counselor roles and duties, as perceived by school leadership (Amatea and Clark, 2005; Benigno, 2017) tend to be confused in what education and training school counselors have received and how to best utilize their knowledge and skills.

Blake's (2020) study of high school counselors established that much of the school counselors' daily and weekly schedule is directed by school leadership, with their time being devoted to administrative tasks such as state and district testing coordination and scheduling. These are roles that fall outside of the American School Counselor Association (2019)-defined national model. Lowery, et al. (2018) reported that principals often assign these additional duties due to constraints and personnel shortages which results in the reduction of counselors' time for implementation of comprehensive school counseling programs (Fye et al., 2017; Hilts et al., 2019). These additional roles have also been linked to reduced job satisfaction and burnout (Holman et al., 2019). With these findings, it is also important for school counselors to be able to recognize and acknowledge, monitor, and address their symptoms of fatigue and burnout (ASCA, 2019).

As counselors are responsible for providing school counseling services that support professional and ethical standards (Kim and Lambie, 2018), it is essential for them to keep up to date with program knowledge and skills through professional development opportunities and training, while also being an advocate for their profession. Cotton-Royal concluded the following:

> In order to maintain currency on best practices and recent endeavors in the profession of school counseling, school counselors should consistently be involved in professional development that meets their specific needs (ASCA, 2019). Professional development encompasses a variety of educational opportunities designed to develop and enhance a professional's knowledge and skills. It is often the primary modality used by school systems to strengthen the foundational skills and performance of educators.
>
> (2020: 3)

School counselors are in a unique position to advocate for individual students, underrepresented student populations, campus, and district-level policies, and local and state legislative practices and policies. By developing and implementing a comprehensive counseling program, with the utilization of the ASCA (2019) framework as the foundation, counselors are better able to serve their students and align their roles within the context of the school system. Alignment of campus and district missions also aids in creating those valuable and significant partnerships with administration, staff, community, and other system stakeholders while validating the importance and function of the school counselor position. Trusty and Brown (2005) delineated advocacy competencies for school counselors, which included dispositional statements, along with the knowledge and skills essential to becoming effective advocates. Through professional development and training, school counselors are better able to have both the communication and writing skills necessary to be successful in their advocacy roles (Fye et al., 2017).

Furthermore, school reform and the establishment of national policies and strategies (Herr, 2001; Warren, 2018) would continue to set the standards, and national guidelines, for preparing professional school counselors for the roles they were trained in. As part of the recommendations at both the state and national levels, Carey and Dimmitt (2012) recommended a student-to-counselor ratio mandate, in combination with required data collection and its use in local and state decision making, that would aid in ensuring all students have the access they need to college and career counseling, including meeting the students' social and emotional needs.

Leadership in Practice

While the global pandemic brought about significant changes to many school counseling programs and how school counselors were accomplishing the numerous responsibilities that were both assigned and mandated, the continued necessity and the crucial role that school counselors play in the lives and mental health of so many students continued to increase. Savitz-Romer et al. (2020) reported that a *prominent theme* that developed from the students' detachment with school counselors was a lack of essential academic, social-emotional, and postsecondary counseling. Like many other educational professionals, school counselors had limited guidance on the mechanics of effectively delivering counseling services through an online virtual platform. Transitioning to remote learning required continuous adjustments which necessitated school counselors to creatively think about engaging and motivating students while providing relevant and responsive services.

In an effort to meet the needs of students and their mental health, it became imperative that, like most educators, school counselors had to embrace technology and learn how to traverse the plethora of online programs. By utilizing innovative online tools, school counselors could communicate both directly and indirectly and stay connected with students and families. To present counseling lessons, school counselors had to have even greater flexibility regarding scheduling and the amount of time afforded to work with individuals or groups of students. For some school counselors, this limited amount of time resulted in the development of videos comprising topics such as social-emotional learning that would cover a core portion of the counseling curriculum (Meyers, 2020). Providing counseling services while using engaging videos or webinars, as well as using live chat services such as Zoom or Google Meet, and incorporating a variety of other academic and mental health resources, helped to support the needs of the students.

While safeguarding the students' mental, emotional, and physical welfare was essential, it also became paramount for school counselors and their own personal health, including their emotional health. Though contending with the uncertainty, worry, stress, and tasked with providing support and guidance to others through this challenging time, school counselors needed resources and strategies that could be incorporated easily into their already hectic lives and that were easily accessible. One of the most essential recommended resources became the need to focus on self care (ACA, n.d.b). As noted by the ACA, it is difficult for counselors to meet the needs of others if they were not taking care of their own needs and focusing on their own healthy mental well-being. The ACA's recommendations included:

- Finding the time to enjoy activities such as reading, spending time outdoors, baking, journaling, or creating arts and crafts.
- Utilizing grounding exercises or calming apps to help manage emotions.
- Seeking professional help for support and validation of feelings and emotional experiences.
- Creating new routines to fit with a new or adjusted schedule.
- Allowing oneself to be realistic and flexible regarding tasks and self-expectations during uncertain times.
- Encouraging individuals to reach out for support and to know that there are others experiencing the same things.

In addition to existing resources for school counselors, there was increased support through national, state, and local levels. As school districts began to shut down, the American School Counselor Association (ASCA, n.d.) created various resources geared towards the virtual learning platforms. It included such resources as virtual school counseling toolkits, additional materials, and lessons across the expanse of grade levels. They also provided articles featured in *School Counselor* magazine and *ASCA Aspects*. The ASCA offered open access to resources and professional development training through online webinars and presentations for ASCA members and non-members. Likewise, the US Department of

Education (n.d.) provided COVID-19 resources for school districts, students, families, and state and local education agencies, delivering individual guidance and support to school counselors, educators, and administration.

The results of a survey from the Harvard Graduate School of Education of almost 950 school counselors indicated how the COVID-19 pandemic has impacted school counselors' ability to do their job and adequately meet the needs of the students they serve. Thus, the challenges school counselors faced during the pandemic impacted both counselors' and students' mental well-being. Research findings by Savitz-Romer et al. (2020) suggested the following:

- Counselors were unable to spend as much time working directly with their students on academic and career planning development and social-emotional subjects.
- Counselors indicated that they seldom received clear direction from school or district administration.
- Counselors conveyed a lack of collaborative effort involved in COVID-19 planning and school support services.

To help bridge the expanding gaps that the pandemic has magnified, it is essential to note that school leaders work collaboratively with the school counseling members to articulate a comprehensive counseling plan with outlined and well-defined expectations and input from stakeholders. Utilizing school counselors in the specialty areas in which they are trained and prioritizing the counselors' time to best suit students' needs, and ensuring counselors have access to professional development, resources, and support systems that are adaptable to the changing learning environment is paramount.

Mental and Behavioral Health Considerations

With students returning to *in-person* school, the impacts of the pandemic on the mental health of students have begun to surface. According to Sheasley (2021), there have been increased mental health difficulties and a decline in postsecondary enrollment. Rath and Beland (2020) reported this decrease in enrollment being significant for those students who are first-generation or low-income. Even though there is a limited amount of research regarding the roles, working conditions, and expectations of school counselors during COVID-19, scholarship findings indicated the positive impact and influence that school counselors have on their students and their effectiveness. This research, while focused on teachers, emphasized that working conditions either enable or limit their efficacy (Johnson et al., 2011).

With the uptick of increased mental health issues and disruptive behaviors, often what follows is potential violence or fights. According to Bonnie Rubenstein, these mental health and behavioral issues are a result of the lack of structure, losses, and stressors that many of the students encountered during the coronavirus pandemic (Warner School of Education, 2001). Many families struggled with the day-to-day lack of *normalcy*, loss of interactions with friends and family, loss of jobs or financial challenges, and even loss of loved ones due to illness or death.

Adults can support students by fostering a sense of safety and security and through positive and nurturing interactions. Flexibility is also an important factor while navigating the daily changes resulting from the pandemic (Warner School of Education, 2021). As counselors are a vital and necessary component of the educational staff, it is essential that students have access to school counselors. For students with unmet mental health needs, the barriers to social and educational development continue to rise. As school counselors have received specialized training to provide a variety of services including education, intervention, and social-emotional support, they are also integral in providing referral services to families. Likewise, they play an important role in the way of advocacy and fostering an environment that promotes access to mental health services with those services being accepted, accessible, and as a positive component of a student's overall mental health and well-being. School counselors are uniquely positioned and have the ability to assist in bridging the gaps between the students and resources within their communities. The results of these interactions aid to reduce the stigma of mental health while also helping to ensure the developmental needs of all students are met.

Through leadership, advocacy, and collaboration with administration and faculty, school counselors possess those qualities to be agencies of change for supporting the mental health challenges that affect many students within the school setting. For the sake of accomplishing these tasks, it is necessary for school counselors and school leaders, in a conjoined effort, to make data-driven decisions regarding programming and services offered (ASCA, 2019). Through evaluation of services and delineating outcomes, the resulting communication with all stakeholders involved leads to more effective and integrated planning with developing a mental health model within the school system. These mental health models, as recommended by Mellin et al. (2010) should also include collaboration with other mental health professionals while providing and implementing a tiered system of mental health supports (Vaillancourt et al., 2016).

Ethical Considerations

As the pandemic took hold of the world and forced students to remain home, school counselors had a continuing obligation to provide services to their students. For many school counselors, providing services virtually posed many ethical challenges in addition to providing services. The Ethical Standards for School Counselors (ASCA, 2022) proposes that school counselors should incorporate an ethical decision-making model when faced with a dilemma. Thorough documentation of the steps taken, and processes involved, through a decision-making model, is also recommended. (Hicks et al., 2014; ASCA, 2022).

Cottone and Claus (2000) stated that while there are over 30 various decision-making models available to school counselors, there is no set criteria or rationale for selecting one model over another. Stone (2005) has listed the Solutions to Ethical Problems in Schools (STEPS) as one model designed to meet the needs of school counselors. This model, created by Carolyn Stone (2005) includes nine steps and provides counselors with a well-defined methodology for ethical decision making (Brown et al., 2017). The steps involved are:

1 Define the problem emotionally and intellectually.
2 Apply the ASCA and ACA ethical codes and the law.
3 Consider the students' chronological and developmental levels.
4 Consider the setting, parental rights, and minors' rights.
5 Apply moral principles.
6 Determine your potential courses of action and their consequences.
7 Evaluate the selected actions.
8 Consult.
9 Implement the course of action.

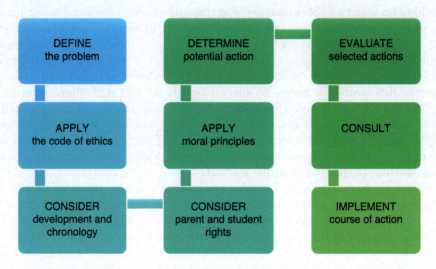

Figure 3.1 Solutions to Ethical Problems in Schools (STEPS).
Note: Carol Stone (2013). Created by J. Nelson (2023).

Furthermore, the ASCA *Ethical Standards for School Counselors* (2022), includes the following guidelines, to address virtual school counseling:

A.16 Virtual/Distance School Counseling

School counselors:

a Adhere to the same ethical guidelines in a virtual/distance setting as school counselors in face-to-face settings.
b Recognize and acknowledge the challenges and limitations of virtual/distance school counseling.
c Implement procedures for students to follow in both emergency and non-emergency situations when the school counselor is not available.
d Recognize and mitigate the limitation of virtual/distance school counseling and confidentiality, which may include unintended viewers or recipients.
e Inform both the student and parent/guardian of the benefits and limitations of virtual/distance counseling.
f Educate students on how to participate in the electronic school counseling relationship to minimize and prevent potential misunderstandings that could occur due to lack of verbal cues or inability to read body language or other visual cues that provide contextual meaning to the school counseling process and school counseling relationship.
g Recognize the challenges in virtual/distance/hybrid settings of assisting students considering suicide, including but not limited to identifying their physical location, keeping them engaged on the call or device, contacting their parents/guardians and getting help to their location.

As these ethical codes were developed as guiding principles and out of a need to help counselors resolve issues in a consistent manner according to Freeman et al. (2004), school counselors may find that more complex ethical dilemmas may occur during times of crisis or other major events. To find a solution to a situation that may appear ambiguous, it is important for an individual to not only know and understand the ethical codes as set forth by ASCA and the state within which they are practicing, but also to consult with a variety of sources. These sources may include reviewing school district policy, discussions with other colleagues, or seeking consultation (Lambie et al., 2011).

School counselors must likewise work with district administration in establishing protocols during times of crisis or at-home learning and virtual instruction. It may be necessary to review and receive additional education and instruction, related to the legal regulations concerned within the Family Educational Rights and Privacy Act (FERPA, 1974) and the Health Insurance Portability and Accountability Act (HIPAA, 1996), to protect confidential student information from being disclosed, regardless of whether it is educational or health-related in nature.

Knowledge and guidance regarding the privacy policies for the online platforms provided through the school district, and the limitations of the platform, are other factors involved when reviewing ethical considerations. Verifying the platform is HIPAA compliant and maintaining confidentiality is yet another way to mitigate the confidentiality limits that school counselors may be facing when providing virtual or distance counseling.

Before starting any type of virtual or distance counseling with students, counselors should obtain permission from the parent or guardian. This informed consent should be in writing, with the permission form being created in conjunction with district policies and guidelines with accessibility online. The permission form should include language specific to virtual or distance counseling and include statements concerning confidentiality and the potential limitations of confidentiality.

District administration and school counselors should also have policies and procedures in place in the event that a student or parent will need to be contacted directly. Identification of how school district personnel will make those connections, either from an online platform or through an alternate service provider or application, is important in protecting personnel and school counselors' personal privacy and potential for liability in using their own personal phone number. ASCA sustains that school counselors have an ethical imperative to maintain a professional distance from students and parents. Professional distance is the appropriate familiarity and closeness a school counselor engages in with students and their family members. When professional distance is violated, then dual relationships occur (ASCA, 2022: A.5).

Likewise, maintaining district and school websites that include information and resources for students and parents is crucial in the event of both emergency and non-emergency situations and what to do when school counselors or other district personnel are not available. Educating students and parents regarding policies and procedures, while also providing as much information on the school counseling website as possible, can help to alleviate any unforeseeable issues that could potentially arise.

Cultural Complexities

The American School Counselor Association (ASCA) *Ethical Standards for School Counselors* (2022) states in the Preamble that:

> School counselors are advocates, leaders, collaborators and consultants who create systemic change by providing equitable educational access and success by connecting their school counseling programs to the district's mission and improvement plans. School counselors demonstrate their belief that all students have the ability to learn by advocating for an education system that provides optimal learning environments for all students.
>
> (2022: 1)

As a means of implementing an effective and comprehensive school counseling program and through providing services to all students, school systems must be willing to adopt and utilize the ASCA (2019) Model Framework. This framework is poised on themes of collaboration, leadership, advocacy to the profession and the students that are supported, and systemic change. For school counselors, advocacy and working toward resolving social justice go hand in hand. School counselors engage in supportive practices that create equal access and provide opportunities for all students. These agents of change also serve in leadership roles, act as consultants, and serve as collaborators, with positive ripple effects being seen within and throughout the school community as a result of their direction. Integrating these themes, through the ASCA Model Framework, school counselors are better able to support inclusivity, equity, and access for all students.

While the school counselor's primary role is to support the academic, career, and social-emotional development of all students through effective implementation of comprehensive school counseling services (ASCA, 2019), school counselors also have an ethical obligation within their role of service to advance access, equity, and systemic change, as defined in the American School Counselor Association Ethical Standards (2022):

> School counselors are advocates, leaders, collaborators, and consultants who create systemic change by providing equitable educational access and success by connecting their school counseling programs to the district's mission and improvement plans. School counselors demonstrate their belief that all students have the ability to learn by advocating for an education system that provides optimal learning environments for all students.
>
> (ASCA, 2022: preamble, para. 2)

While the pandemic accelerated the integration and use of digital technology across a broad spectrum worldwide, it also forced school systems to close their buildings with a massive shift to online learning platforms. With this momentous move also came the realization of exposed inequities to access and utilization of technology for many students. According to a survey by the Education Week Research Center (2020), there are significant gaps between schools with and without resources, such as basic technology and remote instruction. The survey also reflected that 64 percent of American administrators and teachers, in school districts with large populations of low-income students, faced more significant issues through a lack of technology or access to resources and equipment. These same faculty members, in the highest poverty area schools, reported that nearly one-third of their students were not logging into their schoolwork while at home, or making a connection with their teachers.

Even before the COVID-19 pandemic, students in vulnerable communities – particularly those already marginalized by race or socio-economic status – were already facing inequality (Simon, 2021). It was reported that 30 percent of Hispanic students and 40 percent of

African American students in the United States K–12 school had non-existent online instruction during COVID shutdowns as compared to 10 percent of white students (Dorn et al., 2020). With the existence of substantial educational gaps and inequalities pre-pandemic, these differentials continue to create even larger barriers for advancement in educational endeavors with potential deprivation of future income for these students. Simon (2021) shared this statement from one of the individuals that was interviewed: "'COVID just revealed how serious those inequities are,' said GSE Dean Bridget Long, the Saris Professor of Education and Economics. 'It has disproportionately hurt low-income students, students with special needs, and school systems that are under-resourced.'"

As school districts begin to re-open and students return to the classroom, school counselors are tasked with an even larger leadership role. Leadership is the core ingredient that moves the implementation of a comprehensive school counseling program, according to Reese (2021). Through the continual emergence of ramifications that have been brought on by the pandemic, the plague of inequities, discrimination, and injustices affecting large numbers of students has become even more clear and brought to the national forefront. It is vital that school counselors, working in conjunction with school administration and stakeholders, work together to create a better system and meet the unique needs of students of color and those living in poverty. Addressing the faulty foundational issues in education is pivotal and begins with advocacy and social justice work (Rutledge, 2020). Young and Kneale stated, "Working as a school counselor leader requires moving beyond transformative school counseling roles to initiating school wide or district wide school counseling systemic strategies and being present at the decision-making tables" (2013: 3).

As noted in an earlier version of the ASCA National Model (2012):

> Systemic change occurs when inequitable policies, procedures, and attitudes are changed, promoting equity and access to educational opportunities for all students. Systemic barriers can be school-based, district-based, or at the state or federal level. Change happens through the sustained involvement of all critical players.
>
> (ASCA, 2012: 9)

School counselors must continue to educate themselves in the areas of trauma, multiculturalism, and cultivate a culture of inclusivity for all. According to Rutledge (2020), taking a proactive approach to combat foreseen issues after incidents of racial injustices have occurred is just one step of the many needed for transformation and change to happen. Rutledge (2020) also suggests evaluating programs that are currently in place and conducting an "equity inventory" to identify possible issues or gaps currently in existence. Developing program goals and shifting the focus towards social justice and "dismantling inequitable practices and procedures" as stated by Rutledge (2020), is another recommendation for positively impacting the counseling program.

Strategic Considerations

The American Counseling Association (ACA) and the Council for Accreditation of Counseling and Related Educational Programs (CACREP), both governing entities for setting the standards for counselors and accreditation standards for counselor education programs, promote and provide direction in how graduate schools can teach counselors in training the skills necessary to provide competent and ethical services to clients. Additionally, professional counselors are trained to advocate on behalf of individuals receiving counseling services to address systemic, institutional, attitudinal, and social barriers that impede access, equity, and success. Graduate-level counseling programs across the nation are held to a higher standard and expectation to "ensure that graduate counseling students are prepared to address social injustices in schools and communities" (Rutledge, 2020). The American Counseling Association Code of Ethics, Standard A.7.a, states "When appropriate, counselors advocate at individual, group, institutional, and societal levels to address potential barriers and obstacles that inhibit access and/or the growth and development of clients" (ACA, 2014: 5).

Conclusion

Leadership, advocacy, collaboration, and systemic changes are all roles that define the makeup of the professional school counselor. These roles are cohesive and interwoven throughout the work that is done to provide comprehensive services to all students. When executed from a social justice standpoint, these practices can begin to break down those systems that are currently in place that present barriers to equity, inclusion, and diversity. A vital first step is to have those difficult conversations and discussions centered around advocacy and social justice. The second crucial step that must happen, for change to occur, is the formulation, implementation, and execution of social justice advocacy in action across all systems. Through advocacy and social justice education, training, and awareness, increased efficacy and competence emerge.

Without the immediate interventions and support of vulnerable and at-risk student populations, these inequities will continue to escalate. Dorn et al. (2020), estimate that the dropout rates for Hispanic and African American students will continue to rise. In addition to the increasing dropout rates, and loss of learning during the pandemic, mental health issues continue to surface. These long-term effects have the potential to extend beyond the pandemic resulting in large-scale economic distress as well as widening the achievement gap. While multiple studies have associated reduced crime and incarceration levels and improved health to economics and earnings (Dorn et al., 2020), the current research projects unfavorable outcomes without changes to the current systems in place.

References

Amatea, E.S. and Clark, M.A. (2005) "Changing schools, changing counselors: a qualitative study of school administrators' conceptions of the school counselor role", *Professional School Counseling*, 9(1): 16–27.
American Counseling Association (2014) *ACA Code of Ethics*. Online. Available HTTP: <https://www.counseling.org/Resources/aca-code-of-ethics.pdf>
American Counseling Association (ACA) (2020) Dr. Seth Hayden. Online. Available HTTP: <https://counseling.online.wfu.edu/faculty/seth-hayden/>
ACA (n.d.a) School Counseling from Home. Online. Available HTTP: <https://www.counseling.org/membership/aca-and-you/school-counselors/school-counseling-from-home>
ACA (n.d.b) Self-Care for Counselors. Online. Available HTTP: <https://www.counseling.org/membership/aca-and-you/school-counselors/self-care-for-counselors>
ASCA (n.d.) School Counseling and School Reentry During COVID-19. Online. Available HTTP: <https://www.schoolcounselor.org/Publications-Research/Publications/Free-ASCA-Resources/COVID-19-Resources>
American School Counselor Association (ASCA) (2019) *ASCA National Model: A Framework for School Counseling Programs* (4th edn), Alexandria, VA: Author.
ASCA (2022) *ASCA Ethical Standards for School Counselors*, Alexandria, VA: Author.

Benigno, S. (2017) "Counselor perceptions: Let us do our job!" *Journal of Education and Learning*, 6(4): 175–180.

Blake, M.K. (2020) "Other duties as assigned: the ambiguous role of the high school counselor", *Sociology of Education*, 93(4): 315–330.

Brown, T., Armstrong, S.A., Bore, S., and Simpson, C. (2017) "Using an ethical decision-making model to address ethical dilemmas in school counseling", *Journal of School Counseling*, 15(13): n13.

Carey, J. and Dimmit, C. (2012) "School counseling and student outcomes: summary of six statewide studies", *Professional School Counseling*, 16(2): 146–153.

Chandler, J.W., Burnham, J.J., Reichel, M.E.K., Dahir, C.A., Stone, C.B., Oliver, D.F., Davis, A.P., and Bledsoe, K.G. (2018) "Assessing the counseling and non-counseling roles of school counselors", *Journal of School Counseling*, 16(7). Online. Available HTTP: <https://files.eric.ed.gov/fulltext/EJ1182095.pdf>

Corey, G., Corey, M.S., and Corey, C. (2015) *Issues and Ethics in the Helping Professions* (9th edn), Boston, MA: CENGAGE Learning Custom Publishing.

Cotton-Royal, L. (2020) *Rural School Counselor Professional Learning Community: Perceptions and Perceived Impact on Professional Identity*. Unpublished thesis, Texas A&M University, College Station, Texas.

Cottone, R.R. and Claus, R.E. (2000) "Ethical decision-making models: a review of the literature", *Journal of Counseling & Development*, 78(3): 275–283.

Dollarhide, C.T. and Saginak, K.A. (2012) *Comprehensive School Counseling Programs: K-12 Delivery Systems in Action* (2nd edn), Upper Saddle River, NJ: Pearson.

Dorn, E., Hancock, B., Sarakatsannis, J., and Viruleg, E. (2020) "COVID-19 and student learning in the United States: the hurt could last a lifetime", McKinsey & Company. Online (June 1). Available HTTP: <https://www.mckinsey.com/industries/education/our-insights/covid-19-and-student-learning-in-the-united-states-the-hurt-could-last-a-lifetime>

Freeman, S.J., Engels, D.W., and Altekruse, M.K. (2004) "Foundations for ethical standards and codes: the role of moral philosophy and theory in ethics", *Counseling and Values*, 48(3): 163–173.

Fye, H., Miller, L., and Rainey, S. (2017) "Predicting school counselors' supports and challenges when implementing the ASCA National Model", *Professional School Counseling*, 21(1): doi.org/10.1177/2156759×X18777671

Jackson-Cherry, L.R. and Erford, B.T. (2018) *Crisis Assessment, Intervention, and Prevention* (3rd edn), Upper Saddle River, NJ: Pearson.

Herr, E.L. (2001) "The impact of national policies, economics, and school reform on comprehensive guidance programs", *Professional School Counseling*, 4(4): 236–245.

Hicks, J.G.F., Noble, N., Berry, S., Talbert, S., Crews, C., Li, J., and Castillo, Y. (2014) "An ethics challenge for school counselors: Part 2", *Journal of School Counseling*, 12(1). Online. Available HTTP: <http://www.jsc.montana.edu/articles/v12n1.pdf>

Hilts, D., Kratsa, K., Joseph, M., Kolbert, J., Crothers, L., and Nice, M. (2019) "School counselors' perceptions of barriers to implementing a RAMP-designated school counseling program", *Professional School Counseling*, 23: 1–11.

Holman, L.F., Nelson, J., and Watts, R. (2019) "Organizational variables contributing to school counselor burnout: an opportunity for leadership, advocacy, collaboration, and systemic change", *The Professional Counselor*, 9(2): 126–141.

Johnson, S.M., Kraft, M.A., and Papay, J.P. (2011) "How context matters in high-need schools: the effects of teachers' working conditions on their professional satisfaction and their students' achievement", *Harvard Graduate School of Education*. Online. Available HTTP: <http://citeseerx.ist.psu.edu/viewdoc/download?doi=10.1.1.394.4333&rep=rep1&type=pdf>

Kim, N., and Lambie, G.W. (2018) "Burnout and implications for professional school counselors", *The Professional Counselor*, 8(3): 277–294.

Kurtz, H. (2020) "National survey tracks impact of coronavirus on schools: 10 key findings", Education Week Research Center. Online. Available HTTP: <https://www.edweek.org/teaching-learning/national-survey-tracks-impact-of-coronavirus-on-schools-10-key-findings/2020/04>

Lambie, G., Ieva, K., Mullen, P., and Hayes, B. (2011) "Ego development, ethical decision-making, and legal and ethical knowledge in school counselors", *Journal of Adult Development*, 18(1): 50–59.

Lowery, K., Quick, M., Boyland, L., Geesa, R.L., and Mayes, R.D. (2018) "'It wasn't mentioned and should have been': principals' preparation to support comprehensive school counseling", *Journal of Organizational & Educational Leadership*, 3(2), Article 3. Online. Available HTTP: <https://digitalcommons.gardner-webb.edu/joel/vol3/iss2/3>

Mellin, E.A., Bronstein, L., Anderson-Butcher, D., Amorose, A.J., Ball, A., and Green, J. (2010) "Measuring interprofessional team collaboration in expanded school mental health: model refinement and scale development", *Journal of Interprofessional Care*, 24(5): 514–523.

Meyers, L. (2020), "School counseling in the time of the coronavirus", Online (September 28). Available HTTP: <https://ct.counseling.org/2020/09/school-counseling-in-the-time-of-the-coronavirus/>

Ministry of Health T.R. (2020) *COVID-19 (SARS-CoV-2 Enfeksiyonu) Rehberi*. Online. Available HTTP: <https://hsgm.saglik.gov.tr/depo/birimler/goc_sagligi/covid19/rehber/COVID-19_Rehberi20200414_eng_v4_002_14.05.2020.pdf>

Rath, A., Beland, A. (2020) "'The process doesn't look the same': high school guidance counselors on why the pandemic has made applying for college harder". *Boston Globe News*. Online (December 9). Available HTTP: <https://www.wgbh.org/news/local-news/2020/12/08/the-process-doesnt-look-the-same-high-school-guidance-counselors-on-why-the-pandemic-has-made-applying-for-college-harder>

Reese, D.M. (2021) "School counselor preparation to support inclusivity, equity and access for students of color with disabilities", *Frontiers in Education*, 6. Online (March 12). Available HTTP: <https://doi.org/10.3389/feduc.2021.588528>

Robertson, D., Lloyd-Hazlett, J., Zambrano, E., and McClendon, L.S. (2016) "Program directors' perceptions on school counselor roles", *Journal of Professional Counseling: Practice, Theory, and Research*, 43(2): 1–13.

Rutledge, M. (2020) "Change is gonna come", *ASCA School Counselor Digital*. Online (July/August). Available HTTP: <https://www.ascaschoolcounselor-digital.org/ascaschoolcounselor/july_august_2020/MobilePagedArticle.action?articleId=1601128#articleId1601128>

Savitz-Romer, M., Rowan-Kenyon, H.T., Nicola, T.P., Carroll, S., and Hecht, L. (2020) "Expanding support beyond the virtual classroom: lessons and recommendations from school counselors during the COVID-19 crisis", Harvard Graduate School of Education & Boston College Lynch School of Education and Human Development.

Sheasley, C. (2021) "'Somebody cares': how schools are helping with student well-being", *Christian Monitor*, Online (March 24). Available HTTP: <https://www.csmonitor.com/USA/Education/2021/0324/Somebody-cares-How-schools-are-helping-with-student-well-being>

Simon, C. (2021) "Remote learning turned spotlight on gaps in resources, funding, and tech – but also offered hints on reform", Online (July 9). Available HTTP: <https://news.harvard.edu/gazette/story/2021/07/how-covid-taught-america-about-inequity-in-education/>

Stone, C. (2005 [2010]) *Ethics and Law for School Counselors*, Alexandria, VA: American School Counselor Association.

Stone, C. (2013) *School Counseling Principles: Ethics and Law* (3rd edn), Alexandria, VA: American School Counselor Association.

Trusty, J. and Brown, D. (2005) "Advocacy competencies for professional school counselors", *Professional School Counseling*, 8(3): 259–265.

US Department of Education (n.d.) "COVID-19 resources for schools, students, and families". Online. Available HTTP: <https://www.ed.gov/Coronavirus>

Vaillancourt, K., Cowan, K., and Skalski, A. (2016) "Providing mental health services within a multitiered system of support". Online. Available HTTP: <https://cmhacy.org/wp-content/uploads/2016/03/B2-Utilizing-School-Wide-Positive-Behavior-Intervention-MTSS-Key-Points-CASP-Sanderling.pdf>

Warner School of Education (2021) "School counseling expert offers tips for supporting students as behavioral, mental health concerns arise during the lingering COVID-19 pandemic", University of

Rochester. Online. Available HTTP: <https://www.warner.rochester.edu/newsevents/story/2911/school-counseling-expert-offers-tips-for-supporting-students-as-behavioral-mental-health-concerns-arise-during-lingering-covid-1>

Warren, J. (2018) *School Consultation for Student Success: A Cognitive Behavioral Approach*, New York: Springer.

Warren, J., Jones, S., and Unger, D. (2020) "Strengthening Professional School Counseling: A Call to Action", *Professional Issues in Counseling*, VI(Article 1): 61–76.

WHO (2020a) "Naming the coronavirus disease (COVID-19) and the virus that causes it". World Health Organization. Online. Available HTTP: <https://www.who.int/emergencies/diseases/novel-coronavirus-2019/technical-guidance/naming-the-coronavirus-disease-(covid-2019)-and-the-virus-that-causes-it>

WHO (2020b) "Annex to considerations in adjusting public health and social measures in the context of COVID-19". World Health Organization. Online. Available HTTP: <https://www.who.int/publications/i/item/considerations-for-public-health-and-social-measures-in-the-workplace-in-the-context-of-covid-19>

Young, A. and Kneale, M.M. (2013) *School Counselor Leadership: The Essential Practice*. Alexandria, VA: American School Counselor Association.

4 Restorative Practices that Support Student Mental Health Concerns

Christina Shaw

Leadership Quote

There is always a reason for a behavior. When students' voices are heard, we can make sense of their behaviors.

Judy A. Nelson

Aspirational Statements

- Restorative Practices (RP) in schools allows students to be seen, heard, and understood. RP provides healing and restoration of previous trauma and experiences.
- School counselors and administrators should advocate for RP in their schools to provide a place for students to feel connected and psychologically safe.
- Psychological safety in the classroom is the belief that you will not be ridiculed or teased for something said or done by other classmates and teachers.

Introduction and Background

History and Origin of Restorative Practices

Restorative Practices (RP) address the need to be listened to by peers, the ability to speak for one another, and recognition of the needs of another. They address the ability to understand the needs and purpose of the misbehavior and how to repair the harm to the one who was harmed (Amstutz and Mullet, 2015; Lenertz, 2018). "The overarching goals of RP are to build healthy relationships and repair those relationships if harm arises in any given community (e.g., the classroom)" (Silverman and Mee, 2018: 132).

RP have been used to build relationships between students and their academic success and sense of connection to school (Brown, 2015). Teachers who spend time with their students and use restorative circles support social-emotional needs, social skills, and behavior regulation, and build relationships (Golson, 2018; Kehoe et al., 2018; Motsinger, 2018; Roseberry, 2018). When students form relationships with their teachers, they are more successful academically and behaviorally (Golson, 2018; Motsinger, 2018; Roseberry, 2018). Educators can build and maintain relationships with their students through using RP (Amstutz and Mullet, 2015; Brackett et al., 2011; Brown, 2015; Gulliaume, 2013).

DOI: 10.4324/9781003219750-5

Students are heard and can express their feelings with a restorative model, whereas students are unheard with punitive and exclusionary disciplinary methods (Disney, 2018; Golson, 2018). Roseberry (2018) urged educators to listen actively to students, who can tell teachers what they need to be successful. Not only do RP provide opportunities for students to be heard; participation in restorative circles has been shown to increase students' sense of community in a school environment (Smith et al., 2018). Smith et al. (2018) affirmed the need to provide students with restorative circles in the classroom because the circles provide a space for listening to the voice of every student and provide opportunities for students to connect and converse with one another. Research by Smith et al. (2018) led to the conclusion that restorative circles can build trust in the classroom; more risks are taken because of the trust that is built in the circles. Kehoe et al. (2018) found that circles promoted student dialogue, healthy relationships, and mutual respect among teachers and students. Professional school counselors (PSCs) can advocate for the students by providing training for school staff to better understand the need for RP to be implemented on campus and in the classrooms.

The PSCs lead the schools by advocating for the climate and culture of the campus, when proactive approach is instilled. Jean-Pierre and Parris-Drummond (2018) asserted that RP are preventive and responsive. The true essence of a restorative approach is to strengthen relationships and cultivate social engagement (Reimer, 2018). RP are a preventive means to correct students' misbehaviors as students acquire empathy, social-emotional skills, and conflict resolution skills (Jean-Pierre and Parris-Drummond, 2018). Although there are benefits to implementing restorative circles, Lenertz (2018) encouraged further exploration of circles in secondary schools.

Leadership Program Values and Standards

School counselors act as educational leaders to provide advocacy and support to students' needs and remove barriers that would adhere to student success.

> They apply their emotional intelligence to ensuring that participation occurs in constructive ways, and they confront unproductive behaviors with openness and empathy, helping others feel valued and supported during change processes. Accomplished school counselors are leaders who strive to implement a vision in which every student succeeds.
>
> (NBPT, 2017: 51)

School counselors serve as productive leaders on their school sites to provide positive change, advocacy, and vision for all students to succeed. RP are one evidence-based tool that aligns with these standards.

Leadership in Practice

The purpose is for PSCs to lead RP efforts at their schools, because the role of PSCs is advocacy for social justice that would provide more equitable systems in schools (Smith et al., 2018). School counselors should be at the forefront of school and district decision making committees. This opportunity allows for their insight on students' needs to make changes to policies to support all learners.

No other professional in the school setting is more skilled than PSCs to facilitate an RP circle on campus. Circle facilitators skills are the ability to *hold space* and be able to facilitate more dialogue and work through uncomfortable moments (Smith et al., 2018). Although PSCs are the most skilled school professionals to facilitate RP circles, PSCs can facilitate RP committees to ensure these elements and principles are being implemented and modeled to the rest of the educators on campus. Additionally, PSCs can provide leadership in RP check-in circles with the staff to model the process.

Through the American School Counselor Association (ASCA) National Model (2019a), PSCs advocate for students through planning and assessing their attendance, discipline, and opportunities for resources. The implementation of RP on campus provides an opportunity to address this ASCA competency. Students who experience RP are engaged in reflecting on their own behaviors, which evolves into self-discipline (Jean-Pierre and Parris-Drummond, 2018). Students who are involved in RP take responsibility for their actions and gain empathy for others who are involved in their misbehaviors (Kehoe et al., 2018). As a result, they acquire a sense of self-awareness and self-reflection of their behaviors with others (Kehoe et al., 2018). RP can influence students' behaviors through self-reflection, self-discipline, and how they treat others (Jean-Pierre and Parris-Drummond, 2018; Kehoe et al., 2018).

Mental and Behavioral Health Considerations

How Do RP Address Behavioral Health Needs?

Stress or fear prohibits students from learning and denies the ability to focus, which causes one to be less successful in school (National Scientific Council on the Developing Child, 2010). According to the Council and their research on brain development, when stress and fear are heightened, the prefrontal cortex is affected, which "is critical for the emergence of executive functions – a cluster of abilities such as making, following, and altering plans; controlling and focusing attention; inhibiting impulsive behaviors; and developing the ability to hold and incorporate new information in decision-making" (2010: 3). Hopkins (2011) found that stress and fear inhibited the ability to obtain and process new information. If classrooms operate in a space where fear and stress exist as well as a lack of connections, then students perceive these environments to be filled with hostility and insecurity (Hopkins, 2011). When the brain is in the reactive (fight, flight, or freeze) state, the learning function is shut down to focus on how the body can survive. The cerebral cortex, the thinking part of the brain, is not active, while the fear and stress is signaling the limbic system. This significantly affects the student's ability to learn and academic achievement.

How Do RP Address Mental Health – Trauma and Adversities?

Resiliency factors in children and adolescents help them to cope with negative life circumstances (Ginsburg and Jablow, 2015). Protective factors are those that are present in a child's life to help in coping with adverse life experiences and in nurturing resiliency (Borto, 2011). The most common protective factors to cultivate resilience are present in the individual, family, and community (Borto, 2011). The child who possesses individual protective factors usually has these traits: positive self-esteem and concept, internal control, communication skills, good mental and physical health, problem-solving skills, optimistic positive attention from others, and the ability to adapt (Borto, 2011). Borto (2011) explained that people with a sense of hope in the face of adversity maintain a positive outlook. In times of stress, caregivers can provide assurance to children through their security and allow the children to express their feelings and concerns (Imran, 2020). Educators can build on the strengths of students to increase resiliency equilibrium (Acosta et al., 2016; Zimmerman, 2013).

Strong relationships with adults are a proven protective factor for building resiliency in youth. The term supportive adult refers to any adult who is available to an adolescent. Two notable ways in which a youth benefits from this relationship are time away and reinterpreting experiences (Borto, 2011). The first way is through the youth being away from an adverse environment and receiving support from an adult from whom they might not receive that support in their own household. Second, the youth can receive a different perspective and change their narrative with support from a caring adult (Borto, 2011). Through storytelling by a student to a supportive adult, the youth will feel validation, will be able to process events, and will receive guidance (Borto, 2011). These relational benefits provide a framework for building resiliency in the youth. Educators who understand the framework of resiliency can promote positive adolescent development (Zimmerman, 2013). PSCs can provide trauma informed training or advocate to provide this knowledge to their campus staff. The use of RP is one such way to facilitate a trauma informed space.

Relationships between teachers and students can be a factor for students to become more resilient and academically successful in school (Bernstein-Yamashiro and Noan, 2013; Donlevy, 2001). Borto (2011) found several themes in supportive adult relationships to adolescents: "being there, being non-judgmental, listening to them, taking special interest in them, providing encouragement, safety, and support, problem solving, and serving as a role model" (2011: 192). These themes are important for teachers to understand so they can support students and cultivate resiliency (Bernstein-Yamashiro and Noan, 2013; Borto, 2011; Donlevy, 2001). PSCs can provide this understanding through the modeled RP check-in circles and asking the teachers what elements they value in their relationships with others and how they feel when those values are met. Additionally, correlate that to the relationships and culture of their classrooms, values are important to be present even in the classroom.

Bernier et al. (2014) used advisory lessons that focused on resiliency-based curricula to foster students' sense of resilience and coping skills. The relationships between teachers and students were intentional during resiliency-based lessons. As teachers spent time getting to know their students, they calmed anxieties and implemented cooperative activities that bonded students with each other (Brown, 2005). In research by Borto (2011), positive relationships with peers provided students emotional security, increased self-esteem, and the ability to practice social skills, which strengthened resilience and coping skills.

Confident, caring adults can preserve students' resiliency, which nurtures them throughout their lives (Ginsburg and Jablow, 2015). Resiliency is the ability to bounce back from adverse experiences. Ginsburg and Jablow (2015) suggested seven "critical Cs" to support resilience in students: "competence, confidence, connections, character, contributions, coping, and control" (2015: 21). Deficiencies in these seven traits can be precursors to negative behaviors as students cope with stress. When these "critical Cs" are in place and modeled by caring adults, the adolescent may become more productive and make better decisions that lead to greater resiliency (Ginsburg and Jablow, 2015). Clayton (2015) used the seven "critical Cs" of resilience as the theoretical framework to identify the actions of master teachers in how to develop resilience in their students. The seven research questions focused on how teachers implemented each "critical C" with their students.

Table 4.1 The Seven Critical Cs

The Seven Critical Cs	How Counselors Help
Competence	Allow students to figure things out. Guide students through situations.
Confidence	Build relationships, maintain consistent classroom expectations, recognize potential, and provide individual and specific praise.
Connections	Provide students with a sense of connection through valuing everyone, meaningful conversations, and celebrating diversity.
Character	Basic understanding of right and wrong. Understanding cause and effect, showing respect, real life explanation for actions, and teaching collaboration.
Contributions	Teach the value of helping others and selflessness in discussions of real-world situations.
Coping	Model appropriate behaviors, provide safe environments, and offer and talk through choices and situations.
Control	Teach students about cause and effect, work together, and encourage independence.

Note: Adapted from Ginsburg and Jablow (2015). Created by J. Nelson, 2023.

Each of the seven "critical Cs" correlates and builds on the others to develop resiliency (Ginsburg, 2011). The foundational first step is competence, the ability of the student to make reasonable and responsible choices (Clayton, 2015). This step is critical in allowing the student to "figure out" things on their own (Clayton, 2015; Ginsburg and Jablow, 2015). A caring adult can help the student to find new ways to show competency and guide the child through a situation (Ginsburg, 2011; Ginsburg and Jablow, 2015). The adult's role in this stage is to offer choices and questions for clarification and to establish comfortable environments (Clayton, 2015). Through these seven "critical Cs" it is important for the PSCs and PSC leaders to share this information and advocate for students to build their confidence, connection, character, contribution, coping skills, and control. This can be accomplished in student support team meetings, MTSS meetings or student check in conferences.

The second step is confidence, which is the belief in one's abilities. This is obtained through real-life experiences for the competent student to feel confidence in their ability (Clayton, 2015). The caring teacher can cultivate confidence in a student through building relationships, consistent classroom expectations, recognizing potential, and providing individual and specific praise (Clayton, 2015). Confidence is the product of established competence and the child's sense of security to feel safe when faced with challenges (Clayton, 2015; Ginsburg, 2011; Ginsburg and Jablow, 2015). When PSCs interact with students daily, they provide opportunities for them to build their confidence through praise and encouragement.

The third step that is critical to cultivate resilience is connection. This step begins with family, then extends to school and community (Clayton, 2015). Healthy adolescent development thrives in opportunities for independent thinking where students have an outlet to speak to trusting adults (Ginsburg and Jablow, 2015). Connection is critical to students to possess empathy, which is established through the reliance of others and forming close relationships with caring adults (Clayton, 2015; Ginsburg, 2011; Ginsburg and Jablow, 2015). Through Clayton's (2015) findings, PSCs can provide students with a sense of connection through valuing everyone, meaningful conversations, and celebrating diversity.

Character, the fourth step, is the basic understanding of what is right and wrong (Clayton, 2015; Ginsburg, 2011; Ginsburg and Jablow, 2015). This step is shown through completion of all prior steps and a strong sense of confidence to make the right decision

(Clayton, 2015). Teachers have identified actions in the classroom to develop character with their students: understanding cause and effect, showing respect, real life explanation for actions, and teaching collaboration (Clayton, 2015). This step is important because it is the action to all of the steps before character. Students show their true character really by their actions (Clayton, 2015; Ginsburg, 2011).

Understanding the importance of the child's contribution to the world is the fifth step (Clayton, 2015; Ginsburg, 2011; Ginsburg and Jablow, 2015). This is the ability to understand one's impact on the world and how one's role contributes and affects others (Clayton, 2015; Ginsburg, 2011; Ginsburg and Jablow, 2015). PSCs have implemented opportunities for students to develop this "critical C" by teaching the value of helping others and selflessness in discussions of real-world situations (Clayton, 2015).

The sixth "critical C" brings the step inward to an ability to handle stressors through coping skills (Clayton, 2015; Ginsburg, 2011; Ginsburg and Jablow, 2015). In this step, resiliency begins to emerge in adolescents through their ability to showcase strategies to cope with difficult situations and adapt to new environments (Clayton, 2015). When this stage is evident, the ability to take positive action against stress, show positive ways to deal with emotions, and live a healthful lifestyle are expressed (Clayton, 2015; Ginsburg, 2011; Ginsburg and Jablow, 2015). PSCs have identified their roles in developing coping skills through modeling appropriate behaviors, providing safe environments, and offering and talking through choices and situations (Clayton, 2015).

The last step is control, which is the understanding that one has control over decisions and outcomes (Clayton, 2015; Ginsburg, 2011; Ginsburg and Jablow, 2015). "The ability to make decisions and realize that outcomes are based on those decisions helps a child to become more resilient" (Clayton, 2015: 37). This step is critical in building resiliency and is crucial in the RP process. It is important for students to know that there is consistency in discipline. Students can help to make decisions and can understand that there are positive and negative consequences for their actions (Clayton, 2015; Ginsburg, 2011; Ginsburg and Jablow, 2015). PSCs have identified ways in which they assisted students to develop control through teaching them about cause and effect, working together, and encouraging independence (Clayton, 2015).

Ethical Considerations

How Do RP Align with the Ethics of a School Counselor?

School counselors are obligated to adhere to the American School Counselor Association's (ASCA) Ethical Standards for School Counselors (2022). Within the ethical standards for school counselors, there is a responsibility to students to support them through RP.

A. RESPONSIBILITY TO STUDENTS

A.1 Supporting Student Development

School counselors:

a Have a primary obligation to the students, who are to be treated with dignity and respect as unique individuals.
[…]
d Provide culturally responsive instruction and appraisal and advisement to students.

> e Provide culturally responsive counseling to students in a brief context and support students and families/guardians in obtaining outside services if students need long-term clinical/mental health counseling.
> [...]
> k Involve diverse networks of support, including but not limited to educational teams, community and tribal agencies and partners, wraparound services and vocational rehabilitation services as needed to best serve students.

RP beliefs align with the ASCA Ethical Standards for School Counselors (2022) through the way students are to be treated. Also, RP is a way to intervene and provide tiers of support that are needed for the student. Additionally, ethically the school counselors can provide support networks in a restorative manner to serve the needs of the student.

The Tier I approach is vital to building connections and relationships (Darling-Hammond et al., 2020; McCarren, 2016; Merrill, 2021; Shaw, 2021). The use of Tier I circles supports students' connections and a sense of responsibility for each other (Seliskar, 2018). Educators use RP by providing students with opportunities to contribute by creating circle questions (McCarren, 2016). A strong presence with consistent communication builds and strengthens relationships, which correlates to student learning (McCarren, 2016). Circles provide an opportunity for all members of the class to connect and communicate, while Tier II conferences are held for only 15 percent of the students who misbehave and need more intensive support (Smith et al., 2015).

Tier II or Tier III restorative circles are intensive practices used to create an honest and respectful conversation that is designed to acknowledge how each person is affected by an incident; they provide opportunities for each person to take ownership and responsibility to repair the harm done (Morrison, 2007). This intensive approach invites everyone to support the one who is responsible for the harm done in the hope that the incident will not reoccur (Morrison, 2007). PSCs use congruent communication during these RP circles to express a situation rather than a student's mistakes, which builds their resiliency to learn and grow from the mistake (Yates and Holloman, 2013).

Cultural Complexities

Cultural Blind Spots

Multicultural and equity considerations within RP begin with community building circles. Educators must provide a space to get to know their students to begin to understand their students' unique needs and stories. Brown (2005) suggested four ways to communicate congruently with young adolescents: (a) use active listening, body language, and facial expressions to match the verbal message; (b) avoid communication roadblocks; (c) respond to the student with empathy; and (d) engage in culturally responsive communication. Terry (2017) stated that RP provided relational skills with English Language learners through social, emotional, and linguistic support. Likewise, Nguyen and Normore (2017) found RP provides more equitable access to social emotional needs of Asian Americans.

Strategic Considerations

How Do RP Align with a School Counselors Schedule, Day, Role, and Efficacy of the Program?

RP align with ASCA ethical standards and positions for school counselors. Within the realm of student discipline, school counselors act as a resource to provide intervention and support for students. School counselors can advocate for understanding of *why* the behavior has occurred, due to their non-threatening relationship with students. "School counselors should be, by policy, designated as neutral and resourceful consultants, mediators and student advocates" (ASCA, 2019b). School counselors should play an effective role in the implementation of RP due to their ability to support students' behavioral prevention and intervention.

School counselors can use a variety of strategies to incorporate RCs in their repertoire of delivering services to students who need them. Meeting individually with students who have been disciplined due to a school infraction is one way to strategize with the student what happened, why it happened, and how the student can correct the situation. Teaching students to apologize, to make amends, to sign a contract to avoid problems in the future, and to make behavioral changes by using a behavior chart for points and prizes are some of the interventions that can be used. Checking in with the counselor to report good behavioral changes is a way to strengthen the student–counselor relationship and to model for the student ways to interact with other staff members.

Counseling students in small groups is another intervention that is particularly useful when students re-enter their home campuses from an off-campus placement. These students often have difficulty integrating back into the mainstream for a variety of reasons: embarrassment, having to answer their peers' questions as to where they have been, feeling that they have missed out on academic skills, and anxiety about being in a large school setting instead of the safety of the smaller off-campus placement. Sometimes teachers are not thrilled to see these students return to their classrooms. Group counseling can prepare students for this, and the students can role-play how to respond to negative attitudes from their teachers. Staffing with teachers before students return from an off-campus placement could head off some of these unfortunate instances that often land a student right back at the alternative campus.

Sometimes wraparound services and/or referrals are helpful. Staffings could include parents, teachers, the school psychologist, and others who might know the student and have important insights to offer. Older students can attend these staffings also. The school counselor should be instrumental in bringing these stakeholders together for the sake of the student's success academically, socially, and emotionally. Perhaps a behavior chart for a younger child could be constructed, or maybe the student needs a referral for psychological testing or outside community counseling. Parents can help identify some of the stressors that might be impacting the academic and behavioral success of the student. Each person in attendance at the staffing could leave with a task at hand and possibly a date to report back to the counselor or to reconvene for a follow-up meeting.

Conclusion

Professional school counselors are skilled at emotional regulation in the presence of persons who are activated and emotionally dysregulated. They are able to express warmth and unconditional positive regard in spite of the dysregulation of the other persons and to listen empathically, invite discussion, and, at the same time, monitor what is going on with the group (Smith et al., 2018). They should share their skills with their school community through advocating that educators understand the importance of RP and how it establishes and builds relationships between educators and students. RP supports student connections to school and can support students' social-emotional development.

Educators serve as role models for appropriate social skills and promote behavioral success with their students (Haggis, 2017). Educators who use strong social skills in a classroom and school environment provide students a sense of connection, care, and relationships that promotes school success (Bucher and Manning, 2005; Faughey, 2020; Haggis, 2017). Gehris et al. (2015) indicated that teachers are the models of how to be treated in a relationship. They model their emotions, which provides direction to students (Gehris et al., 2015). Relationships and trust are the foundations of learning (Bucher and Manning, 2005 Gehris et al., 2015 Haggis, 2017; Smith et al., 2015; Smith et al., 2018). Through trusting relationships, resilience can develop within students (Bernstein-Yamashiro and Noan, 2013; Bucher and Manning, 2005 Ginsburg and Jablow, 2015; Haggis, 2017). Resiliency helps adolescents to cope with negative life circumstances (Ginsburg and Jablow, 2015).

School counselors can promote understanding to the school community that protective factors, such as trusting relationships, help students cope with adverse life experiences. These protective factors are vital in the pandemic due to the ongoing adverse life experiences and stressors (Fegert et al., 2020). Resilient students succeed academically because of relationships that are formed with their parents and educators (Bernstein-Yamashiro and Noan, 2013; Bucher and Manning, 2005; Ginsburg and Jablow, 2015; Haggis, 2017). School counselor leaders are uniquely poised to ensure that all campus level and district level leaders see both the value of RP as well as the value of PSCs leading this important practice on campuses to support the mental health of students.

References

Acosta, J., Chinman, M., Ebener, P., Phillips, A., Xenakis, L., and Malone, P. (2016) "A cluster-randomized trial of restorative practices: an illustration to spur high-quality research and evaluation", *Journal of Educational and Psychological Consultation*, 26(4): 413–430.
American School Counselor Association (ASCA) (2019a) *The ASCA National Model* (4th edn), Alexandria, VA: Author.
ASCA (2019b) "The school couselor and discipline". Online. Available HTTP: <https://www.schoolcounselor.org/Standards-Positions/Position-Statements/ASCA-Position-Statements/The-School-Counselor-and-Discipline>
ASCA (2022) *The ASCA Ethical Standards for School Counselors*. Alexandria, VA: Author.
Amstutz, L., and Mullet, J. (2015) *The Little Book of Restorative Discipline for Schools*. Brattleboro, VT: Good Books.
Bernier, C., Mukai, G., Sinauskas, J., and Wikum, D. (2014) "Building resilience in an at-risk youth population", *Innovative Practice Projects*, Paper 45. Online. Available HTTP: <https://commons.pacificu.edu/ipp/45/>
Bernstein-Yamashiro, B. and Noan, G.G. (2013) "Teacher-student relationships: a growing field of study", *New Directions for Youth Development*, 137: 15–26.
Borto, J. (2011) "Understanding the relationship between important adults and at-risk youth and the impact on resilience", Doctoral dissertation, University of Hartford.
Brackett, M.A., Reyes, M.R., Rivers, S.E., Elbertson, N.A., and Salovey, P. (2011) "Classroom emotional climate, teacher affiliation, and student conduct", *Journal of Classroom Interaction*, 46(1): 27–36.
Brown, D. (2005) "The significance of congruent communication in effective classroom management", *The Clearing House: A Journal of Educational Strategies, Issues and Ideas*, 79(1): 12–15.
Brown, M. (2015) "Talking in circles: a mixed methods study of school-wide restorative practices in two urban middle schools", Doctoral dissertation, Florida Atlantic University.
Bucher, K.T. and Manning, M.L. (2005) "Creating safe schools", *Classroom Management for Middle and Secondary Schools*, 79(1): 55–60.
Clayton, I. (2015) "Actions of master teachers in building student resilience framed within Ginsburg's 7 critical Cs", Doctoral dissertation, Lamar University-Beaumont.

Darling-Hammond, L., Schachner, A., and Edgerton, A. (2020) "Restarting and reinventing school: learning in the time of COVID and beyond", Learning Policy Institute. Online. Available HTTP: <https://restart-reinvent.learningpolicyinstitute.org/>

Disney, F. (2018) "Restorative practices in 21st-century schools: a phenomenological study of circle practice in an urban high school", Doctoral dissertation, University of California, San Diego.

Donlevy, J. (2001) "High-stakes environments and effectives teacher-student relationships: some lessons from special education", *International Journal of Instructional Media*, 28(1): 1–7.

Faughey, D. (2020) "'I got this!' Visual methods as a restorative practice", Academia.edu. Online. Available HTTP: <https://www.academia.edu/44488194/_I_Got_This_Visual_Methods_as_a_Restorative_Practice>

Fegert, J.M., Vitiello, B., Plener, P.L., and Clemens, V. (2020) "Challenges and burden of the Coronavirus 2019 (COVID-19) pandemic for child and adolescent mental health: a narrative review to highlight clinical and research needs in the acute phase and the long return to normality", *Child and Adolescent Psychiatry and Mental Health*, 14. Online. Available HTTP: <https://capmh.biomedcentral.com/articles/10.1186/s13034-020-00329-3>

Gehris, J.S., Gooze, R.A., and Whitaker, R.C. (2015) "Teachers' perceptions about children's movement and learning in early childhood education programmes", *Child Care, Health and Development*, 41(1): 122–131.

Ginsburg, K. (2011) *Building Resilience in Children and Teens: Giving Kids Roots and Wings*, Itasca, IL: American Academy of Pediatrics.

Ginsburg, K. and Jablow, M. (2015) *Building Resilience in Children and Teens: Giving Kids Roots and Wings*, Itasca, IL: American Academy of Pediatrics.

Golson, J. (2018) "Deconstructing exclusionary discipline: a paradigm shift to restorative leadership practices", Doctoral dissertation, Delaware State University, Dover.

Gulliaume, A. (2013) "Beyond compliance and control: creating caring classrooms – Alfie Kohn's alternative to discipline and management", in P. Williams, S. Harris, and V. Farrow (eds), *The Handbook of Educational Theories*, Charlotte, NC: Information Age Publishing, pp. 715–723.

Haggis, D. (2017) "Influencing positive outcomes for troubled youth", *Contemporary Issues in Education Research*, 10(3). Online. Available HTTP: <https://files.eric.ed.gov/fulltext/EJ1147267.pdf>

Hopkins, B. (2011) *The Restorative Classroom: Using Restorative Approaches to Foster Effective Learning*, Abingdon, UK: Routledge.

Imran, N., Zeshan, M., and Pervaiz, Z. (2020) "Mental health considerations for children and adolescents in COVID-19 pandemic", *Pakistan Journal of Medical Sciences*, 36: S67–S72.

Jean-Pierre, J. and Parris-Drummond, S. (2018) "Alternative school discipline principles and interventions: an overview of the literature", *McGill Journal of Education*, 53(3): 414–433.

Kehoe, M., Bourke-Taylor, H., and Broderick, D. (2018) "Developing student social skills using restorative practices: a new framework called H.E.A.R.T.", *Social Psychology of Education*, 21(1): 189–207.

Lenertz, M. (2018) "The impact of proactive community circles on student academic achievement and student behavior in an elementary setting", Doctoral dissertation, Brandman University.

McCarren, E. (2016) "Care tactics: the role of perceived teacher care in students' experiences in secondary school online courses", Doctoral dissertation, University of Hawaii-Manoa.

Merrill, S. (2021) "Too much focus on 'learning loss' will be a historic mistake", Edutopia. Online. Available HTTP: <https://www.edutopia.org/article/too-much-focus-learning-loss-will-be-historic-mistake>

Morrison, B. (2007) *Restoring Safe School Communities: A Whole School Response to Bullying, Violence, And Alienation*. Alexandria, NSW, Australia: Federation Press.

Motsinger, S. (2018) "Social-emotional learning and restorative practices and its impact on perceptions of teacher and student relationships", Doctoral dissertation, San Diego State University.

National Board for Professional Teaching Standards (NBPT) (2017) *School Counseling Standards*. Online. Available HTTP: <https://www.nbpts.org/wp-content/uploads/2017/07/ECYA-SC.pdf>

National Scientific Council on the Developing Child (2010) "Persistent fear and anxiety can affect young children's learning and development", Working Paper 9, Center on the Developing Child, Harvard University. Online. Available HTTP: <https://developingchild.harvard.edu/wp-content/uploads/2010/05/Persistent-Fear-and-Anxiety-Can-Affect-Young-Childrens-Learning-and-Development.pdf>

Nguyen, H.O. and Normore, A. (2017) "The 'at-promise' model minority student: providing equity, restorative practices, and access to mental health supports", in A.H. Normore and I. Lahera (eds) *Restorative Practice Meets Social Justice: Un-silencing the Voices of "At-Promise" Student Populations*, Charlotte, NC: Information Age Publishing.

Reimer, K. (2018) *Adult Intentions, Student Perceptions: How Restorative Justice is Used in Schools to Control and Engage*, Charlotte, NC: Information Age Publishing.

Roseberry, D.B. (2018) "Student perception of the effects of out-of-school suspension on academic motivation", Doctoral dissertation, University of Louisville. Online. Available HTTP: 10.18297/etd/3107

Seliskar, H. (2018) "Moving from bad kid island to second chance community: a case study of an alternative and restorative school", Doctoral dissertation, Kent State University.

Shaw, C. (2021) "A mixed-methods case study exploring secondary educators' perspectives and uses of restorative practices, including insights on current influences for teacher-student relationships and student connections to school", Doctoral dissertation, Concordia University-Texas.

Silverman, J. and Mee, M. (2018) "Using restorative practices to prepare teachers to meet the needs of young adolescents", *Education Sciences*, 8(3): 131–137.

Smith, D., Frey, N., and Fisher, D. (2015) *Better Than Carrots or Sticks: Restorative Practices for Positive Classroom Management*, Alexandria, VA: Association for Supervision and Curriculum Development.

Smith, L., Garnett, B., Herbert, A., Grudev, N., Vogel, J., Keefner, W., Barnett, A., and Baker, T. (2018) "The hand of professional school counseling meets the glove of restorative practices: a call to the profession", Professional School Counseling, 21(1). Online. Available HTTP: <https://journals.sagepub.com/doi/10.1177/2156759×X18761899>

Terry, M. (2017) "Restorative practices and English language learners: language development in relational contexts", in A.H. Normore and I. Lahera (eds) (2017) *Restorative Practice Meets Social Justice: Un-silencing the Voices of "At-Promise" Student Populations*, Charlotte, NC: Information Age Publishing, pp. 89–106.

Yates, P. and Holloman, H. (2013) "Haim Ginott: congruent communication", in P. Williams, S. Harris, and V. Farrow (eds), *The Handbook of Educational Theories*, Charlotte, NC: Information Age Publishing, pp. 725–733.

Zimmerman, M. (2013) "Resiliency theory: a strengths-based approach to research and practice for adolescent health", *Health Education & Behavior*, 40(4): 381–383.

Section II

Integrating Mental Health in the Development and Training of School Counselors

Because administrative leaders recognize that school counselors are integral to the healthy growth and development of students in their schools, collective choice in promoting and supporting excellent training sources and on-going maintenance of skills and practices are critical. Section II provides a beginning to the end focus on administrative leaders adopting a commitment to expose and incorporate leadership models that promote a mental health concentration in school counselors, the development of the school counselor professionals, and the training and continuing education which prepares and sustains school counselors in becoming and operating as mental health professionals in schools, as priority in today's times. Additionally, the post-graduation mentoring and supervision emphasis will ensure the continued professional development of novice counselors.

How there is continued debate and insecurity experienced, as to whether or not school counselors are equipped to be providers of mental health, is astounding and quite baffling. The training in graduate school is one or two courses different from the mental health counselors' preparation. School counselors and administrative leaders must reshape this line of thinking and own that school counselors are prepared to identify, intervene, stabilize, and refer any stakeholder, including our students, who need mental health support and services.

Lisa A. Wines

Counselor educators who train school counselors understand that the ultimate roles of those trainees will necessitate an excellent understanding of counseling skills and interventions designed to promote positive mental health. In fact, training programs do not train students how to register students, act as disciplinarians, substitute teach, or act as coordinators of programs such as testing and grade placement.

Judy A. Nelson

No two school years are the same, no two graduating classes are the same, and no two school districts or campuses are the same. Thus, it is imperative that professional school counselors and administrative leaders regularly reflect and plan prescribed professional development opportunities to support this ongoing growth.

Natalie Fikac

DOI: 10.4324/9781003219750-6

Section II

Integrating Mental Health in
the Development and Learning
of School Counselors

5 Leadership Models for School Counselors to Promote Mental Health

Sandy Benavidez and Natalie Fikac

Leadership Quotes

Leaders focus on the value of others. — Judy Nelson

True success is having a successor. — Natalie Fikac

You cannot pour from an empty cup. — Natalie Fikac

Aspirational Statements

- Essential skills such as advocacy, collaboration, and systemic change assume a certain degree of leadership, leadership may be considered the foundation of the other essential skills.
- Transformational leadership puts the leader and the group members in an egalitarian framework whereby power is shared and the goal of the group is to achieve ongoing, large-scale transformation beyond simple task completion.
- Transformational leadership promotes school counselors as visionaries who engage with others in a constant practice of change and development.

Introduction and Background

Conceptual Framework for Transformational Leadership

Transformational leaders are recognized as change agents who are good role models, who can create and articulate a clear vision for an organization, who empower followers to achieve a higher standard, who act in ways that make others want to trust them, and who give meaning to organizational life. In a study by Strear et al. (2018), successful school counselors' experience held many similarities. Resonating themes involved responsibility for leadership; had clear, focused goals; self-defined their roles as a counselor; secured support from others; demonstrated the ability to grow from resistance; and were willing to expand

DOI: 10.4324/9781003219750-7

their leadership skills. School counselors described as transformational leaders also consistently lead comprehensive counseling programs. Additionally, programs that had both district and administrator buy-in resulted in greater counselor gains and ultimately student improvement.

As participating school counselors articulated their positionality in the comprehensive school counseling program implementation process, five subthemes were illuminated. These sub themes included supporting district-level comprehensive school counseling program implementation: (a) shared vision, (b) individualized support, (c) systemic training, (d) data support, and (e) administrative support and communication (Strear et al., 2018). Helping school counselors to understand the application of leadership to their work is key to their realizing new roles and transformed comprehensive programs. The increase of pedagogy must come from deliberate professional development opportunities that hold transformational leadership as its primary focus. Although school counselor leadership training and opportunities are increasing in presence, transformational offerings for those tasked with leading school counselors continues to be sparse. Successful transformational school counselor programming implementation and leadership involve the following sub themes.

Shared Vision

Aligning the visions for their school counseling programs with the unique vision of each school site is essential, thus increasing investment and understanding of school counseling services in the greater school community. School counselors must be instrumental in creating school mission and vision statements along with other campus leaders and then demonstrating how the comprehensive school counseling program aligns with the overall mission of the school.

Individualized Support

School counselors need a collective, shared voice that addresses the individual needs of each campus or district. Each school community has a unique set of constraints, barriers, and needs. Transformational leaders learn about what school counselors are already doing to help identify areas of their existing programs that align with a comprehensive program, reduce specific barriers prohibiting congruence in key areas, and create an action plan for each school.

Systemic Training

In order to build and support dynamic school counseling comprehensive programs, transformational leaders design, deliver, or lead training efforts that establish a consistent foundational understanding. They utilize the American School Counseling Association (ASCA) national standards as a guide and consult when needed to address components in areas they may lack competence. Training should be ongoing and consistent, where school counselors, school counselor leaders, and administration collaborate to strengthen services.

Data Support

Transformational leaders believe in the importance of data for demonstrating the purpose, process, and outcomes of school counseling services. Enhanced school counseling data collection also assists school counselors in communicating with stakeholders about the integral roles of school counselors and the possible effects of comprehensive programs on students' educational success.

Administrative Leaders' Support and Communication

Transformational leaders emphasize the importance of open channels of communication at the district and school levels, this includes combining school counselors and administrators in district-level meetings to establish shared goals. Clear administrative support from the top down (i.e., central office administrators → site administrators → school counselors → stakeholders) is essential to drive a collective voice from administrators and counselors. This partnership is seen as an effective strategy to aid in the communication of the roles of school counselors to the greater school community and public.

Transformational Leaders as Servant Leaders

Effective educational leaders are advocates, mentors, and role models for students. To become effective leaders, school counselors can adopt the servant leadership framework to acknowledge the assets of school counselors and students and use those assets to provide support and guidance. Often referred to as the grandfather of the servant leadership philosophy, Harris et al. (2017) defined the servant leader as someone who:

> is [a] servant first ... begins with the natural feeling that one wants to serve, to serve first. Then conscious choice brings one to aspire to lead. He or she is sharply different from the person who is leader first.
>
> (2017: 52)

At its core, servant leadership encourages the leader to serve others, ensuring others' priorities and needs are placed before the leader's own needs. The servant leader emphasizes the growth of the team, while striving to put followers first, and focuses on others' personal development. Transformational leaders are servant leaders. They ensure the needs of the people they are charged with leading, have everything they need to be dynamic school counselors. The greatest leaders are selfless and invest in people.

Leadership Program Values and Standards

"Who we are is how we lead." Brown (2018) coined this phrase based on thousands of pieces of research data in her text *Dare to Lead*. School counselors have a professional and personal responsibility to understand the values that they lead by. School counselor leaders must name their values for a deeper understanding of what is driving decisions, visions, and goals. Taking values work one step further by operationalizing values is equally as important. A school counselor can ask themselves, what does it look like when I am living into my values, what does it look like when I am living outside of my values and how do my personal values align with the values of the school counseling team, division, or department? Once school counselor leaders name and operationalize their personal values, they lead their school counseling teams through the same process and serve as integrity partners in this important work. When school counselors name and understand their personal values, candid conversations can occur and a robust vision and mission statement can be laid out for the guidance and counseling department, division, team, etc. A truly transformational and servant leader continually participates and evaluates their own personal development so that the school counseling team and ultimately students benefit from a transformative and comprehensive school counseling program. These vision and mission statements should incorporate transformative leadership program values and how the needs of the students, or whole child are addressed and served.

Leadership in Practice

School counselor leaders and school counselors understand that the use of literature and research should be used to guide and inform their practices. Oftentimes we learn from others who we have been led by what leadership is and isn't. One cannot discount the importance of strong mentorships. School counselor leaders must cultivate opportunities to grow the leadership skill sets of the school counselors they are leading. This begins with the school counselor leader modeling strong transformational and servant leadership. A study of school counselors engaging in educational leadership found "those who were successful took responsibility for leadership; had clear, focused goals; self-defined their roles as a counselor; secured support from others; demonstrated the ability to grow from resistance; and were willing to expand their leadership skills" (Dollarhide et al., 2008: 267).

Mental and Behavioral Health Considerations

Leading is a work of heart and leading a team of professional school counselors is a work of hearts. It is essential for leaders to continually evaluate their own mental and behavioral health. Common terminology including secondary traumatic stress, compassion fatigue and moral injury are used when a helper experiences their own set of wellness needs. A leader must model self-care and self-preservation often. A leader can include wellness tips, tools, strategies, and trainings regularly for the counseling team at meetings and in weekly emails. Advocating for wellness days at the school district level helps to develop a culture to develop positive mindsets and habits around self preservation. Adding additional wellness days that all staff can utilize during times of burnout and overwhelm will benefit the entire school community. "You cannot pour from an empty cup" (Fikac, pers. comm., 2022) is a quote often used to illustrate the need for all leaders to take care of themselves. A professional school counselor leader or professional school counselor is uniquely poised in the school community to promote this important concept and to share strategies to support mental and behavioral health for all.

Ethical Considerations

Hatch et al. (2018) evaluated questions presented to school counselor leaders, where the most asked question involved what counselors should focus on learning to become a highly skilled counselor. The highest leverage responses included: collecting and analyzing data and effectively marketing your school counseling program are essential skills for school counselors today. School counselors and leaders can work extremely hard, but if they don't demonstrate and share the impact of the work, stakeholders will never understand the benefit of a comprehensive school counseling program. Learning about data and marketing allows you to both measure and share program results for future improvement and to ensure the sustainability of your role as a school counselor and leader.

According to the ASCA *Ethical Standards for School Counselors* (2022):

> **A.2 Confidentiality**
>
> School counselors:
>
> a Promote awareness of school counselors' ethical standards and legal mandates regarding confidentiality and the appropriate rationale and procedures for disclosure of student data and information to school staff.

A.3 Comprehensive School Counseling Program

School counselors:

a Provide students with a culturally responsive school counseling program that promotes academic, career and social/emotional development and equitable opportunity and achievement outcomes for all students.
b Collaborate with administration, teachers, staff and stakeholders for equitable school improvement goals.
c Use data-collection tools adhering to standards of confidentiality as expressed in A.2.
d Review and use school and student data to assess and address needs, including but not limited to data on strengths and disparities that may exist related to gender, race, ethnicity, socioeconomic status, disability and/or other relevant classifications.
e Deliver research-based interventions to help close achievement, attainment, information, attendance, discipline, resource and opportunity gaps.
f Collect and analyze participation, ASCA Mindsets & Behaviors and outcome data to determine the progress and effectiveness of the school counseling program.
g Share data outcomes with stakeholders. (School counselors ensure the school counseling annual student outcome goals and action plans are aligned with the district's school improvement goals.)

The transformational leader guides school counselors to recognize how their own leadership aids in the development of transformational comprehensive school programs. When a leader's own belief system collides with what is right, transformational leaders lean on facts and ethics to guide their decision-making. Knowing what is expected of counselors is a solid first step in bridging the occasional administrator-school counselor gap.

Currently there is limited to no counselor pedagogy infused in university-based administrator preparation or certification programs which can further drive the wedge in programmatic changes. This truth should not be used as a crutch but rather a catalyst to engage in collaborative dialogue with counselors to advocate from the most knowledgeable lens possible.

C. School Counselor Directors/Administrators/Supervisors

School counselor directors/administrators/supervisors support school counselors in their charge by:

a Advocating both within and outside of their schools or districts for adequate resources to implement a school counseling program and meet students' needs and the school community's needs.
b Advocating for fair and open distribution of resources among programs supervised, using an allocation procedure that is nondiscriminatory, equitable, informed by comprehensive data and consistently applied.
c Taking reasonable steps to ensure school and other resources are available to provide staff supervision and training.

> d Providing opportunities for professional development in current research related to school counseling practices, competencies and ethics.
> e Taking steps to eliminate conditions or practices in their schools or organizations that may violate, discourage or interfere with compliance with the laws and ethics related to the school counseling profession or equitable outcomes for students.
> f Monitoring school and organizational policies, regulations and procedures to ensure practices are consistent with the ASCA Ethical Standards for School Counselors.
> g Using and/or advocating for a performance appraisal instrument aligned with the ASCA School Counselor Professional Standards & Competencies that assesses school counselors' knowledge, skills and attitudes.
> h Understanding the ASCA Ethical Standards for School Counselors, the ASCA National Model and the ASCA School Counselor Professional Standards & Competencies.
> i Providing staff with opportunities and support to develop knowledge and understanding of historic and systemic oppression, social justice and cultural models (e.g., multicultural counseling, anti-racism, culturally sustaining practices) to further develop skills for systemic change and equitable outcomes for all students.
> j Collaborating and consulting with school counseling graduate programs to support appropriate site placement for supervisees and ensure high-quality training that is essential for school counselor preparation.

Cultural Complexities

Very often in the field of school counseling, culture and ethics intersect. As the United States population continues to become more and more diverse, the need for effective training and supervision practices in cultural competence among school counselors is evident (Sue and Sue, 2008). Through the utilization of professional development and ongoing supervision, school counselors can gain multicultural competence allowing them to become leaders within their schools to advocate for the development and implementation of culturally responsive school practices and curriculum (Paisley and McMahon, 2001).

Transformative leaders can (a) openly discuss one's own culture and how this impacts their beliefs and worldview; (b) explore cultural countertransference issues; and (c) provide a safe environment for racial and ethnic identity development (Constantine, 1997). Broaching topics of diversity, inclusion, equity and belonging begins with leadership. Transformative leaders do not shy away from crucial conversations, but rather they openly engage within their respective capacities. The American School Counselor Association (ASCA) has developed an online module that reviews three aspects which include self-reflection and personal bias, the role of the school counselor, and systemic change through the ASCA National Model (2019). The learning objectives are detailed:

> **Module 1: Self-Reflection & Personal Bias**
>
> - Identify and acknowledge personal limitations and biases, and articulate how they may affect the work of a school counselor
> - Identify those around ourselves who affect our personal bias
> - Complete a self-reflection and personal bias assessment

Module 2: The Role of the School Counselor

- Identify the role of the school counselor in implementing systemic change through a framework of the ASCA National Model
- Contemplate the role of the school counselor as it exists within your school and/or district
- Demonstrate your belief that all students have the ability to learn by advocating for an education system that provides optimal learning environments for all students
- Collaborate with administrators, teachers and other staff in the school and district to create systemic change
- Explain the need for multicultural education in K–12 schools

Module 3: Systemic Change through the ASCA National Model

- Act as a systems change agent to create an environment promoting and supporting student success
- Use data to identify how school, district and state educational policies, procedures and practices support and/or impede student success
- Use data to demonstrate a need for systemic change in areas such as course enrollment patterns; equity and access; and achievement, opportunity and/or information gaps
- Develop and implement a plan to address personal and/or institutional resistance to change that better supports student success
- Discuss ways systemic racism manifests in schools
- Evaluate and assess the current systems in your school
- Promote equity and access for all students
- Identify the knowledge, skills, and attitudes needed to address systemic barriers and mitigate racism in schools.

(ASCA, 2019).

In order to embark on the journey to cultural competency, transformational leaders must be comfortable with their own identity and ensure the comfort of their school counselors. Additionally, it is within the purview of the counselor leader to honor the recommendations of the Council for Accredited Counseling and Related Educational Programs (CACREP) instituted standards for counseling programs which require multicultural training within the counseling curriculum. The American School Counselor Association places an impetus on the ethical obligation for school counselors to serve as advocates, leaders, collaborators, coaches, and consultants who create systemic change by providing equitable educational access. This occurs through comprehensive school counseling programming that connects directly to district mission and improvement plans. Through this work, school counselors have the incredible opportunity to be solution-focused in a way that supports all students. According to the *ASCA Ethical Standards for School Counselors* (2022):

A.1 Supporting Student Development

School counselors:

h Respect students' and families' values, beliefs and cultural background, as well as students' sexual orientation, gender identity and gender expression, and exercise great care to avoid imposing personal biases, beliefs or values rooted in one's religion, culture or ethnicity.

Underserved and At-Risk Populations

School counselors:

a Strive to contribute to a safe, respectful, nondiscriminatory school environment in which all members of the school community demonstrate respect and civility.

A.10 Marginalized Populations

School counselors:

a Advocate with and on behalf of students to ensure they remain safe at home, in their communities and at school. A high standard of care includes determining what information is shared with parents/guardians and when information creates an unsafe environment for students.
b Actively work to establish a safe, equitable, affirming school environment in which all members of the school community demonstrate respect, inclusion and acceptance.
[...]
e Understand and advocate for all students' right to be treated in a manner that honors and respects their identity and expression, including but not limited to race, gender identity, gender expression, sexual orientation, language and ability status, and to be free from any form of discipline, harassment or discrimination based on their identity or expression.
f Advocate for the equitable right and access to free, appropriate public education for all youth in which students are not stigmatized or isolated based on race, gender identity, gender expression, sexual orientation, language, immigration status, juvenile justice/court involvement, housing, socioeconomic status, ability, foster care, transportation, special education, mental health and/or any other exceptionality or special need.
h Actively advocate for systemic and other changes needed for equitable participation and outcomes in educational programs when disproportionality exists regarding enrollment in such programs by race, gender identity, gender expression, sexual

orientation, language, immigration status, juvenile justice/court involvement, housing, socioeconomic status, ability, foster care, transportation, special education, mental health and/or any other exceptionality or special need.

B.1 Responsibilities to Parents/Guardians

School counselors:

b Respect the rights and responsibilities of custodial and noncustodial parents/guardians and, as appropriate, establish a collaborative relationship to facilitate and advocate for students' maximum growth in the areas of academic, career and social/emotional development.

B.2 Responsibilities to the School

School counselors:

a Develop and maintain professional relationships and systems of communication with faculty, staff and administrators to support students.
b Design and deliver comprehensive school counseling programs that are integral to the school's academic mission, informed by analysis of student data, based on the ASCA National Model.
c Advocate for a school counseling program free of non-school-counseling assignments identified by "The ASCA National Model: A Framework for School Counseling Programs."
d Exercise leadership to create systemic change to create a safe and supportive environment and equitable outcomes for all students.
e Collaborate with appropriate officials to remove barriers that may impede the effectiveness of the school and/or the school counseling program in promoting equitable student outcomes.
f Provide support, consultation and mentoring to professionals in need of assistance when appropriate to enhance school climate and student outcomes.
g Inform appropriate officials, in accordance with federal and state law and school and district policy, of conditions that may be potentially disruptive or damaging to the school's mission, personnel and property, while honoring the confidentiality between students and school counselors to the extent possible.
h Advocate for administrators to place licensed/certified school counselors who are competent, qualified and hold a master's degree or higher in school counseling from an accredited institution.
i Advocate for equitable school counseling program policies and practices for all students and stakeholders.

j Advocate for the use of vetted, bilingual/multilingual translators to represent languages used by families in the school community and support broader cultural communication and engagement.
k Affirm the abilities of all students and advocate for their learning needs, supporting the provision of appropriate accommodations and accessibility.
l Provide culturally responsive information to families to increase understanding, improve communication, promote engagement and improve student outcomes.
m promote culturally sustaining practices to help create a safe and inclusive school environment with equitable outcomes for all students.
n Adhere to educational/psychological research practices, confidentiality safeguards, security practices and school district policies when conducting research.
o Use school and community resources to promote equity and access for all students.
p Use inclusive language in all forms of communication and ensure students and stakeholders have access to materials in their preferred languages when possible.
q Collaborate as needed to provide optimum services with other school and community professionals with legitimate educational interests (e.g., school nurse, school psychologist, school social worker, speech-language pathologist), following all local, state and federal laws.
r Strive to address and remedy the work environment and conditions that do not reflect the school counseling profession's ethics, using advocacy and problem-solving skills.

Strategic Considerations

Most university school counseling programs do not include specific training, coursework, or instruction on the important topic of leadership. Many school counselor leaders also have not served in leadership positions prior to leading teams of five to several hundred school counselors. The role of a school counselor is unique, thus the role of being a school counselor leader is equally unique. School counselor leaders must seek out opportunities to research, explore, develop and learn leadership skills. "True success is having a successor" (Fikac, pers. comm., 2022). The Leadership WISE (Wellness, Innovation, Support, Education) Academy is one strategic consideration and opportunity. Leadership WISE is an annual leading, learning, growth, consultation and coaching academy. This academy provides an opportunity for school counselor leaders and school counselors to sharpen their skill sets and build tools to lead their school counseling programs in a data-driven, heart-centered and transformative way (www.wellnessfirst.org).

Conclusion

School counselors are inherently leaders. They are poised and positioned to serve as transformational and servant leaders on behalf of students and the school community as a whole. Their unique skill sets include empathic listening, problem solving, data-driven decision making, student centered problem solving and advocacy. As the needs of school communities are ever changing, the important role of a school counselor is also ever changing. One thing remains the same; a school counselor leader and school counselor must find ways to cultivate and nurture their leadership skills.

References

American School Counselor Association (2019) *ASCA National Model: A Framework for School Counseling Programs* (4th edn), Alexandria, VA: Author.

American School Counselor Association (2022) *Ethical Standards for School Counselors*. Online. Available HTTP: <https://schoolcounselor.org/getmedia/44f30280-ffe8-4b41-9ad8-f15909c3d164/EthicalStandards.pdf>

Brown, B. (2018) *Dare to Lead*, Random House: New York.

Constantine, M.G. (1997) "Facilitating multicultural competency in counseling supervision: operationalizing a practical framework", in D.B. Pope-Davis and H.L.K. Coleman (eds) *Multicultural Counseling Competencies: Assessment, Education and Training, and Supervision*, Thousand Oaks, California: Sage, pp. 310–324.

Dollarhide, C.T., Gibson, D.M., and Saginak, K.A. (2008) "New counselors' leadership efforts in school counseling: themes from a year-long qualitative study", *Professional School Counseling*, 11(4). Online. Available HTTP: <https://doi.org/10.1177/2156759X0801100407>

Harris, P.N., Hockaday, M.S., and McCall, M.H. (2017) "Black girls matter: counseling black females through a servant leadership framework", *Professional School Counseling*, 21(1b). Online. Available HTTP: <https://doi.org/10.1177/2156759X18773595>

Hatch, T., Duarte, D., and De Gregario, L. (2018) *Hatching Results for Elementary School Counseling: Implementing Core Curriculum and Other Tier One Activities*. Thousand Oaks, California: SAGE.

Paisley, P.O. and McMahon, G. (2001) "School counseling for the 21st century: challenges and opportunities", *Professional School Counseling*, 5: 106–115.

Strear, M.M., Van Velsor, P., DeCino, D.A., and Peters, G. (2018) "Transformative school counselor leadership: an intrinsic case study", *Professional School Counseling*, 22(1). Online. Available HTTP: <https://doi.org/10.1177/2156759X18808626>

Sue, D.W. and Sue, D. (2008) *Counseling the Culturally Diverse: Theory and Practice* (5th edn), New York: Wiley & Sons.

6 Training School Counselors in Graduate Programs to be Mental Health Conscious

Judy A. Nelson and Lisa A. Wines

Leadership Quote

Training new leaders should be the greatest satisfaction of counselor educators.
                                                                Judy A. Nelson

---

Aspirational Statements

- Education and training, by way of course development as written by professors, should be degreed counselor educators, credentialed in school counseling, have served as a school counselor in the field, and are dedicated to the advocacy and training of school counselors, adhering to and conveying the trends, core concepts, ethics, and evidenced-based approaches in the school counseling profession.
- Universities with departments in counseling should offer courses in comprehensive school counseling programming, crisis intervention, and counseling children that require field-based assignments in local area schools.
- Administrators, responsible for the hiring of school counselors, should care about the curriculum taught to school counselors, by reviewing their transcript, along with the acquired skills, which directly affect the personhood of a counselor-in-training and ultimately impacts your agreement towards the continuing education of the school counselor.
- Administrators, with school counselors, should embrace the idea of distributed leadership with specialized acumen for each, which in turn, does not support hierarchical, top-down or delegated leadership approaches.
- School counselors in training must understand that addressing their internal comes before addressing anyone else's internal. There is no preaching without practice!

Introduction and Background

Course development and its inherent considerations is an undertaking large enough to require intentionality and strategic planning. What do researchers believe is required for graduates of a school counseling program to know in preparation of this advanced degree

DOI: 10.4324/9781003219750-8

and credential. In the book, *Online Counselor Education: A Guide for Students*, written by Carl Sheperis and R.J. Davis (2015), all facets of online programming for counselors were described. Moreover, this publication referenced the necessity in evaluating courses of online programs and faculty experience and research, along with reviewing specific indicators of quality counselor education programs. What this suggests is an advancement in the need for courses and quality programming in counselor education.

In a review of literature, there were fewer articles addressing counseling course development in traditional brick-and-mortar schools. Furlonger et al. (2018) went more in-depth than most researchers in authenticating the essentials needed in counseling course development of consumers (students) from diverse cultural backgrounds. The authors were in agreement that there were "certain sources that influenced [counseling] preparation courses; that were acknowledged as the first source being the general literature" (2018: 45). It was discovered that training on theoretical concepts, the integration of researcher-practitioner utilizing evidence-based frameworks, and major changes in [counseling] practice (cultural considerations, teletherapy, and brief counseling interventions) were necessary components to course development (Furlonger et al., 2018). The second source was ethical guidelines of relevant counseling associations, and the third source was accreditation standards in the field.

School counselor development and training, in curriculum and disposition, begins with the knowledge base required for students to attain their graduate degree. In summary, school counselors should be exposed to curriculum covering and scaffolding the following eight summative learner outcomes: 1) history and philosophy of counseling; 2) theory, practices, and interventions of counseling, human growth, consultation, collaboration, assessment, leadership, and career development; 3) cultural, social, and environmental factors – inclusive of trends and factors that impact learners' development; 4) characteristics, exceptionalities, behavioral, and educational needs of all students, special populations, and dynamic families; 5) selection and implementation of a responsive comprehensive school counseling program model that infuses academic and school counseling curriculum, along with integration of career and college readiness components; 6) reflective, ethical, consultative, and supervised practice during and post-graduation; 7) careful incorporation of technology that supports communication, training, data management, and learning systems; 8) responding to legal and ethical considerations (CACREP, 2024; Texas Education Agency, 2018). While there seems to be a commitment in these areas in the literature and in counseling standards, this lens is focused on outward professional development of the school counselor in training – with a concentration on counseling the youth and persons served, as opposed to addressing the mental health conditions of the school counselors themselves – within the curriculum to start, while they are in the seat of being trained by faculty or professors.

Leadership Program Values and Standards

Course development should have a model for creation that infuses relevant standards in the field and that makes credentialing nationally and internationally portable. Online course development should have standards and a rubric that are specific for review for the continuous improvement of online and blended courses (Quality Matters, 2018). In counselor education, regardless of whether your program is accredited, it is best practice to softly align course deliverables with the Council for the Accreditation for Counseling and Related Educational Programs (CACREP, 2024). Thus, if a counseling department ever decides to transition to accreditation, which authenticates and adds a high-quality value to your program, the work by way of course development has been essentially completed. Whether it is a new course or a course needing revision, the upcoming process can still be followed. The standards, outlined, should not halt creativity in assignment creation or prevent various instructional strategies appropriate to teaching college or graduate-level students. It should include a blueprinting process that allows counseling department leaders and faculty an opportunity to review its design for the purpose of essential elements in the field being addressed, for cross-training in appropriate and yet vast settings (Quality Matters, 2018).

CACREP (2024), in mission and core values, is dedicated to:

- encouraging and promoting the continuing development and improvement of preparation programs;
- preparing counseling and related professionals to provide services consistent with the ideal of optimal human development;
- the development of preparation standards;
- the encouragement of excellence in program development;
- the accreditation of professional preparation programs.
- advancing the counseling profession through quality and excellence in counselor education;
- ensuring a fair, consistent, and ethical decision-making process;
- serving as a responsible leader in protecting the public;
- promoting practices that reflect openness to growth, change, and collaboration; and
- creating and strengthening standards that reflect the needs of society, respect the diversity of instructional approaches and strategies, and encourage program improvement and best practices establishes standards appropriate for the training of all counselors.

These CACREP (2024) latest standards are specifically taken from Section 2: Academic Quality; Section 3: Foundational Counseling Curriculum; Section 4: Professional Practice; and Section 5: Entry Level Specialized Practice Areas, and they address systematic and continuous assessment of graduate students content, competence, skill, dispositional development, and culturally-relevant complexities in school counseling. These standards are below:

Section 2.C. Counselor education program faculty continuously and systematically assess how students individually demonstrate progress toward and mastery of knowledge, skills, and professional dispositions as required for program graduates.

Section 3. The curriculum for entry-level programs provides for obtaining essential knowledge, skills, and attitudes necessary to function effectively as a professional counselor. Curriculum knowledge domains and outcome expectations are frequently interrelated and not mutually exclusive. Ethical behavior, diversity, equity, inclusion, and critical thinking are integral to counselor preparation and should be infused throughout the curriculum. Diversity refers to all aspects of intersectional and cultural identity. Counselor preparation programs address culturally sustaining content and strategies across the eight foundational curriculum areas.

Section 4.A. The counselor education program provides on-going support to help students find field experience sites that are sufficient to provide the quality, quantity, and variety of expected experiences to prepare students for their roles and responsibilities as professional counselors within their specialized practice areas.

Section 5H. The school counseling specialized practice area addresses the following areas:

1. models of school counseling programs
2. models of PK-12 comprehensive career development
3. models of school-based collaboration and consultation
4. development of school counseling program mission statements and objectives
5. design and evaluation of school counseling curriculum, lesson plan development, diverse classroom management strategies, and differentiated instructional strategies
6. school counselor roles as leaders, advocates, and systems change agents in PK-12 schools
7. qualities and styles of effective leadership in schools
8. advocacy for school counseling roles
9. school counselor roles and responsibilities in relation to the school crisis and management plans
10. school counselor consultation with families, PK-12 and post-secondary school personnel, community agencies, and other referral sources
11. skills to critically examine the connections between social, familial, emotional, and behavior problems and academic achievement
12. skills to screen PK-12 students for characteristics, risk factors, and warning signs of mental health and behavioral disorders
13. strategies for implementing and coordinating peer school-based interventions
14. techniques of social/emotional and trauma informed counseling in school settings
15. evidence-based and culturally sustaining interventions to promote academic development
16. approaches to increase promotion and graduation rates
17. interventions to promote postsecondary and career readiness
18. strategies to facilitate school and postsecondary transitions
19. strategies to promote equity in student achievement and access to postsecondary education opportunities

In addition to the CACREP Standards (2024), the American School Counselor Association (ASCA) provides a number of resources for counselor leaders. One of these is the online, self-paced course titled, *School Counseling Leadership Specialist Training*, comprising nine modules, available on the ASCA website (ASCA, 2020b). The training incorporates leadership attributes, theory, how to access sources of personal power, development of self-awareness, creating systemic change, collaborating with other leaders, challenges of leadership, and promoting the comprehensive school counseling program.

The ASCA also has standards for school counselor training programs (ASCA, 2022a) that must be considered as faculty create or revise their curriculum. Seven standards encompass the following topics: Standard 1: Foundational Knowledge (learner and learning); Standard 2: Core Theories and Concepts (content, instructional practice, and professional responsibility). These standards comprise the basics of any school counselor training at the university level.

Standard 6, in particular, addresses professional practice and includes the concept of school counselors as leaders. Candidates demonstrate the appropriate scope of school counseling practice in varied educational settings, understand their role as a leader, collaborator, advocate, and agent for systemic change, and engage in opportunities to support their professional growth and identity development.

Leadership in Practice

If administrators and school counselors are to work together for the benefit of the educational system and ultimately its students, both must understand the curriculum, standards, and type of training that school counselors receive. In some university educational leadership and counseling programs, future administrators take a course that specifically outlines the training, duties, and relevant roles of the school counselor, and school counselor trainees take a course in leadership. These programs are bound to enhance the collaboration of the administration and school counselors including excellent communication, like-minded goals, and a commitment to continuous improvement.

Leadership as an Added Component to School Counselor Curriculum

School counseling programs that include a leadership component either through a stand-alone leadership course or infusing leadership concepts throughout the program, offer the best opportunity for school counselors to collaborate with administrators, to be leaders in their own right, and to contribute exponentially to the vision and mission of the school. It is incumbent upon counselor educators to develop courses that do not impose inappropriate duties on school counselors or suggest that school counselors are simply available to do whatever administrators believe they should be doing. Training school counselors to be confident about their role, their program, and their leadership abilities is essential.

Program Handbook as a Leadership Tool

One of the tools that encourages this type of leadership is the program handbook which teaches students the protocol for their professional behavior as students. This is important in that it helps students realize that they are developing into professionals with responsibilities, ethics, and the ability to make sound professional judgments. The *Publication Manual of the American Psychological Association*, 7th edition, (2020) should be required as a text in each counselor education course. School counselors in training must learn the value of excellent communication, both spoken and written. Learning to write technical information formally using the APA style manual ensures that credit will be given to original sources, that ideas will be communicated in straightforward language, that data will be used to provide program assessment, and that tables and figures will enhance the data, making it clearer.

Course Syllabus as a Training and Instructional Strategy

Another important tool is the syllabus for each course with the following information incorporated:

- Course Overview and Introduction
- Standards in Profession
- Learning Objectives and Competencies
- Assessment and Measurement of the Objectives
- Instructional Materials (required and recommended)

- Learning Activities
- Learner Interaction (with professor and peers)
- Course Technology
- Learner Support
- Accessibility and Usability

Often the syllabus is a working document, but students have the right to know when changes are made and the reasons for those changes. The syllabus should be constructed in a manner that is easy to read and understand with assignments, directions, and due dates clearly outlined. Some professors use a syllabus quiz to make sure students have read the important information included. This is particularly helpful in a fully online course.

Choosing a textbook as well as recommended readings is an important part of preparing the syllabus. Textbooks should be current and written from a stance of expertise. For example *School Counselors as Practitioners: Building on Theory, Standards, and Experience for Optimal Performance* (Wines and Nelson, 2019) and *Responding to Critical Cases in School Counseling: Building on Theory, Standards, and Experience for Optimal Interventions* (Nelson and Wines, 2021). These books include chapters written by school counselors and counselor educators with extensive experience in the field. Incorporating journal articles and chapters from original works exposes students to state-of-the art and evidence-based information in the field.

Including guest speakers in the syllabus calendar is another way to expose students to experts in specific counseling strategies or interventions. School counselors in training want to know what it is like to be a school counselor in a high school, middle school, and elementary school. They also often want to know how to go about getting a job as a school counselor and how to talk to prospective principals about what the expectations are in that particular district and school campus. Some students are interested in becoming licensed as a professional counselor as well as their license or certification in school counseling and would like to hear from speakers who have been both school counselors and licensed professional counselors. Tapping into the resources in the community creates strong bonds among university professors, students, and engaging speakers.

Four Types of Course Design

Course development necessitates hours of careful planning whether the course is online, hybrid, face-to-face, or a flipped classroom. Professors frequently are given extra time or funding to construct new courses. Online courses are constructed on a platform such as Blackboard Collaborate, Kaltura Virtual Classroom, Adobe Connect, and WizlQ. There are many other platforms, and with the advent of the pandemic, virtual classrooms have made giant strides in connecting students and professors to each other and to the content of a course. In an online course, platforms must provide ways to store readings and videos, technical options for posting discussions, a venue for students to turn in assignments, and a gradebook. Professors must help students understand that inappropriate discussions will not be tolerated in an online course. Students sometimes feel anonymous in an online course and might be more forthcoming with criticism of other students, political comments, and personal stories that are not relevant or appropriate for class time. Monitoring student activities and discussion in an online course takes time and attention to detail. Professors are wise to create office hours, synchronous class discussion time, and other time sensitive activities to avoid being available to students anytime of the day or night. Additionally, it is challenging for professors to track attendance in an online course. Some specific strategies are to count discussion threads that are posted on time or submitting other assignments on time as being present in the course. Professors can also post lectures and require that they be viewed by a certain time.

Sometimes professors find that a hybrid course works well with their students and the content provided. In a hybrid course, students might meet online part of the required time in a course and partly face-to-face. All assignments can be submitted to the online platform and an online gradebook can be utilized while discussion might be during the face-to-face portion of the course. A benefit to a hybrid course is that it gives students time to work independently, particularly if the assignments include a good deal of reading, writing papers, and activities out in the community. Similarly, professors who flip their classrooms assign all readings, research, videos, recorded lectures and other content to be completed outside of class time. This frees up class time to be used for activities, problem-solving, and discussion.

Another benefit of the online platforms is creating mini courses that lead to micro-credentialing. For example, a student who enrolls in and completes four courses in substance abuse could receive a certificate of substance abuse work. These micro-credentials do not license a student to be a substance abuse counselor; however, they certify that a counselor has completed substantial work in one particular area. School counseling programs might offer micro-credentialing in early childhood, trauma-informed school counseling, crisis counseling, counselor leadership, and so forth.

Face-to-face courses meet entirely in person. Students are expected to be present in class for each meeting unless ill or perhaps attending a required work-related event. The syllabus should make clear what the expectations are for attendance and what the consequences are for absenteeism. Most students do not maintain engagement in a course that is entirely lectures, since most graduate courses meet weekly for approximately three hours. Professors who teach interesting and engaging face-to-face classes incorporate activities, discussion, group work, short videos, role-playing, and other interesting teaching strategies that not only help students learn the main concepts, but also keep them interested in the course material.

Certifications, Licensure, Regulations, and Continuing Education

Requirements

One of the responsibilities of counselor educators is to assist students to understand and adhere to the requirements necessary for certification and/or licensure. Each state has specific laws and regulations regarding academic requirements, state and national testing, internship hours and licensure hours required, as well as specific guidelines for supervision hours. On the American Counseling Association (ACA, n.d.) and the American School Counselor Association (ASCA, n.d.) websites, students and counselor educators can access the addresses, phone numbers, and web addresses of the state behavioral health departments. While ultimately it is the responsibility of the trainee to meet these requirements, counselor educators must guide students through the processes.

In some states, school counselors are licensed, and in other states, they are certified. Some states require some years of teaching experience while others do not. The number of hours required to become a school counselor vary from state to state and are generally established in law and regulations; however, most require a master's degree in school counseling while some require a master's degree in another field with a certificate in school counseling. It is important for trainees to be familiar with these laws and regulations in order to comply with the requirements. In many programs, students who are enrolled in the school counseling track also have the opportunity to take additional hours to become licensed as a professional counselor. Each state's behavioral health website includes the rules and regulations of becoming a school counselor and a licensed professional counselor. Again, there are specific requirements attached to both of these designations.

The practicum and supervision courses in graduate training are helpful in demonstrating to students how to accrue hours, document these hours, and complete the required forms for the university. The face-to-face counseling hours and supervision hours in these courses are excellent ways for school counselor trainees to understand the importance of accuracy in reporting, organization in note taking and record keeping, and the process of storing client information safely and confidentially. Additionally, counselor educators can use these courses to inform trainees on state certification and licensure requirements. The importance of graduate instructors with school counseling experience cannot be overstated. The school setting is a unique environment with very specific counseling and organizational skills required. In addition to counseling students in groups and individually, school counselors manage the *comprehensive school counseling program* which is consistent with the goals and vision of the school and the school district.

Portability and Standardized Certification or Licensure

Portability has been a topic of interest in the counseling field for many years (https://www.nbcc.org/portability/faq). Portability refers to certification and licensure requirements that would be streamlined across states. This would provide greater access to clients in need and would provide the ability of counselors to move from one state to another without having to sit for additional exams, take additional coursework, or adhere to singular state laws. The American Counseling Association, the Council for Accreditation of Counseling and Related Education Programs, and the American Association of State Licensing Boards have put forth a number of models that would make portability a reality, but as of this writing, significant barriers and inconsistencies continue to exist and to create problems for counselors.

Continuing Education Units

While students do not accrue continuing education units (CEUs) until they are fully licensed and must have them to renew their license during each renewal rotation, they certainly can establish the habit of engaging in personal and professional growth. As it has been clearly reiterated in this chapter, the counseling profession requires personal growth as one moves through the counselor education program. Stagnation in personal growth for counselors is a disservice to the self and to potential clients. Counselor educators have a responsibility to help students grow and evolve as they move through their coursework. Professors can use several strategies to accomplish students' growth and development. One strategy is to encourage students to join at least one professional organization. Often the state chapter of the American Counseling Association is ideal because students feel more confident to attend events and conferences where they know others, and they might even become active through committee work or running for office. Professors can also take students to state, regional, or local workshops and conferences to exhibit how important engagement in professional organizations is. Professors also might engage students in the research and publication process by having them collect data and assist with reporting results in the form of an article for publication. These strategies are all excellent ways to show students what it means to be a professional.

Mental and Behavioral Health Considerations

Addressing Mental Health Consciousness and Incorporating Mental Health Training in School Counselor Preparation

Mental Health Consciousness

As aforementioned in the eight summative learner outcomes, programs are specifically developed to address these eight core counseling areas, with sometimes a minimal incorporation of school counseling courses (i.e. one or two courses). Courses in these areas should not only require graduates to learn how to work with the students they are to serve, there should be assignments incorporated in every core area that addresses a school counselor's internal well-being. Below are suggestions for personal reflections, assignment stems, or modifications to the current curriculum that may be helpful in accomplishing such.

- History and philosophy of counseling:
  - What are your current cultural beliefs and philosophy about you personally receiving counseling services?
  - What stigma has been passed down in your family about counseling and the benefits associated with these services?
  - Have you or someone you know received counseling services? What were your experiences with enduring or observing their process?
- Theory, practices, and interventions of counseling, human growth, consultation, collaboration, assessment, leadership, and career development:
  - What theory and interventions would or have worked well with you?
  - What practices do you currently or formerly have that lead to physical, behavioral, cognitive, and emotional dysfunction?
  - What was your most challenging stage of development and what have you done to remedy these experiences so as not to affect your personal or professional life?
  - Create a scale and rate yourself on the ability to work with others; to consult when confused about a topic or task; and to collaborate with others.
  - Do you believe in tests and assessments? How have tests and assessments been beneficial and detrimental to self-concepts of intelligence, personality, ability, talent, or performance indicators?
- Cultural, social, and environmental factors – inclusive of trends and factors that impact learners' development:
  - Describe what you have been taught in your family system regarding cultural differences? Choose 3–5 populations you can recall receiving lessons about from peers or family members. Describe what those lessons were and how they permeate who you are today?
  - Do you believe you can effectively counsel a student about stressful or debilitating environmental factors, when you have not addressed your own? Explain in detail your thoughts and feelings related to this.
  - Becoming a school counselor may challenge your thinking as confidence. Do you believe you can learn the counseling curriculum, and fully carry out the duties of a school counselor? What factors or barriers are in the way of your academic performance?
  - Are you an introvert, extrovert, or both? How might these distinctions contribute or take-away from your development as a professional school counselor?

- Characteristics, exceptionalities, behavioral, and educational needs of all students, special populations and dynamic families:
  - In honest reflection, how would you describe your character development over time? Has there been congruence or incongruence in what you have told people and your actions?
  - The six pillars of character are trust, respect, responsibility, fairness, caring, and citizenship. Create a scale and rate yourself accordingly and then provide a description as to why you scored yourself as you did.
  - People have talents and exceptionalities. Describe yours and how you would use these talents and exceptionalities in your work with students or the public.
  - What behaviors do you currently and formerly have that need or have needed adjusting or modification? Think about the narrative expressed over the years by family and friends and how might that impact your professional work with others?
  - Some people have conditions that are observable and other conditions are internal. Do you or someone you know have a condition where special considerations were needed or afforded?
  - What do you think about dynamic or blended families? What are your ideas about marriage/divorce? List all the topics in counseling that you know will be difficult for you to work with and your plan of remediation for these internal barriers.
- Selection and implementation of a responsive comprehensive school counseling program model that infuses academic and school counseling curriculum, along with integration of career and college readiness components:
  - In what ways were academic curriculum and social emotional behavioral learning curriculum taught to you in school? What do you recall learning?
  - Did you have critical or crisis experiences in school? How did your school counselor/school help you?
  - In grade school, were you introduced to college and career options and how much barring did that exposure have on your choices?
- Reflective, consultative, and supervised practice during and post-graduation:
  - Do you engage in reflective and self-awareness practices? Do you believe you use a lens of honesty with yourself? Can you objectively evaluate your personhood (beliefs about others, biases, treatment of others, self-centered life approaches) and professional practice (including self-talk and written and verbal feedback from others)? If not, what consultative, collaborative, and steps to seek out supervision would you take in order to locate this information and place it out in front for review and personal transformation?
  - Are you a perfectionist or privileged? Do you believe that you are doing life right? Do you hold an elitist or self-righteous attitude toward others? If so, what are the inherent consequences personally and professionally?
  - Is your life currently streamlined, personally and professionally? Do you live in duality – meaning one way at work and one way at home? What are the advantages or disadvantages of code-switching or to living less than your authentic self?
  - In schools, sometimes there exists a work-place culture that embodies unwritten rules. As a school counselor in training, how will you approach rejecting and transforming those unwritten rules that are unjust, biased, and systemic to stakeholders or administrators?
  - Supervision should be on-going – while in training and post graduate school. How will you ensure remaining accountable and practicing professionally through seeking supervision?

- Careful incorporation of technology that supports communication, training, data management, and learning systems:
  - When using technology in your personal life, are you affected emotionally by online affiliates or adverse content? If so, how do you manage these outcomes, along with the time you invest in social media?
  - Do you sponsor technology use in personal and professional relationships? Have you lost connection to in-person or phone conversations? Have you allowed technological or media use to cloud or change your judgment in relationships?
  - Do you see texting as a form of credible evidence? How about the content you post or allow followers and educational stakeholders to witness – do you see this as providing fuel for others to box-you-in or categorize you or your character? Do you think this content has the potential to personally or professionally debilitate or assassinate your character or ability to promote or maintain employment?
- Responding to legal and ethical considerations:
  - Review current standards of ethical practice in school counseling. Identify and share which will be challenging for you to follow or abide by?
  - Are you a conscious responder to difficult issues or emotional? How might that have legal and ethical ramifications?
  - Historically, what has been your process to make life decisions? Do you operate by an ethical decision making model and if not, which would you adopt in school counseling?
  - How do you see the privacy or confidentiality of information shared by others? In your past, how often were you conveying information that you should not, or perpetuating defacement or slander of the reputation of another? Do you think that engaging in this form of defamation is ever necessary? Please explain how and in what situations discussing unfavorable content about another person would?

Preparing to assist students with mental health needs

According to the American School Counselor Association (ASCA):

> School counselors recognize and respond to the need for mental health services that promote social/emotional wellness and development for all students. School counselors advocate for the mental health needs of all students by offering instruction that enhances awareness of mental health, appraisal and advice addressing academic, career and social/emotional development; short-term counseling interventions; and referrals to community resources for long-term support.
>
> (ASCA, 2020a)

For the most part, school counselor trainees receive the same coursework as students who are preparing for licensure as clinical mental health counselors or marriage and family counselors. Each specialty includes the general counseling courses and then the courses specific to the licensure or certification desired. School counselors take the same general counseling courses as other specialties, and some programs make it possible to earn the requirements for both school counseling and licensure as a professional counselor in one master's program. Therefore, it would be inappropriate for school counseling graduates to feel that they are not adequately prepared to counsel students or for stakeholders to assume that school counselors are not capable of responding to crisis situations or of recognizing serious mental health issues. It is incumbent on counselor educators and school counselors to train school communities on the expertise of those graduating from school counseling programs.

When school counselors do not practice their mental health counseling skills, students who need support might go unnoticed until a crisis occurs. The worst-case scenarios for untreated mental health issues include suicidal ideation, attempts, and completions; drug use; sexual acting out; behavioral acting out; truancy; failing grades; and dropping out of school. Students who have serious mental health issues have much better outcomes if those issues are addressed early, and school counselors have the potential to recognize symptoms and behaviors that need immediate attention.

If a school counselor's time is dominated by clerical and administrative tasks, the ability of that counselor to intervene appropriately when students need assistance is suppressed. These non-counseling duties are also a way to suppress the identity of the school counselor as an educational expert and a mental health provider. When a school counselor's skills are not recognized and used appropriately, students suffer and counselors burn out (Falls-Holman et al., 2019).

Ethical Considerations

The counselor educator and student relationship evolve over time. During the first courses trainees take, the professors are most likely more directive and hands-on. However, by the time students are in the internship, they are making decisions on their own while consulting with their peers and their professors. This relationship moves from the teacher and student perspective to more of a collegial nature. At a certain point, professors might invite students to present at conferences or write journal articles with them, thus including them in the professional world, not simply the academic world. Similar to a parent's relationship responsibility to a child, the responsibility for a positive relationship between professor and student lies mainly with the professor. Providing encouraging corrective feedback and treating students with respect is of the utmost importance regardless of race, ethnicity, religion, sexuality, ability, and so forth. When professors struggle with a student's behaviors or background, the professor must seek consultation or supervision.

In the Academy, school counselor trainees are supervised by their professors, and, during the internship, they are supervised by a site supervisor as well. While counselor educators who teach school counseling courses most likely have more supervisory training and experience than the site supervisors, both roles are important. The counselor educator must track the accrued hours on site, make site visits to see the trainee in action, consult with the site supervisor, and assist the site supervisor with an evaluation that is accurate. In addition, the professor holds class, listens to the challenges that the students bring to class, and leads discussion about the topics relevant to the group of students. On the other hand, the site supervisor has direct observations of the student including organizational and time management skills, relationships with staff and students, the handling of crisis situations, and making professional judgments. Making the final decisions about the quality of the work the trainee has put forth will determine the student's grade, but more importantly those decisions will help determine the success or failure of the student as a school counselor.

Unfortunately, once school counseling trainees graduate, most of them may receive administrative supervision but probably will not receive clinical supervision. This immediately sets up the opportunity for graduates to fail in their skills, interventions, and program management. Additionally, it smacks of a lack of ethical behavior and guidelines.

After all, those graduates who seek licensure as professional counselors or marriage and family counselors enjoy several years of postgraduate supervision before being officially licensed. Therefore, why shouldn't school counselors benefit from these same supervisory experiences?

There are several ways to overcome these supervision obstacles, and counselor educators can assist. In many school counseling programs, students have the option of taking the same hours that are required for licensure as a professional counselor. Sometimes the school counselor can use counseling hours accrued in the school setting and obtain weekly supervision right after graduation and for up to 2 or 3 years. Another possibility is for novice school counselors to form consultation groups that conduct peer consultation on a weekly or monthly basis. The best school leaders and administrators ensure that novice school counselors have some form of clinical supervision. The first several years of being a school counselor can be extremely overwhelming, and it is imperative that novice school counselors have some form of clinical supervision whether it occurs in groups or individually.

Another ethical consideration is the ethics of being informed. School counselors do not live and work in a vacuum; therefore, it is incumbent upon practicing school counselors to update their skills and interventions as well as to be informed about local, state, national, and global events that might impact their students. Counselor educators must model these behaviors for their students. Impressing on students the importance of the continuation of learning beyond the counselor education experience is imperative. Counselor educators should encourage membership and participation in professional organizations, attendance at conferences and workshops, and a commitment to keeping abreast of events that might influence students. While many newsworthy events might have personal and political overtones, it is important for the school counselor to put aside their biases in order to support students and their educational success.

Cultural Complexities

Multicultural proficiency is a complex set of skills, beliefs, and attitudes that promotes a social justice lens through which to work with diverse populations of students. School counselors must always strive to attain the highest level of multicultural proficiency by attending training and workshops post-graduation; by immersing oneself in the demographics of the school setting; and by setting aside personal biases that might negatively impact relationships with students. It is incumbent on counselor educators to model excellent multicultural proficiency and to assist students who struggle with their own biases. In general, schools are demographically diverse with many races, ethnicities, languages, sexual orientations, and abilities represented.

Counselor education programs generally offer one course that specifically addresses multiculturalism. However, the best school counseling programs infuse multicultural concepts in every course so that trainees are constantly challenged to address diversity. Trainees must understand that all students and their families are unique and will not respond to a cookie cutter set of interventions. Counselor educators should offer many opportunities for trainees to work with diverse groups in their classes and during internship. In light of the civil unrest that exists in this day and age, professors must be willing to have those courageous conversations with students in order to ensure that their clientele will be served and respected no matter what their race, ethnicity, sexual orientation, and ability might be.

Strategic Considerations

Considerations for the actual implementation of master's and doctoral programs in school counseling require the following components: thoughtful planning, coordination among professors who teach in the program, and partnerships with school districts for the purpose of recruitment and internship placement. The first component, thoughtful planning, includes choosing textbooks, activities, and assignments for courses that are relevant to school counselor trainees as well as utilizing public school and community resources to enhance the courses. Secondly, professors who teach school counseling courses must have experience as school counselors. Nothing is more frustrating to students than to feel that the person who should be the expert in the course admits to having no prior experience in school counseling. Recruitment of qualified counselor educators is a top priority. The last component of developing a rigorous and useful curriculum is to engage the school districts and other community resources in the area. Students can actually help with this endeavor if short visits to neighborhood schools are embedded in the curriculum as well as interviews of seasoned school counselors.

Another integral strategic consideration is recruitment of excellent students. School counseling programs at various universities have a plethora of ways to recruit and retain students who will make good school counselors. Many counselor educators go out into the community and make presentations about their programs in which attendees have ample time to learn about a career in school counseling and ask specific questions about programs, tuition, time management, and so forth. Multimedia can also be used to advertise school counseling programs. Emails, banners, postcards, billboards, blogs, flyers, and infomercials are additional ways to encourage prospective students to learn more.

In addition to recruitment, professors must make decisions about the mode of course offerings. Some programs are mostly online with some specified residency time; others are totally face-to-face, while still others are a combination of the two. The time of day that courses are offered will impact prospective students' ability to make a commitment to a program. In some states, several years of teaching experience are required, meaning that most of those potential students will be teaching during the day and will need to attend classes in the evenings. Some programs send professors out to the school districts to teach their courses. In large metropolitan areas, this is convenient and can help students cut down on travel time and parking issues. Programs around the nation vary in many of the particulars that induce promising students to choose one university over another. These decisions are personal and depend on work load, child care, domestic and family obligations, financial capabilities, and many other considerations. Students are well advised to discuss with their significant others the time and financial costs of an advanced degree.

Counselor educators have a responsibility to engage local school districts in the training of school counselors. Relationships with school districts provide the best training experiences for promising school counselors as well as free school counseling services to local school districts. A collaborative relationship with administrators and other school staff as well as the community at large will be an immense benefit to everyone involved. Internships in the school community are necessary, as are opportunities to acquire direct clinical counseling hours. Training the school supervisors to assist in this broad endeavor is essential. Training sessions can be offered online or face-to-face, but should be a requirement of school counseling supervision. When classes are offered with local school districts, counselor educators find it efficient to be able to touch base frequently with district administrators.

Conclusion

Ultimately, counselor educators are the mentors and consultants to their students during the program and after students graduate. They are role models of professionalism and ethical behavior, and they exhibit excellent professional judgment throughout the program. Students will find themselves involved in complex cases, ethical dilemmas, and frustrating situations, and they will seek out the professors who guided and mentored them during their training to help them work through these complicated matters. As school counselor graduates grow and develop, they will become the leaders that they look up to in their mentors, the counselor educators who guided them through their training.

References

American Counseling Association (n.d.) *Licensure Requirements for Professional Counselors, A State by State Report*. Online. Available HTTP: <https://www.counseling.org/knowledge-center/licensure-requirements>

American Psychological Association (2020) *Publication Manual of the American Psychological Association 2020: The Official Guide to APA style* (7th edn), Washington, DC: American Psychological Association.

American School Counselor Association (ASCA) (n.d.) "State certification requirements". Online. Available HTTP: <https://www.schoolcounselor.org/About-School-Counseling/State-Requirements-Programs/State-Licensure-Requirements>

American School Counselor Association (2020a) "The American School Counselor Association Position Statements: The School Counselor and Mental Health". Online. Available HTTP: <https://www.schoolcounselor.org/Standards-Positions/Position-Statements/ASCA-Position-Statements/The-School-Counselor-and-Student-Mental-Health#:~:text=School%20counselors%20advocate%20for%20the,resources%20for%20long%2Dterm%20support>

ASCA (2020b) *School Counseling Leadership Specialist Training*. <https://www.schoolcounselor.org/Events-Professional-Development/Professional-Development/ASCA-U-Specialist-Training/School-Counseling-Leadership-Specialist>

ASCA (2022a) *ASCA Standards for School Counselor Preparation Programs*. Online. Available HTTP: <https://www.schoolcounselor.org/getmedia/573d7c2c-1622-4d25-a5ac-ac74d2e614ca/ASCA-Standards-for-School-Counselor-Preparation-Programs.pdf>

ASCA (2022b) *ASCA Ethical Standards for School Counselors*. Alexandria, VA: Author.

Council for Accreditation of Counseling and Related Educational Programs (CACREP) (2024) *CACREP 2024 Standards*, Alexandria, VA: Author.

Falls-Holman, L., Nelson, J., and Watts, R. (2019) "Organizational variables contributing to school counselor burnout: an opportunity for leadership, advocacy, collaboration, and systemic change", *The Professional Counselor*, 9(2): 126–141.

Furlonger, B., Snell, T., Di Mattia, M., and Reupert, A. (2018) "What should be considered when designing and developing a counselling course for adults from diverse professional and cultural backgrounds?", *Australian Journal of Adult Learning*, 58: 41–65.

Nelson, J. and Wines, L. (2021) *Responding to Critical Cases in School Counseling: Building on Theory, Standards, and Experience for Optimal Interventions*, New York: Routledge.

Quality Matters (2018) "QM Rubrics & Standards". Online. Available HTTP: <https://www.qualitymatters.org/qa-resources/rubric-standards>

Sheperis, C. and Davis, R.J. (2015) *Online Counselor Education: A Guide for Students*, Newbury Park, CA: Sage.

Texas Education Agency (2018) *The Texas Model for Comprehensive School Counseling Programs*, 5th edn, Austin, TX: Author.

Wines, L. and Nelson, J. (eds) (2019) *School Counselors as Practitioners: Building on Theory, Standards, and Experience for Optimal Performance*, New York: Routledge.

7 Student Development and Performance in Academics, Intrapersonal, and Dispositions for School Counselors-in-Training to Address Mental Health Needs

Lisa A. Wines

Leadership Quotes

Forging a school counselor-in-training forward into a career of helping and serving, is being curious about their mental-health status, and sometimes even challenging the root causes of their intrapersonal relationship, personhood, practices, ways of living, attitudes, ethics, experiences, and values – all of which remains the most intimate vantage point and point of view accessible in their work with the public. The question becomes, is that intimate vantage point harmful or helpful to others?

Lisa A. Wines

Developing school counselors might have ideas about all the ways in which they will make this world a better place. But really, prior to that idea, is first knowing all the ways in which you need to become better and all the ways in which you made yourself better.

Lisa A. Wines

Aspirational Statements

- University counseling department leaders should consider less about revenue generated by enrollment counts and hold more true to the mental health needs of the student and the public by training, gate-keeping, and aiding credential competent, credible, professional school counselors-in-training.
- Counselors-in-training realize that feedback provided by faculty and supervisors are both positive and constructive. Growth in their mental health and wellness does not truly take shape if only strengths and positive feedback are focused upon.
- School district directors of counseling should explore, with potential applicants, if areas were needed for remediation or necessitated plans of growth during their training.

Introduction and Background

Student development, in the field of school counseling, requires faculty to implement and support rigorous processes that should entail screening and gauging fitness for the field prior to acceptance/enrollment through graduation. It is often that "affectual and intellectual achievements are separated" (Reid, 2009: 292). These achievements are quite essential to merge and coalesce. Additionally, these processes of review should be implemented on an on-going basis. Particularly if accredited, departments of counseling often have some form of an established committee, specifically for students' development within their academic, intrapersonal, dispositional performance.

Academic performance, inclusive of didactic and experiential-based learning, is the measurement of students' trajectory and the level of curriculum mastery in courses taken on the degree plan. Intrapersonal development is the initiation and exploration of a student's relationship with self (e.g. loving self; having confidence and esteem; ability to address and see oneself and the student-client; adaptability; to nurture the total body by soothing physical and emotional suffering; process and come to terms with adverse experiences), their ability do life, and access skills required for a healthy body, mindset, lifestyle, and habits. Dispositional performance is the monitoring and investigation of students' posture, attitude, and behavior. All of these areas have an impact on the mental-health status of these growing professionals, and similarly the mental-health instability has an effect on the academic, intrapersonal, and dispositional performance of school counseling graduate students.

Leadership Program Values and Standards

School counselor preparation and programs, designed for educating and training, are authenticated by ethical and accreditation standards. The profile of an exemplary school counseling student should consist of someone who is of high ethical and moral competence, a critical and panoramic thinker, a fused self – both personally and professionally, culturally permissible, emotional and intellectually intelligent, and someone who sees themselves as a receiver of and contributor to the human experience.

The most current American School Counselor Association (ASCA) Standards for School Counselor Preparation Programs (2019, 2022), the American School Counselor Association Ethical Standards for School Counselor Education Faculty (2018), the Council for the Accreditation of Educator Preparation (CAEP, 2022), and Association for Advancing Quality Education Programs (AAQEP, 2018) have agreeable written language that candidates are required to demonstrate specific knowledge, skills, and dispositions appropriate to an advanced counseling degree and relevant credentials in counseling or school counseling. These standards, across all bodies, are coalesced, generally required, and are described here below:

- Demonstration of competence (capacity, efficiency, mental stability), successful disposition (attitude, communication/speech, and expressed beliefs), and professional behavior (ethical/legal, technological, conduct toward self and others, research/evidence-based, academic integrity).
- Prioritization of relationship building (consultation, collaboration, mentoring) and culturally responsive practices (ethnic heritage, complex identities, dynamic lifestyles, non-traditional ways of being, sociological orientation).
- Guidance toward and monitoring of reflective and self-aware practices (identification of mental health imbalance, positive mental health practices, personal sustenance, accountability).
- Implementation of an admission (matriculation, diverse recruitment), monitoring (stage reviews, supervision, feedback), and gatekeeping processes (professional fitness).

- Offers comprehensive curricula (school counseling core concepts and comprehensive programs, role development, theory) and practice-based field experience (complex and layered exposure).

Leadership in Practice

This section provides a description of the student development committee members, and the complex layers to how the process of student development is conducted. The following information provides the role of student development committee members, role of student development processes, admissions process for student development, incidence or infraction type that require faculty referral (see Appendix A) of students to the committee for review; written, participatory, technological, literary, and cumulative sanctions, and the four stages of review – the Kokoro Way.

Role of Student Development Committee Members

The student development committee member should be diverse with internal and external representation in the department of counseling. Following are potential member roles and their responsibilities:

- Chair of Student Development Committee/Member – School Counseling Faculty Representative:
  - coordinates committee meetings and student hearings;
  - sets meeting agendas and follows hearing protocol;
  - is responsible for maintaining records for incident reporting, committee meetings, and student hearings;
  - creates student decision letters with stated sanctions for department chair review (see Appendix C).
- School Counseling Faculty Representative/Member:
  - uploads documents in a confidential file sharing drive one/shared drive;
  - keeps meeting minutes.
- Admission Representative/Member:
  - is responsible for presenting readmission cases for probation and suspended students.
- Accreditation or Program Outcomes Representative/Member:
  - develops or revises meeting process/protocol/manual (see Appendix B) for committee and chair;
  - creates the final annual report to share with faculty for continuous program improvement, either at the beginning or end of each school year.

Role of Student Development Process

The process of student development requires faculty or an appointed committee to monitor the progress of students in the program and to respond to student concerns others may have. Generally comprised of diverse faculty members, the deliverables of this ethical committee are to support and monitor the developmental and academic progress of graduate school counseling students. Because training persons to become school counselors is not an easy feat, a developmental approach entails providing students with an overview of concerns; offering immediate feedback in writing, in-person, and or online; providing opportunities to influence critical thinking and professional behavior; and allowing students to respond or change their course of action. Committee members may find a punitive approach as a perfect option, simply because the student infraction was too egregious. Generally, a punitive approach might entail a preference to dismiss students from the program who demonstrate a dearth in competence (incompetent) at any stage of development or a level of harsh responses written in program policies that are exclusionary in nature.

For more than a decent amount of objectivity and unbiased approaches, the committee's composition can have appointed external members who are from other departments within the college. Key functions are staged, and purposed to gatekeep via tracking, reviewing, intervening, remediating, and if necessary, placing on probation or suspension. These concerns often are generated by faculty, former or current students, staff, or off-campus site supervisors. Following is a layout which describes the order, mitigation, and responsive operations of this working body.

1 Create and update student development policies – that are approved by leadership, in alignment with university student affairs processes and procedures – particularly within rules and regulations regarding due process and when referrals remain within the department or are catapulted forward to university level committees.
2 Create a system (preferably electronic) of referring and efficient responding.
3 Regularly monitor grade point average.
4 Respond to dispositional concerns.
5 Respond to evident intrapersonal conflicts or conflicts that misaligned from the values of the profession.
6 Ensure a timely response to reporters/referees when referrals or incident reports have been submitted.
7 Provide judicious notifications to students when academic or disposition meetings are convening, program requirements have not been met, referrals were made, or incident reports have been submitted.
8 Decide on and enforce sanctioning options (e.g. remediation plan) and issue in an ethical manner, with a distinction of it being developmental or disciplinary/punitive in nature.
9 Utilize anonymity in file sharing or electronic data-tracking systems necessary to document the number of referrals/incidents, students reviewed, reason for referral, and outcomes of faculty or student hearings. Updates and reporting information is usually limited to sharing within the department of counseling (i.e. faculty, department chair, dean) or at the university level within the student affairs division.
10 Utilizing all options, maintain student retention in the program.

Ultimately, student development is continuous, beginning in the matriculation stage through the ending or completion stage, whereas data accrual and review is practiced and prioritized for all students enrolled. It is vital for committee members to agree on the type of culture and reputation they desire to have and consider if they can distinguish a developmental or punitive approach in student reviews. Regardless of whether developmental or punitive, due process is always in order and must be evident in department procedures or student hearings.

Student Development in Admission Process

Most school counseling programs have general criteria that the admissions committee typically screens for: a completed application, an application fee, letter of interest and recommendation(s), transcripts of a baccalaureate degree from an accredited program with standards for a particular grade point average, and oftentimes, specific scores on the graduate record examination (GRE). Terms like candidate and applicant are used interchangeably to describe an individual interested in pursuing a professional degree, which can prepare you for licensure or certifications, beyond the undergraduate degree. There are predetermined admission criteria and standards which are described below:

1 **Completed Application** – this can demonstrate an applicant's ability to follow instruction. Affixing the signature and date is one of the most important elements of the application. Like grade school, demographic and the contact information provided may not always be accurate, so a statement of providing accurate contact information and a commitment to updating it when there are future changes, may be explicitly stated on the application. States may have a general application process (i.e. Apply Texas) so that one electronic application can be completed for multiple schools. Some university or departmental programs may require an additional application through other technological mediums (i.e. TK20) and requires both university and departmental level acceptance.
2 **Application Fee** – most standardly, this applied fee enables the admission committee to review applications and make candidate decisions. These fees, generally, are never allocated to compensate admission committee members.
3 **Grade Point Average (GPA)** – there may be a minimum GPA, like a 2.8 on undergraduate coursework, or 3.2 on graduate coursework, or an overall GPA of 3.5 on the last 30 hours on undergraduate coursework. Criteria, if the GPA does not meet standards, must be established by admission committees.
4 **Graduate Record Exam (GRE)** – this examination assesses reasoning, critical, and analytical thinking. These scores may be required by university programs or departments if the GPA does not meet the standard. Formulas may be used, with minimum acquired scores, to support the issuance of a letter of acceptance.
5 **Letter of Interest** – a statement of purpose, written by the applicant, may be required. Applicants should know the reasons for interest in the program; intelligence, aptitude, or ability; the intention behind and the goals set toward pursuing that particular path; articulate strength, experiences, an ability to appreciate diversity, and character traits.
6 **Letter of Recommendation(s)** – Any number of recommendations may be helpful and necessary for acceptance. Individuals who are asked to submit on a candidate's behalf can be professors, mentors, or supervisors. It can also be a Likert-scaled recommendation form. Whoever is selected should know much of the information presented in the letter of interest. These letters are often written in narrative or electronic format.

There are other plausible criteria that have historically been debated among faculty as to whether applicants should be required to submit additional items with their application materials. Requiring these additional items may or may not be exercised by administrative leaders, but are gate-keeping components in the field, which some may believe would be used in discriminatory, unfair, non-confidential ways. Following is a brief list of these additional items that departments of counseling should not only be considered as a part of general admissions criteria, but as foundational to the student review process. The descriptions provided are not exhaustive, and admission committees could adjust as deemed appropriate.

1 **Letter of Practical Response** – this is a letter in which applicants are required to read a prompt or case scenario and formulate a practical response that is reflective of reasonableness, is ethical, and in alignment with standards in the field.
2 **Video Submission** – this is a pre-recorded video, in which applicants are required to respond to open-ended questions that aid in understanding their levels of professionalism, personal beliefs, interest in the field of counseling, and/or problem-solving skills.
3 **Interview** – the interview is an opportunity for admissions committee members to design an interview protocol, utilize a rubric for their fair and ethical review, with a professional response provided to interviewee as to how criteria was met or ways to improve in an interview process.
4 **Documentation of Therapy Services** – this is a form of documentation (i.e. self-reported or actual evidence) that the applicant would provide demonstrating their commitment to self (to heal), transparency (to reduce stigma in receiving services) and subscription (to engage) in the field by receiving counseling services or leading by example.

These various forms of additional criteria allow faculty, who serve on the admission committee, to utilize general and additional criteria for selecting school counseling graduate students. All processes can be electronic – just keep in mind that when applicants are required to hand-write information – you are able to acquire information, such as psychological, behavioral, character, and abilities known as graphology.

Admissions committees should publish criteria for application requirements to potential program candidates. An overall rubric – for collective criteria, must accompany a rubric, which will help determine fitness for the program and serve as tools for decision making in the acceptance and enrollment process.

Student Referral or Incident Reporting

Student referrals or reporting incidents experienced with school counseling students can be a difficult decision for student peers, faculty, staff, or outside districts/agencies to make. There are two primary options:

1 Reporting person recognizes a student has an academic, intrapersonal, or dispositional concern. As a faculty member determines, it might be necessary to meet with a student to address it – document it, scan, file, and/or store any supporting evidence or documentation.
2 Instructor/Faculty addresses concerns *and* consults with another professional or faculty member with similar credentials – disclosing no personally identifiable information. Determination may be made to refer or make an incident report.

Departments, faculty, supervisors, and student development committees should maintain the following as governing values and staples inherent in the process of grooming and raising students up in the school counseling profession (student development).

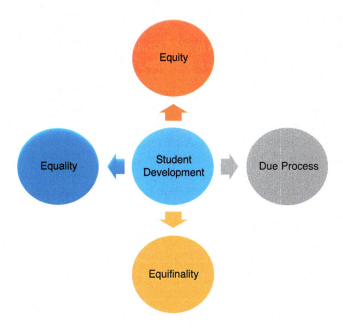

Figure 7.1 Essential Governing Values, Staples, and Principles of Student Development.
Note. Created by Lisa Wines, 2023.

Due process, equality, equity, and equifinality are essential in shaping school counselors today. Due process is the advance notification of what the committee or departmental concerns are; it is providing transparency of what the process of development, decisions, or outcomes will be; it is clearly conveying what happens when a failure to address the concerns is exercised by the student; and clearly communicating how a student will be affected if adherence to plans is circumvented or not completed as required by the committee. Equality is a consistent effort to provide the same resources and opportunities to all students. Equity is seeing the diversity in the circumstances of students, an additional provision if you will, that perhaps recognizes gaps in resources or access, and serves as a commitment to level the playing field among all students. Equifinality, embodies the notion that there are diverse pathways that can arrive at the same outcomes. In no way should these governing values, staples, and principles fall dormant or by the wayside in developing students in school counseling programs.

Additionally, departments, faculty, supervisors, and student development committees know that this process requires a level of investment: in your role, your commitment to the student, and your commitment to serving as gatekeeper to the profession and public. It also can be very time consuming – to appropriately track incidents for factual reporting, then spending time in fair-minded contemplation or consideration of the situation or concern and sorting through options, not to mention professionally and appropriately seeking confidential consultation and anonymous reporting with administrative leaders or other counselors with like credentialing, who can shed light on their knowledge or expertise – perhaps simply how might they respond to a situation as such. One critical element here is whether the professor of record (faculty member) decides to handle the intervention inside of the course or to send a referral to the committee for review. From there, the committee should respond departmentally and then refer to the university level – particularly if a student refuses to comply.

There are some common reasons why (infractions or violations) students might obtain a referral to the student development committee, and therefore subsequently and consequently endure the sanctioning process. Table 7.1 is not exhaustive, but serves as a reflection of what has been witnessed in departments of counseling regarding student issues. These categories of incidence or infraction types are deemed as students being deficient or not adequately adjusted in the areas of academic performance, intrapersonal development, and dispositional performance. These are factual (evidence-based) accounts, directly linked to being observed, witnessed, or conceptualized by faculty, and are assessed markers of students' mental-health status – therefore gauging their mental-health instability. These incidents or infractions are opportunities to develop students and create more well-adjusted school counseling professionals in the field.

Table 7.1 School Counseling Student Infraction or Incident Types

Academic Performance Incident/Infraction Type #1	Intrapersonal Development Incident/Infraction Type #2	Dispositional Development Incident/Infraction Type #3
Low grade point average	Failure to explore, adequately respond in course assignments, and understand personal mental-health status as it relates to counseling standards	Unprofessional communication or lacking filters in written and all expressed forms of communication (actions or behavior; social media or technology)
Academic misconduct, dishonesty, or plagiarism (initiator, participant, non-reporting observer)	Misrepresentation of self, living in duality, or without authenticity	Unprofessional, negative, instigating, or patronizing behavior online or in-person; not open to feedback
Earning low scores on counseling skill development, assignments, exams, project-based learning, or field experiences	Believing and using the classroom or counseling office as platforms for opportunities to address personally experienced trauma, identity and gender preferences or conundrums, and/or adverse experiences	Compromised or lack of respect toward faculty, staff, and off-site supervisors
Failure to adhere to assignment requirements, course or site policies, rules, regulations, and state law	Inability to accept accountability for thoughts, emotions, and actions; rigid and inflexible	Dysregulated emotions or lacking impulse or self-control in class or school settings (fighting, disrespect, or theft)
Argues, manipulates, or attempts to influence adjustment of grades or scores via unreasonably contesting and challenging grading	Lacking ethics or cultural sensitivity	Exhibiting minimal boundaries and engages in inappropriate risk-taking
Not meeting accreditation, state-testing competencies for licensure or certification, or Program Standards	Lacks motivation, initiative, or resourcefulness necessary for success	Lacks timely submission of record keeping, inaccurate documentation, HIPAA or FERPA violation
Placed on a remediation plan, probation, suspension, or program expulsion		

Created by L. Wines, 2023.

The infractions or incidents, suggested in Table 7.1, for example, can be individually separated or labeled as incident 1.a or 1.b, depending upon the need of the department or district. Any issue or concern represented in the table can be subject to review through referral or incident reporting. The referral or incident form (see Appendix B) is to be completed – preferably electronically – whereas the data input on the form can be aggregated, disaggregated, and interpreted by counseling department faculty. Additionally, students can have secondary referring reasons that need a committee's responsiveness, like ethical breaches, legal violations, cultural insensitivities, challenges with professionalism, and/or off-site concerns (i.e. practicum or internship placement).

Student Sanctions

It is widely understood that where there are infractions, there are consequences. In school counseling and university programs, these are called sanctions. Defining the meaning of sanction is interesting, as it has both positive and negative connotations. The description that is written non-favorably is defined as a threat toward receiving consequence(s) for disobedience or non-compliance toward policies, rules, and laws. Additionally, the definition of sanction is written favorably, meaning *it is permissible and granted to have* and *that a person is free to perform a certain action*. What a great way to think of a sanction with respect to students being *allowed to accept the outcomes of their choices or decisions made regarding their academic performance, their intrapersonal relationship, and their dispositional performance*. Always consider staging the issuing of these sanctions from least restrictive sanctions to very restrictive/most punitive. Evidence of this approach can only be verified if the process is efficiently documented in each student's file.

Upcoming are five forms of sanctions or requirements, in order to remediate, mitigate, reengage or support students' mental-health stability, and enhance personal and professional growth of students enrolled in the school counseling program. These sanctions are discussed in the student sanction letter (see Appendix C) and can be delivered in five sanctioning formats: 1. written format; 2. participatory format; 3. technological format; 4. literary format; 5. culminating format, with 34 total sanctioning options available for counseling departments' utilization. Among the 34 sanctioning, there are nine written, ten participatory, five technological, seven literary, and three culminating formats options provided.

The following tables provide activities (A) and justifications (J) for these sanctions and can be included in any remediation plan (see Appendix D.1 and D.2), developed by committee members or faculty, by which students are to fulfill. Take attentive note here, that programs have autonomy to decide which of these sanctions are level/priority one, level/priority two, and level/priority three infractions. It is strongly recommended that all sanctions are addressed based on the level of severity, by committee agreement, with administrative leaders' support.

Level/priority 1 is considered as sanctions that are minor. Level 2 are sanctions that are moderate. Level 3 are sanctions considered as major. These can be reversed, whereas level 1 is a major sanction and level 3 a minor sanction. Department committees should gather to decide the level of sanction assigned to the above incident and infraction list, which are appropriate responses for school counseling programs for gatekeeping purposes, inclusive of faculty and committee expertise, all while reaching a cohesive agreement among group members about the level of sanctions to include on the remediation plan.

Table 7.2 Written Format Sanctions

A: Issue a Warning
J: A warning is a form of reprimand that is issued as an initial step to intervention or mitigation for a student-related concern. Depending upon the nature of the incident or referral, this level may be an appropriate response, but always should include language about next steps should a subsequent issue happen.
A: Online Writing Labs
J: This is a virtual sanction – completed in learning management systems (LMS) like Blackboard or Canvas. A lab will allow time to contemplate, reflect, and to increase the likeliness of intentional change. This is committee decided and is neatly aligned with student concerns and can accompany any of the other formats.
A: Create a Written Paper
J: Writing is a form of the student's agreement to do as indicated. It allows time to contemplate, reflect, and to increase the likeliness of intentional change. This paper is committee decided and is neatly aligned with student concerns. This can accompany any of the other formats.
A: Create a Response Paper
J: Submitted narrative responses is a format whereas the student who engaged in the process responds to a prompt or stem. It allows time to contemplate, reflect, and to increase the likeliness of intentional change. This type of paper can accompany watching videos, reflection of therapy sessions, and summary or resonating themes from workshops or professional development. This can accompany any of the other formats.
A: Course or Assignment Failure (Grade of F)
J: Utilize these sanctions if academic dishonesty occurred in any way. This is a natural consequence to cheating or plagiarism. Students have been familiar with these policies since grade school and are required to retake course over. A grade of "F" is final and irreversible or irrevocable.
A: Character Letter
J: This provides an outside person, or community figure head, to act on the behalf of the student. A letter of character is requested by the student and presented to the committee. This correspondence vouches for the student and can reassure committee members that the student has someone outside who knows them and perhaps agrees to assist them in remaining accountable.
A: Journaling
J: Journaling is a reflective exercise known to positively impact mental health. It increases retention/memory, strengthens self-discipline, grows emotional intelligence, develops greater empathy, and enhances self-esteem and confidence.
A: 360 Wrap-a-Round
J: This is a military concept that allows feedback to be provided about an individual as a mechanism for assessment or evaluation. Wrapping around the person is the idea – meaning acquiring unbiased and objective perspectives from individuals, such as colleague, peer, supervisor, mentor, or family member, who have known the student for a minimum of 2 years. The assessment tool can be a list of predetermined questions, responded to in a perception survey format (e.g. electronic or paper) or questions that require narrative or short answer responses. These can be conducted on the phone or virtually by committee members. Participating persons should understand that their responses are protected and never revealed to the student.
A: Responses to Questions
J: Responding to direct questions allows time for best-case responses to surface and increases the likeliness of intentional change. The questions are numbered and require short answers from students. The committee decides the questions and are neatly aligned with student concerns. This can accompany any of the other formats.

Created by L. Wines, 2023.

Table 7.3 Participatory-Format Sanctions

A: Attend workshops, seminars, or professional development (either online or in-person, determined by committee)
J: The topic selected should directly correlate to the reason for student referral and attendance indicates students' exposure to content and to other attendees' engagement. This sanction is a vicarious learning experience.

A: Community Service or Volunteerism
J: This allows a student to be reminded of their initial desire to become a service provider, with the scope of others in focus, and removing themselves altogether. It creates a sensitivity for the human condition and often generates sobriety and humanitarianism (intrapersonal) in thinking, emotions, and actions.

A: Design and Demonstration of a Written Paper
J: This can accommodate any of the other formats. Writing is a form of the student's agreement to do as a written exercise. It allows time to contemplate, reflect, and to increase the likeliness of intentional change. This sanction has the student identify need areas of growth, using embedded research citations. The student establishes a process which will be approached to make the necessary adjustments or changes. Then once written, the student will carry out and demonstrate their application of this plan.

A: Seek Therapy or Group Counseling (number of minimum sessions to be determined by committee)
J: In effort to address the mental health status/stability of our students and to protect the public served, therapy or counseling sessions are not only necessary, but ethical. Committees can decide upon a certain number of sessions and require proof of attendance. Committees can refer to a university-based counseling office or to an outside practitioner or agency.

A: Successful Completion of Counselor Competency Scale-Revised (CCS-R)
J: This is a Likert-scaled tool utilized in the counseling field to assess skills and dispositions. A minimum score needing to be attained on this tool can be stipulated and required from either or both site supervisor and professor on all one or all parts of the tool.

A: Formal Observation, Supervision, or Consultation
J: Students may be required to engage in these modalities for guidance from faculty or other professionals in the field. Specifications of "how to" engage in the experience should be delineated by committee members or faculty. These are all state approved approaches in the profession to solving concerns or dilemmas. This form of supervision or consultation prevents students from taking steps with others that are harmful – personally or professionally.

A: Additional Hours or Assignment Resubmission
J: Different from receiving a grade "F", this is an enrichment requirement and allows students to better understand concepts, processes, standards, and codes of ethics by asking for an in-depth analysis or for additional work to be submitted.

A: Behavioral Plan
J: A behavioral plan is designed to prevent, improve, or modify unwanted behaviors. Goals should be written in specific, measurable, achievable, relevant, and time-conscious formats (SMART). Measurable language inherent in goal statements should be to increase, decrease, or extinguish, with rewards as outcomes stated. The components of this plan are committee decided and frequently monitored by the same working body of professionals.

A: Referral for Medical Attention
J: Departments of counseling may believe students' behavior and/or their conditions require the intercession of a medical practitioner or may need a medical evaluation and explanation. Physiological occurrences, unexplained behaviors, and emotions often require medical review and advice, in which department committees can request from students.

A: Referral for Disability Services
J: Disability services may also be required. Similar to the manifestation determination review (MDR) in K–12 settings, committees and faculty, particularly prior to suspension or expulsion, are obligated to rule-out the possibility of a disability having had an impact on a students' academic, intrapersonal, or dispositional performance. The question at hand: are the areas of concern a manifestation of an unidentified disability? Unidentified means that the committee or faculty are unaware of the disability or any needed accommodations in the program, and therefore may require students to seek and respond to their need for support from disability services.

Table 7.4 Technological-Format Sanctions

A: Video Recording
J: This can be an intermittent or culminating activity. Intermittently, the student can be given a prompt or prompts to respond to in a prerecorded video related to the concern or policy violation. Cumulatively, the video could respond to receiving a remediation plan and how the student plans to fulfill each requirement stipulated or outlined in the plan.
A: View Counseling Videos or YouTube Videos
J: Watching videos allows for auditory and visual learning. The videos should neatly fit with the areas of concern. Retention is maximized and learning is simplified and practical. Audio and visual learning makes up more than 90% of learning compared to text.
A: View a Movie
J: Movies are inspiring, build motivation, and are an inspiration for change. As a student is viewing, learning encourages positive changes and character alignment. Movies have a psychological and emotional impact, creating a sense of relatability to characters in the story.
A: Student Hearing
J: This provides an objective outlet of conveying concerns in incident reports or referral, allows faculty to devise questions specific to students, and creates space for the student to respond and the committee to document those responses. There is a student hearing protocol that should be utilized for structure and consistency.
A: Use of Email, Technology, and/or Virtual Platforms
J: Use of technology, email, and virtual platforms have best-practice clauses for appropriate use. Students may be sent – from a student development department email account – one or more emails requiring a written response. School counseling departments should have resources for referrals (i.e. community practitioners or Internet websites) in electronic format. Technology platforms may be misused and require remediation. Students may not have an appropriate presence online or may need an online hearing using virtual platforms. Online technology can be used for participating in appropriate content, building learning modules, or taking courses relevant to student issues.

Created by L. Wines, 2023.

Table 7.5 Literary-Format Sanctions

A: Read Journal Articles
J: The article(s) selected should be relevant to the student's issue(s). Reading an article provides a field-based perspective on the topic, often delineates vast considerations students should make, sets evidence-based outcomes, increases motivation, and promotes retention of information in the brain. Select literature that provides insight into reasons for referral or incident reporting. Journals, and their articles, should have a current publication date (present to 5 years ago) and many require one of the written activities.
A: Assigned Website(s) Reading
J: With pertinent information relevant to the student's issues, these websites are assigned for reading and review. These websites could be informational, interactive, and maximize retention.
A: Counseling Vignette or Case Study
J: Provides opportunity for students to outline actions or steps, to clarify judgment, and enhance objectivity (reducing bias). It is a way to explore options and variables that makes each student's case unique.
A: Juxtaposition of Seminal and Current Literature
J: This can accommodate any of the other formats. This provides an opportunity to compare the trends and best practices in the literature. Looking at the literature substantiates the culture of the profession and the areas to avoid within that professional context.
A: Listen to Audio Book
J: This is for the auditory learner and will increase retention. Audio books have counseling specific content or specific self-help content aligned with the student's need or presenting issue. The audio book should have a predetermined approval by the committee.

(Continued)

Table 7.5 (Continued)

A:	Read and/or Compare Ethical Codes, Policies, Standards, and/or Laws
J:	Assigning students any part or whole of these documents to review, which can be essential to their growth and development. These documents can convey areas where there was direct violation or misunderstanding made by students – perhaps of the standard itself or of the language in the documents. Comparison, analysis, and evaluation are the higher order thinking skills necessary in working school counseling.
A:	Read Department, District, or Agency Policy
J:	School counseling programs should provide opportunities in the remediation and sanctioning process for students to become acquainted with department, district, or agency policies. If the area of concern was a direct violation to any of these policies, then an appropriate response would have students obtain a copy, review, interpret the meaning, and perhaps craft a response.

Created by L. Wines, 2023.

Table 7.6 Culminating-Format Sanctions

A:	Program Probation
J:	This option is based on academic performance and usually provides a range of time (e.g. a semester) to improve the semester GPA (SGPA) and/or a student's cumulative GPA (CGPA). SGPA and CGPA is only calculated with graduate-level courses (undergraduate coursework is not calculated). Students with full graduate admission status who fail to achieve and maintain the counseling department's minimum CGPA (usually a 3.0) at the completion of a determined number of graduate hours, should be placed on academic probation (AP1). A student might need one full term or semester (time) to fulfill the remediation plan. For probation to apply to dispositional performance, policies would have to be written to reflect such, and in a way that is measurable and allows change to occur. Students on probation may have had one or more level 1 infractions. Students can enroll in courses but may not apply for admission to candidacy or for graduation. The probationary status applies regardless to whether the student receives a letter of notification from the graduate office.
A:	Program Suspension
J:	A student might need one full term or semester (time) to fulfill the remediation plan (e.g. access counseling services and provide evidence that counseling has been ongoing). The time also might be used to complete an incomplete course or complete sanctions as described in the various formats. To require a full-term suspension demonstrates to the student that the problems the faculty have observed need time to be corrected. For suspension to apply to dispositional performance, policies would have to be written to reflect such, and in a way that is measurable and allows change to occur. Students on probation may have had one or more level 2 infractions. Students who earn a minimum grade point average (GPA) on all graduate courses in the next enrolled semester and whose CGPA is below that minimum grade point average, will be placed on academic probation for a second time (AP2). For example, an AP1 student who fails to earn a 3.25 GPA in the next enrolled semester, and whose CGPA is less than 3.0, will be suspended. Students must garner administrative approval (department chair or dean) to return or readmit into the program. Failure to meet requirements leads to program expulsion.
A:	Program Expulsion
J:	Program expulsion may happen once a student has returned from comportment of another issue and is required if a student engages in a blatant ethical violation, an egregious – yet severe – level 3 infraction, or if the program suspension was not fully utilized to correct the student's issues. Expulsion indicates a student's inability to reapply or return to the program, as due process is evident throughout the entire process (i.e. from referral to student development to program expulsion).

Created by L. Wines, 2023.

Provided by the student to the committee should be evidence of a fulfilled remediation plan, as well as explanations for the outcomes of non-compliance or non-completion. Student appeals must be reviewed by the faculty committee. If the student is not satisfied with those recommendations, then the appeal might be appropriate to send to the Dean's office.

Human resources would be the last review for an appeal. All steps to an appeal must be followed by faculty committee, the Dean's office, and lastly, human resources.

Issues of Plagiarism and Academic Dishonesty

Universities and departmental programs often have issues of plagiarism, academic dishonesty, and collusion addressed within student code of conduct policies, program handbooks, or manuals (Appendix A). Because universities nationally and internationally have varying descriptions of plagiarism and academic dishonesty, the suggestion here is to refer to university college and departmental policies in creating the standard of practice and expectations for students in school counseling programs to abide by and follow without waiver. That withstanding, what has consistently been unaddressed, are the descriptions or degrees of variance within the levels of severity stipulated inside of these codes of honor.

Universities often have programs, such as Turn-It-In (www.turnitin.com) or Blackboard Safe Assign (https://www.blackboard.com/teaching-learning/learning-management/safe-assign), that are electronic databases that house student submissions and can identify information gathered from the internet or other sources – which can help faculty members in school counseling determine the integrity of assignment submissions and to help authenticate that it is the students' original work and not the work belonging to or taken from another student, or an online website, such as Course Hero. For example, when a Safe Assign Score is higher than 35 percent, there should be a process of determining if it is major or minor plagiarism. Regardless of the Safe Assign score being greater than 35 percent, all work in question should be categorized as either minor or major.

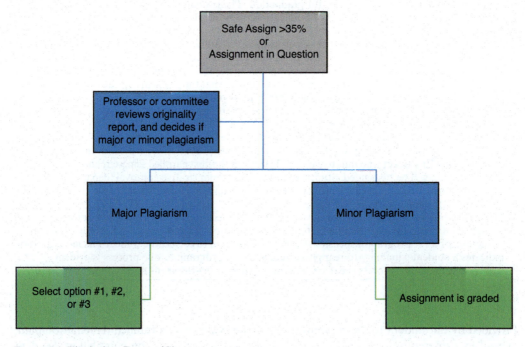

Figure 7.2 Plagiarism Process/Chart.
Note: Created by Lisa Wines and Robika Mylroie.

When there is a Safe Assign Score greater than 35 percent, the student development faculty committee or professor of record reviews originality reports and decides if it is major or minor plagiarism. Following, are the definitions of minor or major plagiarism:

> **Minor Plagiarism:** Indication of copied material reflective of author names, American Psychological Association (APA) headers, in-text citations, (with references) or incorrect citations and/or references.
>
> **Major Plagiarism:** An intent to plagiarize was evident. Students have content directly placed in text or submission. Examples are content from the student's previously submitted work (self-plagiarism), content from former or current students' assignment submissions, using content without proper citation, or borrowing course content from Course Hero and other online sources.

If determined as major plagiarism, one of the following options should be selected:

> **Option #1:** Redo the entire assignment for partial credit (i.e. may earn up to a certain percentage of the original point value). When the student takes accountability for their actions and admits their wrong-doing or extenuating circumstances that led to their choice to plagiarize. It is an openness to explore what they did wrong and developmental in nature.
>
> **Option #2:** Issue a zero on the assignment. The student took some responsibility for plagiarism. Depending on the circumstances, the professor has the option to assign a "0" for any instance of plagiarism. For example, in instances of student-to-student plagiarism, an automatic "0" should be assigned regardless of how the student obtained original work.
>
> **Option #3:** Course failure is the outcome when the student is apathetic, refuses to describe any particulars or details, fails to take ownership, is flippant or disinterested, finds fault in faculty members, Safe Assign score is >90%, and/or the student is repeating (second offense) or simultaneously involved in plagiarism in other classes. Students should be referred to the Student Academic, Intrapersonal, and Dispositional Committee.

Remediation Plan Format

Remediation planning begins when a faculty committee has received an incident report, created a student file, read over the infraction types, and scheduled a student hearing. Then, prior to the student hearing, the committee should convene to cover the student hearing protocol and to understand what type of questions each committee member will ask to better understand the student's response, perspective, or point-of-view to the content of the report made by either a peer, professor of record, advisor, or other faculty member. After thoroughly following the student hearing protocol, the student should be notified, in writing, the outcomes of the hearing and the plan of action as summoned by the committee to the student in question. This is called the remediation plan and it has several components:

1 Reasons for Referral
2 Infractions/Incidents
3 Hearing Outcomes
4 Sanctions and Justifications
5 Time for Completion (Each Sanction and Entire for Remediation Plan)
6 Failure to Comply Statement (Addressing Refusal, the Inclusion of Attorney or Advocate, and Escalated Referral to University-Level Student Services Division)

Case Vignette by Aleister Lonnie Gamble

This information presented in this case vignette are not true and developed strictly with the intent of educational purpose only. Victor is in his final year of graduate school and is ready to walk away from the dream he has held for over 20 years. The dream began after his mom was diagnosed with Major Depressive Disorder when he was only 10 years old. From the day his mom received her diagnosis, therapy became a part of his life. Victor knew his mom struggled on her journey, the years of weekly sessions, the long line of referrals, changing medications, losing jobs, months staying with family, and even an in-patient stay at the local hospital. However, by the time Victor entered high school, she had become a *changed* woman in his eyes. She started being a mom again, better yet she was like herself again! To Victor, the reason behind her recovery was 75 percent of the fact she *finally* had a good counselor and he wanted to be just like that – a good counselor. However, the past 2 months had made those years of growth and determination seem trivial and naive.

At first, it was bearable. A couple of his clients prematurely terminated, the bulk of his caseload was still in pre-contemplation of change, and the paperwork was only slightly daunting. However, by the end of the first month, Victor was having trouble getting to his internship site on time, and often felt exhausted in dread of having to go into session. He wanted so badly to impact change, to give his patients back their lives! And yet, no matter what he tried, he seemed to only have one patient that *might* be ready for termination in another month. He tried to get his mind off from the fact that there are so many people in need of help, and yet it seemed impossible at times to help them.

The breaking point occurred as Victor was driving home from his site one night when a song came on the radio that made him pull over. He sat in his car on the side of the interstate, trying to get his breath. This was not Victor's first panic attack; they had come back with a vengeance over the past few weeks and often woke him up in the middle of night, but this was different. It was different because Victor wanted this to be the absolute last time it happened to him. This time the thoughts seemed to engulf him, "How can I be an instrument of change when I can't even drive home? How much longer before they all know I can't do this? How much longer should I even try? What if I am doing more harm than good?" The biggest question of them all was, "What if I can't do this career?".

He finally decided to drive home and go to bed. The next day in the middle of his third session, the threshold broke. He had a panic attack in front of his patient. While this was actually managed well by him and the patient, Victor could not bear to tell his site supervisor what had happened. He felt so ashamed and decided to leave right after that session ended. Victor called out sick the next 3 days, until his supervisor called to check in. Over the call, he tried to explain the dread, the panic attacks, the loss of sleep, the pressure, the physical pain even, but he realized it had come out a sobbing mess that would certainly warrant ethical concern. As his site supervisor suggested personal therapy, Victor felt as though his whole body was on fire with anger. Thank you for your advice; he mustered to get out as he politely ended the call. Victor didn't want to go to any type of therapy anymore.

Suggested Sanctions for Case Vignette

Clearly, Victor needs help and should have notified his site supervisor to such immediately (Incident/Infraction #2). This may be beyond what his site supervisor or faculty supervisor can provide. Because he has already missed client sessions (Incident/Infraction #1) and does not appear able to continue his internship duties, the supervisor or faculty of record should obtain this information through processes of supervision – essentially through case updates – and make an incident report. The faculty review committee in receipt of this referral/report should meet with one another to discuss the nature of the referral and the totality of infractions made. Making sure the governing values and staples are at the crux of their work with the student (i.e. due process, equality, equity, and equifinality), a student hearing should be scheduled with the student. The hearing protocol should be precisely followed and documented in notes. The committee should meet, post the student hearing, to discuss the sanctions that appropriately respond to the incident or infraction. This will help Victor decide if counseling is indeed the career path for him, guarantee that his clients' best interests are protected, and explore how his family-of-origin might be impacting his current situation.

While any number of the written, participatory, technological, or literary sanctions seem befitting, the faculty review committee might recommend the following plan for Victor. A program of suspension of one full term is in order. This is the only way that his clients can be protected from observing their counselor's own anxiety and depression in session and from abandonment due to Victor not showing up for sessions. The clients' needs must come first. While Victor is on suspension, counseling should be required for the full term with proof of attendance and regular updates from the counselor as to Victor's progress. Additionally, the review committee can offer a wide variety of written, participatory, and technological sanctions to help Victor assess his ability and desire to proceed in the counseling program. At the end of the suspension, Victor should be required to meet with the committee to review his progress and to determine if continuing in the program is viable.

Four Stages of Review – The Kokoro Way

In Japanese culture, Kokoro harmoniously integrates the heart and mind. As trainers of school counselors, there has been less emphasis placed on the totality of counselor development, being etched or grounded in, a fusion of one's heart-center (i.e. intentions, true feelings, the unmodified self) and the mind (i.e. way of thinking, reasonableness, and fair-mindedness). The critical endeavor with a *Kokoroian Student* implies that the student should have accepted understanding and great expectation for the upcoming educational experience. Meaning that they comprehend that their mind, body, and spirit are indivisible and that as a Kokoroian Student, they should connoisseur this alignment and congruence everywhere always – in their educational, professional, and personal life.

Faculty members are the Sensi of these students – are quite learned, have known life, collected experience, and impressive teaching – all readily available to the Kokoroian Student. Faculty members are *sens*ible, *sens*itive, and common-*sens*ical. With this Sensi mindset in place, faculty members of school counseling programs are charged to review students from their submission of an application to program matriculation, through graduation or program completion. For school counselors-in-training to be within departmental compliance, programs usually require students to maintain a "B" average or a 3.0 GPA. Other requirements available for faculty review are students being required to sufficiently demonstrate counseling skills (i.e. Counselor Competency Scale-Revised) or to furnish a portfolio of works, prior to graduation or obtaining their license or certification – with established academic-based standards. Programs may have specific standards and expectations for dispositional aptness, meaning the behavior and attitude of the student remained consistent with expected and acceptable dispositional-based standards for all students enrolled. Final requirements consist of field experience curricula – which are performance-based, and often are courses like residency, practicum, and internship.

Each stage, described herein, has an established protocol by which faculty implements a fair and equitable review process. Another way to conceptualize this is through stage review for school counselor Kokoro development. Faculty members are to: Access (Stage 1); Mold (Stage 2); Chisel (Stage 3); and Refine (Stage 4). These stages are conducive to synthesizing the mind, body, and spirit of school counselors in training, referred to earlier as The Kokoro Way. Additionally, to better understand these stages, phases, or gateways, which are described here as stages, they were linked to Jean Piaget's Theory of Cognitive Development (sensorimotor, preoperational, concrete operational, formal operational) and to a seminal work in counselor development, written by Rønnestad and Skovholt (2003).

Stage 1: Access

Applicants apply to a school counseling program and engage in a process of seeking acceptance to the program. Applicants are screened for initial fit, based on the admission process previously mentioned. Acceptance allows faculty members to have granted access by beginning to review and develop these applicants at this beginning stage.

Using this model as described, once students matriculate into the program, John Piaget's Theory of Cognitive Development Sensorimotor Stage and Rønnestad and Skovholt's (2003) The Layperson Helper Phase are integrated, whereas students are catapulted into a stage where they begin to investigate, both intentionally and in course-work design, their inner self (i.e. with a focus on mental health stability or instability), using some of their basic cognitive processes (i.e. sensation, attention, and perception), and senses (i.e. eye-sight, hearing, and smelling) as a starting place for school counselor development. According to Rabindran and Madanagopal (2020) in this stage,

> infants [in counselor training] think [by] using their senses and motor actions [guided by their brain]. They [have] learned about the world [around them] by touching, looking, and listening. These [infants in the field], try to develop simple concepts of objects ... [whereas] the [t]rial and error method [are] the major basis of learning
>
> (2020: 2153)

Overall, this stage provides school counselors-in-training with a true and basic understanding of human beings in general, and a realistic understanding of themselves as human beings, in ways that neither they nor counselor educators should circumvent or try to avoid.

Additionally, at a fundamental level, school counselors-in-training generally have only had the experience of helping and supporting others they are in direct or tangential

Student Development and Performance 103

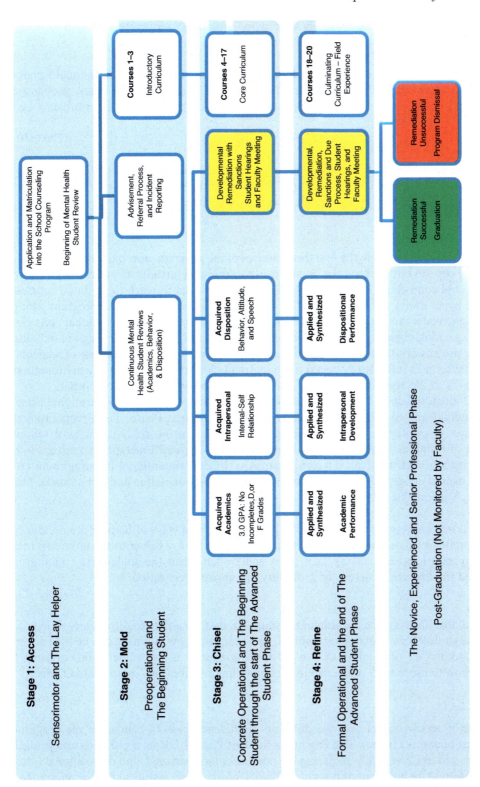

Figure 7.3 Stage Review for School Counselor Kokoro Development.

Note. Adapted from John Piaget's Theory of Cognitive Development, and seminal work by Rønnestad and Skovholt (2003). Created by Lisa Wines, 2023.

relationships with (i.e. family, friends, and work affiliates) – equivalent to that of a lay person. According to Rønnestad and Skovholt (2003), a lay person is:

> [a]ll people [who] have experience helping others before they enter professional [school counselor] training ... in such as parents, children, friends, and colleagues; people are continually engaged in trying to help others to make decisions, resolve problems and improve relationships.
>
> (2003: 10)

Student development, in this stage of review, is at a fundamental level for the school counselor-in-training; that they primarily bring with them their senses to understand themselves and those they will counsel or serve in the future.

Stage 2: Mold

This stage of review occurs in the first three courses of the program, approximately 15 percent of the total courses outlined to take. Students are learning an introductory curriculum to the field of school counseling. Faculty members, who are assigned to teach these initial courses, should be hyper-aware of how students are acclimating and settling into the program, along with a heightened awareness of students' academic, intrapersonal, and dispositional progress. At this stage, molding is initiated. Advisement, referrals, and incident reporting are ongoing within the process of student development and stage review. Although the review of students' mental health status has already begun upon matriculation (the access stage), a continuation of this review in the areas of academics, intrapersonal, and disposition, are in order.

Stage 2 integrates John Piaget's Theory of Cognitive Development Preoperational Stage and Rønnestad and Skovholt's (2003) The Beginning Student Phase. The Preoperational Stage hones in on key behaviors, such as imitation (mirroring the student as a school counselor in training), using symbolism (understanding expressed metaphors and similes), applying verbal evocation (can develop a narrative through intentional listening), and engaging in mental imagery (being able to empathize and place oneself in another's shoes). The Beginning Student Phase is when:

> [t]he student knows that the lay [persons] conceptions and ways of helping are no longer appropriate or valid. To move from the known role of the lay helper to the unknown role of the professional is a taxing task often acutely felt when the student [in training] is assigned the first client. Issues of suitability are normatively raised.
>
> (2003: 12–13)

Combined, this stage is quite the vulnerable stage – in that the ability to distinguish periods of time in the student's narrative is not optimal, to understand how language can be used as the primary mechanism of symbolism – wordsmithing even – is not understood, or simply knowing how to use the gift of the gab in the counseling relationship – is an abstract concept.

Stage 3: Chisel

This stage of review occurs over the duration of students' next 14 courses of the program (70 percent of courses taken). The Beginning Student Phase students are shaped and pruned during this process, essentially acquiring the academic, intrapersonal, and dispositional fortitude and meeting the high expectations of the field. Unfortunately, a student may be referred for a critical incident or can have a remediation plan, with sanctions, put into place. Students are learning an essential core counseling curriculum that moves toward the base of the iceberg, into topics in counseling that students may find personally jarring or difficult. During this stage, faculty members are consistently reviewing students' academic, intrapersonal, and dispositional progress. Additionally, in the chisel stage, options to incident report, host committee members' meetings, and facilitate student hearings, are quintessential. Remediation plans and sanctions should be developmentally appropriate, to the student, their violation and level, with cultural implications accepted and responded to as needed.

This stage assimilates John Piaget's Theory of Cognitive Development Concrete Operational Stage and Rønnestad and Skovholt's (2003) The Beginning Student Phase through the peak of The Advance Student Phase. These phases are indicative of students striving toward perfectionism, to get it right, at a thorough level. In fact, "[students] are typically not relaxed, [non] risk-taking, [nor] spontaneous (2003: 14–15). School counselors in training are concrete and exact, thereby understanding timelines, environment, and frequency. Furthermore, the chisel stage as labeled, Rønnestad and Skovholt's (2003) noted as dichotomous, in that:

Beginning students typically find the start of professional training to be exciting, but also intensely challenging. Theories/research, clients, professional elders (professors/supervisors/mentors/personal therapists), one's own personal life, peers/colleagues, and the social/cultural environment combine to impact and sometimes overwhelm the beginning student.
(2003: 11)

The Beginning Student Phase student is open, understands that holistic growth is in order, and gathers that complexities need mastering and refining (Rønnestad and Skovholt, 2003). As a student in school counselor training slowly graduates upward to The Advanced Student Phase, which is one headed toward field experiences like practicum or internship, they reach the status of intern. At the onset, Rønnestad and Skovholt (2003) believed,

the central task at this phase is to function at a basic established/professional level. Many students, however, have higher aspirations for their functioning and want not only to avoid making mistakes, but to excel in their work. Many feel pressure to do things more perfectly than ever before.
(2003: 14)

Stage 4: Refine

This stage of review, refinement, occurs over the duration of students' last few courses in the program (15 percent of courses taken). This is a culminating stage, often experienced while in the field, and is an applied knowledge that is synthesized across academic learning, intrapersonal development, and dispositional performance. It combines John Piaget's Theory of Cognitive Development Formal Operational Stage and Rønnestad and Skovholt's (2003) The Advanced Student Phase. Synthesis of what you have read, heard, seen, and experienced, is an acquired advanced skillset. Yet, still, students may be referred or may have a remediation plan. It is often hoped that students who are training to become school counselors, fail to need remediation or circumvent, altogether, being referred to the Student Development Committee. They are refined: students have reconciled their own adverse experiences, processed through these adversities in a way that contributes to safe practices and not causing those served any harm. Students can clearly see how it all comes together. Students at this stage of refinement have learned cumulative counseling curriculum and comprehensive practice-based approaches that they can test, adopt, reject, or revise for their work, ahead, in the field.

Students are entrepreneurs of being theory enhanced, abstract thinkers, logical, and strategic. Toward the end of The Advanced Student Phase, school counselors in training are looking for models, master therapist, experienced school counselors – essentially senior practitioners (Sensi) for differentiating themselves (here's who I do not wish to be), critically assessing and evaluating models, and rejecting aspects of their learning (Rønnestad and Skovholt, 2003).

The Novice, Experienced, and Senior Professional Phase

The final three phases of counselor development, according to Rønnestad and Skovholt (2003), are the Novice, Experienced, and Senior Professional. Although these phases are beyond the school counselor graduate experience and will be journeyed through post educational experiences and post successful remediation.

In closing, there are four stages which are being recommended for school counselor Kokoro development. These stages are designed to review students' academic, intrapersonal, and dispositional performance. Appropriately understood, the integration of Jean Piaget's Theory of Cognitive Development (sensorimotor, preoperational, concrete operational, formal operational) and to the seminal work in counselor development, written by Rønnestad and Skovholt (2003) aides in conveying that school counselor growth occurs in stages, from beginning to end, a combination of concrete to abstract learning and conceptualizing, across academic, intrapersonal, and dispositional domains.

Mental and Behavioral Health Considerations

Albeit true, this entire chapter supports early identification of academic, intrapersonal, disposition, and mental health status in school counseling students, who are beginning the process of application throughout graduation. This section describes mental health training, justifications for why academic, interpersonal, and dispositional performance should serve as beginning markers to identify mental health status instability, ways in which departments of counseling are recommended to shift their lens from not only equipping school counselors in training to work with the students, parents, teachers, and administrators – as opposed to students having inherent within the structure of counseling programs, formal approaches to intentionally address their students mental health needs. Chapter 6 discussed ways to infuse this internal exploration and critical self-analysis into all counseling course curricula and assignments.

Mental Health Training

Programs in school counseling are designed to educate students on how to become a counselor in the school setting. Historically, it was an anomaly, and quite rare to have school counselors addressing mental health needs in schools. As the complex, multifaceted, yet dimensional society quickly changes, school counselors not only need to address the mental health needs of students in schools, but as they are being trained as a school counselor, their mental health should equally be addressed. Faculty who are identified to teach counselor education curricula should always take time to infuse mental health considerations, even if not a direct part of curriculum. Further, in courses that focus on counseling skillset development (i.e. counseling skills course, residency courses, and field experience courses), the priority remains that school counselors-in-training are charged to focus on themselves as an instrument, not only of change for others around them (change agent), but as an instrument in need of personal transformation. School counselors-in-training engage in a mindset shift, with a will to engage in the process of "cleaning around their own door-step", meaning correcting all that is not serving them or addressing persons or circumstances that lack positive contribution to being better than they were yesterday.

Academic and Dispositional Progress as Indicators of Mental Health

Faculty members, typically counselor educators or those who hold credentials in counseling, relate to how academic and dispositional progress can serve as an indicator of students' mental health status. Mental health status, in general, is the current state in which patients' or clients' emotional, cognitive, appearance, judgment, and insight are observed, documented, and responsibly treated if evidence or outcomes dictate each occurs outside of the normal limit. Many counselor educators are licensed mental health professionals and have a trained eye for these mental health faculties.

School counseling programs should recognize students' academic progress (i.e. struggling in classes; obtaining low grades), intrapersonal, and dispositional progress as potential indicators. Persons with poor performance, intrapersonal conflicts, and negative dispositions tend to experience anxiety, mood swings, feel guilty, and/or depressed. Although there may be other available mental health conditions, the idea is not to automatically exclude the impact mental health has on these three areas.

Shift Educational Lens from External Processes to Internal Exploration and Modification

Perhaps more often than counselor education faculty has been unwilling to admit, the educational lens of school counselors-in-training has primarily focused on how to counsel, support, transform, mitigate, make safe, and resource student concerns and issues. No longer should the lens remain on external processes of counseling and helping, but rather make the shift toward internal exploration and modification of oneself, thereby increasingly checking one's mental health status. In the field of school counseling, it is not uncommon that parents and students are interested in knowing whether school counselors have experienced situations like theirs or whether or not the school counselor has walked a mile in their shoes. This internal exploration, and modification, when necessary, provides school counselors with an opportunity to address unfavorable experiences that could lead to academic, interpersonal, or dispositional conflicts. A bigger question goes unanswered: how can school counselors-in-training be placed into a professional setting to work as a counselor without having addressed their own issues – particularly within their educational trajectory in counseling? The direction of the field, as a consideration, is an invitation to move what was ancillary to primary. Intentionally focusing on school counselors' mental health stability and development, in addition to academics and dispositional performance.

Critical Analysis of Self

During the training and development of school counselors, there should be an internal focus on what exactly is the truth (truth-telling) for the student. Another way to begin this type of critical self-analysis is for students to ask themselves, am I living truly open and transparently? A final overarching question for students is, have I accepted the experiences of my life, as they are? In other words, are your garnered experiences, both favorable and unfavorable, used as a platform for in-depth analysis? By enduring a self-engaged process of critical analysis, this directly strengthens the school counselor in training's professional capacity to fully operate in schools.

Ethical Considerations

There are many key ethical considerations in navigating the development of students in a school counseling program. A few considerations, discussed here, are gatekeeping, violation of policy, following stated guidelines, dual roles and relationships, confidentiality and disclosure, and legal and advocate representation. These often become ethical dilemmas if not recognized at the onset, and efficiently responded to, once evident.

Gatekeeping as Protection for the Public

Protecting the public by making certain graduate students enrolled in school counseling programs are in their best capacity – mentally, behaviorally, and emotionally – is a responsibility held by all faculty members charged to gatekeep the counseling profession. The justifiable purpose is not only grooming school counselors to become solid professionals, but also, to create experiential learning opportunities that are reflection-based and designed to better understand their mental health status.

Failure to protect the public from graduates who are, nonetheless, unhealthy, or who have not addressed their personal issues, places innocent persons in jeopardy and compromises their inherent right to non-maleficence and beneficence – the core values and preamble to our ethical codes. Additionally, counseling programs and the faculty within, review reported incidences, student progress at various stages in the program from admissions through graduation, and work diligently to produce competently skilled, healthy, very sound professionals in the field.

Violation of Policy and Following Stated Guidelines

Policies and stated guidelines (i.e. student code of conduct, department manuals for student development or field experience, or the counseling profession codes of ethics) are essential in institutions of higher learning, counseling practice, and in the field of education. When students violate any type of policy, guideline, or ethical code, maintaining high-standard, responsive practices in addressing these concerns are essential to students' academic, intrapersonal, and dispositional development. In light of equity and fair practice, all students are treated the same; with the same level of care and respect; provided the same opportunities to learn, grow, and reflect; ultimately, following and using these policies and guidelines as basic standards which the committee utilizes as tools to discern information and to ethically operate within these outlined scopes of practice.

Dual Roles and Relationships

In the field of school counseling, it is not unusual that faculty members may run the risk of serving in dual roles. There may be times when the committee members serve as the professor of record. There may be other times where professors feel that navigating course content that explores the mental health status of their students may feel *too clinical* or that the role of professor begins to seem like clinical and diagnostic skills are being utilized.

When professors in counseling programs dual-serve as advisors, instructors, coordinators, and such, these lines are sometimes perceived as unclear or blurred.

Confidentiality and Disclosure

Student incidents and referrals are automatically a part of the student record and should be handled confidentially. These records are typically maintained in the department file or in an electronic database (i.e. TK20 or Taskstream). Disclosure of student referrals, proceedings, or sanctions to faculty members who were not a part of the student development committee should be avoided by removing specifics about each student case – it is usually on a need-to-know basis or being in a position of instruction or advisement with the student. Summative information, however, can be provided to anyone – such as the statistics on the number of referred cases, incident or infraction types – or summative statements that provide an overview to the student case, as opposed to details and specifics.

Legal and Advocate Representation

There may come a time where graduate students in school counseling programs feel that the outcomes of their violations were unjust or unfair. Infrequently, students may be unable to accept responsibility for their choices and believe someone else is there to blame or is at-fault. When this occurs, students may threaten to hire an attorney or bring in an advocate to their student hearing. Always, in these cases, consult with administrative leaders, and university or system attorneys. The directions provided through these consultative and mandated approaches are helpful and can keep objectivity at its highest peak. Other circumstances may be the student feeling unsupported or believing they did not have the accommodations or resources needed in order to be successful in the program. Perhaps the unknown disability of the student manifested as the reason for the student to experience a lack of success. Is the disability a manifestation of poor academic performance, disposition, and/or relational outcomes? If the answer is yes, yet committee members had no clue, then this could be a reason to reconfigure the remediation plan and any sanctions decided upon prior to obtaining this information.

Cultural Complexities

The cultural complexities regarding student development are from an array of gathered experience in serving as chair of student development committees. Culture not only has a strong-hold in counseling relationships (as it should), but it plays a huge part in navigating student issues and concerns. This section addresses two main complexities that interrupt these processes, with dynamic features, and they are the mainstream as the Gold Standard by which many fail to operate within, and whether student development processes are made more challenging due to personality and character not being so easily modified.

Mainstream and The Unacculturated

Graduate students in school counseling programs may have a natural-born citizenship from another country – outside of the United States. This cultural complexity can be challenging because these students may operate and function, only within their up-bringing and customs. They are simply not acculturated to our mainstream way of being and doing – perhaps they cannot relate, do not know, or have a difficulty understanding the *Gold Standard*, and therefore, they seem to not approach situations or problem-solving in a manner that is indicative of an appropriate response. By definition, the *Gold Standard* is the supreme example of something against which others are judged or measured. This difference in frame-of-reference can be the impetus for a referral to the student development committee. When this is the case, committee members should respond appropriately – as they would with any culturally different patient, client, or student – and that is to take these differences into account when rendering sanctions.

Challenges of Modifying Character or Personality

Through the student development process, it may be discovered that the underlying challenges in academic, intrapersonal, and dispositional performance are a representation of true flaws in character or personality. The primary question here is, can processes of student development and remediation change the character or modify the student's personality? Since that question is largely generated in the community of therapists rendering counseling, and there seems to be no clear answer, it is safe to be curious if committee members and remediation processes can impact character flaws or personality deficiencies.

Strategic Considerations

There are several strategic approaches worthy of consideration. The implications of each of the following considerations are that each has a systematic way of task completion or execution. Although prescriptive writing is an option, it is best to leave some fluidity in the processes below, so that each department of counseling can develop a strategic approach and design for orchestrating the following considerations.

Case Identification

Each student enrolled in the school counseling program should have an internal identification (ID) number, utilized to maintain confidentiality. This case ID is an alpha-numerical system that makes tracking and record keeping most private. One example of how this can be done, is to take an alias named Blue Boxelder Ivy, with a date of birth as April 21, 2003. The internal ID may be the combined first initial, birth month, middle initial, birth day, last initial, and birth year: B04B21I03. Departments of counseling get to decide this system and what to do if the student has no middle name or dual-last names.

Committee Meetings

Student reviews should happen at identified periods throughout a school year. When decided, committees meet to review academic, intrapersonal, and dispositional concerns. In alignment with the suggested membership details, these meetings not only review information, but they use the time to plan and schedule student hearings to address incoming referrals.

Student Hearing

The student hearing should be conducted in person or online. The student hearing process/format should be followed, without waiver, and documented by recording and keeping minutes. Correspondence and remediation plans (with included sanctions) should be sent to the student within a certain amount of time, post the hearing date and time. This time period should be evident in the manual written specifically for student development.

Remediation Plan and Sanctioning

The committee members should stay abreast of the students placed on remediation plan and monitor the progress made of students responding to a plan and sanctions. All plans are written developmental in nature and use suggested sanctions as described in this chapter.

Faculty Roles in Data Collection, Tracking, and Review Process

Committee members and department faculty should have a system to file or house referrals, plans for remediation and sanctions, hearing outcomes, meeting agendas, and to aggregate or disaggregate input data. This method of tracking data allows for follow-up, outside referrals made, and to generate reports for faculty members, as needed.

Student Services Referral

Periodically, the student development process in counseling departments was not sufficient to remediate the student, and therefore needs escalation to the Student Services Division at the university level. All documentation will be forwarded, and the student should be notified of this referral. Hopefully, the committee has formed a relationship with the university-level committee, designed to convene on the behalf of all students, undergraduates, and graduates alike.

Student Appeals and Grievance

Periodically, students will want to appeal or file grievances. Students who choose this method of response, should be guided to understand their rights as stated in program manuals and student code of conduct. Sometimes, administration of counseling departments may have misunderstood faculty members' role in gatekeeping the profession and that program probation, suspension, or dismissal may be protecting the public these unfit students are to serve.

Conclusion

This chapter is comprehensive for school counseling departments to utilize for school counselors in training development and growth. It is helpful to understand that this growth begins at conception – essentially at the admissions phase throughout the graduation phase. It is theoretically underpinned by Jean Piaget's Theory of Cognitive Development (sensorimotor, preoperational, concrete operational, formal operational) and by a seminal work in counselor development, written by Rønnestad and Skovholt (2003).

Furthermore, the integration of the spirit of this process, being founded upon due process, equality, equity, and equifinality – all serving as staples to faculty members, as Senseis to The Kokoro Way for students to become, is guiding our future school counselor practitioners exactly to where they should be: with optimal mental health, having addressed their own issues, and understanding how to work with students and families, in an optimal way.

References

American Counseling Association (ACA) *ACA Code of Ethics*, 2014. Online. Available HTTP: <https://www.counseling.org/resources/aca-code-of-ethics.pdf>

American School Counselor Association (ASCA) (2018) *American School Counselor Association Ethical Standards for School Counselor Education Faculty*, Alexandria, VA: Author.

ASCA (Accepted by CAEP 2019; Accepted by AAQEP 2022) *ASCA Standards for School Counselor PreparationPprograms*, Alexandria, VA: Author.

ASCA (2020) *The School Counselor and Mental Health*. Online. Available HTTP: <https://www.schoolcounselor.org/Standards-Positions/Position-Statements/ASCA-Position-Statements/The-School-Counselor-and-Student-Mental-Health>

ASCA (2022) *The ASCA Ethical Standards for School Counselors*, Alexandria, VA: Author.

Association for Advancing Quality Education Programs (AAQEP) (2018) "Standards and Guide". Online. Available HTTP: <https://aaqep.org/standards>

Council for Accreditation of Counseling and Related Educational Programs (CACREP) (2024) *CACREP 2024 Standards*, Alexandria, VA: Author.

Piaget, J. (1936) *Origins of Intelligence in the Child*, London: Routledge & Kegan Paul.

Rabindran, R. and Madanagopal, D. (2020) "Piaget's theory and stages of cognitive development – an overview", *Scholars Journal of Applied Medical Sciences*. Online. Available HTTP: <https://doi.org/10.36347/sjams.2020.v08i09.034>

Reid, S. (2009) "Defining dispositions: mapping student attitudes and strategies in college composition", in P. Portonova, J.M. Riffenberg, and D. Roen, *Contemporary Perspectives on Cognition and Writing*, WAC Clearinghouse Press, pp. 291–312. Online, Available HTTP: <https://wac.colostate.edu/docs/books/cognition/chapter15.pdf>

Rønnestad, M. and Skovholt, T. (2003) "The journey of the counselor and therapist: research findings and perspectives on professional development", *Journal of Career Development*, 30: 5–44.

APPENDIX A

Referral and Incident Form

Student Name:

ID Number:

Date of Incident:

Program of Study:

Total Number of Referrals:

Primary Incident Category:	Academic	Intrapersonal	Dispositional	
Secondary Incident Category:	Ethics	Legal	Culture	
	Professionalism		Off-Site Concerns	

Narrative Description of Incident:

Document Factual Accounts:

  Name of Referring Person:

  Description of Referring Person: Student Staff Faculty Supervisor

  Name of Witness(es):

  Date Student was Contacted:

Remediation Plan: Yes No In-Progress Date:

Sanctions:

APPENDIX B

Template for Student Development Policy Manual

Table of Contents for Policy Manual

Overview of Student Development and Performance in Academics, Intrapersonal, and Dispositions for School Counselors
University and Counseling Department Mission and Vision Statements
Alignment of University and Counseling Department Strategic Planning Goals
American Counseling Association (ACA) and American School Counseling Association (ASCA) Code of Ethics

University Office of Graduate Studies
Rationale for Student Development and Performance in Academics, Intrapersonal, and Dispositions for School Counselors
Student Code of Conduct
Faculty Committee Roles and Responsibilities of Student Development and Performance Faculty Committee
Agenda and Meeting Protocols for Student Development and Performance Faculty Committee
Incidents and Infraction Types and Levels
Incident Reporting or Referral
Student Hearing Protocol
Sanctions (Written, Participatory, Technological, Literary, and Cumulative Formats)
Remediation Plan
University Student Services Referral
Confidentiality, Documentation, and Correspondences
Student Appeals and Grievances

APPENDIX C

Sanction Letter

The **Student Counseling Program Faculty** at _____ is charged with monitoring and responding to the academic performance, intrapersonal development, and dispositional performance, along with professional challenges of our graduate students in the school counseling program. The program faculty facilitate the university and department's mission and vision, along with embodying the leadership and governing ethics, as well as values staples in responding to concerns held by faculty and supervisors.

_____ holds professionalism, academic integrity, self-improvement and transformation in the highest regard. We require that our students uphold the university honor code and in cases where your conduct and performance become in question, the department must review the incident in order to uphold the integrity of the program.

You attended a meeting on _____ and a follow-up meeting on _____. The following areas were addressed during our time together:

(example) did not exhibit professional or ethical behavior in one or more areas as outlined in the course or program.

The School Counseling Program Faculty reviewed your case and as a result, the following sanctions were rendered:

Written Format

Student will earn a grade of F in Course Name and Number, with an earliest graduation date of _____, pending successful completion of coursework.

Participatory Format

Successful Completion of Counselor Competency Scale-Revised (CCS-R)

Technological Format

(example) Submit a recorded video using Zoom, accompanied by a document highlighting talking points by date and time. This video must include the following:

- Integrity in the counseling profession and its importance
- A synopsis of ethical codes and standards from American Counseling Association, state licensing or certification board (whichever applies), and American School Counselor Association that are applicable in your case.
- Ethical and best-practice recommendations regarding academic integrity and what you've learned from this experience.
- Counselor characteristics that should perhaps need further developing, and your plan to do so as you aspire toward entering the field of counseling.

Literary Format

Read Journal Article https://www.tandfonline.com/doi/abs/10.1080/15566382.2004.12033803

Cumulative Format

In closing, future incidences of academic, intrapersonal, or dispositional concerns could, again, be referred to this committee. It is highly recommended that you (list specific directives required). In these instances, prior infractions and sanctions will be a part of the considerations toward your completion in the program. Failure to complete these sanctions can result in further departmental action or consequence. If in disagreement, the chair of the student development committee is your initial point of contact. For now, we hope that this process and opportunity was growth producing and reflective, as we are committed to assisting you in successfully meeting your professional goals.

Thanking you in advance,

Student Counseling Program Faculty

APPENDIX D

Example Remediation Plans

Example 1: Remediation Plan for School Counselors in Training within Clinical Settings

Remediation Form and Growth Plan Clinical mental health counselors-in-training are required to be supervised during their practicum and internship experiences (CACREP, 2024). This approach is optimal, because it allows for more than a year of observing and growing the trainee/supervisee. Both practicing counselors and site supervisors have an ethical obligation to train, mentor, supervise, professionally develop, instruct, and protect the welfare of clients (ACA, 2014). If the trainee/supervisee experience difficulty during this process, it is the opinion and duty of the site supervisor to remediate these professionals-in-training. The supervisor should document his/her concerns and collaborate with other faculty supervisors, faculty members, and administrators to corroborate the sentiment needed for growth. All areas of concern herein are written with precise language in alignment with the standards stipulated in the American Counseling Association Ethical Codes (2014) and are shared with the trainee/supervisee. It is important to note this remediation plan does not address areas of strengths, but only the specific areas needed for necessary improvement/change.

Clinical Skills Problem Areas

Following are the areas of concern presented by the site supervisor responsible for gatekeeping the profession, protecting the welfare of students, and assisting in the development of the trainee or supervisee.

The trainee/supervisee, _____, should:

> choose to be fully present with clients and exercise immediacy when necessary, without an over-anxious will to validate her clinical impressions/diagnosis/suppositions and without the flexibility to consider other alternatives, such as the use of Z-codes. It is important to understand the ways in which clients take our clinical interpretations seriously and how a label can be difficult to receive by many.

Attitude and Dispositional Problem Areas

Following are the areas of concern presented by the site supervisor responsible for gatekeeping the profession and protecting the welfare of clients, along with promoting change and development, personally and professionally, in the trainee/supervisee.

The trainee/supervisee, _____, should:

1 not make decisions or create correspondence of any sort, nor have clients sign this correspondence, on the behalf of the, without the proper letterhead, vetting, nor garnering the appropriate approval from the supervisor or director of counseling program, site supervisor, Supervisor/Director Name. Information placed in this correspondence made guarantees to the client that were not accurate, possible, or truthful.
2 eliminate behaviors that are appear deterministic, or seem slightly pushy, to the degree that some directives and most social cues are not acknowledged, interpreted correctly, or perhaps even ignored.
3 increase insight, raise consciousness, and levels of discernment enough to know what information should not be shared with clients attained during supervision, staffings, or treatment-team processes by anticipating natural consequences and by correctly interpreting potential outcomes.

4 learn to slow down enough in order to manage impulsivity, by engaging and adopting a personal decision-making process or decision tree. The model chosen should have consultation and collaboration with other professionals or supervisors as a necessary part of the decision-making process.
5 manage or eliminate high-levels of curiosity, or an instinctive need-to-know, to the degree that going into areas or systems (e.g. such as taking the privilege to browse administrative areas of the company Square Reader) is understood as unethical and unprofessional.
6 learn to accept constructive criticism/feedback, eliminate behaviors/feelings of defensiveness, and perfectionism. Please be reminded of the purpose of supervisory practices and implemented models of peer-feedback.
7 learn to authentically communicate with the site supervisor, professionally, sharing true thoughts and feelings and knowing the difference in which affairs should be addressed with other interns and which issues should be addressed with the site supervisor.

Application of Appropriate Ethical Codes: American Counseling Association (2014)

Following are the ethical codes that are suggested for your review. This should keep you aware of the expectations set forth by our governing professional organizations and the site supervisor who may need to professionally endorse you as a clinical mental health counselor.

C.2.d. Monitor Effectiveness
C.2.e. Consultations on Ethical Obligations
C.2.f. Continuing Education
C.2.g. Impairment
D.1.c. Interdisciplinary Teams
D.1.d. Establishing Professional and Ethical Obligations
D.1.g. Employer Policies
E.5.d. Refraining from Diagnosis
F.4.c. Standards for Supervisees
F.5. Student and Supervisee Responsibilities
F.5.b. Impairment
F.6. Counseling Supervision Evaluation, Remediation, and Endorsement
F.6.d. Endorsements
F.7.i. Field Placements
F.7.g. Student-to-Student Supervision and Instruction
F.8.d. Addressing Personal Concerns
F.9. Evaluation and Remediation
I.1.b. Ethical Decision Making
I.2.c. Consultation

Growth and Remediation Plan

The supervisee/trainee will review this entire plan and document how these areas have been addressed beginning <u>start date</u> through <u>end date</u>.

> Specifically, the trainee _____ should:
>
> 1. obtain, read, and know all policies of <u>school district or entity name</u> (client, intern, and employee); recall and review her contract and review statements of non-disclosure. Learn to follow instructions, as they are given, consistently and in an unwavering fashion.
> 2. obtain, read, and know the American Counseling Association Code of Ethics (2014), with particular emphasis on the areas mentioned above.
> 3. maintain a journal of how all these areas were concretely addressed with specific dates (e.g. objective evidence is needed like attending workshop, obtaining personal counseling, research articles read or attending a group) and is required to submit to the site supervisor on _____, by the end of the first semester of internship.
> 4. write a paper, with accurate use of APA (headers, in-text citations, references), including six peer-reviewed, current journal articles/literature (within the past 7 years), three that are conceptual in nature and three that are evidenced-based, that addresses all components of this remediation plan.
> 5. submit a video to <u>Supervisor or Director</u> Name on how all these areas were addressed, with an emphasis on the journey, how changes have been made, and the impact of these changes personally and professionally due <u>enter date and time here</u>.

In closing and at this time, my professional practice as supervisor/director is to take a developmental approach with trainees/supervisees. It is expected that name of <u>intern or supervisee</u> remain at the site <u>Name of Site/Location of Site</u> for the <u>Term and Year</u>. Because the aforementioned concerns could place any site at-risk, immediate removal from the site is a viable option. The goal is for <u>Intern Full Name</u> to correct and address all areas of concern. These concerns will be noted on the midterm evaluation and the faculty/professor of record should expect an increase in ratings/scores by the end of the term (final evaluation). Failure to address all components, in detail of this remediation plan, will result in non-endorsement of this counselor-in-training and a recommendation will be made to the university to gate-keep the profession and protect the possible welfare of future clients by not allowing continuation. Amendments to this plan can be made until the end of the course.

Signatures indicate agreement of all that is herein, and demonstrates the site supervisor and supervisee's commitment to work through this remediation plan to address the areas of concern/

_____   _____
Intern or Supervisee Name   Date

_____   _____
Supervisor Name Date   Date

Example 2: University Counseling Department Remediation Plan

SUMMARY OF REFERRAL AND OVERALL STUDENT ISSUE

Departmental Stipulations

The following is a remediation plan that must be completed in order to advance in the program.

It must be completed to move forward in the program. Due to repeated concern, program removal will occur if there is not successful completion.

Remediation Designated

1 Successfully complete the CCS-R with a minimum score of 4 from both site supervisor and professor on all professional behaviors criteria. Some examples of professional behaviors that need to be adjusted are as follows:

   a Submitting requested information by _____
   b Representing circumstances in a truthful manner
   c Professional communication

2 Receives a minimum of a 4 from both site supervisor and professor on the professional skills and therapeutic skills on the CCS-R. Some examples of skills that need to be improved are as follows and should be noted in CCS-R for practicum:

   a Empathic responding (i.e. reflections, summarizing, paraphrasing, etc.)
   b No advice giving
   c Letting the client lead

3 Complete an essay discussing receiving feedback and skills improvement. This essay will be APA style, personal in nature with resources. Additionally, make sure you explore personal defenses surrounding receiving and incorporating feedback and constructive criticism.
4 All course assignments turned in on time with no exceptions.
5 All course assignments submitted as complete (i.e. not with a half-started sentence at the end).
6 Complete presence in class (i.e. gathering water/snacks prior to class beginning, not submitting assignments during class time, staying on camera with appropriate lighting for the duration of the class, etc.).
7 Professional tone and appearance in virtual counseling/telehealth.
8 Following all directions for assignments.
9 Include working with diverse populations into your internship site.

Unsuccessful adherence to this remediation plan will be grounds for dismissal from the program.

APPENDIX E

Student Hearing Protocol

This document is for student development committees. The student hearing protocol should be followed without deviation, and any variation should be documented in the minutes.

- Chair Introduction
- Introductions of Committee Members (*State Name and Role as a Member*)
- Purpose of the Meeting (*Broad in Nature; Confidential; Pulled from Manual and Student Notification Letter*)
- Case Overview (*Specific in Nature; Examples Pulled from Documentation in TK20*)
- Student Response to Concerns (*Expect Non-Verbal/Verbal, Emotional, and Behavioral Reactions*)
- Committee Member Inquiry (*Precise and Accurate According to Student Facts in Case and Student Response*)
- Summary and Student Final Questions (*Share Process of Sanctions/Decisions; Time frame for Follow-up and Decision Letter*)
- Adjourn Meeting

8 Dynamic School Counselor Professional Development Focusing on Continuous Mental Health Education

Natalie Fikac

Leadership Quote

Personal development precedes professional development.

Natalie Fikac

Aspirational Statements

- School counselors are on a unique journey as they continually grow their skills, their craft, their passions and themselves in this ever changing and evolving world.
- School counselors have an opportunity to be innovative in their practice by attending dynamic personal and professional development.

Introduction and Background

The American School Counselor Association (ASCA) defines professional development as "the process of improving and increasing capabilities through access to education and training opportunities" (ASCA, 2019). School counselor professional development needs look different than other positions in education. School counselors navigate the academic needs, social and emotional, mental health and post-secondary needs of their students. These four areas of training and professional development are quite different and require a great deal of planning, thought and intentionality for school counselor leaders to plan for. Each state has its own requirements of the number of continuing education hours to maintain certification and/or licensure. A school counselor leader must be aware of these requirements as they lead the planning and orchestrate opportunities for their teams with a focus on instilling positive mental health for all.

While the professional development requirements of school counselors differ from state to state, there are also opportunities for school counseling programs to be recognized for their hard work. Table 8.1 outlines and compares two examples of program recognition: the Recognizing ASCA Model Program, or RAMP Award (ASCA, 2023) and Texas Counselors Reinforcing Excellence for Students in Texas or CREST Award (TSCA, 2021).

DOI: 10.4324/9781003219750-10

Table 8.1 Criteria for Award-Winning School Counseling Programs

	Recognizing ASCA Model Program (RAMP)	Counselors Reinforcing Excellence for Students in Texas (CREST)
	RAMP and CREST Award Similarities	
What	The Recognized ASCA Model Program (RAMP) recognizes schools committed to delivering comprehensive, data-informed school counseling programs. These programs, which align with the ASCA National Model, exemplify school counseling at its best.	Counselors Reinforcing Excellence for Students in Texas (CREST) is sponsored by the Texas School Counselor Association (TSCA) and awarded to school counseling programs that meet CREST requirements. CREST is a continuous improvement document that school counseling programs can use to demonstrate effective communication and a commitment to obtaining results.
Benefits	• Free ASCA membership for all school counselors in the school for current RAMP schools • An engraved plaque, suitable for display on your office wall • Communication sent to your school's principal and superintendent informing them of your exemplary school counseling program • Template press release to individualize and send to local press • School recognition at ASCA's Annual Conference • Two tickets to the RAMP awards celebration at ASCA's annual conference • Free conference registration for RAMP school principal the year RAMP is awarded • Recognition in ASCA School Counselor magazine and on the ASCA website	• Advocate for your school counseling program and show how it supports student success • Document your school counseling program's role in supporting student success • Show continuous improvement data for your counseling program • Highlight program successes for all stakeholders • Strengthen the campus counseling program by aligning it with the campus improvement plan • Reinforce the school counselor's role in the academic, personal/social, and career development of students • Link your school counseling program to state, national, and legislative standards. • Provide a tool for accountability • Receive recognition at the Texas School Counselor Association/Texas Counseling Association spring conferences • Receive a CREST banner for display on your campus
What information is needed?	• The RAMP application process should be the culmination of the implementation of a school counseling program. Once your school has a program in place, you will need at least one entire academic year to collect the data and information needed to fulfill the RAMP application requirements.[1]	• The CREST application is first and foremost a tool to help you communicate about your comprehensive school counseling program. • The CREST application will provide you an opportunity to explain the design and implementation of your program using images, data elements, and your existing artifacts such as your yearly calendar of activities. • The application rubric provides detailed instructions and citations to pertinent information in the Texas Model.

Section I	**Section I: Vision and Mission Statements** • School counseling vision statement • School counseling mission statement • School and district vision and/or mission statements if available **Section I: Introduction to the School and the Role of the Professional School Counselor** • School information (enrollment/population, address, website, logo, social media, principal name, previous counseling awards) • Information for each counselor (name and contact information, credentials, professional memberships, leadership positions and committees, photo) • Statement regarding the counselor's role on campus (50 words or less) • Example of how the counselor participates in leadership and advocacy (100 words or less)
Section II	**Section II: Annual Student Outcome Goals** • School data summary • Systemic focus • Annual student outcome goals • Reflection **Section II: Program Implementation Cycle** • Description and names of Counseling Advisory Council (CAC) and meeting schedule • An example of the CAC's use of the implementation cycle • A copy of your annual program plan
Section III	**Section III: Classroom and Group Mindsets & Behaviors Action Plan** • Classroom lessons • Small group lessons • Reflection **Section III: Foundational Components** • A copy of your program's mission statement • Your program's definition, rationale and assumptions • Description of how program goals were developed • An example of your needs assessment • A description of your process for evaluating your program

Section IV	**Section IV: Annual Administrative Conference**
	• Completed annual administrative conference template for each school counselor
	• Completed 5-day use-of-time calculators for each school counselor to document previous school year's use-of-time cited on template (one from first semester and one from second semester)
	• Supporting documentation
	• Reflection
	
	Section IV: Four Service Delivery Components
	• An example SMART goal (50 words or less) and a brief list of activities for each service component
	• An example of each of the following:
	   – An activity from any of the components including a data visualization of student outcomes as a result of the activity
	   – A collaboration with parents to support a specific goal or a coordination of efforts with community partners to meet student needs
	   – The school counselor's (or the applicant's) yearly calendar of activities

(Continued)

Table 8.1 (Continued)

	Recognizing ASCA Model Program (RAMP)	Counselors Reinforcing Excellence for Students in Texas (CREST)

Section V	**Section V: Advisory Council**
	• First semester and second semester advisory council agenda templates
	• Council members
	• Council agendas
	• Council meeting minutes
	• Reflection
		Section V: Program Curriculum
		• Select one of the four content areas and explain in detail how your program addresses its scope and sequence:
		  - Describe the data that was used when designing the lesson and how it is connected to one or more counseling program goals
		  - Provide an example of a lesson plan, activity, or unit of instruction
		  - Share an example of how you evaluated the learning outcomes
		  - Describe how the counselor works with stakeholders to ensure that each content area is addressed (100–200 words)

	RAMP Award Additional Requirements	
Section VI	**Section VI: Annual Calendar** • Completed annual calendar template • Calendar aligned with ASCA model • Evidence of calendar communicated to stakeholders	
Section VII	**Section VII: Lesson Plans – Classroom and Group** • Classroom lesson plans • Class lessons data • Small-Group lesson plans • Small-Group data collection plan • Reflection	
Section VIII	**Section VIII: Classroom Instruction Results Form** • The classroom instruction results report shows participation, Mindsets & Behaviors and Outcome data from the three lessons highlighted in Section VII. • Classroom lesson participation data • Classroom lesson Mindsets & Behaviors data • Classroom lesson outcome data • Mindsets & Behaviors data results graph(s) • Outcome data results graph(s) • Reflection	

Section IX	**Section IX: Small-Group Results Report**	
	• The Small-Group results report shows the participation, Mindsets & Behaviors and Outcome data from the Small-Group sessions highlighted in Section VII.	
	• Small-Group participation data	
	• Small-Group Mindsets & Behaviors data	
	• Small-Group Outcome data	
	• Mindsets & Behaviors data results graph(s)	
	• Outcome data results graph(s)	
	• Reflection	
Section X	**Section X: Closing the Gap Action Plan/Results Report**	
	• Mindsets & Behaviors data results graph	
	• Outcome data results graph	
	• Closing-the-Gap Goal Statement	
	• Closing-the-Gap Action Plan	
	• Data Collection Plan	
	• Results data	
	• Mindsets & Behaviors data results graph(s)	
	• Outcome data results graph(s)	
	• Reflection	
Scoring	The application will be scored based on the Fourth Edition scoring rubric (ASCA, 2022). The scoring rubric is based on *The ASCA National Model: A Foundation for School Counseling Programs* (4th edn) and *The ASCA National Model Implementation Guide* (2nd edn).	Each CREST document will be evaluated and scored by members of the TSCA CREST evaluation team comprised of Texas school counselors.
	Each application is scored by a three-person review team overseen by a lead RAMP reviewer.	The rubric's levels (exemplary, proficient, developing, etc.) will correlate to numeric scores. Those scores will be weighted according to the table below to create the final score.
	RAMP status will be awarded to schools that receive scores of 54 or higher (out of a possible 60). Some schools that don't earn RAMP will be invited to resubmit based on the score and the components needing improvement.	• Section I: Introduction to the School and Role of the PSC – 10%
		• Section II: Program Implementation Cycle – 10%
		• Section III: Foundational Components – 25%
		• Section IV: Four Service Delivery Components – 30%
	Schools that resubmit and still don't attain a 54 or higher are eligible to become a Program of Promise and receive mentoring to potentially be eligible for RAMP the following year.	• Section V: Program Curriculum – 20%
		• Section VI: Formatting and Editing – 5%

(Continued)

Table 8.1 (Continued)

Recognizing ASCA Model Program (RAMP)	Counselors Reinforcing Excellence for Students in Texas (CREST)
Schools that earn a 58 or above after the initial review will be designated a RAMP School of Distinction. The application will not be reviewed if all required components are not complete or provided. Following is a list of the individual sections for your application submission. Use the ASCA-provided templates (4th edn). The application must have all 10 components. • Vision and Mission Statements, 6 points • Annual Student Outcome Goals, 7 points • Classroom and Group Mindsets & Behaviors Action Plan, 5 points • Annual Administrative Conference, 5 points • Advisory Council, 6 points • Calendars (Annual and Weekly), 3 points • Lesson Plans (Classroom and Group), 5 points • Classroom Instruction results report, 7 points • Small-Group results report, 7 points • Closing-the-Gap Action Plan/results report, 9 points	CREST Award Additional Opportunities **CREST Leadership** • Successful award of CREST in 2020–2021 • CREST recognition in 3 prior years **CREST Advocacy** • Successful award of CREST in 2020–2021 • CREST recognition in 3 prior years • Presentation at a professional conference (ie. TCA, TSCA, ACA, TASSP, AVID, ESC events etc.) or participation in one or more Advocacy Days at the Texas Capitol

Note: This table is based on the criteria for recognizing excellent school counseling programs from *Recognizing ASCA Model Program* or RAMP Award and Texas' *Counselors Reinforcing Excellence for Students in Texas* or CREST Award.

[1] ASCA templates for each section are available from: https://www.schoolcounselor.org/Recognition/RAMP/Templates. Created by N. Fikac, 2022.

Mentoring plays an essential part in both the personal and professional development of school counselors. School counselor leaders must have a clear understanding of the strengths and areas for growth for each member of their teams. Pairing school counselors with teammates to provide ongoing consultation and coaching can be a great way to build team morale and cultivate trust. Equally important in the mentorship model is ensuring that mentors have scaled up their learning in areas to mentor others, particularly in the area of mental health. School counselor leaders can develop cohorts of specialized trainings for their team. One example could be to have specific cohorts within the school counseling team that specialize in: post-secondary processes, crisis intervention, course selection, trauma-informed care, data collection and analysis, and mental health signs and symptoms including anxiety, depression, etc. When a school counselor leader intentionally creates cohorts of knowledge and passion such as these, the weight of knowing all that a school counselor has to know feels much less heavy and can lead to less burnout. Dr. Brown's research about daring leadership tells us that the number one trust building behavior is asking for help (Brown, 2018). When school counseling teams begin to consult with one another this also increases school counseling staff morale and efficacy.

Leadership Program Values and Standards

As mentioned in a previous chapter, "Who we are is how we lead.". Brown (2018) coined this phrase based on thousands of pieces of data in her text *Dare to Lead*. School counselors have a professional and personal responsibility to understand the values that they lead by. School counselor leaders must name their values for a deeper understanding of what is driving decisions, vision and goals. Taking values work one step farther by operationalizing values is important. School counselors can ask themselves, what does it look like when I am living into my values, what does it look like when I am living outside of my values and how do my personal values align with the values of the school counseling team, division, or department? Once school counselors leaders name and operationalize their personal values, they lead their school counseling teams through the same process and serve as integrity partners in this important work.

When school counselors name and understand their personal values, candid conversations can occur and a robust vision and mission statement can be laid out for the guidance and counseling department, division, team, etc. This process is important in developing a professional development and personal development plan for the guidance and counseling department. When the department is able to name and operationalize its values, this leads to values-based decision making when determining professional development and training goals and aspirations. An authentic and values-driven school counselor leader guides and facilitates this process to ensure that each member of the counseling department's personal and professional development needs are met.

Leadership in Practice

School counselor leaders and school counselors understand the importance of the use of both national and state models to guide and inform their practices. There are many opportunities for school counselor leaders to highlight and showcase the amazing work that they are leading within the school counseling program as showcased above in the RAMP and CREST chart. School counseling leaders lead their teams under a continuous quality improvement (CQI) cycle where strengths and areas of growth are constantly evaluated as the needs of the department and students shifts and changes. This is no different when considering dynamic professional development and training. Leaders who exemplify excellence provide frequent evaluation and reflection opportunities for their teams to ensure that professional development and training is innovative, high quality, and exemplary. School counselor leaders plan for professional development annually based on the cycle of the school year noting important keystone events that might include the list below. School counselor leaders ensure alignment of the needs of the school counseling team, needs of students and school community, national standards, state legislative requirements, as well as an alignment to awareness events.

An example of this might include: a school district has noticed an uptick in the number of reported bullying incidents, and school counselors have spent an additional 10 percent of their time supporting administration and students with bullying incidents in September. The school counselor leader schedules a training in October for the school counselors in partnership with school senior leadership to learn more about bullying and evidence-based interventions as well as multiple campus level events for students and evening events for families of students. This wraparound approach uses data to drive decisions for providing needed training, support and education for staff, students, and families.

Table 8.2 Counseling Awareness Events or Topics

Month	Awareness Events
September	• Childhood Cancer Awareness Month • National Childhood Obesity Awareness Month • National Preparedness Month • National Recovery Month • Self-Improvement Month • Sexual Health Awareness Month • 9/15-10/15: Hispanic Heritage Month
October	• ADHD Awareness Month • Bullying Prevention Month • Communicate with Your Kids Month • Crime Prevention Month • Domestic Violence Awareness Month • Health Literacy Month • LGBT History Month • National Depression and Mental Health Screening Month • Positive Attitude Month
November	• Adoption Awareness Month • Military Family Appreciation Month • National Career Development Month • National Family Caregivers Month • National Homeless Youth Awareness Month • National Runaway Prevention Month • National Scholarship Month • Native American Heritage Month
December	• National Impaired Driving Prevention Month • Safe Toys and Gifts Month
January	• National Mentoring Month • National Thank-You Month
February	• Black History Month • Career and Technical Education Month • Gap Year Awareness Month

(*Continued*)

Table 8.2 (Continued)

Month	Awareness Events
March	• International Boost Self-Esteem Month • National Children's Dental Health Month • Teen Dating Violence Awareness Month • National School Counselor Appreciation Week • Gender Equality Month • National Nutrition Month • Women's History Month • Youth Art Month
April	• Alcohol Awareness Month • Child Abuse Prevention Month • Community Service Month • Counseling Awareness Month • Keep America Beautiful Month • Month of the Military Child • National Autism Awareness Month • National STD Awareness Month • Sexual Assault Awareness and Prevention Month
May	• Asian-Pacific American Heritage Month • Mental Health Awareness Month • Military Appreciation Month • National Bike Month • National Foster Care Month • National Physical Fitness and Sports Month • Teen Pregnancy Prevention Month
June	• Fireworks Safety Month (6/1-7/4) • LGBTQ Pride Month • National Hunger Awareness Month • National Safety Month

Note: This is not an exhaustive list of Awareness Events or Topics. Created by N. Fikac, 2022.

The table above provides monthly unique opportunities for professional school counselors to celebrate, bring awareness to and advocate on behalf of various populations and historical events to bring awareness and capitalize on the opportunity of how a professional school counselor's unique knowledge and skillset can support the entire school community. One such example could include in April during Community Service Involvement Month, the professional school counselor could front load students during guidance lessons in March and staff during a faculty meeting about various community service opportunities within the school community. The professional school counselor could coordinate and support students and staff supporting a local community service in need such as a food bank during the month of April.

Mental and Behavioral Health Considerations

Helping to meet the needs of the whole child is an important role of the school counselor leader and school counselor. If a student is not mentally well, little to no learning will occur in the classroom. School counselor leaders often wonder how much professional development training around mental and behavioral health a school counselor should attend. The answer lies in the role of the school counselor. Is the school counselor functioning as they are intended to as a part of a comprehensive school counseling program? While school counselors are often described as the glue that holds a school campus together, school counselors are often also one of the few positions on a school campus that have received any training or education in the mental and behavioral health space. Other positions that may exist on a campus that have knowledge in this area include the school nurse, a licensed school psychologist (LSSP) or a school social worker. School counselors are often the first person that a parent, student, teacher or administrator turns to when there is a mental or behavioral health need. Thus, school counselor leaders should prioritize training for school counselors in the area of school mental and behavioral health. The Texas Education Agency regularly updates their website with evidence-based trainings located here: https://schoolmentalhealthtx.org/best-practices/

Ethical Considerations

According to the *ASCA Ethical Standards for School Counselors* (2022b):

B.3. Responsibilities to Self

School counselors:

b maintain membership in school counselor professional organizations to stay up to date on current research and to maintain professional competence in current school counseling issues and topics.
[…]
e engage in routine, content-applicable professional development to stay up to date on trends and needs of students and other stakeholders, and regularly attend training on current legal and ethical responsibilities.
f explore and examine implicit biases and the impact on practice and interaction with students; apply learning to program practice and development.
[…]
h recognize the potential for stress and secondary trauma. Practice wellness and self-care through monitoring mental, emotional and physical health, while seeking consultation from an experienced school counseling practitioner and/or others when needed.
i monitor personal behaviors and recognize the high standard of care a professional in this critical position of trust must maintain on and off the job. School counselors are cognizant of and refrain from activity that may diminish their effectiveness within the school community.
j apply an ethical decision-making model and seek consultation and supervision from colleagues and other professionals who are knowledgeable of the profession's practices when ethical questions arise.
k Honor the diversity and identities of students and seek training/supervision when prejudice or biases interfere with providing comprehensive school counseling services to all pre-K–12 students. School counselors will not refuse services to students based solely on personally held beliefs/values rooted in one's religion, culture or ethnicity. School counselors work toward a school climate that embraces diverse identities and promotes equitable outcomes in academic, career and social/emotional development for all students.

School counselors must stay up to date on the ethical requirements of professional development of school counselors, engage in professional development opportunities including training, conferences and research and literature, seek consultation and supervision, and practice self-awareness.

C. SCHOOL COUNSELOR ADMINISTRATORS/SUPERVISORS

School counselor administrators/supervisors support school counselors in their charge by:

a advocating both within and outside of their schools or districts for adequate resources to implement a school counseling program and meet students' needs and the school community's needs.
[...]
c taking reasonable steps to ensure school and other resources are available to provide staff supervision and training.
d providing opportunities for professional development in current research related to school counseling practices, competencies and ethics.
[...]
f monitoring school and organizational policies, regulations and procedures to ensure practices are consistent with the ASCA Ethical Standards for School Counselors.
[...]
i providing staff with opportunities and support to develop knowledge and understanding of historic and systemic oppression, social justice and cultural models (e.g., multicultural counseling, anti-racism, culturally sustaining practices) to further develop skills for systemic change and equitable outcomes for all students.

School counselor leaders must ensure that resources are made available to support school counselor supervision and training, provide relevant professional development opportunities and ensure ethics and laws are not violated for their school counseling teams.

D. SCHOOL COUNSELING INTERN SITE SUPERVISORS

c Use a model of supervision that is developmental, ongoing and includes but is not limited to promoting professional growth, supporting best practices and ethical practice, assessing supervisee performance and developing plans for improvement, consulting on specific cases and assisting in the development of a course of action.

Oftentimes, school counselor leaders also serve as supervisors to school counseling interns. These site supervisors must assist supervisees with professional development opportunities.

Cultural Complexities

School counselor leaders must intentionally provide professional development opportunities for the school counselors that they serve that address cultural issues that can impact the positive mental health of staff and students. This requires the school counselor leader to stay abreast of any new topic or societal need that might arise and practice their own personal exploration and development. These topics include and are not limited to: supporting LGBT students, addressing social justice issues, diversity, equity, inclusion and belonging. The Mental Health Technology Transfer Centers (MHTTCs) in the United States are resources that provide evidence and research-based training, guidance, support, and tools to schools for free. A.10 of the *ASCA Code of Ethical Standards for School Counselors* provides specific guidance for ways for school counselors to serve underserved and at-risk populations that includes advocating, identifying, collaborating and providing support to students who are considered underserved and at-risk.

Strategic Considerations

As mentioned above, school counselor mentoring and the development of cohorts of knowledge and passion within the school counseling team helps to build capacity for the comprehensive school counseling program and trust within the school counseling team. Of equal importance is partnering with local child-serving agencies, university programs, and state programs. Many experts exist in surrounding communities and in local agencies that are able to provide training, guidance, consultation, and support as needed and often for free. Examples could include working with a local mental health authority (LMHA) to provide training and support for school counselors while developing crisis plans, partnering with a local institute of higher education (IHE) to provide training in the areas of post-secondary readiness and post-secondary opportunities and working with local behavioral health hospitals to create referral pathways for students when there is a need for a possible evaluation or inpatient hospitalization. Many times schools and districts operate in silos and do not reach out to local partners for training and support. A well-run multi-tiered system of support (MTSS) includes these vital stakeholders as team members when working to support the mental and behavioral health needs of students.

It is also notable that there is a shortage of school counselors in states across the country. One strategy to create a future workforce is for the school counselor leader to develop and implement an Aspiring School Counselor Academy. This Academy meets regularly with educators within their school district who are interested and/or are in graduate programs to become school counselors. Facilitated and coordinated by the school counselor leader, this provides a direct pathway for graduates to already have a firm knowledge of the vision and mission of the school counseling department and to ensure that the mental health needs of future staff and students will be met. School counselors from the district provide the content for the Academy and lead the training and program. Not only does this further develop the leadership skill sets of the school counselors but it creates buy in for Academy participants.

Conclusion

Providing dynamic school counselor professional development is one of the most important roles of a school counselor leader. With the unique, ever-changing role of school counselors; time is one of the greatest commodities for this role. School counselor leaders must strategically evaluate, plan, and provide exemplary training opportunities for their team. It is very difficult for school counselors to find uninterrupted and sacred time to spend off their campuses to attend professional development and training. School counselor leaders must ensure that this valuable time must include content that is evidence-based, worthwhile, innovative, action oriented, and easy to implement.

References

American School Counselor Association (ASCA) (2019) *2019–2020 National Educational and Health Awareness Dates*. Online. Available HTTP: <https://www.schoolcounselor.org/asca/media/asca/home/2019-20AwarenessCalendar.pdf>

ASCA (2022a) "Fourth Edition: RAMP Applications Submitted in October 2022". Online. Available HTTP: <https://www.schoolcounselor.org/getmedia/15ff9ea7-158d-4297-994b-66a4aee48c59/2022-fourth-edition-rubric.pdf>

ASCA (2022b) *ASCA Ethical Standards for School Counselors*, Alexandria, VA: Author.

ASCA (2023) "Recognized ASCA Model Program". Online. Available HTTP: <https://www.schoolcounselor.org/Recognition/RAMP>

Brown, B. (2018) *Dare to Lead*, London: Vermilion.

Texas School Counselor Association (TSCA) (2021) "CREST 2021 Application Packet". Online. Available HTTP: <https://docs.google.com/document/d/1bsckXX7BSAsJ2hKaf8kNnN3QCT3YR4tPg3DJhVIOiVk/edit>

9 Site Supervision and Mentorship: Practices that Influence Positive Mental Health in Schools

Sandy Benavidez and Kimberly McGough

Leadership Quote

When we serve and grow others, we enter into a delicate professional relationship where words, actions, and guidance have the ability to develop the next generation of counselor leaders or perpetuate a path that may never correct itself.

Sandra Benavidez

Aspirational Statements

- Attunement is defined as "a felt embodied experience that can be individualistic as well as communal, that includes a psychological, emotional, and somatic state of consciousness" (Kossak, 2015: 14). Attunement of our counseling interns is how well it directly impacts their overall success.
- The role of the counselor leader is vast: counselor, educator, supervisor, researcher, advocate, and leader.

Introduction and Background

Counselor supervision has been identified as a critical component in counselor development of performance skills, client conceptualization, self-awareness, and professional behaviors (Bernard, 1979; Bernard and Goodyear, 1998). Supportive site supervisors also provide a level of mentorship that can enhance the counselor intern experience. Mentorship is described as guidance provided by an experienced individual. However, we know and recognize it's so much more than that. Mentorship involves a development of trust, modeling, and consistent support.

In professional settings, when we choose to mentor, we choose to connect with a professional in a way that can join us for a lifetime. Site supervision should include a level of mentorship. Although it can appear regimented and required from an outside perspective, when site supervision is coupled with mentorship, students maximize their learning.

Site supervisors play a key role in developing counselors-in-training who will ultimately promote positive mental health in schools. This position cannot be a regimented practice of focusing on surface level state requirements, but rather one in which modeling, mentorship, and relationship building are at the forefront. Additionally, knowing the school counselor intern's strengths can aid in providing the right kind of mentorship and support in the way the intern needs it most. How do these strengths specifically aid in development? When interns understand what gifts they already hold, site supervisors can assist in maximizing strengths opposed to exclusively focusing on weaknesses.

Site supervisors also have a responsibility for ensuring counselors-in-training are examining their own wellness and mental health and seeking to engage in personal development "with a belief that well counselors are competent counselors who promote students' well-being" (Sangganjanavanich and Balkin, 2013: 67). Therefore, counselor educators not only influence the well-being of counselors-in-training, but the students they work with as well (Moate et al., 2016; Sangganjanavanich and Balkin, 2013). For counselor educators who are not practicing appropriate self-care and wellness strategies, there is a greater likelihood of experiencing stress, which can lead to burnout and impairment. As such, the quality of the teaching and the modeling they provide their students/counselors-in-training is affected, as is the quality of the services received by the clients who are counseled by their students and by the counselor educators themselves (Hill, 2004). Ultimately, the mental health of all parties is tied together.

Leadership Program Values and Standards

School counselors, in the roles of educator and counselor, are responsible for creating and facilitating comprehensive school counseling programs, which can be based on contextual variables including district-level support. According to ASCA (2019), "The primary responsibility of the school counselor director/coordinator in a district or state is to support the development and implementation of school counseling programs" (2019: 1). In a similar vein, Goodman-Scott et al. (2021) reported that most of the district supervisors in their national study were aware of and implementing comprehensive programs at the district level (67 percent), with the majority of those utilizing the ASCA National Model (74 percent). Hence, district-level school counseling supervisors support comprehensive school counseling programs through providing school counselors with direct and indirect support.

Regarding direct support, supervisors provide mentoring, encouragement, consultation, and training while also providing resources and supervision. For instance, ASCA (2019) recommends that supervisors provide school counselors with individual and group supervision to assist in their program implementation. Similarly, from a sample of 11 school counselors using a grounded theory empirical framework, Goodman-Scott et al. (2021) found that school counselors appreciated both formal and impromptu meetings with their district supervisor, reporting that their supervisor helped strengthen their professional identity and roles.

In addition to direct services, supervisors engage in indirect support to assist school counselors in facilitating comprehensive programs (ASCA, 2019). Examples include guiding the school district's vision and implementation of school counseling programs, facilitating school counseling policies and procedures at the district level, and professional advocacy. Specifically, Hurt (2014) described supervisors advocating for lowering school counseling caseloads and educating district and building administrators on school counselors' roles in facilitating comprehensive school counseling programs.

Leadership in Practice

University school counselor programs have rules, requirements, and protocols for site supervision and site supervisors. Some of the typical requirements are as follows. Site supervision training should be offered by the counselor education program at a time and in a venue that is convenient for school counselors who are willing to be site supervisors. One format that can reach the most supervisors is to have a face-to-face meeting with an agenda and a time for questions. Since most supervisors are not compensated monetarily, offering a simple meal or some snacks is customary. Simultaneously this meeting should be videotaped so that those supervisors who are unable to attend can watch the meeting at their convenience. This meeting should be well organized and cover all of the requirements of the supervision experience for the trainees. In some instances, the graduate students attend this meeting with their supervisors, meaning that they hear the same information and have an opportunity to clear up any questions.

Site supervisors meet with their supervisees for an hour each week to discuss cases, go over case notes, and talk about the strengths and challenges for the trainee. This is also a time when supervisors should encourage trainees to self-reflect on their own experiences, current home environments, and mental health status and how those will impact their relationship with the supervisor as well as the students in the school. Documentation of supervision meetings is essential, and it is excellent practice for the next level of supervision which is after graduation and during the accruing of hours for licensure. Additionally, site supervisors must insist on and adhere to specific days and times for the supervision meetings. Trying to have these meetings *on the fly* will be a disservice to the trainee and will result in a poor supervisory experience. The supervisor is usually expected to view group counseling sessions, individual counseling sessions, or even instruction in a classroom by the trainee. This observation can be videotaped or can be viewed in person.

Lastly, site supervisors are generally required to complete an assessment of the supervisee's progress at a midterm point and at the end of a semester. Keeping the supervisee informed throughout the supervisory experience regarding progress is the best way to avoid surprises at the end of the term, and it allows the trainee to improve or overcome challenges during the semester. Most universities supply a checklist and space for comments on the assessment instrument, and it is typical for the supervisor to discuss the evaluation with the supervisee before sending it to the university professor.

It is not always easy for school counselor trainees to earn direct counseling hours in a school setting, particularly if the supervisee is also a teacher in the school (as is still the case in some states). Some ideas about how to accrue direct counseling hours if the student is a teacher include using the conference period, lunch time, before and after school meetings, and weekend programs. All of these ideas require careful planning, and some of them need parent permission forms to be completed.

Mental and Behavioral Health Considerations

The American School Counselor Association (ASCA) (2019) depicts the recommended use of time metric which establishes that counselors should spend 80 percent of their time in direct student services and 20 percent of time in indirect student support. However, historically due to an inability to mandate this recommendation or a lack of understanding from leadership personnel, school counselors are spending more and more time on indirect student services such as serving as state testing coordinators, data managers, data entry clerks, and leading ancillary meetings that don't directly relate to student mental health and wellbeing. Given this inundation of clerical responsibilities paired with the growing student and staff needs, school counselors are experiencing increased rates of mental health distress, burnout, and fatigue.

Researchers (Bardhoshi et al., 2014; Mullen and Gutierrez, 2016; Wilkerson, 2009; Wilkerson and Bellini, 2006) have identified a relationship between burnout and the multiple roles and responsibilities that school counselors perform. However, it is important for school counselors to be aware of and engage in self-care practices that allow them to manage stress so that it does not go unchecked and lead to burnout and the reduction of the administration of services to students (Mullen and Gutierrez, 2016). Likewise, it is important for counselor educators to have an awareness of and participate in wellness practices that aid in managing stress that can lead to burnout and mental health challenges.

The pervasiveness of the global pandemic (beginning in 2019) has only exacerbated the need to promote school counselor self-care practices. Site-supervisors must guide school counselor interns in recognizing how emotional, behavioral, and cognitive well-being are equally as important as overall physical well-being. This task is accomplished by recognizing when counselor interns reveal thoughts or statements of being overwhelmed, appear disconnected or aloof, and by building strong relationships to drive these sometimes uncomfortable discussions. Self-care and wellbeing must be taught. The most effective site supervisors address these principles as a critical first step in the supervision process.

Ethical Considerations

The ASCA Ethical Standards for School Counselors (2022) govern school counselors in their roles as interns, counselors, counselor educators, and supervisors. Section D specifically addresses guidance that site supervisors should consider when agreeing to serve in that capacity. Site supervisors must have an awareness of their strengths, knowledge, and limitations. More than awareness, the ability to recognize how your personal and professional experiences influence your guidance and leadership for school counselor interns is critical. Additionally, site supervisors continuously seek professional growth. They have a discernment which they use as a catalyst to seek continuing education experiences to be a lifelong learner. The following ethical standards drive the role of site supervisors.

D. SCHOOL COUNSELING INTERN SITE SUPERVISORS

Field/intern site supervisors:

a Are licensed or certified school counselors with an understanding of school counseling programs and school counselors' ethical practices.
b Have the education and training to provide school counseling supervision and regularly pursue continuing education activities on both counseling and supervision topics and skills.
c Use a model of supervision that is developmental, ongoing and includes but is not limited to promoting professional growth, supporting best practices and ethical practice, assessing supervisee performance and developing plans for improvement, consulting on specific cases and assisting in the development of a course of action.
[…]

> e Avoid supervisory relationships with individuals with whom they have the inability to remain objective (e.g., family members or close friends).

The global pandemic has reshaped the way counseling and counseling supervision have traditionally been delivered. Although unique situations such as online schools and programs have had experience with virtual delivery, most counselors, supervisors, and interns were abruptly placed in a foreign setting. The ASCA ethical standards anticipated the change in technology and delivery in their 2022 release and provided a broad compass for school counselors across the United States. The new age counselor intern can no longer negate the importance of technology and its platform should be used to provide counseling services.

> **D. SCHOOL COUNSELING INTERN SITE SUPERVISORS**
>
> Field/intern site supervisors:
>
> f Are competent with technology used to perform supervisory responsibilities and online supervision, if applicable. Supervisors protect all electronically transmitted confidential information.
> g Understand there are differences in face-to-face and virtual communication (e.g., absence of verbal and nonverbal cues) that may have an impact on virtual supervision. Supervisors educate supervisees on how to communicate electronically to prevent and avoid potential problems.
> h Provide information about how and when virtual supervisory services will be utilized. Reasonable access to pertinent applications should be provided to school counselors.

Teaching is a major component of the role of the site supervisor. Whether this is in the graduate or postgraduate setting, the number one role as a site supervisor is to teach. This means site supervisors make no assumptions and clearly identify all aspects of the learning and evaluation process. Understanding appropriate data metrics or curating consistent systems in the absence of necessary evaluation tools is an ethical responsibility. Best practice denotes that the site supervisor fully explains policies and practices that influence the intern's final performance along with any opportunities to appeal said processes.

> **D. SCHOOL COUNSELING INTERN SITE SUPERVISORS**
>
> Field/intern site supervisors:
>
> i Ensure performance evaluations are completed in a timely, fair and considerate manner, using data when available and based on clearly stated criteria.
> j Ensure supervisees are aware of policies and procedures related to supervision and evaluation and provide due-process procedures if supervisees request or appeal their evaluations.

Cultural Complexities

As the US population continues to become more and more diverse, the need for effective training and supervision practices in cultural competence among school counselors is evident (Sue and Sue, 2008). Through the utilization of professional development and ongoing supervision, school counselors can gain multicultural competence allowing them to become leaders within their schools to advocate for the development and implementation of culturally responsive school practices and curriculum (Paisley and McMahon, 2001). Supervisors in cross-cultural supervision dyads can optimize the benefits of cross-cultural and multicultural supervision by: a. openly discussing one's own culture and how this impacts their beliefs and worldview with supervisees; b. exploring cultural countertransference issues; and c. providing a safe environment for racial and ethnic identity development (Constantine, 1997). Constantine (1997) examined the extent to which multicultural supervision was conducted at internship sites and ways in which it could be enhanced. Participants in the study reported that spending more time processing issues around cultural differences could have enhanced supervision.

In order to embark on the journey to cultural competency, site supervisors must be comfortable with their own identity and ensure the comfort of their interns. Additionally, it is within the purview of the site supervisor to honor the recommendations of the Council for Accredited Counseling and Related Educational Programs (CACREP) (2024) standards for counseling programs which require multicultural training within the counseling curriculum. The following represent the standards for site supervisors:

SECTION 4: PROFESSIONAL PRACTICE

P. Site supervisors have:

1. a minimum of a master's degree, preferably in counseling, or a related profession; 2. active certifications and/or licenses required for practice preferably in counseling, or a related profession; 3. a minimum of two years post-master's professional experience in the specialized practice area in which the student is enrolled; 4. proficiency in the use of technology utilized for supervision; 5. relevant training for in-person and/or distance counseling supervision; 6. knowledge of the program's expectations, requirements, and evaluation procedures for students.

These standards are necessary in order to meet the cultural complexities inherent within the internship experience. Furthermore, standards allow supervisors to maintain an awareness that their education and training must be dynamic and that factors of culture impact these relationships.

Strategic Considerations

Mentoring School Counselors

The first year in any position can be daunting, especially in the fast paced and demanding role of the school counselor at the beginning of the school year. Acclimating to the school climate and understanding the many facets of the school counseling role are learning curves and adjustments that many first-year school counselors experience the first day in their new role.

To bridge this learning curve, first-year school counselors are assigned a more seasoned school counselor as a mentor, usually by campus administration or a district director of counseling. Moreover, a mentoring relationship can be either formal or informal involving guidance by an experienced and reputable individual to another individual who seeks to develop personally or professionally (Mellen and Murdoch-Eaton, 2015).

The mentor plays a key role in helping the new school counselor understand what is expected by communicating expectations and modeling behavior when working directly and indirectly with faculty and staff, students, parents, and stakeholders. The mentor provides resources for evidence-based practices and data and accountability. Qualitative researchers, Milsom and McCormick (2015) discovered increases in confidence and self-efficacy around the use of data and accountability by school counselors who had mentors.

Grit

Angela Duckworth, the nation's leading researcher on grit, proclaims that, "to be gritty, is to keep putting one foot in front of the other. To be gritty, is to hold fast to an interesting and purposeful goal. To be gritty, is to invest, day after week after year, in challenging practice" (2016: 275). Thus grit, or to be gritty, fits with the journey of a school counselor from graduate school to retirement.

In their quantitative research study on school counselors and grit (N = 1554), Mullen and Crowe (2018) discovered that participants' scores ranged from moderate to high levels of grit (mean score of 3.83) meaning that school counselors persevere through challenges and increasing demands often faced in the school setting to achieve intended goals. Moreover, Mullen and Crowe uncovered that years of experience was positively related to their consistency of interest ($r = .14$, $p < .05$). This key finding indicated the consistency of interest was present despite setbacks or challenges for the participants who have years of experience in the profession. Therefore, school counselors who have been in the field longer, have higher persistence to do and pursue their interests, possibly serving as a protective factor for burnout. Hence, it may be pondered, the impact that a gritty school counselor with years of experience can have on those they supervise and mentor.

Providing Authentic Experiences

For school counselors to be prepared to fulfill the role of the school counselor, it is essential to have a wide array of authentic experiences during practicum and internship. Authentic experiences typically occur when the school counselor in training works alongside the site supervisor in the counseling office. First hand observations and experiences in the counseling office equip school counseling trainees with knowledge and experience on how to handle situations that cannot be experienced in a textbook. For instance, the possibility to observe and assist with a crisis safety plan for a student who is in danger of harming herself is an authentic experience for the counselor in training as textbook crisis training does not adequately address the gravity and impact of observing or assisting with the crisis safety plan firsthand.

Through the encouragement of utilizing evidence-based practices, school counselors in training engage in an authentic experience in which evidence and data outcomes inform practice while enhancing outcomes among students (Zyromski and Mariani, 2016). An example of evidence-based practice includes delivering an evidence-based, group counseling curriculum to a selected group of students. The aspiring school counselor conducts pre- and post-surveys to measure the effectiveness of the group counseling curriculum and the group counseling experience. The data obtained from the surveys will inform the aspiring school counselor on the effectiveness of the group counseling curriculum, but also the experience of the students which will inform future group counseling interventions and experiences for the school counselor in training.

Aspiring School Counselor Institutes

Created by school districts to grow and shape school counselors in conjunction with their graduate school training, aspiring school counseling institutes are increasing in popularity in both urban and suburban school districts. These institutes are designed for district employees who: are enrolled in a school counselor graduate program or have graduated, completed their school counseling certification, and/or are awaiting being hired by the district as a school counselor. The aspiring school counselor institute curriculum is shaped by district policies and procedures, and may include, but is not limited to:

- crisis prevention and intervention strategies;
- social–emotional learning curriculum;
- the district's approach for implementation of the ASCA model or the state's school counseling program model (i.e., The Texas Model of Comprehensive School Counseling Programs);
- training on the district's student data management platform;
- 504 plan documentation and procedures;
- individual planning and 4-year plans;
- FERPA guidelines and ethics training;
- interview tips and strategies;
- evidence-based practices and interventions for group and individual counseling.

Conclusion

As with other school counseling topics, it is to be noted that a gap in the literature exists on aspiring school counselor institutes within the existing body of literature. Literature, however, exists on the topic of aspiring administrator academies, the predecessor for aspiring school counselor institutes. This and other strategic considerations are ripe for research and data-informed results to enhance the training of school counselors as they prepare to launch their new careers. For example, research on authentic school counseling experiences for counselors-in-training and how those impact the behaviors and attitudes of trainees would expand on the internship experience. Additionally, as school counselors become more important to the mental health of students of all ages, researchers might look at how trainees with their limited experiences can learn to provide excellent interventions, strategies, and referrals to students and their families. Counselor educators in university training programs might partner with school districts to collect and analyze these important data.

References

American School Counselor Association (2019) *The ASCA National Model: A Framework for School Counseling Programs* (4th edn), Alexandria, VA: Author.

American School Counselor Association (2022) *ASCA Ethical Standards for School Counselors*. Online. Available HTTP: <https://www.schoolcounselor.org/getmedia/44f30280-ffe8-4b41-9ad8-f15909c3d164/EthicalStandards.pdf>

Bardhoshi, G., Schweinle, A., and Duncan, K. (2014) "Understanding the impact of school factors on school counselor burnout: A mixed-methods study", *Professional Counselor*, 4(5): 426–443.

Bernard, J.M. (1979) "Supervisor training: a discrimination model", *Counselor Education and Supervision*, 19: 740–748.

Bernard, J.M. and Goodyear, R. (1998) *Fundamentals of Clinical Supervision* (2nd edn), Boston, MA: Allyn & Bacon.

Council for Accreditation of Counseling and Related Educational Programs (CACREP) (2024) *CACREP 2024 Standards*, Alexandria, VA: Author.

Constantine, M.G. (1997) "Facilitating multicultural competency in counseling supervision: operationalizing a practical framework", in D.B. Pope-Davis and H.L.K. Coleman (eds), *Multicultural Counseling Competencies: Assessment, Education and Training, and Supervision*, Newbury Park, CA: Sage, pp. 310–324.

Duckworth, A. (2016) *Grit: The Power of Passion and Perseverance*, New York, NY: Scribner.

Goodman-Scott, E., Upton, A.W., and Neuer Colburn, A.A. (2021) "District-level school counseling supervisors' experiences with and perceptions of hiring school counselors", *Professional School Counseling*, 24(1, part 3). Online. Available HTTP: <https://doi.org/10.1177/2156759×X211007656>

Hill, N.R. (2004) "The challenges experienced by pre tenured faculty members in counselor education: A wellness perspective", *Counselor Education and Supervision*, 44(2): 135–146.

Hurt J. (2014) *A phenomenological study of urban middle school counselors and directors of guidance and counseling: Collaborating to understand counselor stress and prevent burnout*, Doctoral dissertation, Liberty University.

Kossak, M. (2015) *Attunement in Expressive Arts Therapy: Toward an Understanding of Embodied Empathy*, Springfield, IL: Charles C Thomas, Publisher, Ltd.

Mellen, A. and Murdoch-Eaton, D. (2015) "Supervisor or mentor: is there a difference? Implications for paediatric practice", *Archives of Disease in Childhood*, 100(9): 1–6.

Milsom, A. and McCormick, K. (2015) "Evaluating an accountability mentoring approach for school counselors", *Professional School Counseling*, 19: 27–35.

Moate, R.M., Gnilka, P.B., West, E.M., and Bruns, K.L. (2016) "Stress and burnout among counselor educators: differences between adaptive perfectionists, maladaptive perfectionists, and non perfectionists", *Journal of Counseling & Development*, 94(2): 161–171.

Mullen, P.R. and Gutierrez, D. (2016) "Burnout, stress and direct student services among school counselors", *The Professional Counselor*, 6(4): 344–359.

Mullen, P.R. and Crowe, A. (2018). A psychometric investigation of the short grit scale with a sample of school counselors. *Measurement and Evaluation in Counseling and Development*, 51(3): 151–162.

Paisley, P.O. and McMahon, G. (2001) "School counseling for the 21st century: Challenges and opportunities", *Professional School Counseling*, 5: 106–115.

Sangganjanavanich, V.F. and Balkin, R.S. (2013) "Burnout and job satisfaction among counselor educators", *The Journal of Humanistic Counseling*, 52(1): 67–79.

Sue, D.W. and Sue, D. (2008) *Counseling the Culturally Diverse: Theory and Practice* (5th edn), Hoboken, NJ: Wiley & Sons.

Wilkerson, K. (2009) "An examination of burnout among school counselors guided by stress-strain-coping theory", *Journal of Counseling & Development*, 87: 428–437.

Wilkerson, K. and Bellini, J. (2006) "Intrapersonal and organizational factors associated with burnout among school counselors", *Journal of Counseling & Development*, 84(4): 440–450.

Zyromski, B. and Mariani, M.A. (2016) *Facilitating Evidence-Based, Data-Driven School Counseling: A Manual for Practice*, Thousand Oaks, CA: Corwin.

Section III

Examining Mental Health Expertise in the Hiring and Retention of Highly Qualified School Counselors

Administrative Leaders and School Counselors understand how critical building a school counselor team is to student success, where the highly-qualified school counselor has a pivotal role in that success. Section III provides information for administrative leaders and school counselors to examine the mental health expertise of their candidate during the hiring and retention process, understanding how to identify necessary components of school counselor character and disposition, how school counselors use mental health expertise in working within the comprehensive school counseling program, and establishing and acculturating school counseling teams with mental health and wellness at the basis of optimal operations.

Although the hiring of school counselors is often faced with time constraints, buddy-buddy or good-ole-boy systems, and a need to fulfill a position, administrative leaders should include school counselors in their hiring committees with approved addendums for interview protocols that incorporate identifying mental health expertise, character, disposition, and values development of school counselors – essentially hiring the best candidate regardless to personal relationships. Exploration of how the candidate intends to incorporate and apply mental health into the comprehensive program is essential.

Lisa A. Wines

Gone should be the days when the principal's best friend has a good friend whose sister is looking for a school counseling position. I know you hear the tongue-in-cheek message here! School counselors should be evaluated for a position based on their expertise, commitment to student growth and development and their own professional growth, and willingness to be a positive and informed team member.

Judy Nelson

The single most important role of a professional school counselor leader or administrative leader is hiring the best candidate to serve on their team. A professional school counselor has knowledge in many areas with mental health at the forefront of this knowledge. The hirer must also be equipped with multifaceted knowledge of the role of a professional school counselor and must know and understand best practices for hiring the right fit.

Natalie Fikac

DOI: 10.4324/9781003219750-12

Section IV

Examining Mental Health Expertise in the Hiring and Retention of Highly Qualified School Counselors

10 Character and Disposition as Necessary Measures of Success for School Counselors as Mental Health Professionals

Jeni Janek

> **Leadership Quote**
>
> Character is built, not inherited.
>
> Judy Nelson

> **Aspirational Statements**
>
> - Inherent personal characteristics along with training, education, and experience mold the counselor leader into an effective and compassionate professional.
> - Pervasive and consistent actions help counselor leaders establish themselves as trusted and reputable leaders long before assuming leadership roles.

Introduction and Background

What makes a great counselor leader able to measure character during the recruitment period? Clues to the answer might be in the following:

1 inherent qualities that may not be easily measured;
2 personality differences in counselor leaders.

Perhaps the closest analogy to demonstrate the power of a great counselor lies with the wind. Though no one can see the wind, we can see the results of its presence whether by the velocity to leave behind a broken path as a result of extreme power or as a gentle breeze providing a reprieve from oppressive heat. The key to regulating the difference in such an impactful force lies in knowing when to blow like a hurricane for protecting a precious soul or to move fields of foliage with a soft and comforting whisper. Because of these intangible and yet powerful traits, it becomes incumbent on school leaders to ensure that leadership in a counseling program consists of a culmination of characteristics that are balanced, dependable, and autonomously synchronized to ensure success. This is not to say that one who leads must be perfect. Quite the contrary, in fact. In many leadership roles, a single mistake could mean disaster and devastation to any business or operation. A leader in a counseling role must know when to identify with subordinates in an intentional effort to exhibit the vulnerability that makes them as human as those whom they lead. Iron-clad practices in a field of humanity are not always well-received. Therefore, the delicate balance of interpersonal skills and elite coordination may best define the persona of a counselor leader. This leader must have a strong awareness of self and others and be mentally well.

Within the recruitment process, focusing on certain aspects of hiring for a leadership position, even a counselor leader or director of counseling, is not unlike searching for a logistically oriented and strategically sound business leader. Qualities that are sought-after for professional integrity include behavioral standards such as punctuality, organization, and strong interpersonal skills.

According to a Wake Forest (2022) article on *Leadership Traits Every Counselor Should Have*, the following traits are listed as desirable for counselors:

1 listening
2 being empathetic
3 building relationships
4 performing assessments
5 coordinating efforts and activities
6 exercising authority
7 being flexible
8 having a sense of humor

This article highlights some very important terminology that also showcases important attributes of an emotionally literate leader who focuses on their own personal mental health and wellness.

Listening is perhaps one of the most obvious virtues of a good counselor, able to listen for what is being said and being aware that there may be times when much can be learned about what is not said. This takes a high degree of skill and a genuine desire to connect at a level that is neither superficial nor self-serving. It's often a challenge to block out the many demands on each leader throughout the day in order to spend time genuinely listening, but it's a necessity for connection and truly understanding peers, superiors, and those whom we serve as servant leaders.

Having empathy almost goes without saying yet is perhaps most at the heart of all sincere communication. Being empathetic is almost adjacent to being incredibly objective. When we can remove our own biases and give ourselves the latitude to escape the bonds of our own meager knowledge and experiences (first realizing that our knowledge and experiences are unique, but certainly not absolute), we can start to see the breadth of perspectives from others. Empathy really goes hand-in-hand with non-judgement, which can be a challenge for many leaders. It's easier to judge someone based on our lived experience and limited knowledge than it is to extend ourselves into what is unfamiliar and unknown.

The skill of building relationships is one that often has an expectation of happening organically and without effort. A characteristic of many great leaders is their ability to expend their full trust sparingly, yet masterfully know when and how to cultivate relationships that encourage fruitful partnerships, keeping the goal of working toward the maximum benefit for those whom they are charged to lead. Building relationships becomes a necessity for not only those important bridge-building opportunities, but also for self-sustenance in a world where allies and enemies may initially present in the same manner. Exceptional leaders realize that the power of relationships also falls within all types of relationships. It's easy to spot those who make connections merely for self-benefit, and are unable to motivate or inspire others with genuine integrity. A leader who conducts themselves in a manner worthy of trust will do so regardless of the company they keep. This allows for their true and reputable intentions to be seen, regardless of the audience. Relationships range from being private to being very public and the demeanor and warmth of a true and caring leader will be evident in both places.

Performing assessments might not carry the most positive connotation upon its first mention, but the reason for this virtue is to have a calculated and purposeful response. Counselor leaders who carry themselves with a disposition of certainty and reliability do so by basing their decisions on data whenever they can. True, that good old "gut instinct" or the intuitive calculation may factor into a given strategy. But by and large, the leader who seeks the best information possible and asks the hard questions can make the best decision for the most people's benefit with the most efficient means in the most appropriate manner. This sounds like a fairly simple formula but is far from easy in the real world. By performing assessments and gauging needs, a leader can truly be most effective.

A strategic counselor is an effective counselor. By coordinating efforts and activities with precise documentation and organization, a counselor leader can effectively structure any given day into the necessary elements for success. Sometimes it is hard to measure this on any day in particular because each day may look so different. Counselors have not historically been heralded for their coordinating efforts for activities in many settings, and yet this aspect of their work is one that is absolutely necessary. One consideration in the coordination of efforts and activities is the partnership between counselor leaders and personnel who assume adjacent leadership positions. If this collaboration is not healthy, then the entirety of the atmosphere suffers because decisions may not be made in unison with goals or the vision for success. It's not often that counselor leaders are considered to have the level of responsibility to assume authority, therefore the ability to coordinate anything can be severely inhibited. When there is a presentation and network built on a trusting and mutual relationship between school leaders where counselor leaders are considered equal, the ultimate result inevitably is growth and success. Even so, exercising authority for the counselor leader is done sparingly in most cases, as our disposition often urges us to find solutions that promote resolve and not diminish empowerment. Employing skills to wield this power can help unify and encourage collaboration.

Even the most strategic counselor will find times where the plan doesn't happen accordingly. Flexibility is the safeguard to minimize the temptation to adhere to rigid schedules and locations, to erroneously believe that outside factors will not deter progress to the original goal. It's lofty and unrealistic to believe that there will not be setbacks and unexpected, uncontrollable changes. A good leader all but anticipates that in the name of growth and success these setbacks will occur, and then knows to not allow the changes to completely derail progress. Problems will occur. Mistakes will happen. Knowing when to focus and regroup and when to adjust to unexpected changes make a stronger leader in any field.

Finally, a sense of humor distinguishes the counselor leader as a human and not a robot. With such high-level work and so much emphasis on detail and expectation, it's easy to distance oneself from this virtue, mistakenly believing that a leader cannot laugh and that they certainly can't laugh at themselves a little.

Each of these shared leadership traits describe a leader who has a high level of emotional intelligence and a leader who is mentally well. Emotional intelligence is an important component of a professional school counselor's character and disposition.

Leadership Program Values and Standards

The American School Counselor Association (ASCA) Ethical Standards (2022) provides a skeletal guideline for how a counselor-leader's behavior should be (relative to our responsibilities). While we have this guidance, it can be more difficult to compose a description of a good counselor leader because we all have such varied personality types, life experiences, and a host of factors that influence how we see the world and how our behavior affects others. Perhaps the section that may best allude to considerations regarding one's disposition and character can be found in the Preamble of the ASCA Ethical Standards for School Counselors (2022) where terms are used to help describe possible characteristics:

> School counselors have unique qualifications and skills to implement a comprehensive school counseling program that addresses pre-K–12 students' academic, career and social/emotional development needs. School counselors are leaders, advocates, collaborators and consultants who create systemic change to ensure equitable educational outcomes through the school counseling program. School counselors demonstrate the belief that all students have the ability to learn by advocating for and contributing to an education system that provides optimal learning environments for all students.
> (ASCA, 2022: Preamble)

Additionally, the STEPS method (Stone, 2010) of decision making contains words that we hear when we read our ethics, but perhaps contemplating the meaning can help us better understand how we think and approach our work. The word beneficence is used to encourage us to seek good. Beneficence is the absence of maleficence or ill will. To have a strong character as a counselor leader, earnestly seeking good for and with others is perhaps the most recognizable hallmark of integrity as a leader. Counselor leaders are expected to first embody this characteristic as they lead, but beneficence goes beyond simply one's work. In order to become a skilled leader in counseling, beneficence should and must be practiced as routinely as breathing in order to align with aspirational ethics. This, with consultation, application of emotional and intellectual skills for decision-making, can help a counselor leader to develop a healthy and true disposition for the work at-hand.

Leadership in Practice

There are many times when a school counselor leader and school counselor are called to lead, such as during a crisis, when advocating for equity for all students, on a leadership team, and so forth. In practice, there are different ways that school counselors lead. These are often tied to the character and disposition of the school counselor leader or school counselor. Below are a few examples of leadership in practice including potential risks and benefits.

Logistical leaders are planners, organizers, and delegators (not taking on everything and handling an overgrown *to do* list). At times, these leaders may not appear fully invested in the process and may not have the ability to showcase their talents. They might focus more on the processes and delegation of meeting the mental health processes within the team and district.

Empathetic leaders embody the struggle for how to manage their own emotional stability while ensuring proper and respectful care for others and those who report to them. This kind of leader might focus too much on the emotional state of their team.

Boundaried leaders maintain healthy boundaries and are better managers, not just the workhorse. Yet they know their own limits and do not feel guilty for saying no or not right now. However, these leaders might not be receptive to new ideas, processes, or mental health needs of the school community and school counseling team.

Each of these character dispositions and leadership styles could potentially lead to deficits in self-care. This means that there is a strong possibility that someone will have to face the effects of overstressed, anxious, and burned-out behaviors from the leadership. The depletion of our stores of energy are not ours alone to deal with. Sometimes we have to hear it in this manner to understand that restoring our battery charges are indeed our responsibility and that the dividends are not just ours, but for those whom we love and cherish closest to us, who feel our energy levels daily; healthy or not. School counselor leaders and school counselors who encompass a strong character disposition stay fully aware of their own limitations as well as the limitations of those that they are leading and offer support, guidance, coordination, and collaboration as needed. These school counselor leaders have a high level of emotional literacy and self-awareness.

Mental and Behavioral Health Considerations

Research (Holman et al., 2019) describes how school counselors feel despondent and disenfranchised when they are used as clerks rather than mental health professionals. The word advocacy can evoke emotions and responses from those who hear it and can sometimes have a connotation of a combative stance. Other times, advocacy carries with it the passion that lets the world know that there is a worthy cause out in the world, and this one is it. One must consider the mental and behavioral health needs of the school counselor and school counselor leader.

Counselor advocacy is not always confrontational. Data speaks volumes for demonstrating needs in any given counseling situation within education. When presented effectively and cooperatively, this data and research can help counselors properly position themselves (with the help of their school-based teams) to carry out their mission and live to the fullest intent of their role. There are times when a leader asks a school counselor to help simply because they trust that the task will be tended to by someone they trust and know will do a good and thorough job. This is not to be taken lightly; the trust element for school leaders (including school counselors) is one that need not be damaged for a simple misunderstanding if this is the case. However, an honest conversation, many times in a logistic and strategic manner, may yield a more efficient and effective way of getting the same job done while allowing the school counselor to tend to matters that are of a more direct impact. School counselors and school counselor leaders should be careful to listen for that trust element and acknowledge this before any refusal or advocacy against a duty. Preserving the integrity of the counselor–leader relationship as a professional and ethical foundation for the school ensures student and staff success. There are considerations for achieving this so that non-counseling duties or clerical tasks are not the sole responsibility of the school counselor. Below are some considerations relative to the approach and resolve of such scenarios:

1 Collaboration with school leaders and decision-makers helps counselors have a valued and active voice in school matters as opposed to silent suffering when delegated assignments are not in alignment with their true responsibilities on campus. Silence about a perceived need in addressing a misconception in the duties of a counselor or the actual purpose of programs conducted through the counselor's office only tips the scales more out of balance regarding inequalities of power that otherwise should be more equitable for the health of the campus.
2 Prior conceptions of school leaders and decision makers impact interactions for those whom they work with. There is a huge power in stereotypes (both positive and/or negative) based

on prior encounters with professionals in education, whether counselors, administrators, or others. A counselor could have a great deal of bridging to do in order to engage their school leader, if said leader had a negative collaboration with a prior individual. Exploring past experiences with leaders may shed light on a counter-transferred perception. Unaddressed, a scenario like this could undermine the success of the campus by way of a damaged relationship. Likewise, if the school counselor embodies a certain expectation of a leader not based on their current assignment but one prior, their understanding of the relationship could certainly be skewed as well. School leaders and counselors must have strong and unified relationships built on mutual respect before the success of any program may be realized.

3 School counselors typically are not aware of their empowerment and the full implications of their important work. Transcripts must be meticulously kept and accurate to the tune of hundreds of entries or updates over the course of a student's time in education. A child who is experiencing grief and trauma may not encounter an adult who is skilled and/or trained in recognizing their needs as a counselor does. A counselor is the only person whom a suicidal teen may confide in, leading to the possibility of treatment and intervention. The responsibilities and outcomes are a direct correlation to the careful planning and considerations for this very important work. Being empowered means digging deep to find the strength to realize this work and not passively stay in a reactionary state. Planning, strategically looking at the work and keeping focus on the goals of a comprehensive school counseling program can help counselors and leaders create sustainable high-impact programs.

Ethical Considerations

ASCA (2022) outlines many ethical standards that align with the assurance that professional school counselors are persons of character and ethical dispositions. The framework of the *ASCA Ethical Standards for School Counselors* rests on the fact that:

> School counselors are leaders, advocates, collaborators and consultants who create systemic change to ensure equitable educational outcomes through the school counseling program and that school counselors demonstrate the belief that all students have the ability to learn by advocating for and contributing to an education system that provides optimal learning environments for all students.
>
> (ASCA, 2022: Preamble)

As described in this chapter and the Wake Forest article, it is imperative that professional school counselors' characters and dispositions include active listening skills, the ability to be empathetic and build relationships, to coordinate efforts and activities, exercise authority, and remain flexible with a sense of humor (Wake Forest, 2022). Each of these traits allow a professional school counselors to serve their school communities and themselves in an ethical manner.

Cultural Complexities

Diversity, Equity, and Inclusion

The disposition and character of a school counselor and school counselor leader can perhaps be most beneficial and prevalent in our efforts to ensure equity and acceptance of all people. People in our establishments constantly observe our behavior and our methods of interacting with others. This includes our presentation of our beliefs and our values. This also includes our social media, our electronic communications, and how we lead. We have hundreds, if not thousands of opportunities to advocate for equality and acceptance. In those times, we can show others our ability to listen and advocate, elicit cooperation and understanding, and use our own characteristics for the purpose of unifying and promoting good will. There are considerations in this work that we all need to be made aware of and help others see as we engage them in these efforts.

Regarding cultural differences:

- Communication is key – being open, honest, and authentic is an important part of communication, especially when cultural differences exist.
- Lived experiences and empathy – conversing, leading and collaborating as a school counselor leader and school counselor provides an opportunity to share lived experiences and practice empathy.
- Protection for those whose lived experiences warrant intentional communications for acceptance; being an ally and champion is key to having a healthy disposition as a counselor leader.

Strategic Considerations

School counselor leaders and school counselors who encompass a strong moral compass and character dispositions are often more successful with the development and management of the comprehensive school counseling program. When a school counselor leader is trusted, leads with integrity, is empathetic to the needs of each campus, and organizes a comprehensive guidance and counseling program they are more likely to continue to thrive and evolve as student needs shift. A school counselor leader who thrives in a space of ambiguity continually analyzes data and strategizes how to best support the school counseling team and get senior leadership buy-in. Analyzing the overall mental health and wellness of the school counseling team is an important lens to consider.

Conclusion

Counseling is a profession that no matter what you do or where you go, your role as a counselor does not change. Many fellow counselors and leaders can share that in any social setting, when around a table sharing livelihoods and professions, when it's revealed that a counselor is in the midst, there ultimately is some reaction or response. The title of counselor carries respect and reverence, an expectation of provision of comfort and strength. Fair or not, the disposition and demeanor of a counselor leader elevates these expectations even more and yet brings a level of influence that reaches to hundreds, if not thousands, through their impact.

References

American School Counselor Association (2022). *American School Counselor Association Ethical Standards for School Counselors*. Online. Available HTTP: <https://www.schoolcounselor.org/About-School-Counseling/Ethical-Legal-Responsibilities/ASCA-Ethical-Standards-for-School-Counselors-(1)>

Baretto, A. (2012) "Counseling for the training of leaders and leadership development: a commentary", *Professional Counselor*, 2(3): 226–234.

Holman, L., Nelson, J., and Watts, R. (2019) "Organizational variables contributing to school counselor burnout: an opportunity for leadership, advocacy, collaboration, and systemic change", *Professional Counselor*, 9: 126–141.

Stone, C. (2005; 2010) *Ethics and Law for School Counselors*, Alexandria, VA: American School Counselor Association.

Texas Education Agency (2022a) *Texas Principal Standards*. Online (October 4). Available HTTP: <https://tpess.org/principal/standards/>.

Texas Education Agency (2022b). *The Texas Model for Comprehensive School Counseling Programs*. Online. Available HTTP: <https://tea.texas.gov/sites/default/files/Pub_2018_Texas-Model_5th-Edition.pdf>

Wake Forest University (2022) *Leadership Traits Every Counselor Should Have*. Online. Available HTTP: <https://counseling.online.wfu.edu/blog/leadership-traits-every-counselor-should-have/>

11 What Directors Need to Know about the Comprehensive School Counseling Programs that Support Student Mental Health

Jennifer Akins

Leadership Quote

School counselors are developers, organizers, assessors, evaluators, and mental health specialists on a school campus. They wear their many hats well!

Judy Nelson

Aspirational Statements

- Comprehensive school counseling programs make a positive difference to student outcomes. Leaders of effective programs are collaborative, intentional, and committed to continuous improvement. School counselors can, and should, wield enormous influence as school leaders and advocates for student success.
- Understanding the purpose and scope of comprehensive school counseling is critical to hiring the best school counselors. Moreover, it is important to recognize that comprehensive school counseling programs are the result of the cooperative efforts of the school community as a whole.
- School counseling competencies are broad and touch every aspect of education and learning. Proficient school counselors must not only have a strong working knowledge of pedagogy and academic advising, but also of mental health and social and emotional wellness. The capacity of the school counselor to prioritize continuous growth in their professional knowledge and expertise will be pivotal in their success throughout their career.
- School counselors are uniquely trained and qualified to detect patterns in student needs and provide responsive services for both prevention and intervention. School counselors work individually, in small groups, or in classroom settings to teach the indispensable skills students need to effectively set and achieve their life and learning goals. In addition, school counselors can be vital sources of training, resources, and professional expertise for the adults in the school community including teachers, staff, administrators, and perhaps most importantly, parents and guardians. Each of these qualities should be assessed in the hiring process.
- Directors and other campus and centrally based administrators must actively engage in the support of comprehensive school counseling programs. Like any successful

> initiative, executing a comprehensive program will require not only an initial investment of time to collaborate on setting goals and priorities but also a commitment to monitor progress, adjust strategies as needed, align efforts with complementary initiatives, and celebrate successes as they occur. Fortunately, research has consistently demonstrated that the outcome will be worth the effort.

Introduction and Background

A growing and well substantiated body of research has demonstrated the effectiveness of comprehensive school counseling programs on student outcomes (ASCA, 2019; Carey and Dimmitt, 2012). At the federal level, school counseling rests under the umbrella of coordinated health, a *whole-child* approach to student wellness and learning. As the *Texas Model for Comprehensive School Counseling Programs* (5th edn) states, "[School counselors] are educational leaders who are responsible for coordination and collaboration with all stakeholders to facilitate the optimal development of all students" (TEA, 2018b: 5). Recent meta-analysis of over 260 research studies found that well-implemented social and emotional learning consistently improves academic performance by 11–13 percentage points (Mahoney and Weissberg, 2018). These programs also have wide public support as shown in a recent poll indicating that 82 percent of US adults say it's important for schools to help students develop interpersonal skills like being cooperative, respectful of others, and persistent at solving problems (ASCD, 2018).

So, what exactly is comprehensive school counseling? The definition we use in Texas states: "through a systematic and planned program, school counselors apply specialized knowledge and skills to provide developmentally appropriate support and interventions for all students" (TEA, 2015: 79). In this definition, the words systematic, planned, and all seem to really get to the heart of the matter. A comprehensive school counseling program is an intentional and data driven process which is centered and focused on assessed student and campus needs. Comprehensive school counseling elements include: needs assessment; program rationale and assumptions; mission and vision; program goals, scope and sequence; a program plan and calendar of activities; and a counselor advisory council to guide implementation and evaluation of the program. It's also important to note that the Texas Education Code (§33.005) specifies that "a school counselor shall work with the school faculty and staff, students, parents, and the community to plan, implement, and evaluate a developmental guidance and counseling program" (TEA, 2015: 79). The Texas Model also provides the helpful Figure 1.2 (2015: 5) which contrasts traditional school counseling to comprehensive school counseling as well as Figure 1.3 which covers the characteristics of high and low performing programs (2015: 12–13).

The ASCA National Model Framework for School Counseling Programs (2019a) points out that the vision for comprehensive school counseling "is shaped by how school counselors view the world and reflects what they believe about students, families, teachers, and the educational process" (2019a: 23). Program goals often "build on courageous conversations about beliefs about student learning and student inequalities and [are] founded in data" (2019a: 25). Moreover, "school counselors work with stakeholders, both inside and outside the school [to] access a vast array of support for student achievement" (2019a: 6). Like the Texas Model, the ASCA Model also spends a considerable effort to explain in detail what is meant by comprehensive school counseling.

Luke and Bernard (2006) found that the "most common components of comprehensive school counseling programs include four functional domains for school counselors: (a) large-group guidance; (b) responsive counseling and consultation; (c) individual advisement; and (d) programmatic planning, coordination, and evaluation, often referred to as systems support" (2006: 283). Within each domain, they explore a focus of activities to help organize the program. They stated that "identifying the correct focus (intervention, conceptualization, or personalization) within a domain activity is typically the most fruitful step in becoming comfortable with the model" (2006: 292).

If all of this sounds like an ambitious undertaking, you are right! Comprehensive school counseling is an intricate response to the needs of students. Researchers have repeatedly focused on the pivotal importance of designing programs based on student needs. Baker & Gerler (2004) wrote, "since student problems are usually complex in terms of causes and needed interventions, a comprehensive, multifaceted continuum of braided interventions is needed" (2004: 27). House and Hayes (2002) again highlighted the necessity of collaboration and teamwork to accomplish the program goals, stating, "systematic change in the education of all students will not occur without the sustained involvement of all the critical players in the school setting, including school counselors," (2002: 252) but note that, "with their school-wide perspective on serving the needs of all students, school counselors are in the best position to assess the school for systemic barriers to academic success for every student" (2002: 252). The Texas Model develops this idea further, stating:

> The school counselor should be the educational professional who has the holistic view of the students' overall academic plans and progress. The school counselor has access to the students' performance in all subjects, their academic history, and their test scores. This comprehensive view of the student can then be utilized to work with students in small groups and individually to assist them in establishing goals and exploring post-secondary options. The individual and group work with students should be connected to the overall goals of a comprehensive school counseling program and based upon developmental needs of the students.
>
> (2002: 3)

Much attention in the literature has been given to the qualities and training needed by the school counselor. While requirements and competencies vary from state to state, some common themes emerge. It is well summarized in the *Texas Evaluation Model for Professional School Counselors (TEMPSC)* (3rd edn) (TSCA, 2020):

> School counselors are committed to promoting human worth, dignity, uniqueness, and potential of all students (American Counseling Association [ACA], 2014). They are committed to understanding the diverse backgrounds and experiences, and other influencing factors that impact their daily living (Texas Education Agency [TEA], 2018). Counselors use their ability to communicate "understanding, acceptance, warmth, and an optimistic attitude" (TEA, 2018, p. 21) with students, to relate effectively with parents, teachers, administrators, and others in advancing student personal, social, educational, and career development.
>
> (2020: 7)

Of critical importance to the school counselor's job are building and maintaining trust, communicating unconditional acceptance, and establishing warmth with those receiving services (Young, 2017). As such, appraisers consider that school counselors' content is more often affective than cognitive, that processes are more often facilitative rather than directive, and that school counselors do not make evaluative judgements about students and others' participating in program activities.

(2020: 15)

It is also worth noting that comprehensive school counseling programs position school counselors as leaders and advocates for social and emotional learning (SEL) and multi-tiered systems of support (MTSS) efforts. In their long-range planning document, TEA recommends districts support: "an integrated and data-driven academic and nonacademic multi-tiered system of support (MTSS) on every campus to identify and connect all students with appropriate support services, including supports for behavioral health, mental health, and intrapersonal and interpersonal effectiveness" (2018a: 15).

Due to the depth and breadth of these responsibilities, school counselors often refer to their work as the *heartbeat* of the school. Their efforts impact and affect not only students' SEL but also that of the adults in those students' lives. Hecht-Weber (2021) captured that:

helping staff members build capacity for identifying, understanding and managing feelings can help bring colleagues the comfort, encouragement, and routine that educators need ... School counselors can lead the way in creating a culture where SEL is central in all classes and throughout the entire school building.

(2021: 30)

Comprehensive school counseling is powerful. In fact, Ockerman et al. (2013) described school counselors as *change agents* and developed the C.A.F.E. supervision model to provide a framework for developing leadership and advocacy as foundational school counselor competencies. They wrote "with a clear identity established, the connected practices of advocacy, leadership and collaboration then result in an equity-focused, data-driven, comprehensive school counseling program" (2013: 47).

One strategy that directors can use to further the development of these competencies in school counselors is to encourage them to apply for recognition of their comprehensive school counseling program. For instance, in Texas, the CREST award presented by the Texas School Counselor Association provides an opportunity for schools to create a document that highlights the ways in which their program aligns to the best practices of the state model. To learn more and see examples visit: https://tsca.txca.org/crest.php. The ASCA model also has an award for comprehensive school counseling called the RAMP. Like CREST, it offers an opportunity to use data and artifacts to demonstrate fidelity to that counseling model. More information is available here: https://www.schoolcounselor.org/Recognition/RAMP. Achieving recognition for comprehensive school counseling programs is also a great way to build school board and community awareness of school counseling and the school counselor's work.

Leadership Program Values

Considering the impact and intricacy of comprehensive school counseling, it is critical that support is provided at the campus and district level. That support begins in an awareness of what comprehensive school counseling programs are and why they are beneficial. As the profession has shifted and expanded the role of school counselors over the last 10 years, it is often necessary to explicitly train existing school counselors, teachers, and administrators about comprehensive school counseling. This presents several opportunities for district directors and other leaders to influence their district's transition to comprehensive school counseling. As the ASCA model (2019) clarifies, "school counseling leadership ... promotes professional identity [and] overcomes challenges of role inconsistency" (2019: 1).

Goodman-Scott et al. found that "supervisors support implementation of comprehensive school counseling programs, including assisting school counselors' transition from preparation to practice" (2021: 1). The study described the dual identity of school counselors as both educators and counselors. The authors pointed out that these roles are "connected and intersecting" (2021: 1). School counselors' capacity to fully inhabit both roles can be based on "contextual variables, including district-level support" (2021: 2).

Through their study, the authors also found that in regard to hiring counselors, two main themes appear to impact the director's preferences: 1. the school counselor's familiarity with and support for the comprehensive school counseling model; and, 2. the school counselor's teaching experiences. In the former, directors tend to listen for evidence of the use of data, leadership, and advocacy. With the latter, directors expressed a desire to hear how teaching experiences supported an awareness of professional identity and school culture. One interesting finding was the perception that a school counselor's prior teaching experience may assist with establishing credibility on the school campus (2021: 4–7).

They further provided a model for district directors to provide direct and indirect support. Direct support includes "mentoring, encouragement, consultation, and training" (2021: 2). Indirect supports include "guiding the district's vision and implementation of school counseling programs, facilitating school counseling policies and procedures at the district level, and professional advocacy" (2021, p. 2). They further noted that "despite supervisors' work in assisting with school counselors' transition from preparation to practice, little research has explored the phenomenon" (2021: 2).

Given the scarcity of additional formal studies, I will share that in my experience, directors may approach the work of supporting school counselors in the following ways:

- Directors may provide support in recruiting and hiring counselors. Directors may be involved in evaluating resumes, identifying candidates, or serving on interview committees. Depending on the size of the district and its practices, directors may handle all hiring decisions or may simply provide screening of candidates. Directors are often asked to provide interview questions. In addition, directors usually manage the counseling intern process. This is a particularly important role if there is an opening at a non-standard time of the year and/or if few experienced candidates are available. Your knowledge of interns and counseling programs will be invaluable. McKinney ISD's intern application and handbook is available here: https://tinyurl.com/misdcounselorintern
- Directors may develop or revise counselor job descriptions and provide training on counselor competencies. Both the Texas Model and the ASCA model have detailed information on competency standards and associated descriptors. The Texas Model also includes a sample job description. These documents may, with the director's guidance, help a campus clarify the specific *look fors* that are important to the campus administration and staff. A director is also usually skilled at helping administrators understand specific terms like solution-focused counseling or trauma-informed practices.
- Directors may be involved in selecting a counselor evaluation model. Some states use or recommend a particular evaluation instrument. Whether you write your own or use a model, it is critically important that school counselors are evaluated using an instrument

that is designed and normed for the school counseling role rather than one that was designed for teachers, administrators, or some other role.
- While a school counselor is primarily oriented towards a specific school, there are many interconnections within the counseling team as a whole. Working together as a district department allows counselors to collaborate in planning, to share resources, and to consult as needed for specific situations. Thinking about the group of counselors in a district as a department rather than just campus staff allows the director to curate resources for certain services. For instance, in my district we use a district wide crisis response team to respond to urgent campus needs. These counselors have received specialized training in grief support and have practiced together regularly both in simulated and in real crisis scenarios. We are also able to draw from the collective strengths of our team to provide teacher training during district professional development days. We have several counselors that have been to train the trainer workshops or have gone to special conferences to be able to turn around their learning to meet district needs. In addition, it has been very beneficial to me to create a counselor advisory council composed of counselor leaders in the district. This group assists me in planning the annual counselor training calendar, selects our counselor book study, and provides mentorship for new counselors. In addition to these ongoing tasks, this group has provided support for special projects such as our district wide counseling framework, our mission, and our department's strategic plan.
- During my early tenure as the Senior Director in my district, I spent a lot of time writing procedural documents. In some instances, I revised existing documents or borrowed and adapted templates from another counselor leader. In other situations, my task was to capture in writing and formalize the processes that had been in place informally for many years. I also completed a thorough review of our board policies and legal mandates. This work enabled me to close gaps and focus our training calendar on areas of need. It also gave me the opportunity to introduce the elements of comprehensive school counseling step by step over time.
- Finally, I have devoted a lot of time to identifying resources in the school and to developing partnerships with outside agencies that can complement and expand the work of the campus' comprehensive school counseling programs.

In addition to these *director moves* there are some important *director views* that need attention as well. To develop effective school counselors, certain skills must be carefully nurtured. House and Hayes (2002) found that "critical to counselors' success will be their skill in consensus building and the ability to work collaboratively with a broad range of professionals and concerned citizens" (2002: 252). They elaborated by stating that:

> creating an effective working relationship among students, professional and support staff, parents, and community members depends upon mutual understanding and an appreciation of the contributions others can make in educating all children. School counselors must learn to build a sense of community within the school, which can serve as a platform from which to advocate for all students.
>
> (2002: 254)

The importance of your efforts as a director to model and highlight community building, to break down silos, and to intentionally include training on communication skills cannot be overstated.

Another critical director view is to integrate the district culture, priorities, and communication style into the development of counseling programs. Pianta and Lopez-Perry (2019) pointed out that "organizational awareness is just as important as self-awareness … When school counselors and district directors have organizational awareness, they are better able to use their understanding of relationships, hierarchies, and decision-making processes to communicate more effectively" (2019: 22). Your perspective from the district level will give you valuable insight that will be critical to your school counselors' success. In fact, the authors go on to say that, "politics are inevitable in any school or district. School counselors and district directors must know how to leverage their influence by navigating through politics to advance their initiatives" (2019: 22). How will you leverage your influence as a school counseling program director? The authors shared their view that "a politically intelligent leader uses a moral compass to influence the organization in the right direction while considering others' wants, needs, values and motivations, and emotions" (2019: 22) This really points us to the concept of advocacy.

Directors must advocate for comprehensive school counseling in strategic and intentional ways. Moreover, they must teach their school counselors how to do it as well! Ockerman et al. (2013) provided a beautiful summary of specific ways to grow advocacy skills in school counseling students:

> Assignments that require students to identify key legislative policies that influence the profession of school counselors can help to advance advocacy skills. Students may write letters to state and local political leaders taking a stand on a particular issue, attend local school board or political town hall meetings, or participate in local lobbying efforts to pass critical legislation. Requiring students to exercise their advocacy skills in practice solidifies the change agent identity, helps them to understand how systemic change and political systems work, and ensures they will have the needed skills to continue these efforts in their professional lives.
>
> (2013: 50)

These tasks could be easily adapted to the needs of practicing school counselors. In fact, appropriate advocacy is a crucial skill for directors and school counselors alike. I want to provide a word of caution as well. Be sure to become familiar with your district's policies and procedures about advocacy efforts and directly train your school counselors on your expectations. Review your ethical standards to ensure you are not exerting undue influence or violating professional boundaries in your efforts to advocate for school counseling programs.

The support of comprehensive school counseling can make a real difference in the perceptions of school counselors and of comprehensive school counseling programs. In the next section, additional ways to practice your leadership are explored.

Leadership in Practice

A critical practice for directors is helping their school counselors tell the story of their comprehensive school counseling program in numbers. I had an *a-ha!* moment a few years back when I heard someone say that "data is an administrator's love language." Though there may be many fears and worries about the process of collecting and using data, it has been my experience that it really makes an impact to provide concrete information to our stakeholders. A common misconception is that school counseling services are soft or unmeasurable or unobservable. While it is true that capturing differences in thinking and feeling requires a bit more creativity and intentionality than capturing differences in concrete behaviors like attendance or turning in assignments, it is absolutely possible to show the outcomes associated with counseling services.

Hatch (2014) wrote "collecting results is an integral part of demonstrating the impact school counselor activities and the program are having on students' attendance, behavior, and achievement" (2014: 52). There are several other benefits that Hatch identified from the data centered approach to comprehensive school counseling programs. School counselors use the power of data to:

- "[ensure] every student receives the benefit of a school counseling program that is preventative in design, developmental in nature, and comprehensive in scope" (2014: 52).
- "share what they learn about the impact of their interventions with other educators" (2014: 52).
- "advocate for systems change, ensuring equity and access to a rigorous education for every student" (2014: 91).

Hatch (2014) also made the practical point that:

> professional school counselors must be adept at interpreting the data, as mistakes in data interpretation could lead to the development of new programs or activities that take time, cost money, and may be unnecessary. Understanding how data elements impact one another and how to look for upward and downward trends is essential to designing interventions.
>
> (2014: 53)

As a director, your attitude towards data will have ripple effects throughout your department. Like any new practice, it takes time and a thoughtful rollout process to implement data collection. In my district, we used a multiyear approach, starting with the simple question of which data is easily and reliably available. We found that counselors often keep records of students seen and could use their calendars to determine numbers of small groups and lessons. We also wanted to identify data that school counselors may not even realize they are collecting such as grade reports, the number of retained students, and the number of seniors that graduate. Over the course of a whole school year, the district counselor advisory council assisted me with learning about data and various time-tracking systems. We thought through implementation issues and developed training on quick data collection techniques and made the why explicit to our team. The next year we did an internal practice year of gathering data. This allowed us to make some tweaks and face some of the worries and concerns. We also made intentional efforts to see data as celebratory in nature rather than as a gotcha. We learned that making time to talk about data and provide lots of examples at each of our meetings was also beneficial. The next year when it was time to share with other stakeholders, the group was far more confident and more prepared to have data discussions.

This focus on data is of strategic value to you as a director because it can make the impact of a comprehensive school counseling program clearer to administrators and other district leaders. It also assists in advocating for the value of the services provided by school counselors. In tight financial times, it is wise to be ready at a moment's notice to quantify what students would lose by cutting school counseling positions. In my district, discussions about data have also helped campuses set priorities, make decisions, and create more balanced plans to share duties.

In addition, when tension or conflict crops up between counselors and administrators, the data can provide some objective feedback to all parties. For instance, I had a situation with an administrator who felt like their counselor was not showing initiative to support the campus improvement plan. I suggested they look through the counselor's data and discuss how her time was being spent. The feedback from that administrator was, "I had no idea she was doing all that!" The counselor was then invited to join the campus leadership team and has shared her data regularly in that setting. This change made it clearer to both parties how the activities on the counseling program plan complemented the campus improvement plan and it provided regular opportunities for the counselor to share her progress, seek support as needed, and make adjustments to better align with administrative priorities.

Helping school counselors navigate conflict with administrators is tricky but important. Most often in my experience, conflict stems from mismatched expectations or a lack of alternative personnel to complete tasks which were traditionally performed by school counselors. While school counselors, and directors for that matter, may not always be able to secure additional staff, there is always opportunity to address communication and relationships. Militello and Janson (2007) summarized the research regarding the significance of counselor–principal relationships. In short, they found that counselors and administrators have "incongruent" ideas about counselor responsibilities and they note that principals hire and evaluate counselors which affects the power dynamic between the pair (2007: 411). Hopefully, however, the authors share that a paradigm shift is beginning which is "marked not by role definition but by mutual value and trust" (2007: 412). To facilitate this trust, the authors recommended structured conversations and training for both groups on effective collaboration strategies (2007: 435).

Dollarhide, et al. (2007) also discussed "critical incidents" in supportive counselor–principal relationship formation. A key finding was that principals' experiences in "witnessing" the impact of the school counselor on "relationships with parents, students, administration, and the entire school" made a difference (2007: 364). By seeing and hearing from those stakeholders, administrators start to form a picture of how the school counselor's professional behaviors and knowledge add "value" to the school, which in turn, leads to trust and support for counselor initiatives (2007: 365). Put another way, the authors argued that "relationship and evidence of systemic influence determine role" (2007: 366). Also worth noting in this study is a list of questions for school counselors to use with administrators during the interview process to give counselors insight into the principal's attitude and experiences with comprehensive school counseling (2007: 369). In a district role, the questions may also benefit individual consultations with administrators about school counselors and their campus programs.

In summary, both studies suggested that school counselors and administrators should spend regular time together to talk and to review impact data. Administrators might be more likely to make time to collaborate if data is directly relevant to campus or district initiatives. Moreover, if the counselor evaluation instrument requires the use and review of data it provides an organic opportunity to share and celebrate the ways comprehensive school counseling has directly improved student outcomes. As a director, your influence, especially around the selection of a counselor evaluation instrument, may be a game changer for your school counselors.

A final leadership practice that directors may utilize is providing explicit leadership training and development to school counselors. Growing leaders requires ongoing support and effort but begins with an understanding of the mindset of the untapped leaders on your team. Young (2019) describes the typical counselor as a *doer*. Indeed, school counselors are often task oriented and responsive to immediate situations like the student at the door or the parent on the phone. Plus, we often like checking things off our to-do list, don't we? But, as Young declared, "doing is a safe zone that does not necessarily require leading" (2019: 12). She elaborates that:

> Doers are like first responders, trained to make a situation better. The attention given improves the situation but not necessarily the outcome. Being a doer isn't enough for school counselors. Student needs demand school counselors move beyond reacting to leading.
> (2019: 12)

Young argued that a school counselor leader is "a responsive change agent who is able to integrate instructional and school counseling best practices to initiate, develop, and implement equitable services to all students" (2019: 12). Further, Young summarized that "a doer reacts; a leader responds with data-informed options resulting in systemic solutions producing self-regulated behaviors for students" (2019: 13). Put another way, doing is not nothing, but merely doing may not result in the tools to accomplish everything we aspire to achieve in the long run. Being a leader is a high bar for any professional to reach! Our school counselors will need training, support, and encouragement to make the shift from doing to leading. However, our students certainly deserve it.

Mental and Behavioral Health Considerations

There is no escaping the fact that school counseling is a work of heart which is deeply connected to the emotional and intellectual labors of caring for the vulnerable. As Lawson and Venart (2005) pointed out, "those who practice in the helping field often have an acute sense of empathy" (2005: 243). We know that students, their families, and educators as well, are often grappling with complex needs and traumas. The counselor can have an "intimate exposure to the struggles and suffering" of those they serve (2005: 243). In the school counselor's attempts to meet those needs and respond to the traumas, there is a real risk of secondary trauma, compassion fatigue, and burnout. Left unaddressed, these become risk factors for counselor impairment.

Freudenberger's (1975) seminal work defined burnout as comprising three elements: emotional exhaustion, depersonalization (depletion of empathy, caring and compassion), and decreased sense of accomplishment (sense of futility, loss of meaning in one's work). Further research offers several different explanations as to why these elements develop. Emily Nagoski and her sister Amelia Nagoski offered this synthesis of the reasons burnout can develop: prolonged stress, lack of social supports, and perceived lack of control, often from socioeconomic factors, trauma and/or grief (Nagoski and Nagoski, 2020). They explained in their recent book:

- Emotions are a neurobiological event with a beginning, middle, and end.
- Emotions are automatic and outside conscious control.
- Emotions are whole-body reactions to stimulus.

Dr. Nagoski explained further, "just because you've dealt with the stressor, doesn't mean you've dealt with the stress itself ... you still need to do something to let your body know you are safe" (2020: 6). Professionals sometimes skip over this processing step in their efforts to respond to the next need or situation. This is a key area where directors can make a difference by providing direct instruction on active stress management and emotion processing techniques such as physical activity, breathing, social connection, the belly laugh, and creative expression. In addition to leading professional development, directors may serve as a consultant, mentor, and accountability partner when counselors need support in applying those skills.

Kristin Neff has researched the link between self-compassion and feelings of self-worth, success, and motivation. School counselors can struggle with feelings of inadequacy or shame in the face of the enormity of their role's responsibilities and the limitations of the services they can provide, especially in schools where many non-counseling duties are assigned. As a director, it's important to help school counselors develop practices for self-compassion. Neff (2021) wrote,

> when we use fierce self-compassion to motivate ourselves, we experience it as encouraging, wise vision ... affirming to our inherent potential. When I can trust that even if I blow it, I won't cruelly turn on myself but will instead be supportive ... I'll draw inspiration and energy from my own loving heart.
>
> (2021: 194)

Neff described a process for taking a self compassion break where we evaluate what we want for ourselves, affirm the issue as a life learning opportunity, and make a supportive gesture for ourselves. This and many other tools, including a self-compassion screening quiz are available at her website: https://self-compassion.org/.

Do not underestimate the power of directly discussing these issues with your school counseling staff. We all know the stigma that exists around mental health, especially for mental health professionals who sometimes believe that as professionals they should not be experiencing anxiety, depression, or other mental health concerns. Lawson and Venart (2005) found that "real life expectations and commonly held myths about counselor invulnerability create barriers to establishing and maintaining strong wellness routines" (2005: 243). By shedding light on these issues, you will be helping to create a culture that is more resilient and more compassionate. As the actress and mental health advocate Glenn Close said, "What mental health needs is more sunlight, more candor, and more unashamed conversation."

In the hiring process, directors and principals may also be able to begin assessing the prospective school counselor's attitudes towards wellness and the way he or she structures their own personal wellness practices. A favorite question that I use in my own interview process is, "tell me about a stress management technique you have taught to others that you use yourself." It may also be helpful to survey your school counselors to see the types of strategies that are most commonly used and which strategies the group wants to learn more about. This will allow you to tailor your professional communications and your school counselor training calendar. You may also find a resident expert that can teach his or her peers. For instance, we have a counselor in my district that is a certified yoga instructor. She has taught the group some simple breathing exercises that were well received and have been beneficial. In my district, we have also benefited from structured time and space to process concerns in a professionally safe environment. Lastly, directors can serve as facilitators and connectors to supports such as:

- Information about employee assistance programs
- Self care professional development and self guided resources

- Referrals to community resources
- Structured individual or group supervision
- Consultation and mentoring to provide supportive accountability for wellness goals

On a final note, it's important to consider your own attitudes towards health and wellness. As the director, you will likely be consulted in some of the most difficult situations. You may be coordinating district crisis response, including grief responses. Your own cup may start to get empty. Your school counselors will watch what you do and how you handle your own self care. I have found a great deal of comfort and support from my local professional connections and my professional association. By networking with other directors and counselor supervisors, I can process some of the more complex situations and ensure that I am providing ethical support to the counselors I serve.

Ethical Considerations

In Texas, our principal standards include a focus on "human capital," which is defined further as the expectation that the principal "is responsible for ensuring there are high-quality teachers and staff in every classroom throughout the school" and ensure the "targeted selection, placement, and retention" of staff (TEA, 2015: 2). This responsibility is reinforced in Ch. 237 of the Texas Education Code and in local district policy.

In considering the ethical responsibilities of hiring school counselors, it's helpful to have an understanding of what qualities administrators may currently use to select school counselors. Beale and Bost's influential 1983 study found that principals ranked teaching experience as the number one most desired attribute of school counselors, followed by ability to communicate, school counseling experience, and former principal's recommendation (1983: 103). Yet, McLothlin and Miller (2008) wrote that "principals are often the primary decision makers ... but do not always have a full understanding of the [counseling] role and function" (2008: 61). So, to increase the ethical approach to hiring school counselors, McLothlin and Miller recommended that "interviews include applicant's educational backgrounds, technological competencies, professional identities, counseling skills, and personal characteristics" (2008: 63). The article lists many sample interview questions for the assessment of each area. They also recommended beginning the communication regarding the role of the school counseling program even in the initial interview, noting that when both the principal and the prospective school counselor share their vision for comprehensive school counseling, it "may aid in the selection of school counselors who complement and support the missions of schools and their administration and may alleviate some of the frustration that stems from parties' holding opposing goals and beliefs" (2008: 64).

In addition to considering each of the factors mentioned above, it's important that directors and principals consider the needs and characteristics of the students on the campus. For instance, if the school has a high percentage of economically disadvantaged students, it would be important to assess the counselor's knowledge of local community resources as well as potential district and campus-based resources for low income students. If the campus has a high percentage of English Language Learners, it would make sense to attempt to recruit a bilingual counselor. As mentioned at the opening of this chapter, selecting the right people for a campus is one the most important and most far-reaching decisions we can ask of the principal role and our district leadership.

Cultural Complexities

Ensuring that the cultural identity and personal characteristics of school counselors mirror the students being served is an aspirational goal for both campus and district leaders. In a widely shared recent study, Mulhern found that "students appear to benefit from being matched with a counselor of the same racial group" (2020). Her findings indicated that "students assigned to a same-race counselor—defined here as a white counselor for white students and a non-white counselor for students who are not white—are about two percentage points more likely to graduate high school, attend college, and persist in college compared to their peers who are assigned to a counselor of a different race" (Mulhern, 2020). In addition, she found an observable improvement in outcomes for students matched with "a counselor who attended a local college or university" (Mulhern, 2020). While the study did not pinpoint the exact reasons these findings may occur specifically for school counselors, she suggested that it may be in line with the proposed reasons provided in research regarding a similar effect that has been observed with students and teachers. Another limitation acknowledged in her study is that her work examined a specific state and it has not yet been replicated by results from a larger and more random sample.

Interestingly, Mulhern explored the idea that specific steps to increase the access of students to counselors that meet these desired qualities may be easier than similar work being done for teacher recruitment since it involves a smaller group of staff. She also suggested that district leaders can develop a talent pool by working in partnership with our higher education colleagues. The major recommendation of her study was to "increase the diversity of the counselor workforce, especially in schools serving large numbers of minority students" (Mulhern, 2020).

Another multicultural consideration that is relevant to the hiring process is to use the interview process to understand the school counselor's efforts to recognize and respond to implicit and explicit bias. The Education Trust (2021) proposes that school counselors must make efforts to address inequities in schools. They wrote,

> ensuring students are supported socially and emotionally is not a matter of teaching students to feel differently about the harms they experience in school, or how to behave – it's a matter of addressing the implicit and explicit biases of educators and adults who interact with students.
>
> (2021: 17)

Principals and directors should be alert for interview responses that demonstrate cultural competency and specific examples of interventions that support equity. The authors note that the school counselor must do more than holding supportive views such as appreciating diversity as well as do more than completing supportive actions such as ensuring their own professional development in areas of cultural awareness. Rather, the authors argued,

> leading from a social justice lens involves public acts that energize others to work toward collaborative multicultural competencies. Leading from an advocacy lens is inclusive of students from underrepresented populations or who may be marginalized. Social justice advocates cannot simply do, they must lead.
>
> (2021: 15)

This is a clarion call indeed to the sensitive and innovative work which results in each and all students achieving success.

Strategic Considerations

The process of understanding and supporting comprehensive school counseling is ongoing work. The director is likely to benefit from conceptualizing the task as a strategic plan spread over a number of years. The plan should incorporate long term and recursive tasks such as assessment of needs, training on a comprehensive model, recruitment both of interns and of qualified candidates as positions become available, and modeling intentional practices for the use of data and accountability for its collection. The plan should also address short term or discrete tasks such as creating or updating job descriptions, developing interview question pools, screening candidates, or selecting a counselor evaluation model. Several of these components are best designed in collaboration with stakeholders including other district leaders, administrators, and your counselor advisory team.

New directors are also strongly encouraged to become active in professional associations. I cannot express adequately how much it has benefited me personally and professionally to be connected with leaders in my region, state, and beyond. It's important for you as a director to fill your own cup and collaborate with experienced individuals. Just like teachers who may be *singletons* in teaching their subjects, most counseling directors may be the only professional in the district with their unique responsibilities. In fact, district to district and state to state, there may be wide variability in the day-to-day tasks and expectations for counseling program leaders. This is why having a wide circle of professional colleagues can be so beneficial. In addition, it has been my experience that making connections to peers in a similar role has raised my awareness of resources that can benefit my counselors, staff, parents and guardians, and students.

Conclusion

Leading comprehensive school counseling programs is a big job. The work is complicated, expansive, and ever-changing. However our reasons to pursue excellence truly center on our hopeful and passionately held aspirations for our students, our families, and our wider community.

Goodwin and Jones (2019) captured the urgency of our work, stating "today's youth feel more anxious, more depressed, more detached, and less hopeful about the future than previous generations" (2019: 82). School counselors can be positioned as advocates and leaders to change this trend. I was particularly drawn to Goodwin and Jones' explanation of providing "power under" students as illustrated below:

> The best approaches, therefore, appear to be multifaceted responses that focus on creating positive school cultures to support students' well-being, providing power under kids rather than asserting power over them. Creating school environments where students feel emotionally safe and valued as individuals not only helps with mental health issues and preventing violence and bullying, but also supports better student achievement.
> (2019: 83)

Another critical reason for this work, despite its challenges, is to empower our students to continue their development beyond their time in public education. Zacarian et al. (2017) wrote, "environments that promote empowerment do so by building students' confidence and capacity to speak up, present, and address issues of their concern, make changes, and take risks" (2017: 63). When we use *power under* to support and equip students to reach for and achieve their goals, they noted that this "gives our students living with trauma, violence and chronic stress a sense of competency and of being valued" (2017: 63). Ultimately, individuals that feel empowered, supported and valued will change the world for the better. As noted by Fullan et al. (2019) "young people are looking for ways to contribute to and shape the world around them and to gain a sense of social connectedness" (2019: 67).

To sum up, as directors we must lead with intention, collaboration, and strategy so that more students, and the variety of adults that love and serve them, will benefit from comprehensive school counseling programs. As I shared in the leadership quote at the beginning of this chapter, hiring and supporting the best school counselors is indeed some of our most important work and we can do that by truly understanding and supporting the things that matter most to our school counselors, their principals, their students, and ultimately their community. Our work is world-building, life-affirming, and hopeful. Thank you my friends and colleagues for the effort you pour into your leadership and advocacy. Together, we can make a lasting difference.

References

American School Counselor Association (ASCA) (2019a) *The ASCA National Model: A Framework for School Counseling Programs* (4th edn), Alexandria, VA: American School Counselor Association.

ASCA (2019b) *Empirical Research Studies Supporting the Value of School Counseling*. Online. Available HTTP: <https://www.schoolcounselor.org/Publications-Research/Research/Impact-of-School-Counseling>

Association for Supervision and Curriculum Development (ASCD) (2018) "Advisory: research alert", *Educational Leadership*, 76(2): 8–9.

Baker, S.B. and Gerler, E.R. (2004) *School Counseling for the Twenty-First Century* (4th edn), Upper Saddle River, NJ. Pearson.

Beale, A.V. and Bost, W.A. (1983) "Selecting school counselors: ranking the characteristics", *NASSP Bulletin*, 67(462): 102–106.

Carey, J. and Dimmitt, C. (2012) "School counseling and student outcomes: summary of six statewide studies", *Professional School Counseling*, 16(2): 146–153.

Dollarhide, C.T., Smith, A.T. and Lemberger, M.E. (2007) "Critical incidents in the development of supportive principals: facilitating school counselor-principal relationships", *Professional School Counseling*, 10(4): 360–369.

Education Trust (2021) "Social/emotional and academic development through an equity lens", *ASCA School Counselor*, 57(3): 15–18.

Freudenberger, H.J. (1975) "The staff burn-out syndrome in alternative institutions", *Psychotherapy: Theory, Research and Practice*, 12(1): 73–82.

Fullan, M., Garner, M. and Drummy, M. (2019) "Going deeper", *Educational Leadership*, 76(8): 64–69.

Goodman-Scott, E., Upton, A.W., and Neuer Colburn, A. (2021) "District-level school counseling supervisors' experiences with and perceptions of hiring school counselors", *Professional School Counseling*, 24(1b): 1–11.

Goodwin, B. and Jones, L.M. (2019) "Beyond locks and drills", *Educational Leadership*, 77(2): 82–83.

Hatch, T. (2014) *The Use of Data in School Counseling: Hatching Results for Students, Programs, and the Profession*, Thousand Oaks, CA: Corwin.

Hecht-Weber, K. (2021) "Proactive SEL", *Counselor News: The Official Publication of the New Jersey Counseling Association*. Online. Available HTTP: <https://www.schoolcounselor.org/Newsletters/September-2021/Proactive-SEL?st=NJ>

House, R.M. and Hayes, R.L. (2002) "School counselors: becoming key players in school reforms", *Professional School Counseling*, 5(4): 249–256.

Lawson, G. and Venart, N. (2005) "Preventing counselor impairment: vulnerability, wellness, and resilience", *VISTAS Online*, 53. Online. Available from: <https://www.counseling.org/knowledge-center/vistas/by-subject2/vistas-professional-development/docs/default-source/vistas/vistas_2005_vistas05-art53>

Luke, M. and Bernard, J. (2006) "The school counseling supervision model: an extension of the discrimination model", *Counselor Education and Supervision*, 45(4): 282–295.

Mahoney, J.L. and Weissberg, R.P. (2018) "SEL: what the research says", *Educational Leadership*, 76(2): 34–35.

McLothlin, J.M. and Miller, L.G. (2008) "Hiring effective secondary school counselors", *NASSP Bulletin*, 92(1): 61–72.

Militello, M. and Janson, C. (2007) "Socially focused, situationally driven practice: a study of distributed leadership among school principals and counselors", *Journal of School Leadership*, 17(4): 409–442.

Mulhern, C. (2020) "Better school counselors, better outcomes", *Education Next*, 20(3). Online. Available HTTP: <https://www.educationnext.org/better-school-counselors-better-outcomes-quality-varies-can-matter-as-much-as-with-teachers/>

Nagoski, E. and Nagoski, A. (2020) *Burnout: The Secret to Unlocking the Stress Cycle*, New York, NY: Random House Books.

Neff, K. (2021) "Fierce self-compassion: how women can harness kindness to speak up, claim their power, and thrive", New York, NY: Harper Collins.

Ockerman, M.S., Mason, E.C. and Chen-Hayes, S.F. (2013) "School counseling supervision in challenging times: the CAFE Supervisor Model, *The Journal of Counselor Preparation and Supervision*, 5(2). Online. Available HTTP: <http://dx.doi.org/10.7729/51.0024>

Pianta, R. and Lopez-Perry, C. (2019) "Sharpen your influence", *ASCA School Counselor*, 57(2): 20–23.

Texas Education Agency (TEA) (2015) *Texas Principal Standards Handout*. Austin, TX: Texas Education Agency. Online. Available HTTP: <https://www.region10.org/r10website/assets/File/Texas%20Principal%20Standards%20Handout%20030415.pdf>

TEA (2018a) *Building a Stronger Texas: Long Range Plan for Education*. Online. Available HTTP: <https://tea.texas.gov/node/104198>

TEA (2018b) *The Texas Model for Comprehensive School Counseling Programs* (5th edn), Austin, TX: Texas Counseling Association. Online. Available HTTP: <https://tea.texas.gov/sites/default/files/Pub_2018_Texas-Model_5th-Edition.pdf>

Texas School Counselor Association (2020) *The Texas Evaluation Model for Professional School Counselors (TEMPSC)* (3rd edn) Austin, TX: Texas Counseling Association.

Young, A. (2019) "From doer to leader", *ASCA School Counselor*, 57(2): 10–15.

Young, M.E. (2016) *Learning the Art of Helping: Building Blocks and Techniques* (6th edn), Boston, MA: Pearson Education, Inc.

Zacarian, D., Alvarez-Ortiz, L., and Haynes, J. (2017) *Teaching to Strengths. Supporting Students Living with Trauma, Violence and Chronic Stress*. Alexandria, VA: ASCD.

12 Interviewing and Placement of School Counselors to Include Mental Health Practices

Amy Cmaidalka, Laurie Rodriguez, and Carla Voelkel

> **Leadership Quote**
>
> Ancillary means providing necessary support to an organization. School counselors are not add-on positions or afterthoughts, but rather they provide the specialized support that keeps schools running. Schools without school counselors would be like hospitals without ambulances.
>
> Judy Nelson

> **Aspirational Statement**
>
> - Do more than is expected. Show gratitude always. Work hard and be nice.

Introduction and Background

School counselors play a critical role on a campus leadership team. They ensure that students are provided with a safe and caring environment, and they are often the glue that holds a school together. If you are a school counselor leader or campus leader, hiring the right person for the important position of school counseling can be one of the most crucial decisions you make.

Over the years, the role of school counselor has drastically changed in response to societal trends. District and campus administrators must be familiar with current state regulations and the responsibilities of school counselors. The profession has shifted from being ancillary and reactive to one that addresses the academic, career, and social-emotional development of all students in a school through a comprehensive school counseling program.

As practitioners, we know today's school counselors are critical partners in creating effective school change within a campus culture, and they are necessary to assist with the overall social and emotional health of both students and staff (McGlothlin and Miller, 2008). This chapter will provide practical considerations for creating a hiring model grounded in best practices.

DOI: 10.4324/9781003219750-15

Leadership Values and Standards

To ensure a culture of learning for all, leadership matters most. School counselor leaders and school counselors play a critical role in collaborative school leadership, campuses, and districts. Although leaders might have different roles on a school campus, those who are highly effective remain focused on the same purpose, and they share the vision, mission, beliefs, and goals of the organization.

Collaborative leaders who believe all students can learn at high levels are continuously involved in an improvement cycle that includes identifying concerns, disaggregating data, planning, taking action, evaluating action steps, and making adjustments. While this process takes time, it produces results. As part of collaborative school leadership, school counselors must have authentic and effective relationships with campus administration, work interdependently to achieve campus goals, and hold themselves accountable.

Dickinson ISD provides a *Profile of a Leader* when considering the best candidates for positions in their school district. This profile is used to illustrate multiple types of leadership on a school campus. Dickinson ISD describes a leader as being visionary, strategic, inspirational, courageous, and inclusive. Each of these descriptors align with the district improvement plan and descriptors operationalize traits for each descriptor. For example, a Dickinson ISD leader who is courageous maintains high standards of excellence in the areas of honesty, integrity and fairness, stewardship, trust, respect and confidentiality, and perseveres when times are difficult. This document is used during the interviewing process to select applicants who align with the leadership traits identified by the district.

Leadership in Practice

Dispelling the Divide between School Counselors and Administrators

How does this profile of leadership connect to school counselors? The role of school counselors in public schools today is very different than in previous years. No longer are they the keeper of the master schedule, campus testing coordinator, and intervention facilitator. School counselors are leaders who advocate, consult, and collaborate with multiple stakeholders to ensure students are successful and campus goals are attained, while maintaining a focus on the social and emotional well-being of students and the school community. They ensure that the needs of the whole child are met.

Venturing beyond the traditional administrative school counseling role is a major shift in thinking for district and campus administrators, and it is a shift that is variable across the state and nation. For over 25 years, *The Texas Model for Comprehensive School Counseling Programs* (TEA, 2018) has been in existence, and in 2001, Texas Education Code placed a statutory requirement for all Texas public schools to implement a comprehensive school counseling program. This requirement has transformed counseling programs in some school districts, yet in others, district and campus leaders still lack familiarity with the model, and counselors continue to be given responsibilities that are traditional and reactive rather than developmental and preventive.

In May 2021, during the 87th Texas Legislative Session, Senate Bill 179 was approved and is now law. This legislation requires the board of trustees of each school district to adopt a policy that requires a school counselor to spend at least 80 percent of the school counselor's total work time on duties that are components of a comprehensive counseling program. This includes providing the following:

- **Guidance Curriculum** to help students develop their full educational potential, including the student's interests and career objectives;
- **Responsive Services** to intervene on behalf of any student whose immediate personal concerns or problems put the student's continued educational, career, personal, or social development at risk;
- **Individual Planning** to guide a student as the student plans, monitors, and manages the student's own educational, career, personal, and social development; and
- **System Support** to facilitate the efforts of teachers, staff, parents, and other members of the community in promoting the educational, career, personal, and social development of students.

(Texas Constitution and Statutes, n.d.: 33.005)

As campuses replace school counselors who are leaving public school settings or expand existing counseling programs, it is imperative that district and campus administrators have a clear understanding of the critical components that make up a comprehensive guidance and counseling model. Professional school counselors can be intentional leaders who work and plan collaboratively with campus leadership teams to effectively meet the needs of students and staff.

Counselors as Leaders during the Interviewing Process

To grow and excel as a school counselor leader working alongside campus leaders, school counselors must venture beyond the walls of the counseling office. They must be committed to continuous learning with other counselors and the campus leadership team, and they must be innovative and willing to take risks. In addition, they must actively participate with campus and district leadership in training and activities aligned to district initiatives and the district strategic plan. Ensuring that school counselors are hired to serve in this capacity begins with having an intentional, effective and productive interviewing process. For current and future school counselors, the interview process is a first step to demonstrate leadership traits and qualities. For current school counselor leaders, hiring the right school counselors for your district is essential.

In preparing for the interview and placement process, interview committees ask specific questions to determine leadership aptitude, and will look for counseling applicants who are the best fit for their campuses. School counseling applicants must understand the campus and district vision, goals, and needs prior to interviewing. Completing a leadership self-assessment is often also helpful for applicants. Below are some questions to help both school counselor applicants and school counselor leaders consider who might be the best fit for the school district and campus. According to Young (2013), the questions below can also serve as an excellent source of written response interview questions.

- What is your individual professional vision for school counseling?
- How do your vision and personal beliefs align with the district and/or campus goals?
- How do you use data to make informed decisions, and what types of data do you use?
- How will you help ensure access and equity for all students?
- What traditional leadership characteristics do you possess? Are you trustworthy, confident, intelligent, and organized?

- Does your counseling skill set include a dedicated work ethic, resourceful problem-solving, systemic collaboration, interpersonal influence, social justice advocacy, and professional efficacy? What are personal examples of your skill set?
- Are you an effective communicator? What are specific examples?

(Young, 2013: 35–40)

Meeting the multiple needs of students and families in school today is extremely challenging, and campus administrators cannot do it alone. As school counselor leaders and administrators begin the process for hiring and selecting professional school counselors, they must outline their vision for a comprehensive school counseling model program, remove traditional barriers that prevent it from becoming operational, and be committed to establishing collaborative relationships with counselors and utilizing their leadership skills beyond the counseling office. With this approach, comprehensive school counseling programs can become a reality, and school transformation will occur.

Interview Process Model

Once a person has applied for the professional school counselor position, it is the responsibility of the school counselor leader to make sure that all applicants are interviewed fairly, equitably, and consistently. When establishing interview procedures for hiring a school counselor, expectations for the role of the school counselor must be established at the school district level prior to starting the process. Once the critical theoretical groundwork has been done (i.e. establishing leadership values and reviewing the answers to the leadership questions above), then the actual interview process model begins, as outlined below.

A. Review the Professional School Counselor Job Description

An intentional school counselor job description forms a basis for interviewing and placement, and becomes the transparent tool to convey intricacies of the role. The following are steps to take to ensure that the job description is accurate and aligned with the true role of a school counselor:

1. Typically, school districts make available job descriptions when a position is posted. Prior to interviewing and accepting a position, candidates should have the description of the intended job and its roles and responsibilities so that applicants can make an informed decision on the position.
2. Campus administrators must analyze the core roles and responsibilities and reference the American School Counseling Association (ASCA, n.d.) article entitled, *The Role of the School Counselor* as the skillset is determined. An excellent resource for considering appropriate and inappropriate counselor duties can be found on the ASCA website. Ideally, the district will align these two resources when developing the school counselor job description.
3. The interviewers should provide a candidate with the candidate's school counseling position evaluation tool, which can provide a lens to shape the candidate's understanding of the position and how one might be evaluated.
4. Screening and selecting interview applicants is the first step to this process and one of the most important. Consider creating a candidate evaluation criteria matrix. If there are a significant number of applications for a position, using a candidate evaluation criteria

matrix will allow for sorting through dozens of potential candidates in an equitable manner, while reducing bias, and allow the selection for only the most appropriately qualified candidates to actually interview.

B. Determine the Minimum Qualifications

Minimum qualifications refer to the necessary education, work experience, skills, and knowledge required to perform the essential duties and responsibilities of the role. These qualifications should be the foundation for determining which applicants are qualified to move forward in the hiring process. Minimum qualifications begin the screening process to ensure professional fit for the job.

1 A rubric should be developed in conjunction with the school counselor job roles and responsibilities. Applicants must meet required minimum qualifications to be considered a candidate.
2 Eliminate inflated job qualifications because it can limit the diversification of your applicant pool and may adversely affect applicants from historically underrepresented and marginalized populations.
3 Minimum qualifications should be limited to "must haves" such as technical experience, base-level education, and certifications. Examples of this include, an earned Master's degree in School Counseling, a school counselor state certification, classroom teacher experience, etc.

C. Determine Preferred Qualifications

Preferred qualifications can include specific skills, expertise, and education that might indicate optimal performance. They are typically added to attract the ideal candidate but should be considered a plus or bonus and not used as a threshold to automatically disregard candidates who do not meet them.

1 Each preferred qualification should be evaluated separately, and applicants do not have to meet the desired requirements to move forward to the interview process.
2 If a candidate meets the preferred qualifications, in conjunction with the minimum qualifications, then this candidate is usually optimal and could become a top candidate for the position.

D. Determine How the Qualifications Actually Relate to the Job

The purpose of this step is to identify the relevance of the qualification and confirm whether it is necessary to perform the essential duties of the job. Use this section to identify and document the following:

1 What percentage of the time would the qualification be used?
2 Does this qualification match the day-to-day functions and duties?
3 Would on the job training or other professional development benefit the applicant if the minimum qualification is not met?
4 What kind of skill is it – a performance skill (applied to role), competency, or technical skill? Why does the applicant need the skill?

E. Determine Evaluation Criteria

The purpose of this step in the interview process is to numerically increase equity and to minimize bias by identifying various ways applicants may meet the qualification. Use this section to discuss and identify the following:

1 When assigning rubric scores, use scores such as highly-qualified, met standard, and below standard.
2 What kinds of things should the interviewees look for to provide evidence that indicates the candidate meets the needed qualification?
3 Are the qualifications too exclusive or geared towards a narrow audience? (ie. Is it knowledge only internal applicants would have?)
4 Are the qualifications too specific? (ie. If the requirement is two years of experience, will we miss out on a great candidate with only 1.5 years of experience?)
5 Are the qualifications transferable? Meaning, in what other way has the candidate attained a skill (i.e. through another industry or field) or could the candidate attain the skill or knowledge – post hire – to meet this requirement?
6 Are the qualifications written for a more senior or higher level of expertise than necessary?
7 If the counselor is relocating to your state, does the school counselor need an opportunity to obtain the knowledge or state certification?
8 Is this qualification based on the skills or expertise learned over time by the person who previously held the position? Can we train up on this knowledge for this qualification?

F. Create Interview Questions

Interview questions provide an opportunity to highlight the applicant's abilities as reflected in the job description, compared to their professional experience. Consider using the sample interview questions provided by ASCA (n.d.):

1 Professional school counselors must be excellent communicators. Consider written questions or scenarios that help the committee determine an applicant's written and verbal communication skills. Sample questions might include a selection from the aforementioned bulleted list regarding school counselors as leaders, as well as the following:

   a Tell us how you imagine a typical day as a professional school counselor.
   b Why did you choose to become a professional school counselor?
   c Where do you see yourself in 2, 3, 5, 10 years?
   d Describe your process when a student expressing suicidal ideation.
   e How would you respond to a parent who is irate that has been advised to speak with you?

2 Consider interview questions and concepts that address unintentional biases and questions to address diversity, equity, and inclusion.
3 Consider other ways to get to know the candidate including a professional school counselor portfolio, containing artifacts like a collection of experience-based materials, reflection papers on counseling philosophy, and other components that highlight the candidate's work history, philosophy, professional ethics, abilities or talent, and perspective. Some universities require the development of a portfolio as part of their graduate program requirements and a physical or electrical copy could be shared as a part of the interview

process. If the district decides to use a portfolio, clear directions regarding the required components and matrix examples should be provided to the candidate (perhaps via the job posting itself).

G. Consider an Applicant Presentation

Prior to the interview, candidates can create a PowerPoint or Prezi presentation on a trending topic in school counseling or of passion for the applicant. Providing a criteria for the presentation is necessary, with an interest in determining specific skills that are often used for candidate presentations. When asking applicants to create a presentation, ensure that there is a level of personal research that must be conducted about the campus and or district in the process. Below are a few examples:

1 Candidate choice on their preferred open-ended school counseling topic, relevant and trending in the field. (ie. Social media trends, self-esteem issues, post-secondary opportunities, group counseling, etc.)
2 Year-at-a-glance program design that includes the outline of guidance curriculum, small groups, responsive services, individual planning, and system support.
3 Systematic responsive services plan that addresses the needs of students while referring to data to support.
4 Interactive website that explains the candidate's role as a school counselor, program design, ways to communicate in case support is needed, handouts, resources, or calendar.
5 Program implementation cycle created to meet the needs of the desired campus including supporting documents and data that supports the campus. Utilizing a specific model such as the Texas model.

H. Create a Scoring Rubric

The scoring rubric is one of the most important pieces to this process. The rubric for scoring can be divided into two parts: the interview questions and applicant presentation. It is recommended to place the rubric in Survey Monkey or another online platform available to the district for immediate electronic scoring and feedback of the interview committee as opposed to calculating scores via hand and organizing from highest scores to lowest. A rubric should be determined as developmental, holistic, used as a checklist, or analytical. A rubric should have the following components inherent in its design:

1 An overall description of the rubric.
2 Items for rating that identified components of the interview questions and presentation criteria.
3 Mastery level via a Likert scale like exemplary (4), proficient (3), marginal (2), or below level (1).
4 A description of the level of mastery for the items identified as being rated.

I. Diverse Representation for Interview Committee

Select and train a group of diverse interview committee members that represent the various campus stakeholders and school community. When the interview committee is trained, documentation of their attendance and a copy of the training should be provided to human resources if needed and stored on campus for future reference and modifications. The members of this committee should relatively understand the role of the school counselors and believe in the necessity of that role. The district's Counseling Advisory Committee (CAC) is a great resource for training the interview committee members.

1. Key responsibilities of the interview team are inclusive (avoid bias), objective (follow a structured and streamlined approach), and confidential (non-disclosure agreement).
2. Best practices include having a diverse hiring committee. These members should include campus administration, district leaders that represent the counseling program, professional school counselors, and teachers.
3. Interview questions need to be agreed upon and used for all candidates. Once the diverse interview committee is established and interview questions are agreed upon, interviewing begins.
4. The interview committee reviews human resources protocols. These protocols often are confidential and appropriate for note taking. In every interview, there is a basic agenda that is followed for clear expectations: introductions and a copy of the interview questions. Each member should ask a question in round robin style. The hiring committee takes notes during the process. At the end of the interview, the candidate is thanked for their time and clear information is shared of next steps for the position.
5. After all candidates have been interviewed, a decision is made. If there are multiple candidates that would be a good fit, then candidates move to a second interview with members of the district cabinet for a final selection. Each school district shall establish its own processes once a candidate is selected.

J. Selecting the Best School Counseling Candidate

The final and most important part of interviewing and placing professional school counselors is the final selection of the best school counseling candidate. Once the interview committee comes to consensus on the best candidate and an offer is made, and the offer is accepted, the imperative work of onboarding and developing relationships with the campus principal is essential.

College Board is a mission-driven not-for-profit organization that connects students to college success and opportunity as stated on their website (https://www.collegeboard.org/). The site includes many resources for school personnel for the enhancement of student accomplishments and college and career planning. The site offers many resources for school personnel. One resource that is primarily interested in how well principals and school counselors interact for the benefit of students is a toolkit that is available to anyone (College Board, 2021).

The following sections in *Enhancing the Principal School Counselor Relationship: A Toolkit* (College Board, 2021) encourage continuous engagement and relationship building: a. articulating purpose, vision, and mission; b. effective communication; c. ensuring equity; d. cultivating trust and respect; e. collaborating and sharing decision making; f. advancing student achievement; g. supporting a new principal or school counselor; and h. continuing improvement and advanced practices (2021: 6). This resource can be particularly effective when principals are considering the hiring of a new counselor. The contents which include templates and activities suggest to a principal that they consider what type of professional would be willing to build a relationship with me that will include the topics in this toolkit. These topics address the importance of the relationship that a school counselor and principal build together for the benefit of all students.

Mental and Behavioral Health Considerations

Interviewing and hiring school counselors have mental and behavioral health considerations that are local to the candidate and the administrative leaders who are a part of the interview committee or charged to make the final decision. Interviews should be uplifting, engaging, and positive experiences. The idea of rigor going to the point of discomfort, creating psychological loopholes (i.e. designing questions in a way that promotes failure in responses) in questioning, or asking personal questions not appropriate for a colleague's knowledge are forbidden. If you are an administrative leader determined to hire only those you prefer, this could be a discriminatory practice which never promotes positive mental health. Further, if administrative leaders only desire members of their team to be seen and never truly heard, this can create workplace stress.

How would you know if your candidate has mental or behavioral health considerations that could impede performance? Self-care is a measure of positive or negative mental health considerations. Asking candidates about their hobbies, travel for pleasure, relaxation habits, and ways they de-stress is an appropriate measure of how well the candidate takes care of himself/herself. Self-awareness is one of the most important attributes for school counselors to exhibit to be ethically able to respond to their clients, the school system, and the community-at-large. The interview team would want to explore comments such as a candidate declaring that he/she does not have time to take care of personal needs or that he/she is a workaholic and never has time for hobbies or relaxation. These types of comments could be made to impress on the team as to what a hard worker the candidate is, or they could be warning signs of a person who is not self-aware and able to ask for help when needed.

Additionally, applicants must have the desire and the know-how to be mental health professionals and not simply academic deans or registrars. Only candidates who are committed to identifying and responding to students' mental health concerns should be considered. Aspiring school counselors have the training to respond to mental health challenges and critical incidents and feel confident in their ability to do so. More than ever, school personnel find that they are being asked to respond to school and community crises such as gang violence, weapons, substance use, racial unrest, sexual concerns, abuse in the homes, suicidal ideation, natural and manmade disasters, and other serious situations that impact students. The school counselor should be a leader in these responses and should steer crisis committees and response teams through emergencies that require training, planning, and certainty in reaction to them.

Ethical Considerations

The interviewing process should be grounded in a framework of ethical considerations of doing the right and ethical thing such as interviewing only qualified applicants for the right reason to select the most qualified candidate using a fair and equitable process. If the interview team fails to consider all potentially ethical pitfalls, then the team risks unintentionally creating a biased process. There are several kinds of biases to consider when developing an ethical hiring process as enumerated on the University of Washington Human Resources website (https://hr.uw.edu/diversity/hiring/).

Types of Bias

Institutional Bias

This reflects a type of *tunnel vision* regarding the school or district that is in the process of interviewing potential school counselors. Tacking on desired qualifications to a job description might create a disadvantage to those who are underrepresented in the field. For example, stating that a desired qualification is a degree at a level higher than is necessary for the position creates an uneven playing field for those who don't have that degree, but who might be excellent school counselors. Another type of institutional bias is to give preference to an applicant who appears to have knowledge about the school or district or perhaps have relationships with leaders in the district.

Explicit Bias

This is intentional and based on personal beliefs, values, and life experiences. A person with this type of bias ignores the possibility that other perspectives have value and should be considered. In general, a school leader who is interviewing for school counseling positions will prefer applicants who are similar to themselves. Leaders with explicit biases might interview only candidates with certain backgrounds and might intentionally dismiss candidates who do not have much experience. They might give preference to an applicant who graduated from a certain school, who knows some of the friends of the interviewer, or who attends the same church as the interviewer. Since we are naturally drawn to people who have similar values and similar backgrounds, the interviewing committee members should address these potential biases before they begin the interview process.

Implicit Bias

This usually goes unnoticed by people in general because they simply are not aware of their biases, and, in fact, their biases actually conflict with their stated values. It is not unusual for all of us to have some biases based on our upbringing, life experiences, and current living situations. The interviewing committee might work diligently to establish a fair and equitable hiring process, but unnoticed biases can create negative screening and hiring protocols. The committee leader should discuss the possibility of implicit bias and ask all members to individually assess their own biases that might impact the interview process.

Pitfalls to Avoid

One specific pitfall to avoid during the interview process is intentionally excluding an applicant for some biased reason that might even be based on one person's previous knowledge of the applicant. School professionals generally have pretty extensive networks that extend beyond their campuses and school districts. Many school employees have been employed in more than one district and often receive background information on potential candidates prior to the interview selection process. Other times, school professionals know the candidate based on her or his work in another capacity. However, school professionals must not succumb to the temptation to select candidates based solely on one colleague's experience. If the candidate meets the minimum qualifying material and the hiring committee selects their application to move forward as a team, then the candidate receives an interview. One person's judgment, perception or experience must not interfere with the opportunity to find the best candidate for the position.

Another pitfall is giving a courtesy interview to a candidate for whom the interview team has pre-determined the candidate's inappropriateness for the specific position. Sometimes this type of interview is completed to avoid hurting a colleague's feelings or because the interview team has been told by senior leadership to interview a candidate for a personal or political reason. Avoiding courtesy interviews saves time for everyone and is the ethical and sound thing to do.

The interview committee likely has every intention of being fair and equitable. The interview committee has also established their belief structure regarding the nature and role of the professional school counselor. It is important for the interview committee and school counselor leader leading this work to determine whether members of the team have reviewed their understanding of unconscious bias. Biases are a natural part of human existence. Our own biases can result from our life experiences, including exposure to other cultures and belief systems, and we may not be aware of how these biases impact our lives in both our personal and professional circles. The interview committee must be aware of potential biases that affect the hiring process. The school counselor leader must check in with the team and plan for avoiding bias or lose a qualified applicant.

Addressing, Recognizing, and Responding to Unconscious Biases

Once the school counselor leader acknowledges a potential issue of unconscious bias, she or he can plan for how to mitigate or address it during the interview process. According to the *Harvard Business Review* (Knight, 2017), there are a number of ways to reduce bias in the interview process: 1. seek to understand personal biases and discuss these with the interview committee members before the interview process begins; 2. rework the job description to make it more inclusive; 3. make the screening process a blind review which means that the interview committee begins by just looking at the qualifications of the applicants and not their gender, race, or ethnicity, etc.; 4. ask applicants to solve work-related problems using situations that are common in a school counselor's day at work; 5. standardize the interview questions so that all applicants are judged on the same information; 6. consider likeability since that will be important in a school setting and in a leadership role; 7. consider diversity goals since research shows that a diverse workforce is an asset to an organization.

Cultural Complexities

When school counselor leaders consider multicultural principles, they must assume that every interview committee member has individual implicit bias and put practices in place to audit the biases. Addressing implicit biases as described in the previous section is an important first step.

Diversity, Equity, and Inclusion Focused Questions and Guidelines for Quality Responses

Diversity, Equity, and Inclusion-related (DEI) interview questions are not utilized to assess an applicant's personal identity, but to assess the applicant's skills and knowledge on the value and importance of diversity, equity, and inclusion. The overall goal of including these principles in the interviewing process is to create an environment of inclusion and to hire people who are aligned with the values of the school district. When considering a personal diversity statement assessment in the application or diversity questions in your interview process there are a few consideration including: explaining why the value of diversity is important in the school counselor role, utilizing scenario or technical questions vs. broad open-ended questions, ensuring the questions are relevant to the position and team culture, assessment of the candidate's skills and knowledge of the value of DEI, not the candidate's personal identity or proximity to diverse populations, and setting and developing guidelines for a quality answer with the hiring team prior to screening candidates to ensure equitable assessment of the candidate's responses (University of Washington, 2020).

Samples of DEI focused questions and guidelines of a quality answer

Below are a few sample DEI focused questions and guidelines to consider for a quality answer from the website of the University of Washington Human Resources Department (University of Washington, 2020):

> 1 How have you committed yourself to understanding and aiding in the pursuit of equity and inclusion in your professional and or personal life?

Guidelines of a quality answer include answers that include specific actions or steps taken to pursue equity, an explanation of motivation to be inclusive in their professional life, and demonstration of a knowledge and understanding of what exactly equity and inclusion are. Candidates who provide quality answers are able to articulate and explain the connection between equity/inclusion and their personal and/or professional opportunities, can acknowledge that this work can be challenging, and can demonstrate specific classes, tools, resources, and training used to gained more understanding.

> 2 What steps have you taken to mitigate your biases in the workplace?

Guidelines of a quality answer include a clearly demonstrated knowledge of bias in general and different types of bias. Additionally, candidates with quality answers have the ability to articulate and explain self-awareness of their own biases. These candidates can also measure their success or failure of mitigating their biases in the workplace, can acknowledge the challenges around recognizing and minimizing biases in the workplace, and understand and can articulate knowledge of the personal impact of biases, and the steps and resources that can help mitigate bias.

> 3 Oftentimes, including a scenario in the interview process is also helpful. Here is an example: You are in a departmental meeting/training where a co-worker communicates that they feel targeted by the facilitator's micro-aggressions. They express that they feel they need to communicate this to the facilitator after everyone else has left. They seem uneasy and very much affected. What is your response?

Guidelines of a quality answer include an answer that is actionable such as using first person language, demonstrating the importance of validating their coworkers' feelings, and sharing candidate's personal challenges or difficulties of the scenario, clearly stating if they are an ally or advocate and how they can support their co-worker.

Utilizing these sample interviewing questions, or others like them, will ensure that the interviewing committee considers the important aspects of diversity, equity, and inclusion.

Strategic Considerations

Through a solid support system, school counselor leaders can grow their own school counselors. The counseling team is a family. A special bond should exist between all school counselors and the school counselor leader. Campus level leaders must understand the roles and responsibilities of a professional school counselor. Once those are established, school leaders support growth by supporting and advocating for this position.

Community partnerships are key in growing a solid circle of care and support for students, staff, and families. School counselor leaders, campus leaders and professional school counselors must work together to seek out local agencies and child serving agencies that can support the comprehensive guidance and counseling program.

Conclusion

One key element to discuss is the campus leadership perceptions of how the school counselor should allocate their time – this will frame the interview and selection process. (Leuwerke et al., 2009). Campus leaders who view the school counselor position as administrative will ask different questions than campus leaders who view the school counselor as a social and emotional mental health practitioner. Even the name of the position influences the perceptions of the competency level, e.g. whether the title is guidance counselor, school counselor, or professional school counselor (Zyromski et al., 2019).

As a comprehensive school counseling program, data analysis occurs on a regular basis. This data is used to see strengths, weaknesses and opportunities for change and growth. School counselors also conduct data analyses to audit and grow their own campus program. Through ongoing needs assessments, surveys, and data, the placement of school counselors is determined through a collaborative approach in the best interest of students.

Mental and behavioral health are extremely important to consider during the interview process. It is crucial to emphasize that the district and administrators continuously advocate for overall wellness. Through a staff wellness multi-tiered system of support, a variety of interventions are put in place to support all staff. Mental and behavioral health considerations must be reviewed prior to interviewing to guarantee staff and students will be supported by the candidate. The professional school counselor plays a unique role in supporting staff and students. This candidate needs to be a champion for mental and behavioral health.

School counselor leaders must ensure that all stakeholders understand and support the school counselor hiring process and that hired school counselors are supported as they grow and nurture their skill sets while supporting the needs of the whole child.

References

American School Counselor Association (n.d.a) "Sample interview questions for school counselors". Online. Available HTTP: <https://www.schoolcounselor.org/About-School-Counseling/Careers-in-School-Counseling/Sample-Interview-Questions>

American School Counseling Association (n.d.b) "The role of the school counselor". Online. Available HTTP: <https://www.schoolcounselor.org/getmedia/ee8b2e1b-d021-4575-982c-c84402cb2cd2/Role-Statement.pdf>

College Board (2021) "Enhancing the Principal–School Counselor relationship: a toolkit". Online. Available HTTP: <https://counselors.collegeboard.org/media/pdf/enhancing-principal-school-counselor-relationship-toolkit.pdf>

Dickinson ISD (2022) *Profile of a Leader*. Online. Available HTTP: <https://www.dickinsonisd.org/upload/page/0805/Profile%20of%20a%20Leader.pdf>

Knight, R. (2017) "7 practical ways to reduce bias in your hiring process". Online. Available HTTP: <https://hbr.org/2017/06/7-practical-ways-to-reduce-bias-in-your-hiring-process>

Leuwerke, W., Walker J., and Shi, Q. (2009) "Informing principals: the impact of different types of information on principals' perceptions of professional school counselors", *Professional School Counseling*, 12(4). Online. Available HTTP: doi:<10.1177/2156759×X0901200404>

Levin-Epstein, M. (2019) "Exploring the dynamics of an evolving relationship", *Principal Leadership*, December: 1–5.

McGlothlin J. and Miller, L. (2008) "Hiring effective secondary school counselors", *NASSP Bulletin*, 92: 61–72.

Texas Education Agency (TEA) (2018) *The Texas Model for Comprehensive School Counseling Programs* (5th edn), Austin, Texas: Author.

Texas Constitution and Statutes (n.d.) "Education Code". Online. Available HTTP: <https://statutes.capitol.texas.gov/Docs/ED/htm/ED.33.htm>

University of Washington (2020) "Tools for evaluating applicants". Online (July 27). Available HTTP: <https://hr.uw.edu/diversity/hiring/tools-for-evaluating-applicants/>

Young, A. (2013) *Building-Level Leadership*. ASCA. Online. Available HTTP: <https://www.schoolcounselor.org/getmedia/b17aaa18-60f0-42f8-ad1e-52552e0959b7/Building-Level.pdf>

Zyromski, B., Hudson, T.D., Baker, E., and Granello, D.H. (2019) "Guidance counselors or school counselors: how the name of the profession influences perceptions of competence", *Professional School Counseling*, 22(1), 2156759×X19855654.

13 Creating and Maintaining the Best School Counseling Team for Mental Health and Wellness

Monya Crow and Jill Adams

Leadership Quote

Leadership is not an action. It is who you are and what you do! Building a team means knowing who you serve, understanding where they need support, what their strengths are and creating systems to transform and guide them to being the best version of themselves.

Jill Adams and Monya Crow

Aspirational Statements

- Consultation and collaboration with other stakeholders are core tenets of a successful Professional School Counselor department.
- School counseling leaders are responsible for advocating for Professional School Counselors with intentionality and stewardship.
- Hiring practices and support post-hiring are critical to the success of new counselors and supporting the systems of the mental health roles in a school and district.
- Consultation and collaboration are essential.
- Professional School Counselors are an essential role on the interdisciplinary school team with expertise in the academic, social, and emotional needs of students from a developmental and whole child lens.

Introduction and Background

The role of the professional school counselor has evolved due to the ever-increasing social-emotional and mental health needs of students and families and the shift from solely academic advising to the whole child approach. Federal and state legislative efforts, to bridge the gaps between siloed home and school roles, asked families and schools to begin to seek each other out for a greater partnership than ever before in public education. The new partnership is full of resources, equipment, and collaboration. In response, the role of the school counselor has evolved to meet the needs of both families and the school community at large. Legislatively, safety in schools has become a practice and foundational piece of the school day. This is not only physical safety but *felt safety* where students don't just need to be told they are safe, but students need to feel safe and included. According to the Trust Based Relational Intervention (TBRI) model (Purvis et al., 2013), students need to feel safe at school in order to learn. This is achieved through relationships with trusted adults where adults are looked to in order to connect to students, empower them to problem solve, and correct and guide them safely toward their future. There have been plenty of quips and memes about checking on the adults in a school setting, but this has become more true and less fodder. Staff members are receiving students with whatever they bring to the table and are expected to ensure learning, safety, basic needs, social skills, and so many other life lessons that propel students to be thriving as they leave our walls. With this comes a responsibility to ensure our students aren't hungry, have someone who loves them at school, pass their state exams, have friends, and know how to navigate relationships and conflict. And these responsibilities are the tip of the iceberg. As the magnitude of an educational role increases, so does the level of support needed to ensure that the caregivers have their own oxygen! Supporting a rockstar counseling team is multi-faceted: supporting counselors from a leadership level, equipping the mental health professionals in a school or district, and taking the time to be intentional and preventive with the supports needed for staff. Even our mental health professionals need check-ins, processing and resources to ensure they are able to perform the job expected of them.

Leadership Program Values and Standards

Heart-Centered Leadership

The school counselor role is rooted in meeting the needs of the person in front of them. The core of all school counseling work is centered in the heart. Heart-centered leadership is driven by the ASCA code of ethics which states "all students have the right to be respected, be treated with dignity and have access to a comprehensive school counseling program" (ASCA, 2022).

Heart-centered leadership is about connecting, supporting, uplifting, and rooting for the rise of the team you lead (Brown, 2018). It is free from judgment, free from shame and free from fear. In heart-centered leadership, it is never "let me know if you need anything" it is "I know how you like your coffee" and that paves the way for a leader to communicate through both the love language (Chapman and White, 2011) and strengths of the school counseling individuals and teams.

Servant Leadership

As a counselor leader, there is a decision point as to whether you are a supervisor or a leader. Supervision is ensuring compliance and leadership is encouraging growth, vulnerability, and consultation. The word servant leadership is often overused, which contributes to it becoming trite, however it does encompass and encumber what it takes to support the role of a school counselor. In a school setting, it is critical to be aware and aligned to district vision, mission, and goals as well as the culture and climate of the stakeholders being served. When looking at the characteristics of a servant leader, they are quite parallel to the heart of a school counselor.

In 1991, Robert Greenleaf's writings outlined a set of ten characteristics of the servant-leader that are of critical importance. These ten characteristics include: *listening*; *empathy*; *healing relationships*; *awareness* of self and others; reliance on *persuasion* rather than position of authority or coercion; the ability to *conceptualize* ideas rather than just thinking operationally; *foresight* or the ability to understand how the past, present, and future intertwine in decision-making; *stewardship* or a commitment to serving others; *commitment to growth* of people by nurturing the personal and professional growth of others; and *building community* for their work group. These ten characteristics of servant-leadership are by no means exhaustive. However, they do serve to communicate the power and promise that this concept offers to those who are open to its invitation and challenge (Spears Center, 2022).

Having a lens that you are there to serve and support the people in your department guides how you prioritize initiatives and how you spend your time supporting them. Allowing your team to have voice in the department is foundational to servant leadership. Voice doesn't have to mean being the complaint department but it does mean allowing people to problem solve to help drive department development and seek solutions that benefit the people in the role. The voice can be everything from the interview process to systemic protocols to supporting new counselors. Without being hierarchical, it is important to create a system of people in your department to support and consult with each other, drive department work and create space for collaboration so everyone isn't operating in a silo. This can be in the form of lead counselors at different levels, mentors for new cohorts of counselors, and your go-to people that you've identified in a strengths-based way to do some behind the scenes work. With advocacy and leadership as core competencies in the role of school counselors (TEA, 2018), growing these traits in your counseling teams only proves to strengthen the comprehensive school counseling programs at the campus and district levels.

The flip side of intentional leadership and walking alongside your team members is not becoming all things to all people. It is important to model this for your team as well as to truly set healthy boundaries so that you are not answering questions such as "are we still meeting today?" or "Can you resend the link for the form due tomorrow?" Often in new counselors, there is such a desire to do a good job, there are very diffuse or unhealthy boundaries. Training, teaching, and modeling is an excellent way to support new counselors in maintaining a healthy start to their role and ensuring they stay the course in a positive and professional way.

Leadership in Practice

Hiring the Right People

The starting point of building your rock star team is your screening and hiring processes. This is something that you may want to have your current counselors help develop, because these are the people who will be walking with them on their campuses and teams. As a district leader, it is also important to have the opportunity to have interactions with all possible candidates. Some districts might use a team to screen candidates without the leadership having the opportunity to meet with each candidate. The downfall of this approach is that there is not a multi-faceted approach to look at a candidate from a variety of lenses.

Your screening process may be somewhat determined by your human resources department, but it is critical to advocate for a process that draws out the characteristics and components that are critical in the counseling and mental health roles.

Considerations when developing your screening process:

- What traits are a part of your department philosophy and expectations?
  - Some departments want experience, while others are okay with being brand new to the profession. Some place more value on the academic advising and some home in on the mental health pieces. This is something that is critical for your team to be able to

articulate so your counselor/mental health pool shares the common vision of your department and district.
- Start with a brainstorm of the type of counselors you want in your department. Ask for input from the people who are already in the role!

- What questions do you ask them and why?
  - Don't be afraid to bring in scenarios that may trip up even the most veteran professionals. Often, it isn't the exact answer, but the evidence of consultation and problem solving when there isn't an exact answer ... which in our profession, is there ever?
  - When developing a rubric for scoring, consider not just the answer to the question but do you see evidence of important traits? Consultation is a huge foundational piece in our district so this is something that we have in almost every rubric. It's not always having the right answer off the top of your head, but knowing who to ask when it isn't black and white. Kid centered is the goal of any candidate! We always say, we can teach skills, but we cannot teach heart!

- What answers do you need to hear so you know they are right for your team?
  - Build in room for overall impression related to interpersonal skills, student-focused answers, clarity, and an ability to engage and build rapport with whomever is in front of them. These are the people who will be receiving students, families, and staff on some of their hardest days.

- How do you meet every person who may be a part of your team?
  - We conquered this with the group interview! A group interview serves two purposes. One is to meet and interact with each candidate, even if it is for a short period of time. Secondly, a group interview allows you to see interpersonal skill sets that are imperative in these roles. Our favorite question to ask is "Tell me your favorite story about a kid that you have worked with in any role." This question will draw out who is kid-centered – "This kid was so strong and resilient!" Versus who is me-centered – "They were better off after having worked with me."

As mentioned before, collaboration is key, and this is a place where it really matters. So what does that look like? District counseling leaders screen candidates for skill set and alignment with department vision and mission. A pool of candidates is created so that campus principals and counselors can interview for campus fit. What this yields is a team member that will thrive at both the department and campus level.

Teaching Them to Fish

If a leader *answers the call* at every turn, it can easily become enabling instead of building capacity. A core component of serving others is to recognize *what they bring to the table*. That might include: "I worry that he/she will be mad at me" or "I am afraid people will think I don't know what I am doing!" In order to support and grow through some often unhealthy mindsets, professional learning is a foundational piece of creating the best counseling department ever. Philosophy and "How WE do it" must be developed with repeated exposure and conversations. Because it is sometimes difficult to pull all counselors for professional learning throughout the year, professional learning has to be valued, multi-modal and just-in-time. As district leaders, letting people know that attendance at professional learning is a non-negotiable can be a difficult conversation with campus administrators but is a *hill to die on* because it is an investment in the team that is necessary to support the many needs of campuses and students.

As technology has evolved, professional learning can be offered in a variety of ways. Some may be in-person, some may be virtual, and some may be housed in digital self-paced modalities. Especially with all of the beginning of the year professional learning, it can feel like an inordinate amount of information that your team members are likely to forget because it was so much. All of it can feel and may be essential when it comes to protocols, mandates, and policies, which doesn't even give space for philosophy, team-building, and leadership development. Micro-learning throughout the year is an effective and efficient way to provide information and learning to your team. This can be in the form of a weekly/biweekly virtual Q & A, post-lead counselor team meetings, a year-at-a glance, or other weekly newsletters or emails. Knowing how your teams best receive information and making sure that you aren't either *fire-hosing* or providing too much information in too many places is foundational to effective professional learning. In addition, managing a clearing house like an online handbook is a great reference tool for the counseling team to look to for answers on protocols and absolutes. There are a variety of tools that will allow for leadership to update a document which in turn, updates that information in the handbook allowing for point-in-time information.

Tough Conversations

When we delve into the role of the counselor, social worker, or mental health professional on a campus, there are a variety of audiences with whom these roles will have tough conversations. It is vital for counseling leadership to walk through scenarios and pitfalls of critical conversations with parents, administrators, teachers, and students. In training the team to have tough conversations, *where they get stuck* must be a part of the conversation. Often what a person is bringing to the table is overlooked. When a professional is confronted by an angry parent or teacher, that can trigger feelings of fear or inadequacy. Support for moving through those conversations is rooted in valuing each person as a professional and building confidence.

Tough conversations are best taught by examples and role playing. This means that a professional learning scenario is set up to walk through the conversations that school professionals are bound to have. What might a professional and supportive response be for the following scenarios?

- When a parent says, "I'm not going to have this?"
- When a co-worker says, "They are just being lazy."
- When your Principal says, "_____."
- When a student says, "My teacher hates me."

Becoming Unstuck

1 *Lean in.* Despite feeling like moving out of a tough conversation is the most comfortable, the very best thing to do is to lean into it. It is common when confronted with conflict to retreat, but all too often that results in straining the relationship. Rather than saying to an angry parent, "Ma'am our policy states ... .", what about "Ms. Jones, I want to make sure that I am hearing all of the concerns you have."

2 *Who is your Bat phone?* Consultation is a foundational piece of any counselor, social worker, or mental health professional role. Not only does it help to bounce ideas off and

with sticky situations with a colleague, ethically, we are required to. Identify early on who your go-to people are.

3 *Get comfortable saying "I don't know."* All too often we get stuck when we feel like we are supposed to know an answer to something and we don't. One of the best tools to get unstuck is to be honest and say "I don't know." That may be in response to a student who is seeking direction or to a parent who demands an answer. In either of these situations, the professional can say "I don't know … but I will find out and follow up with you as soon as possible."

- At the root of every tough conversation, the question must be "What is best for the student?" With that at the core, all approaches and decisions will head in the right direction.

Modeling and Seed Planting

1. Cohort Model

In order to grow the best counseling department ever, counseling leaders must spend time growing counselors as leaders. As mentioned earlier, there is a huge difference between the approach being "Let me know if you need anything" and "I know how they like their coffee." One cohesive and supportive approach to the team members that are new to the department, is to utilize a cohort model for growth and development. This model has many benefits to the new team members and department at large. The basic tenets of the cohort model are:

- Meets quarterly each school year.
- Have a plan for each meeting that includes microlearning and review of all protocols and philosophies.
- Guest speakers: those who came before … ask your veteran counselors to come and present to the new counselors and share tips and tricks as well as to build relationships with each other.
- What topics do they need to hear?
  - Transitioning from teacher to counselor: "I'm sure they didn't mean that" vs "What was that like for you to hear that?"
  - CPS reporting musts
  - How to support … angry parents, unsuccessful students etc.

2. Lead Meetings

The connection between what a department needs in a school counselor and what a campus needs can be achieved with a meeting in the middle agreement. This is a comprehensive plan that outlines in detail the *what* of the school counselor combined with what a campus needs from a counselor (504, RtI, lunch duty, etc.). Lead counselors can be utilized for so much more than just disseminating information; developing them to be consultants and leaders for their teams is critical when leading departments.

One of the best collaboration partnerships is that between a campus counselor and the campus administration. This dynamic blends the critical element of both the what and why of behavior as well as academics and overall success. Lead counselors are an excellent resource to build the collaborative model that becomes a working document and understanding between campus administrators and campus counselors. This agreement outlines what the goals are for the counselor for the year as it relates to the national or state counseling model, identifies any non-counseling duties and shows outcome measures.

3. Work Groups

We referenced earlier the cautionary tale of being all things to all people with regard to access and availability but instead, striking a balance. Along those lines, counseling leadership cannot *build all the airplanes* either as that distracts from the leadership role and capacity. Having said that, when given the right framework, the counselors can and will build the airplanes they need to fly. Not only is this supportive for the counseling department leadership, it creates ownership and buy-in from your team.

Start with the framework of who, what, when, where and why:

- *Who?* Who will participate in what workgroups? Diversify your groups based on elementary, middle school, and high school as well as expertise.
- *What?* Query your team to find out what systems they need to streamline their work and create clarity and efficiency.
  - Diversity, equity, and inclusion
  - Academic
  - Social emotional learning
  - Protocols
- *When?* How long will each work group take? Will this work happen during the summer? What needs to be completed in person? What can they do on their own? And what is the compensation for their work?
- *Where?* Secure space for your team to be able to work and collaborate.
- *Why?* Work groups must be rooted in the philosophy of the district and the department. This opportunity also strengthens the relationships between counselors as well as allowing for *share fairs* where ideas and toolboxes can be shared.

Recognition and Praise

Recognition comes back to KNOWING your team as people and also being aware of accomplishments on their campuses. Authenticity and relevance are critical when it comes to recognition! Recognition can come in many forms and can be as simple as presence in a conversation, acknowledgment of the essential nature of the role, and celebrating wins. Before you can have recognition, you have to take the time to get to know your team. One of the most valuable statements you can have in your toolbox is, "I'm never too busy for you." Recognition can range from state awards to a simple note, and all are equally impactful.

In the state of Texas, winners of the CREST award (Counselors Reinforcing Excellence for Students in Texas) represent exemplary counseling programs as defined by the Texas Model for School Counseling.

Some additional ideas that celebrate your team are:

- Notecards each week
  - "I still have it!"
  - "It made my day."
  - "I had no idea you thought I did a good job!"
  - "It meant the world to me!"

- Celebration lunch: an end of the year time to get together as a team and counselors share their goal attainments and wins!

- Door prizes: you would be amazed at how excited a counselor can get over a package of new highlighters or stick notes. Even at regular counselor meetings, door prizes, however small, are a great way to say "We see and appreciate you!" With budgets often lean, many door prizes can be donated through community partnerships (i.e. restaurant coupons etc.)

Mental and Behavioral Health Considerations

Cover your mouth with the oxygen mask first ... With the increase in trauma societally and legislative support for more training on mental health and wellness, it can be common for the helping professionals to become overwhelmed themselves. Compassion fatigue is a very real place whereby a helping professional begins to feel negative or adverse reactions to the situations or people in their care. As a leader, it is imperative that counselors are educated on the signs and symptoms of compassion fatigue and how to prevent it. One of the best protective factors against compassion fatigue is having healthy boundaries. Healthy boundaries are reflected in knowing when to say no, supporting your team to grow and learn versus enabling, putting your work down and taking a break and recognizing and adhering to your limits.

When you hit the wall, be honest. A positive outcome of creating a safe and cohesive counseling team, is that when they hit the brick wall, and they will, they will reach out for help. So in that instance, what does support for your team look like?

- Open door policy: Do you invite your team members to talk to you? Do they feel comfortable reaching out based on the relationships you have built?
- Count me in: What is your philosophy? Do you model that "we can do this?"
- Philosophy from the beginning: "Talk about the problem when it's not a problem." Prepare your team for the bumps. It is much easier to talk about a bump or a brick wall BEFORE it happens. Then when it does, your team will recall, "mama said there would be days like this."
- Lead on purpose, not "let me know if you need anything."
- Be approachable despite being at central admin and not seeing them every day.
- Know how they take their coffee.

The challenge with leading a department or team of counselors that you don't see every day can be a lack of connection. Any department that hopes to be the best ever has to foster cohesiveness and an overall feeling that *we are one*. As the leader it is imperative to know your counselors. Who responds best to positive reinforcement? Who responds best to a direct approach? Who is on the struggle bus?

Ethical Considerations

The ethical nature of any counseling team is paramount. Without ethics at the forefront of all decisions, reckless actions and diffuse boundaries are in play. As counseling leaders, when we look at a framework for hiring, it is imperative that it be a collaborative process. In order to retain the best of the best, you hire the best of the best and support them every step of the way. Your hiring practices must be intentional and targeted. A common question a prospective candidate may ask is "What type of support does the department offer for new counselors? What type of Professional Learning is offered?" *Sink or Swim* will never build the type of team that is dynamic or sustainable. In order to keep a great team going, it must include: on-going training and support; access and availability with boundaries; leaning into the bumps in the road and brick walls; and cheering them on every step of the way. The following standards from the ASCA Ethical Standards for School Counselors (2022) should guide leaders as they support school counselors and the CSCPs:

C. SCHOOL COUNSELOR DIRECTORS/ADMINISTRATORS/ SUPERVISOR

School counselor directors/administrators/supervisors support school counselors in their charge by:

a Advocating both within and outside of their schools or districts for adequate resources to implement a school counseling program and meet students' needs and the school community's needs.
b Advocating for fair and open distribution of resources among programs supervised, using an allocation procedure that is nondiscriminatory, equitable, informed by comprehensive data and consistently applied.
c Taking reasonable steps to ensure school and other resources are available to provide staff supervision and training.
d Providing opportunities for professional development in current research related to school counseling practices, competencies, and ethics.

Cultural Complexities

As we look at multicultural complexities, there is no role more equipped than a counselor or social worker to meet these needs. As more districts are hiring positions dedicated to diversity, equity, and inclusion (DEI), the counseling department is a vital part of this work. These concepts are not what we do, they are who we are. Ethically, we operate from a place of unconditional positive regard (Rogers, 1961). This is a posture and approach that is rooted in neutrality and person-centeredness.

People, in general, like to engage with people who look like them, act like them, and have experiences that mirror their own. To create a diverse counseling team is important for students to interact with those counselors who have commonalities with them and who can model for students the idea that "I'm here for you; I understand you; and I believe in you." Some students might not hear these types of statements anywhere else in their lives. Conversely, students who see a diverse counseling team collaborating, working together, solving problems together receive a powerful lesson in the opportunities we all have when DEI are an everyday part of life. The expectation then is that you students can be equitable, diverse, and inclusive as well, and that's what is expected of you.

Strategic Considerations

There are many nuts and bolts to consider in your hiring and retention processes. The first step is to create a calendar or *year-at-a-glance* for both your hiring processes as well as for each role in your department. This will be a pacing guide for both you and your team members to help to ensure deadlines are met and programs completed. A second important consideration is where will you find your potential candidates? A great place to start is to partner with your institutions of higher education to develop and operate an intern program to allow you to grow your own.

If supported by your school district, creating a pool of counselors that campus administrators can select from allows for a guarantee of the counselor skill set while allowing for campuses to interview for fit. Once you have created your counseling pool, there are considerations for campus fit. Often, through collaborative relationships, district counseling leadership and campus administration, talk through prospective candidates and good fit.

Conclusion

Just like the student-centered approach, where all decisions are rooted in what is best for kids, what is best for counselors and the department as a whole comes first. With a counselor-centered approach, there is a large probability that you will create the best school counseling team ever. As a district or campus leader, investing in growing your people as they walk the role and providing ongoing support and learning for your team as well as advocating for the role to other stakeholders is the best way to make your team the best it can be! Once the stakeholders in a school community understand the power of the counseling role, the gains can be exponential for students and families. District leaders operate from a place of advocacy, cheerleading, empathizing and defining because at the end of the day, people always ask, "Who takes care of the caretakers?" and the answer is "WE get to!!"

References

American School Counselor Association (ASCA) (2022) *ASCA Ethical Standards for School Counselors*, Alexandria, VA: Author.
Brown, B. (2018) *Dare to Lead*, New York, NY: Penguin Random House, LLC.
Chapman, G. and White, P. (2011) *The 5 Languages of Appreciation in the Workplace: Empowering Organizations by Encouraging People*, Chicago: Northfield Pub.
Greenleaf, R.K. (1991 [1970]) *The Servant as Leader*, Indianapolis, IN: The Robert K. Greenleaf Center.
Purvis, K., Cross, D., Dansereau, D., and Parris, S. (2013) "Trust-based relational intervention (TBRI): A systemic approach to complex developmental trauma", *Child & Youth Services*, 34, 360–386.
Rogers, C. (1961) *On Becoming A Person: A Therapist's View of Psychotherapy*, Boston: Houghton Mifflin.
Spears, L. (2010) "Character and servant leadership: ten characteristics of effective, caring leaders", *The Journal of Virtues & Leadership*, 1, 25–30.
Spears Center (2022) "Ten characteristics of a servant-leader". Online. Available HTTP: <https://www.spearscenter.org/46-uncategorised/136-ten-characteristics-of-servant-leadership>
Texas Education Agency (TEA) (2018). *The Texas Model for Comprehensive School Counseling Programs* (5th edn), Austin, TX: Author.

Section IV

Developing, Designing, Implementing, and Evaluating Comprehensive School Counseling Programs Utilizing a Mental Health Perspective

School counselors develop, design, implement, manage, and evaluate the comprehensive school counseling program in their schools. When administrative leaders insist that programs are based on student needs, focused on all students, and evaluated each year for effectiveness, school counselors, then, are more free to contribute substantially to the continuous improvement of schools. Section IV highlights how to manage programs that support mental health in schools, infusing crisis plans whereas mental health is at the crux, data collection and analysis processes, and measures of accountability, along with outlining and managing budgets, partnerships, and other funding sources that foster agendas for mental health. Administrative leaders embrace that school counselors are who direct their programs and are considered to be leaders in their trained disciplines within the school environment.

> Campus comprehensive school counseling programs do not operate in silos and should act as a district-wide effort. Administrative leaders who only allow for school counselors do to part or some, as opposed to all, encroach on violating professional codes of ethics that promote educators to operate *precisely* within their scope of practice.
>
> Lisa A. Wines

> When school counselors manage their programs correctly and are willing to audit their programs each year, progress toward assisting all students will be made. Using data to evaluate progress and where progress is lacking, the school counselor is able to advocate for more resources including time, access to students, and funding.
>
> Judy A. Nelson

Data drives all decisions. Professional school counselors and administrative leaders are willing to lean into vulnerability to take a deeper look at data that may uncover underlying issues in order to better develop, design, implement, manage, and continually evaluate the comprehensive school counseling program in their schools. Data is what speaks to our most senior leaders and school boards who can make final decisions about addressing the needs of our students.

Natalie Fikac

Section IV

Developing, Designing, Implementing, and Evaluating Comprehensive School Counseling Programs Utilizing a Mental Health Perspective

14 Managing Programs that Support Mental Health

Tisha Kolek

Leadership Quote

School counselors contribute substantially to the continuous improvement of schools through their leadership of comprehensive school counseling programs. Students and teachers alike are changed for the better when they interact with school counselors.

Judy Nelson

Aspirational Statements

- School counselors are helpers by nature and therefore do not always fully realize their leadership potential and its significant relevance (or direct correlation) to effective school counseling programming.
- As school counselors advocate for comprehensive counseling program support from various stakeholder groups, they should remember to begin with their "why" the programming aspect is significant and necessary.
- When school counselors empower others (students, staff, parents, and community members) they will, in turn, empower themselves and then as a result, create successful and sustainable comprehensive counseling programs.

Introduction and Background

Change is a process, not an event. Too often, change is treated as a one-time event. Enthusiasm is generated about a possible change, an event is held to launch the change, but then everyday events that follow smother any follow-through. People are good at holding *first annuals* but often forget to finish the tasks. Make no mistake – change is a process, not an event. Sufficient time must be built into the change schedule if the change is to be successful. Perseverance is a virtue (Gysbers and Henderson, 2012: 43).

Counselors' first commitment to making a change in the profession of professional school counseling is to see themselves as leaders. Leaders of their campus, experts in the field of social, emotional, and personal growth of students, and advocates for the support that students need to achieve their potential. With school counselors often being the only ones in the role of supporting student mental health at their campus or even on a small team of just a few professionals, counselors must comfortably assume the role of leadership for these tasks in this area that they have been well-trained and educated to support. Fellow educators look to counselors for assistance to help students in the classroom with their challenges that are unique to each individual. How often do staff members stop by the counseling office to seek expertise and guidance regarding the needs of a student? Staff look to counselors for assistance every day, particularly in addressing the mental health of students. Staff are communicating the worth and value of a counselor every time they seek assistance. Assume the role of leadership. Step into the domain with confidence and well deserved merit because of the unique role that school counselors have at every campus.

Leadership Program Values and Standards

School counselors are leaders of their programs which support the academic, social, and emotional needs of school age students. With the diverse needs of the students of today, effective programming that equitably meets the needs of all students on a counselor's caseload is critical. For counselors to serve students and meet their ever-changing needs, comprehensive programming is imperative. School counselors will need to grow their leadership skills and seek additional training and learning to advocate for effective counseling programs. Historically, leadership is defined as a person who holds a certain title or office. For a comprehensive counseling program to achieve success, counselors will need to see that they are the leaders and program managers of the counseling program that meets the needs of *all* students.

Stephen Covey

Stephen Covey says that people think of leadership as a position which might negatively impact their view of themselves as leaders (FranklinCovey, n.d.). This is where a paradigm shift must occur to be relevant to the current model of leadership that exists today. Counselors are leaders. They lead the counseling initiatives by working with other leaders on campus and in the district to implement effective programming. Through their advocacy and programming knowledge, they then create the structures of the program as aligned to state and national model standards as well as mandates. Managing the school counseling program involves assessing program strengths and weaknesses and maneuvering adjustments for maximum positive impact and results. From creating social emotional programming for positive student mental health, college and career exploration to crisis management and response, counselors are the experts of the school counseling program for all such aspects. Serving in this role with a leadership mindset enables the program to be successful to meet the needs of the students. According to the ASCA National Model (2019a) professional standards and competencies, leadership behaviors are as follows:

> **B-PF 7. Demonstrate leadership through the development and implementation of a school counseling program**
>
> a Identify sources of power and authority and formal and informal leadership
> b Identify and demonstrate professional and personal qualities and skills of effective leaders

> c Apply a model of leadership to a school counseling program
> d Create the organizational structure and components of an effective school counseling program aligned with the ASCA National Model
> e Apply the results of a school counseling program assessment to inform the design and implementation of the school counseling program
> f Use leadership skills to facilitate positive change for the school counseling program
> g Define the role of the school counselor and the school counseling program in the school crisis plan
> h Serve as a leader in the school and community to promote and support student success
> i Participate in the school improvement process to bring the school counseling perspective to the development of school goals
>
> (2019a: 4)

As stated above, counselors will demonstrate leadership through the development and implementation of a school counseling program. All competencies included in B-PF 7 are instrumental in program development and implementation. When one aspect of program implementation is not intentionally included in the plan, the program will not be as successful. The first three items are identifying leaders to help support and advocate for programming as well as exhibiting personal leadership in the counseling role. The next two (d and e) are designing and implementing the ASCA National Model (2019a). It is also important to align the national model to include state required counseling program requirements. For the next aspect (f), it is important for the school counselor to step into the role as the leader of the counseling program. Communicating, advocating, and monitoring the counseling program is critical. Item (g) is essential as well. Defining the school counselor role for all stakeholders is an ongoing task. The role of the counselor should easily be accessed through the campus website, the counselor literature, as well as the counseling program itself.

Leadership in Practice

What is Leadership?

What is leadership? What is the definition of a leader? When we ask these questions to educators and even more specifically, counselors, we often think of position or title. We think of principal, assistant principal, superintendents, and so on. Counselors, oftentimes, do not think of themselves as leaders. However, as more students need support for emotional, social, and academic concerns, counselors are skilled and educated for the task. Counselors are leaders in this arena. They are ready to offer assistance to meet the needs of students, as varied as those needs can be. As the school counseling program continues to evolve with the ever-changing society influences and needs, it is crucial that counselors seek leadership training and continued professional development. All school counseling professionals can continue to refine their skills of leadership to further empower the counseling programming.

How Do Counselors Advocate?

When counselors advocate for effective and equitable programming for students, a philosophical approach can help facilitate the success in a more collaborative environment. Simon Sinek (2009) speaks to the golden circle concept in many of his books such as, *Start*

With Why: How Great Leaders Inspire Everyone to Take Action. He speaks to the golden circle model as an attempt to explain how some people inspire others and create successful opportunities. When examining this model and applying the implementation of the comprehensive counseling program, a different advocacy and leadership approach emerges. As we build capacity in our programs by advocating and educating our stakeholders, which are defined as our staff, students, and parents, counselors need to be prescriptive and intentional. Using this model will help to achieve that.

As we design and implement our counseling programs, we need to increase capacity with help for program initiatives. Many counselors have caseloads upwards of 500 students. Therefore, counselors should recruit additional help with programming. The way to do this is to inspire others so that more adults on a campus are supporting the students' holistic needs of social, emotional, and academic support. When we increase awareness of the critical importance of effective counseling initiatives, using the golden circle is key. Sinek (2009) states that everyone knows what they do and oftentimes professionals will start to inspire others with their *what*. Sinek says, however, people can be more influential when starting with the *why*. He states there are three questions that should be reflected upon to influence and inspire others to add value to opportunities.

These three questions are the following: *What do you do? How do you do what you do? and Why do you do what you do?* Counselors should define their why when seeking to improve or enhance counseling programs that they lead. The why is what we share with others to inspire capacity building so that the program has ancillary support. Example: According to student survey data, drug use and abuse has increased by 20 percent over the last 5 years in our high school. The counseling program wants to provide support with specific initiatives, like guest speakers and curriculum embedded in a freshman elective class to address the school wide concern. When counselors advocate for the additional focused support to be considered, counselors will be able to positively influence decision makers when the why is shared first. For example:

- *Why?* Our students are struggling in our community with drug use and abuse. This concern will keep our students from achieving their potential success during their high school years and beyond.
- *What?* We need to implement a prevention curriculum and educate our students.
- *How?* Embedding curriculum into all physical education classes, including athletics, PE, dance, and so forth will ensure that our students are taught the skills needed to avoid usage.

Now consider this. Using this same scenario, think how the advocacy for substance use support might have a different outcome if the counselor stated the how, then the what, and finally the why in the same leadership discussion. Different effect, right? When beginning with the why, the conversation appeals to the part of the brain that controls emotions, behavior and decision making. This neuroscience approach can inspire others to support initiatives as they are needed in our comprehensive programs. Sinek says that it is the most important message that an individual can communicate as this is what inspires others into action. Action is what counselors need to increase accessibility and effectiveness of counseling programs.

How Do Counselors Build Program Capacity?

Increasing program capacity and reach is yet another factor to strategically think of when designing, implementing, and analyzing a counseling program. Utilizing FranklinCovey's

"4 Essential Roles of Leadership" model (FranklinCovey, n.d.) can be a game changer. It is known that the world is constantly evolving, as are the issues that our students face each day. As such, counselors are facing varied situations and issues each day that they serve students, staff, and parents in the counseling role. The vast changes in our society throttled by technology, generational changes, and access to various information bytes greatly impacts the mental health of students and the work that counselors do. With such propensity for swift changes, counselors who access a leadership framework can lead their programs with strategic influence and success. The 4 Essential Roles model leans on four distinct roles that leaders play that are highly predictive of success. Covey calls them essential because leaders consciously lead themselves and their teams in alignment with these roles, and then they lay the foundation for effective leadership.

The Four Essential Roles of Leadership are:

1 *Inspire Trust*: Be the credible leader others choose to follow – one with both character and competence.
2 *Create Vision*: Clearly define where the counseling program is going and how the program is going to get there.
3 *Execute Strategy*: Consistently achieve results with and through others using disciplined processes.
4 *Coach Potential*: Unleash the ability of each person on the team (campus) to improve performance, solve problems, and grow careers.

As counselors lean into inspiring trust, credibility is developed when counselors have both character and competence. This is when counselors shape a culture of high trust. When high trust with stakeholders is established, comprehensive programming goals and initiatives are the most accessible by students. This is always the goal. That is why this leadership role for counseling is critical to develop, be mindful of, and most of all valued. Trust is the foundational glue through which all other aspects of the program are achieved.

The second leadership role is creating vision. When counselors align the counselor program vision to the campus and district goals, then program alignment for desired outcomes will have the greatest potential. Every counselor and leader who supports counselors must have a vision, because leadership, by definition, requires change. Effective leaders in counseling create a shared vision and strategy and communicate it at all levels. This is imperative to program success. Communicating the goals, the plans, the success with appropriate audiences ensures that trust and credibility are maintained and that the vision is still the focus and relevant.

The third leadership role is executing strategy. This role is necessary to implement the counseling program. Once the *year-at-a-glance* program has been created and communicated to all stakeholders, the next step is implementing the aligned initiatives. This is the actionable step. During this phase, monitoring quality programming, seeking feedback, making necessary changes, and strategizing optimal outcomes are all relevant and integral aspects of this leadership role for counselors. Counselors are the managers of the comprehensive program for the campus and should be seen as such in how they lead each aspect. Execution is perhaps the role that counselors will lean into for most of the school year as this is the actionable stage of the programming for students, staff, and families.

The fourth role is coaching potential. This is a role that counselors and counselor leaders should be most mindful of as it is the role that builds capacity for the campus program and for the counseling profession. Most counselors are challenged by having large caseloads of students. Although ASCA (2019c) recommends a 250-to-1 ratio of students to school counselors, the national average is actually 424-to-1 for the 2019–2020 school year (ASCA, 2022a) So, this leadership role is important for counselors to embrace for two reasons. The first reason is that counselors can offer more individualized programming if they have recruited programming help from other campus educators with whom they work. Teachers, librarians, coaches, teacher assistants, parent volunteers, community volunteers can all become programming partners to ensure that more students can benefit from the social, emotional, and academic lessons, assemblies, meetings, and so forth that need to be offered every year.

Building an army for the counseling program to work alongside the professional school counselor is just one way that counselors can increase their capacity. So coaching potential in others to assist with the program goals and initiatives has positive strategic potential. The second reason this role is critical is that counselors can see the potential in other educators that have the skills and the heart to become counselors. When counselors recruit and encourage their peers to consider the counseling profession as a future career, real change can occur. As the mental health and academic needs of our students increase, counselors will be in high demand. Recruiting those with natural talent and disposition to join our profession and advocate for our students is a must in today's educational climate. This is how counselors unleash the ability of different key staff members on their campus to improve performance and increase programming access.

How Do We Measure Success?

Successful programming is the thread of any program. The counseling program is always in draft form – evolving over time. After every program initiative, a school counselor and/or school counselor leader should assess the activity or support. With large caseloads across our nation, school counselors need to be mindful of their time, resources, and efforts to be the most effective. A question that is instrumental to reflect upon is this: How are students different because of the school counseling program? Using data and stakeholder feedback answers this question with limited bias.

Seek evidence of impact. How should counselors do this? According to resources provided in the state of Missouri for professional school counselors, they lead counselors to ask three questions that help provide evidence of the impact of school counseling programs on student outcomes. The first question asked is: To what extent is the school counseling program in place and being implemented? The second question asked is: Is the program being managed and conducted with fully certified and capable school counseling personnel? The third question asked is: Is there a plan or system in place to use relevant student data to determine program impact on student outcomes? Conducting this analysis is critical to achieving the four aspects of quality programming: building a foundation, management of the counseling program, delivery of the services, and accountability of student outcomes and campus performance. Quality programming, highly skilled counselors, and measured programming are the keys to equitable comprehensive counseling programs at any level.

Mental and Behavioral Health Considerations

What is the school counselor's role in planning, implementing, and evaluating the comprehensive counseling program that supports the mental and behavioral health needs of all students? According to ASCA's 2020 article titled, *The School Counselor and Student Mental Health* (ASCA, 2020), the school counselor leads this work at the campus and district level. They are the professional staff members who are designing and enhancing the program to meet the social and emotional needs of students. This includes educating the staff, parents, and even the students on mental wellness, appropriate mental health supports, and even supporting each other on the campus so that all students feel safe, seen, and heard. A school counselor creates such a program over time by staying current with wellness trends and best practices, collaborating and connecting to local resources for student referrals, as well as providing professional development on a regular basis for all staff so they are empowered to also provide a safe educational environment for students. In this same ASCA article, the following bulleted statements are critical for school counselors to act on throughout the school year.

- Adhere to appropriate guidelines regarding confidentiality, the distinction between public and private information and consultation.
- Help identify and address students' mental health issues while working within the:
  - ASCA Ethical Standards for School Counselors (2022b)
  - ASCA Professional Standards & Competencies for School Counselors (2019b)
  - National, state and local legislation, which guides school counselors' informed decision-making and standardizes professional practice to protect both the student and school counselor.
- Seek to continually update their professional knowledge regarding the students' social/emotional needs, including best practices in universal screening for mental health risk.
- Advocate for ethical use of valid and reliable universal screening instruments with concerns for cultural sensitivity and bias if state legislation or school board policy requires universal screening programs for mental health risk factors.

(ASCA, 2020)

Oftentimes, counselors may be the only available resource for a student to access mental health support. For this very reason, a school counselor must maintain current training and seek research-based practices through regular professional development. A school counselor has unique education and professional skills to provide short-term trauma, grief, or crisis support to students in times of need. It is imperative for counselors to seek relevant referrals for students for long-term care and support. Therefore, connecting and collaborating with area professionals who are licensed to provide therapy and treatment is part of the leadership role of a professional counselor. This program aspect ties back to establishing trust as well as executing strategy that was previously mentioned in leadership development related to the work of a school counselor. The student trusting your support and skills and then helping them to access appropriate resources is a program aspect that should be developed and refined over time so that capacity is built for equitable access for students.

Ethical Considerations

How do professional school counselors effectively and accurately promote the comprehensive school counseling program? And more importantly, why should the program be promoted? The counseling program has evolved over the last 120 years or so. In the early 1900s, the counseling program was primarily provided to students to offer testing, student planning, and vocational guidance (TEA, 2018: 4). Fast forward 100 plus years and the counseling competencies now include a prescribed professional identity, a model to provide guidance curriculum, responsive services, as well as individual planning for all students. The evolution of the program is significant. Even when comparing the program in 2023 to the program in the early 2000s, one realizes that 20 years ago, the focus was on conservatism, academic guidance, use of student data, and advocacy. Many stakeholders, including parents, school leaders, and teachers experienced the program of the 2000s as a student and not the program that we have evolved to today. For this very reason, it is important that school counselors lead the program regarding high ethical standards along with a strong advocacy presence for program education. Counselors can achieve this positive promotion of programming to stakeholders in a successful fashion when adhering and staying mindful of the bulleted statements above. The ASCA Ethical Standards for School Counselors (ASCA, 2022) outlines the following for the management of comprehensive and data-driven school counseling programs:

A.3 Comprehensive Data-Informed Program

School counselors:

b Collaborate with administration, teachers, staff and stakeholders for equitable school improvement goals.
c Use data-collection tools adhering to standards of confidentiality as expressed in A.2.
d Review and use school and student data to assess and address needs, including but not limited to data on strengths and disparities that may exist related to gender, race, ethnicity, socioeconomic status, disability and/or other relevant classifications.
e Deliver research-based interventions to help close achievement, attainment, information, attendance, discipline, resource and opportunity gaps.
f Collect and analyze participation, ASCA Mindsets & Behaviors and outcome data to determine the progress and effectiveness of the school counseling program.
g Share data outcomes with stakeholders.

Cultural Complexities

Is there a way for school counselors to attend to diversity? As referenced in *Developing and Managing Your School Counselor Program*, the answer is *yes*. Authors Norman Gysbers and Patricia Henderson (2012) share the following:

> The demographics of the school community and, perhaps more important, the demographics of the student population as a whole set the standard for appropriate representation in the guidance and counseling program improvement process and for assessing the appropriateness of current guidance and counseling program participation. The makeup of the steering committee, advisory committee, and work groups that are leading, providing input, and analyzing the program data should reflect the diversity in the community and the school. Not only should the community representatives reflect the ethnic makeup of the community, but they should as much as possible reflect the various family configurations, lifestyles, economic levels, and educational levels.
>
> (2012: 126–127)

The authors go on to state that we need more diverse multicultural practices to respond and support the students with a sensitivity and appropriateness that nurtures all students, including those who are underserved as well as overserved. Leadership voice of the school counselor helps to ensure that equitable practices and programming are accessible by all. The school counselor has the most strategic position to see the needs of the campus as well as access to data to monitor trends that may speak to inequities. It is for this very reason that the counselor leans on all four of the leadership roles. The counselor should build trust, create a vision of an equally accessible counseling program, execute the strategic initiatives to support the needs of students, and coach the potential in others through professional development and program advocacy. *The 4 Essential Roles of Leadership* (FranklinCovey, n.d.) will enable the counselor to lead the campus through the program development that is rich in culture, community, and ethnicity for inclusivity of all.

Strategic Considerations

Two trends are likely to continue in this profession of school counseling. The first trend is that students will continue to have complex needs with their social, emotional, and academic development. More than ever, mental health issues are a concern for parents, students, and educators. The Centers for Disease Control and Prevention (2022) released a study on the mental health status of youth during the pandemic of 2019. More than one-third of high school participants in the study reported experiencing poor mental health during the pandemic including these experiences during the past year: 44 percent reported feeling sad or hopeless; 55 percent experienced emotional or psychological abuse by a parent or other adult in the home; and 11 percent experienced physical abuse by a parent of other adult in the home (CDC, 2022). The need for competent mental health interventions is more critical than ever, and school counselors are trained to assess mental health needs and to collaborate with partners to provide the services that will impact student success.

Thus, the second trend is that the comprehensive counseling program will need to continue to evolve to meet the complex needs of students. When students have social and emotional support, then academic learning and gains can be achieved. Professional school counselors are the resources that students need at every grade level. And our legislators and school leaders are continuing to support the work that professional school counselors can provide to students and families, but school counselors cannot manage this work on their own. School counselors should be building programs with a capacity mindset, a mindset that begins with a foundational program that continues to grow and expand with resources, initiatives, and supports. School counselors should seek partnerships with local mental health authorities, state agencies, community-based licensed professionals, counselor interns, institutions of higher education, and so forth. These partnerships should be nurtured and developed to add value and services to the school so that the counselor is able to build a program and system that has capacity and reach. Reach to meet the individual needs of more students than they alone can provide. Reach for specialized support and services that are beyond the certification and skills of the professional school counselor. Systems and structures to support such needs and increase the varied services that students may require is a focus each year for the school counselor to assess and analyze based upon data (surveys, student data, and trends). Building a program that is data driven and based upon standards that promotes and enhances the learning process for all students is the vision of a comprehensive counseling program and is the role of the professional school counselor at every campus level.

Conclusion

As school counseling continues to evolve to support the needs of students, it is important to embrace the role of leadership at the campus and district level. More students have equitable opportunities of access and reach when counselors build comprehensive school counseling programs. School counselors play a critical role in ensuring schools provide a safe, caring environment and that students have the necessary mindsets and behaviors to advance academic achievement outcomes. School counselors should strive to work collaboratively with stakeholders to ensure equity, access, and academic success of all students (ASCA, 2019a).

References

American School Counselor Association (ASCA) (2017) *The School Counselor and School Counseling Programs*, Alexandria, VA: Author.
ASCA (2019a) *ASCA National Model: A Framework for School Counseling Programs* (4th edn), Alexandria, VA: Author.
ASCA (2019b) *ASCA School Counselor Professional Standards & Competencies*, Alexandria, VA: Author.
ASCA (2019c) National Student to School Counselor Ratio 1986–2019. Online. Available HTTP: <https://www.schoolcounselor.org/getmedia/>.
ASCA (2020) *The School Counselor and Student Mental Health*. Online. Available HTTP: <https://www.schoolcounselor.org/Standards-Positions/Position-Statements/ASCA-Position-Statements/The-School-Counselor-and-Student-Mental-Health>
ASCA (2022a) "School counselor roles & ratios". Online. Available HTTP: <https://www.schoolcounselor.org/About-School-Counseling/School-Counselor-Roles-Ratios>
ASCA (2022b) *ASCA Ethical Standards for School Counselors*. Online. Available HTTP: <https://www.schoolcounselor.org/getmedia/f041cbd0-7004-47a5-ba01-3a5d657c6743/Ethical-Standards.pdf>
Centers for Disease Control and Prevention (CDC) (2022) "New CDC data illuminate youth mental health threats during the COVID-19 pandemic". Online. Available HTTP: <https://www.cdc.gov/media/releases/2022/p0331-youth-mental-health-covid-19.html>
FranklinCovey (n.d.) "The 4 essential roles of leadership". Online. Available HTTP: <https://www.franklincovey.com/solutions/4essentialroles/>
Gysbers, N.C. and Henderson, P. (2012) "A comprehensive school guidance and counseling program: getting organized to get there from where you are", in *Developing & Managing Your School Guidance & Counseling Program* (5th edn), Alexandria, VA: American Counseling Association, pp. 43; 126–127.
Sinek, S. (2009) *Start with Why: How Great Leaders Inspire Everyone to Take Action*, New York: Penguin.
Texas Education Agency (TEA) (2018) *The Texas Model for Comprehensive School Counseling Programs*, Austin, TX: Author.

15 Mental Health Considerations for District and School Level Crisis Prevention, Intervention, and Postvention Plans

Benny Malone

> **Leadership Quote**
>
> The inevitability of crisis is a given. However, how we intentionally hold our own humanity in what can be a protocol-driven process is what separates trauma-informed, healing-centered leadership from business as usual.
>
> MHTTC School Mental Health Crisis Leadership Lessons

> **Aspirational Statements**
>
> - Crisis response has a way of feeling reactionary, even when there is adequate planning on the front end.
> - Traditionally, crisis planning is a process by which the likelihood of an event is assessed, considering location, circumstance, and context. From that point, a set of protocols based on best practice may be developed.
> - The role of leadership within this process is to prioritize, communicate, and provide direction. What is often not considered in the process is how we are to be as leaders (e.g., relational leadership); who we involve in our thinking (e.g., inclusive leadership); and in what ways our plans will mitigate/increase risk, increase/decrease safety, and also potentially traumatize/heal those we serve (e.g., complexity thinking).

Introduction and Background

A comprehensive crisis intervention plan should contain three distinctive elements: prevention measures, intervention measures, and postvention measures. The literature regarding school crisis planning varies in how school districts label and describe local crisis intervention plans. The National Education Association publishes the *NEA's School Crisis Guide*, which uses a quadrant format for its four components – Prevent, Prepare, Respond, and Recover (NEA, n.d.). Yet, as a subtitle to the online document, the program is described as what to do before, during, and after any school or community crisis. Terms including comprehensive school crisis intervention plan and comprehensive school safety plan are used interchangeably across the literature and are used in that manner in this chapter.

206 Benny Malone

The content of this chapter is based in part on my experience in a large Texas suburban school district as the director of the district's guidance and counseling program, elementary school counselor, and teacher of students with an emotional disability. Throughout my professional career, I have had broad experience in advocacy, professional organization leadership, school counselor training both locally and through state-wide conferences, and parent education programming. I also have a personal as well as a professional interest in mental health issues of children and adolescents and am a trained volunteer educator for the National Alliance for Mental Illness (NAMI).

Evidence of Need for School Crisis Planning

My first year as the director of a large suburban school district counseling department was in 1999. I came to the director's job with 25 years' experience in counseling, social work, and special education teaching, all relating to children and adolescents experiencing social, emotional, and/or learning difficulties. That first year as director was a turning point in my career. The Columbine School Shooting had recently occurred on April 20, 1999, four short months before I began my new leadership role as director. School year 1999–2000 began with the school district leadership, my counseling department colleagues, and other related services departments embarking on the joint charge to sharpen our focus on crisis intervention planning.

Everyone was horrified, dismayed, and saddened at the terrible display of violence perpetrated by two students and unleashed on unsuspecting classmates and teachers. Following Columbine, we reviewed old crisis plans and updated them. Administrators received training and provided training to campus staff on crisis intervention. We established a Superintendent's Student Leadership Conference and asked students to tell us about the problems in our schools that were less visible to staff than to students. New policies, ongoing staff training, and student participation were key elements in our post-Columbine crisis planning. We felt rather good about our plan until September 11, 2001, when New York City's Twin Towers were attacked and destroyed by a foreign terrorist group. Safety planning became a top concern in every facet of society, while hypervigilance was embedded as a core thought and behavior pattern in millions of American families.

Joint Impact on Families and Schools

Table 15.1 charts the evidence of stressors that families, and therefore schools, have encountered in the past 20 years, 2001–2020. Note the steady trending upward in the five categories of crisis events listed in the table. Every state has experienced its measure of crises since 2001. Rural, urban, and suburban schools and communities have been impacted. Families have had good cause to worry about the health and safety of their children.

Table 15.1 Large Scale Disasters and Crisis Events with Potential Impact on U.S. Schools 2001 to 2020

5-Year Interval	Natural Disasters*	School Shootings+	Terrorism and Threats^	U.S. Involvement in Wars=	Public Health Epidemics#
2016–2020	28	393	33	9	3
2011–2015	13	147	29	11	1
2006–2010	6	198	17	5	1
2001–2005	8	148	13	3	0

Source: * Wikipedia (n.d.a); + NCES (n.d.); ^ Wikipedia (n.d.b); = Kelly (2020); # CFR (n.d.)

If families are facing major stressors, such as a natural disaster, risk of violence at school, fear of being threatened (whether globally or personally), parents deployed for extended assignments in war zones, or a serious health crisis in a parent or child, schools will face them too. In 1999, the shooting at Columbine High School scared us with its one event and caused schools everywhere to engage in new crisis planning. That number has jumped to an astounding 393 school shootings in the most recent 5-year period, 2016–2020, a shocking average of six to seven shootings each month for 5 years! In fact, the categories of stressful events families have faced all climbed upward except U.S. Involvement in Wars, which decreased from 11 to 9 during the 2016–2020 interval. All five of the categories also have the potential to cause major financial strain on families when community-wide catastrophes spike unemployment, foreclosures, and homelessness as we have seen most recently with the COVID-19 pandemic.

The big picture of stressors that impact families become major concerns for schools. Each natural disaster, shooting, bullying, deployment, or serious family illness reveals the face of an individual student to teachers and classmates. Floods, hurricanes, tornadoes, and wildfires have literally resulted in families and children losing everything – housing, possessions, means of transportation, employment, pets, even loved ones. Looking behind the school shooting data reveals that a shooting may occur because of situations such as disputes among two or more students, suicide–murder pacts and suicide attempts, bullying gone too far, dating-related conflicts, anger toward staff over grades or disciplinary action, or illegal student activity involving drugs or contraband (NCES, n.d.).

Perhaps global terrorism is more of an adult worry, but the student version of being targeted and threatened is bullying. Deployment of military forces from a small-town military installation may result in an entire classroom of students who miss, worry about, and grow up without a parent. If one classmate's parent does not return home safe and sound, the anxiety level of many students will likely increase. Finally, we now universally recognize the devastation of an unknown and unchecked public health crisis. In-depth planning by school districts for public health crises that could close schools for an extended period of time was not a high priority issue before the COVID pandemic. Our schools are now beginning to rise out of COVID's educational disaster, but what a learning curve we've endured! In addition, many schools lacked the student health leadership offered by a professional nurse on campus. Data collected from the 2015–2016 school year revealed that only 52 percent of schools had a full-time school nurse, despite the American Academy of Pediatrics' recommendation in that same year that schools have at least one full-time registered nurse available for meeting students' health needs (NCES, 2020). It is discouraging that 4 years later in 2020, an ABC investigative news report revealed that 25 percent of schools nationwide still have no school nurse on staff (ABC, 2020).

Leadership Program Values

Understanding Local School District Values

The values I held as the director of guidance and counseling programs were aligned with those I witnessed in leaders across my school district. Working as collaborative teams evolved into a natural effort when creating, developing, implementing, or evaluating a program, whether the task was the responsibility of an elementary school grade level team, a central office curriculum council, or the IT department planning committee. My school district's *in situ* values are listed below.

- Adhere to a whole child educational philosophy with programs designed to foster academic, physical, social, behavioral, and emotional development for every student.
- Follow a practice of teaming across educational disciplines when developing policy guidelines and procedures.
- Seek feedback from students, parents, and community members when developing broad scope programs such as a district-wide comprehensive crisis plan.
- Ensure administrative commitment to complete and consistent implementation of the district-wide comprehensive counseling program based on best practices.

School Counselor Leadership in Practice

My state's mandated guide, *The Texas Model for Comprehensive School Counseling Programs*, 5th edition (TEA, 2018), and the American School Counselor Association's (ASCA) guide, *The ASCA National Model: A Framework for School Counseling Programs*, 4th edition (2019b), identify school counselors as leaders in a district's efforts to develop a comprehensive prevention, intervention, and postvention crisis plan, precisely because school counselors must first develop a comprehensive counseling program for their individual campuses. The school counseling program is a big part of a crisis and safety plan. Its development comes first and is designed to address the needs of all students, taking into account the campus demographics and best practices for service delivery and program content. Both the ASCA and Texas models include program delivery components to guide counselors in developing and implementing a comprehensive counseling program for all students.

The guidance and counseling services provided to students, whether in large, small, or individual settings, establish the foundation for responding to all three components of a comprehensive crisis plan – prevention, intervention, and postvention. These three components are appropriate steps for the counselor in delivering services to one student or to the entire student body. The ASCA National Model (2019b) divides its framework in four parts: Define, Manage, Deliver, and Assess. The *Texas Model* includes four delivery components based on specific services that align with student needs: Guidance Curriculum, Responsive Services, Individual Planning, and System Support. Each model is available online as listed in the references:

- *ASCA Executive Summary – Outline of Conceptual Model and Four Components* (2019a)
- *Texas Model PDF format – Conceptual Model and Four Service Delivery Components* (TEA, 2018b)

Leadership and Best Practices

The term *Best Practices* identifies professional standards for counselor training and preparation as well as specific components of a comprehensive counseling program. Such a program needs to fit the overall campus demographic characteristics, as well as address the academic, social, behavioral, and emotional needs of all students.

School counselors must hold a master's degree in counseling or a related field and be licensed or certified according to each state's professional standards board. Counselors also seek periodic update training, attend professional conferences, and participate in professional organizations. School counselors are trained to adapt and implement a program that addresses the needs of all students in their individual schools.

Texas Model, Codified in Statute

Texas has been a leader in advancing best practices in school counseling as an essential program for supporting student success in elementary and secondary schools. The first *Texas Model* was introduced by the Texas Education Agency (TEA) in 1991, and over the past 30 years, has been updated, strengthened, and implemented across Texas school districts. The biggest boost to comprehensive guidance and counseling in Texas schools came in 2001 when the *Texas Model* was passed and codified in the Texas Education Code (TEC) by the state legislature (Texas Constitution and Statutes, n.d.: 33.003–33.007). In later legislative sessions, additional laws were passed that broadened school counselor responsibilities in areas important to strengthening preventive crisis measures.

- TEC Chapter 37 requires disciplinary alternative education programs and counseling for students with behavioral needs including offenses involving drugs or alcohol.
- TEC §11.252 requires a campus to provide suicide prevention, conflict resolution, and violence prevention programs and have policies related to sexual abuse and maltreatment of students.

The model was updated two more times at the recommendation of the Texas Education Agency in order to address the evolving needs of Texas students and include new legal requirements of the Texas Education Code. The current and 5th edition was published in 2018 and is the most comprehensive edition of the model. A large body of research, program evaluation, and school counselor input backs the *Texas Model*. A major counselor professional organization, the Texas Counseling Association, provided strong leadership in creating this latest edition. To purchase a copy of the *Texas Model*, 5th edition, contact the Texas Counseling Association at www.txca.org or 800-580-8144.

School Counselor Leadership as Advocates for Campus Programs

It was an amazing time to serve as the director of guidance and counseling in 2001 when the *Texas Model* actually became state law in Texas. Counselors in my large suburban school district became strong advocates for implementing the new law patterned after our *Texas Model*. It was a time for educating school administrators, teachers, and parents about the value-added curriculum designed specifically to support the social, behavioral, and emotional development of students. Some states, including Texas, do not mandate the hiring of school counselors as essential staff. However, in my state, *The Texas Model for Comprehensive School Counseling Programs* (2018) itself is mandated. When this situation exists in a state, as it does in Texas, school counselors become stronger advocates for the program on their own campuses, precisely because the model is the law, and the law is the model. The barriers many counselors had faced, especially being assigned time consuming non-counseling duties, began to fall. School counselor leadership skills are honed through advocating for their students to have a best practices program implemented in a complete and consistent manner.

A positive relationship with administrators and teachers enhances a counselor's opportunity and success in achieving full implementation of the counseling program. Counselors help teachers and principals understand the counselor's role as unique in purpose and responsibilities. Counselors share wisdom and knowledge with principals about social, emotional, and psychological needs of children and adolescents and alert them to potentially harmful trends affecting youth in the local community and society-at-large. School counselors also share suggestions and collaborate with teachers who are concerned about individual students, assist them in working with a student's parents, and identify additional resources to help the student, family, and teacher.

Often the counselor's first advocacy task is to help principals and other school staff understand the comprehensive counseling program and its value to the whole child concept of education. While counselors are instrumental in helping students achieve a positive school experience through academic success, their role should not include non-counseling duties that take away from their time and ability to implement all components of the counseling program. Planning for crisis prevention, intervention, and postvention, whether for large school crises and disasters or an individual student's social, emotional, or behavioral crisis, requires counselor involvement in a leadership capacity to ensure a safe school environment.

Crisis Plan Prevention Measures

In addition to developing and implementing a comprehensive school counseling program, first and foremost, my district involved counselors in other prevention roles at the campus and district levels. The prevention measures described below include examples of counselor leadership in cross-disciplinary teaming, staff training, networking with community organizations, parent involvement, and implementation of programs to support positive school climate and work environments across the district.

Related Services Collaboration

A crisis prevention approach in my district meant that leaders of the related services departments – counselors, psychologists, diagnosticians, and nurses came together to make sure we coordinated with each other on topics that impacted all of us. With the district leadership's blessings, we initiated regular monthly meetings and called ourselves the CPDN committee. We wrote uniform procedures for ADHD best practices, responded jointly to student and faculty deaths, and regularly reviewed our procedures to ensure they were properly aligned with regulations required by HIPAA. We established lines of communication, shared common staff training opportunities, and collaborated on seeking district support for new policies, procedures, or programs to address emerging social and emotional needs of students. The outcome of this unity in our approach strengthened our understanding of the broader needs district-wide. The counseling department in our district had the largest number of staff compared to other professionals that were part of the CPDN committee. Additionally, counselors worked in every school building in the district and had strong relationships with both campus administrators and teachers. School counselors were often the professional sought out first by the other related staff when called in to evaluate a student who was at risk.

Contracted Social Workers for Home Support

According to Miriam Nisenbaum, the executive director of the Texas chapter of the National Association of Social Workers, there are only around 700 school social workers in the state because Texas doesn't require schools to have them (Houston Public Media, 2018). However, collaboration with our county's Youth Services Program provided my school district with 20 trained social workers who were part of the overall district crisis plan. Their role in prevention services came through school counselor referrals when it was apparent that both the student who was at risk and his family needed social services that a school could not directly provide.

Social workers offered transportation to therapy appointments when a family had no means of transportation. In family crises such as a fire, flood, or homelessness, social workers provided food, clothing, and a place for the family to live until the family became more stable. The social workers' responses served to help a student return to school more quickly because emergency services were made available to the whole family. This also helped the student return to school with a sense of normalcy in place. Professional, practical support from social workers outside the limited resources of a school district shortens a crisis, at least from a student's perspective. In my district, our Youth Services Specialists (YSS) were employees of the county but under contract with the school district and assigned to the guidance and counseling department.

As the director of the guidance and counseling program, I supervised the YSS at the central office level and assigned them to individual schools. The campus counselor was the liaison for YSS services needed by students on that particular campus. Another model for providing social workers to schools is Communities in Schools (CIS) which is active in 25 states and the District of Columbia. This organization is an American non-profit that works within public and charter schools to help at-risk students to stay in school and perform well. Access this link for more information about CIS: https://www.communitiesinschools.org.

Parent Involvement Programs

Encouraging parent involvement is an important area led by school counselors which supports a school's crisis prevention efforts. Counselors offer parents free workshops and speakers on current social/emotional topics that concern parents, provide parenting classes that focus on developmental stages of childhood and strategies for improving parent–child communication, and provide information on post-secondary education topics including financial aid, admission examinations, and application procedures.

Parents not only find that counselor presentations are helpful learning experiences, but they also allow the school counselor to be seen as a specialist in the social, emotional, and academic issues that concern parents. If a need arises for a parent to seek help for a child's adjustment at school or a parent has worries about the child's motivation or behavior at home or school, they will know who the school counselor is and will have an understanding of the help counselors provide professionally and in confidence. A positive relationship with the school counselor leads to trust and a willingness to heed a recommendation for appropriate help outside the school. Such parents in turn are supportive of the school counseling program and can be the advocate another parent needs to seek help for their troubled child, another step toward good prevention measures for avoiding school crises.

Staff Wellness Program

At times a school district employee may experience personal issues that cause added stress and worry that follow a person to work. This situation may occur in any type of business or employment setting. In my district, the counseling department set up a free short-term employee assistance program to help our teachers and staff problem-solve personal or family situations that were troubling the employee. School counselors who were licensed to provide private counseling in addition to being certified school counselors volunteered to meet with employees requesting assistance from what we called our Staff Wellness Program.

The participating counselors were given a small stipend for their additional professional time. Appointments were scheduled after school hours and were held in the central office Guidance and Counseling department. The appointments were confidential and not part of any employee's performance evaluation. The wellness counselor helped with defining and understanding the employee's concerns, provided community referrals, and encouraged the employee to follow through in seeking outside help.

The Staff Wellness Program also provided access after school hours to high school athletic facilities for personal exercise opportunities. Campus staff programs such as exercise walking groups and healthy eating programs were instituted and led by campus faculty members. One multi-talented school counselor taught an exceedingly popular salsa dancing class after school on his campus. The Staff Wellness Program was a very inexpensive district program that supported employee health and morale. It added to the overall positive school climate that is necessary to sustain helpful prevention measures in a crisis plan.

Crisis Plan Intervention Measures

The counselor's role and involvement during an active crisis may differ based on whether it is a situation impacting a single student or many students. The priority for intervention always must be based on what is needed first by those most severely impacted.

Individual Personal Crisis Intervention

The counselor may be the first responder in individual crisis situations. Counselors must ask themselves the following question before intervening in personal crisis situations. *"Where and how are my unique counselor training and skills needed most?"* The following four examples are representative of situations a counselor may encounter any day on the job.

- Speak calmly with and help de-escalate a student who is in a highly emotional state.
- Walk with a teacher to the safety of a private office after the teacher's emotional breakdown in the classroom to help the teacher recover from and process the personal crisis that just occurred.
- Notify the principal for backup and ensure the safety of nearby students and staff while trying to speak to an irate parent who is screaming at a student or school staff member.
- Meet with a distraught parent sharing the news of a child's death, serious car accident involving a family member, or incident of domestic violence resulting in a police response to the home.

From my experience when encountering situations like these, I intuitively remembered three mantras I learned from my own mentors.

1 Seek first to understand.
2 Listen more. Talk less.
3 Do no harm.

School counselors must always think on their feet. In highly charged emotional situations, you cannot assume you have an immediate solution to the crisis a student, family member, or teacher is telling about or showing you. If you are lucky and listen and observe very well, your client may just tell you what he or she needs, feels, and fears in the moment. Understanding these priority concerns of the client will speed up your intervention decisions and steps.

A shorter time living through an initial traumatic event may help reduce the long-term impact of trauma experienced as a result of the individual's personal crisis.

When a student begins to exhibit significant changes in behavior or motivation at school, the counselor is often contacted by the teacher or parent to discuss their concerns about the changes. School counselors naturally take a broad look when a student's grades drop suddenly, problems in attendance or tardiness come into the picture, non-participation or sleeping in class begin to occur, or a student's behavior towards adults and classmates dramatically changes. If an at-risk committee only addresses topics like failure to pay attention in class, not completing homework, lack of parent involvement, or even *laziness* or a *bad attitude* toward school, the counselor should seek more information about the student. There are multiple situations that may display a set of descriptors like these. They may include:

- Family changes caused by death, illness, divorce, parent loss of employment, or other significant family situation may impact a student's school performance.
- A student may be the victim of physical or cyber bullying that is unknown to the school or parents.
- A student may be experiencing early symptoms of a mental disorder such as depression, bipolar disorder, or First Episode Psychosis.
- The student may be the victim of physical, sexual, or emotional abuse, or severe neglect.
- The student may have an undiagnosed physical illness.
- The student may be abusing substances.
- The student may have an undiagnosed severe learning disability.

Small counseling group participation is often very therapeutic for students experiencing major family changes. They benefit from learning that they are not alone and receiving support from their peers. The skills used by the counselor should include a mix of hands-on activities and cognitive processing to help the students with their confusing and painful feelings. Strategies such as role playing, art, active games, group writing, and expressive movement through music help a child or teen learn ways to self-calm in times of stress. In the other situations listed, a counselor's intervention may include making a report of suspected abuse to Children's Protective Services; scheduling an individual counseling session with the student; scheduling a phone or office conference with parents; or consulting with the teacher or diagnostician about a possible referral for a special education evaluation.

Unexpected Large Crisis Intervention

If an unexpected crisis such as a shooting, explosion on campus, or violence involving a student crowd occurs, school counselors will most likely respond as part of a team. If the crisis event occurs on one or many campuses, the principal will most likely be the team leader in each individual setting. Communication lines established in advance are a priority. The school counselor's assignment may be to assist classroom teachers in establishing a calm atmosphere with students in a classroom by providing age-appropriate situational information; giving reassurance and guidance about safety measures for students in the classroom; and helping students call parents on their personal cell phones. If a classroom is locked down for safety and there are injured students or adults, counselors should provide first aid, offer comfort, and ensure that the appropriate team leader is notified about the injuries.

Each school plan for intervening in an active crisis will vary based on the size of the district and the individual campus. Other team assignments of a school counselor may include being the liaison with community resources, communication contact for students' families, or providing responsive services in a triage area. This last example was a role many school and community counselors played when the Houston Astrodome became an evacuation center for 27,000 families who fled from the devastation of Hurricane Katrina. Counselors volunteered their counseling skills listening, comforting, encouraging, and sharing of themselves with families who had experienced horrific trauma.

Natural Disasters Intervention

Crisis intervention measures taken as a result of a natural disaster hitting a community typically involve a larger number of students and families needing recovery services. The major difference between a sudden shooting, explosion, or violent outburst, and a national disaster is that with the latter, some forewarning may be given. In situations where forewarning combined with an opportunity for community-wide preparation exists, primarily postvention measures may be needed from the school counselor and the campus as a whole. Immediate needs for intervention are often met through government agencies and private organizations that provide disaster relief services. However, disasters such as tornadoes and earthquakes give little warning in advance of the event. If those kinds of natural disasters are likely to occur in a particular geographic area, municipal governments likely have major emergency plans and even special departments that coordinate the initial emergency response. As an important part of the community, school districts should have similar plans in place in order to coordinate with local programs.

My school district was significantly involved in providing counseling services to many students and families who relocated to our area after Hurricane Katrina. Some of our schools experienced a huge jump in enrollment in just a few days after families settled in shelters, apartments, or homes of friends and family members living in the school district. The complete story of this large crisis intervention and postvention experience in my school district is included in an earlier book, also edited by Judy Nelson and Lisa Wines, entitled *Responding to Critical Cases in School Counseling*. Judy Nelson and I co-authored the chapter about the Hurricane Katrina–Houston suburban school district connection (Nelson and Wines, 2021).

In the crisis situation involving Hurricane Katrina, the school district and surrounding community became the major resource for meeting the needs of displaced families and students. A natural disaster may happen to someone else, and you are the provider of services. In other instances, the disaster happens to you and others provide resources and services to the families and students you know and care about. If a campus or school district is on the helping side of this continuum, you can be sure that a school counselor is serving others in their time of need.

Maslow's Hierarchy of Human Needs

When a natural disaster or major crisis hits a community or an individual student crisis interferes with his or her ability to learn and be successful, faculty and staff need to consider Maslow's Hierarchy of Human Needs. Physiological needs are universal and ground the lowest level of Maslow's hierarchy pyramid. Physiological needs include air, food, water, sleep, and shelter, and are fundamental to human survival. Physiological needs are naturally the most important needs for the person (student) who is deprived of them. They must be met first for the individual to survive and thrive.

Maslow theorized that safety is the next most important human need. Safety needs include physical safety, emotional security, financial certainty, and safety of possessions. When safety needs are not met, the student(s) likely will stay hyper-focused, anxious, and continually worried about safety in the surrounding environment. This need is vital to a student who has experienced a significant threat or crisis regarding personal safety. To be successful in school, all students must know they are in a safe environment surrounded by adults who will provide physical and emotional security (Mcleod, 2023).

School systems have never been required to be the entity who provides all of Maslow's lower-level needs to children and adolescents. However, schools must be able to recognize when these needs are not met and link community resources to those students who are homeless, do not have enough food to eat, or may be victims of abuse. Maslow's "lower-level need" does not mean less important. It means first and foremost. It is critical that schools are aware of every child who comes to school hungry or has no place to sleep at night or is being abused. The school must take steps to ensure his or her special needs are met quickly.

Below is a list of four simple questions that form a basic assessment of student needs following an event like those in Table 15.1. The questions should be asked, regardless of whether the crisis impacted one student or many.

1 Is the student hungry or lacking sleep?
2 Does the student have a home to go to when the school day is over?
3 Is the student afraid to go home?
4 Is my school a safe place for students right now?

The school counselor plays a critical role in ensuring that these basic questions are asked when an at-risk assessment is conducted, again whether it is concern for a single student, a subgroup identified from school demographic data, or the whole school. Because of a counselor's special training and perspective gained from having a professional focus on social, behavioral, and emotional needs of students, he or she is likely to be the first to ask these questions. If an at-risk committee assessing any student showing significant behavioral and motivation changes at school does not ask these four questions, the committee may never discover that a student's fundamental needs are unmet.

Crisis Plan Postvention Measures

The narrow definition of *postvention* makes this topic unique in the trio of important measures that make up a campus comprehensive crisis plan. The term originally gained acceptance as a specific therapeutic intervention for individuals who were family members or had a close relationship with a person who died by suicide. The theoretical concept of postvention is based on the work of psychologist Edwin Shneidman. Shneidman is known as the father of contemporary suicidology and founded the American Association of Suicidology (AAS). The AAS promotes research, public awareness programs, public education, and training for professionals and volunteers. In addition, AAS serves as a national clearinghouse for information on suicide. This website is an excellent resource for school counselors seeking to learn more about the risk factors for suicide and postvention strategies. In many studies and articles on suicide, postvention is treated as both prevention and intervention to stop contagious suicidality. Further information on AAS is available at this link: https://suicidology.org/about-aas/.

The purpose and definition of postvention completes the package for prevention and intervention measures to include in crisis planning. Its inclusion in a comprehensive crisis plan offers support for family members and closely related peers of the individual who died by suicide. Both the prevention and intervention measures target individuals experiencing "suicidal bereavement." In professional literature, this phrase is used to differentiate this particular kind of psychological pain as a special type of grieving felt by those who continue living after a loved one or close friend dies by suicide.

Documented Suicide Risk Factors

An analysis of the top 20 risk factors demonstrating an association with suicide were reported in a mega study, entitled *The Interpersonal Theory of Suicide*. Six of the 20 factors are likely familiar to the counselors who pay close attention to students who are considered at risk on their campuses. The table below explains how a counselor's knowledge of the needs of troubled students can enhance his or her timely ability to provide postvention services. When a counselor knows the risk factors AND knows the student, intervention and support are more likely to help a student move past the desire for suicide in the moment.

Table 15.2 Counselor Knowledge of Risk Factors for Suicide in Students

Risk Factor	At Risk Student
Mental Disorder	Student is receiving special education services as a student with an emotional disability (i.e. mental disorder in medical terminology).
Previous Suicide Attempt	Student has past history of trauma events or earlier suicide attempts.
Family History of Suicide	Awareness of certain past and current family history of death by suicide in a close family member or friend.
Exposure to Suicide	Awareness of lethal and/or non-lethal incidents of suicide within the school-wide community.
Genetic Dysfunction in Serotonin	Presence of a diagnosis of a mental disorder often indicates a genetic component to dysfunction of the neurotransmitter serotonin.
Impulsivity	Awareness and possible previous counseling intervention with students who have impulsivity and behavioral control issues.

Source: Van Orden et al. (2010); Sadkowski et al. (2013). Created by B. Malone, 2022.

Survivors of Suicide and Those with Other Risks

The risk factor Family History of Suicide calls attention to those left behind following a lethal suicide. Those who survive the death by suicide of someone they love are at risk of becoming victims themselves. What this means for school crisis planning is that the follow-up after a student or teacher suicide then becomes part of both prevention and intervention measures in general as well as being included in postvention measures.

Additionally, other students with any of the six risk factors for suicide should also receive postvention contact by the school counselor if a suicide has occurred in the school community. A suicide in the campus community adds to the pre-existing risk factors that may already be present with a student. A school community suicide risk factor for that student is significant even if he or she and the person who died did not share a close relationship. All school counselors should be knowledgeable of these significant research findings. Students and staff with any of the six risk factors for suicide are your clients during the postvention period.

To be clear, school counselors are not trained to conduct the specialized therapeutic postvention support groups and individual long-term postvention therapy. However, you are the front-line advocate for ensuring that a student who needs this intervention gets it in the appropriate setting outside of school. It means that you will periodically check in with this student and seek to form a positive relationship as the student's touch point on campus anytime stressful or destructive thoughts seem overwhelming. See them *before* the next crisis happens. Your ability to offer safety, support, and hope in the moment for your student is built on their trust in you not to judge, belittle, or ignore the needs they bring to you. In addition to intervention at this moment, you are providing prevention of a future potential decision to end one's life. Research reveals that there are two parts to an action to take one's life – suicidal desire and capability to act. They do not automatically appear together. The one thing that should be your priority response when this student comes to you is to reduce the capability to act. Your strong counseling skills are what you need to bring calm, momentary hope, and a promise of support that will help your student take one step at a time, one day at a time.

Mental and Behavioral Health Considerations

Childhood Trauma

School counselors also possess an awareness and understanding of the effects of traumatic events on students. Childhood trauma results when a child witnesses or personally experiences an event that threatens his or her life or bodily integrity. Table 15.1 events that may happen only one time but are extremely destructive with a high threat or danger level may result in severe trauma to a child, adolescent, or adult. Likewise, ongoing stress, such as living in a dangerous neighborhood, being the victim of bullying at school, or constantly feeling fearful of abuse at home, can also be traumatic. Adults may not experience or process a trauma the same as children or adolescents. Staff training to help teachers and administrators become more knowledgeable of how a family, school, or community disaster or crisis may trigger a traumatic response in students is clearly a topic that school counselors should be providing. Many new behaviors that a student exhibits in the aftermath of a trauma-causing event will likely be observable in a classroom, on the playground, or in the cafeteria, or other sites of interaction with others. These behaviors include:

- anger issues
- attention problems
- changes in appetite
- development of new fears
- increased thoughts about death or safety
- irritability
- loss of interest in normal activities
- problems sleeping
- sadness
- school refusal
- symptoms like headaches and stomachaches.

(Morin, 2022)

- Traumatic events, especially when experienced multiple times, may lead to Post Traumatic Stress Disorder (PTSD) in children and teens, a psychological disorder which may continue into adulthood. A study published in 2015 showed that, "the more adverse childhood experiences a person has, the higher their risk of health and wellness problems later in life" (Morin, 2022).

This body of research is known as Adverse Childhood Experiences (ACES). Childhood abuse is recognized as a repetitive form of trauma for a student. The Veterans Administration, which has researched and developed programs for addressing PTSD in military families, reported that 3–15 percent of girls and 1–6 percent of boys develop PTSD following traumatic events. The trauma-causing impact of different kinds of child abuse is a serious concern for school counselors. The VA reported the following statistics below charted in Table 15.3. These statistics are based on 3 million reports of child abuse made annually to Children's Protective Services (CPS). The reports involved 5.5 million children. Proof of abuse was confirmed in 30 percent of the reported cases (PTSD, n.d.).

Table 15.3 Percentage of Valid Child Abuse Reports by Type of Abuse

Categories of Abuse Reported	% of Abuse Reports Validated by CPS
Neglect	65%
Physical Abuse	18%
Sexual Abuse	10%
Psychological Abuse (mental, emotional)	7%

Note: Report by Veterans Administration. Created by B. Malone, 2022.

One of the challenges in supporting students who are victims of child abuse is that school personnel do not know it is happening unless physical injuries are apparent or an outcry is made by the student. If a disaster or school shooting or public health threat occurs, it is much more likely that the school will learn about this student's experience.

Another difference in assessing abuse in a student's life as a trauma is that it happens to an individual rather than to a classroom, grade level, or entire student body. Suspicions that a student may be showing signs of a personal traumatic event should trigger an immediate referral to the school counselor. Teachers do not need to know the nature of a serious situation which a student has been through in the past or is currently experiencing in order to make the referral. They need to be observant of changes in a student's behavior and give a heads up to the school counselor. The school counselor is trained in how to respond to social and emotional distress in students and knows of available supportive resources within the school system and the community at large.

My colleague Judy Nelson and I created the *At-Risk Protocol for Early Warning Signs in Students*. It is a one-page checklist that guides a school counselor in collecting objective data such as a student's grades, attendance, and discipline as well as identifying appropriate subjective data. Subjective data includes input from teachers, parents, or peers who have expressed concerns about changes in a student's personality or behavior. A copy of the *At-Risk Protocol* and instructions for its use may be found at the end of this chapter.

Ethical Considerations

The following ethical considerations from the *ASCA Ethical Standards for School Counselors* (2022) are relevant to school counselors responding to critical events including suicide, violence, abuse, and natural disasters.

> **A.5 Sustaining Healthy Relationships and Managing Boundaries**
>
> School counselors:
>
> a Collaborate with all relevant stakeholders, including students, school faculty/staff and parents/guardians, when students need assistance, including when early warning signs of student distress are identified.

b Provide a list of outside agencies and resources in their community, or the closest available, to students and parents/guardians when students need or request additional support. School counselors provide multiple referral options or the district-vetted list of referral options and are careful not to indicate an endorsement or preference for one individual or practice. School counselors encourage parents/guardians to research outside professionals' skills/experience to inform their personal decision regarding the best source of assistance for their student.

A.9. Serious and Foreseeable Harm to Self and Others

School counselors:

a Inform parents/guardians and school administration when a student poses a serious and foreseeable risk of harm to self or others. This notification is to be done after careful deliberation and consultation with appropriate professionals, such as other school counselors, the school nurse, school psychologist, school social worker, school resource officer or child protective services. Even if the danger appears relatively remote, parents/guardians must be notified. The consequence of the risk of not giving parents/guardians a chance to intervene on behalf of their child is too great.
b Recognize the level of suicide risk (e.g., low, medium, high) is difficult to accurately quantify. If required to use a risk assessment, it must be completed with the realization that it is an information-gathering tool and only one element in the risk-assessment process. When reporting risk-assessment results to parents/guardians, school counselors do not negate the risk of students' potential harm to self even if the assessment reveals a low risk, as students may minimize risk to avoid further scrutiny and/or parental/guardian notification. The purpose of reporting any risk-assessment results to parents/guardians is to underscore the need for parents/guardians to act, not to report a judgment of risk.
c Collaborate with school administration to ensure a student has proper supervision and support. If parents/guardians will not provide proper support, the school counselor takes necessary steps to underscore to parents/guardians the necessity to seek help and, at times, may include a report to child protective services.
d Provide culturally responsive mental health resources to parents/guardians.
e Report to administration and/or appropriate authorities (e.g., law enforcement) when a student discloses a perpetrated or a perceived threat to another person's physical or mental well-being. This threat may include but is not limited to verbal abuse, physical abuse, sexual abuse, dating violence, bullying or harassment. The school counselor follows applicable federal and state laws and school and district policy.

A.11. Bullying, Harassment, Discrimination, Bias and Hate Incidents

School counselors:

a Recognize that bullying, discrimination, bias and hate incidents rooted in race, gender, sexual orientation and ethnicity are violations of federal law and many state and local laws and district policies.
b Advocate for schoolwide policies, protocols and training for response to bullying, harassment and bias incidents centered in safety, belonging and justice.
c Advocate for accessible, effective tools for students or community to report incidents of bullying, hate or bias.
d Report all incidents of bullying, dating violence or harassment to the administration, recognizing these behaviors may fall under Title IX of the Education Amendments of 1972 or other federal and state laws as illegal and require administrator intervention.
e Recognize that bias incidents are not only potentially traumatizing for students but can lead to significant damage and disruption of the school environment. Facilitate and monitor schoolwide prevention of bullying, harassment, discrimination, hate and bias through active practices that support a positive school climate, culture and belonging.

A.12 Child Abuse

School counselors:

a Report to the proper authorities, as mandated by the state, all suspected cases of child abuse and neglect, recognizing that certainty is not required, only reasonable suspicion. School counselors are held to a higher standard regarding their absolute duty as a mandated reporter to report suspected child abuse and neglect.

Cultural Complexities

I live in one of the most diverse cities in the United States. My suburban school district had approximately 100,000 students attending 75 schools at the time of my retirement in 2008. Over 60 languages were spoken by our students. Many of the elementary schools had large enrollments of English Language Learners (ELL). School counselors had many responsibilities working with these students. Many of our counselors spoke more than one language. Then and now the school district ethnicity statistics of enrolled students is closely aligned with the state-wide ethnicity of Texas students. In 2018, Hispanic students accounted for the largest percentage of total enrollment in Texas public schools in 2019–2020 (52.8 percent), followed by White (27.0 percent), African American (12.6 percent), Asian (4.6 percent), and multiracial (2.5 percent) students. Professional training on working and learning in a multicultural environment was always a frequent topic for administrators, teachers, and students.

The Director of the district's ELL department came to the monthly counselor meetings for all elementary counselors and secondary coordinating counselors. It was an important time during which counselors shared what was happening at the campus level regarding barriers that hindered meeting student and family needs. The ELL director updated counselors on federal and state rules and laws as well as district procedures for enrolling new non-English speaking students, access to translators, and scheduled programs for families. Our district had a strong parent education program. The bilingual counselors taught parent classes on their campuses in the fall and spring semesters. It provided parents with an opportunity to be addressed in their own language, meet other parents who were in classes with their own children, and get to know the school counselor as the go-to person for offering help when they needed it.

One research study reported findings on the diversity–cultural competency content found in US state-required school crisis plans during the years 2009–2015. The study obtained data from 40 of the 50 states. The study set out to determine how many state-required school crisis model plans included content related to cultural sensitivity. Information from the review of the state plans was summarized under seven major coding categories. The results from reviewing 33 of the 40 state plans were described as including topics that were "related to human diversity and cultural sensitivity," but "the focus was peripheral." The content of the state's model plans most frequently reported addressed only three of the seven major categories. The content topics most frequently found in the state-required plans are listed below.

- assisting students with mental and physical disabilities;
- tapping into community resources representative of diverse cultural groups; and
- strengthening communication by addressing cross-cultural language and communication issues.

The seven broad coding categories offer guidance to help counselors identify important factors that should be addressed during the process of creating the crisis plan itself. The content included in the plan will show the path to the training needs of campus staff. Individual self-reflection, awareness of hidden biases, and the desire to better understand, appreciate, and respect others represents a personal journey. When cultural experiences, ethnicity, and ableness are different from one's own, and the effort to understand is neglected, a school climate will deteriorate for both staff and students. A focus on diversity issues will be needed to help school staff gain new understanding of cross-cultural differences that are found in our nation's schools. The seven major categories below may guide school counselors in helping a campus move towards a more culturally competent workplace and student environment.

1 Recognition of the importance of culture
2 Cultural composition of community profile
3 Cross-cultural language and communication issues
4 Cultural competence training
5 Information about cultures
6 Tapping into community resources representing diverse cultural groups
7 Evaluation of plan's cultural competence

The researchers concluded that coupling research with practical applications is needed to strengthen cultural competence of all school stakeholders participating in writing and implementing school crisis plans. Strengthening the cultural competence of school administrators, teachers, community first responders, and students, in the long run, will lead to improved support services for all students and families (Annandale et al., 2011).

The findings and recommendations of this study should cause school counselors as leaders to advocate for including cross-cultural intervention measures in every school crisis plan. Our country continues to evolve in strength with the richness of the unique diversity found in our communities and schools.

Strategic Considerations

Each district's crisis plan must represent its own demographics and student needs. The enrollment size of a district is often an indicator for whether or not certain provisions are included in its written crisis plan. The larger the district, the greater will be the number of individual focus points in a district's plan. Based on surveys that assess small, medium, and large school districts' crisis plans, it appears that small districts have less complexity built into their crisis plans. The percentage of met standards in medium and large districts is greater across the board when compared to small districts (CDC, 2016).

An example of this variation is extracted from the SHPPS, 2016 data and is listed in Table 15.4. It is important for district and school guidance and counseling leaders to note the lower compliance of smaller districts to these three significant areas for crisis planning. Similar variations by district size are consistent across the SHPPS, 2016 report. No district of any size that completed the survey met the 95 percent compliance standard for provision of post-crisis mental health services.

Table 15.4 Inclusion of Certain National Standards in School Crisis Plans for Students and Staff: Comparison by District Size

District Enrollment Size*	Provisions for Special Needs and Mental Health Services	Mental Health Services Provided Post-Crisis	District Funding for Staff Training in Crisis Preparedness
Small District Compliance	78%	75.8%	88.4%
Medium District Compliance	90.3%	88.0%	92.6%
Large District Compliance	90.7%	88.6%	97.4%

Note: Extracted from SHPPS (2016). Small District--≤4,999; Medium District--5,000–9,999; Large District--≥10,000. Created by B. Malone.

The data from the School Survey on Crime and Safety (SSOCS) (Diliberti et al., 2019) also supports the report from the SHPPS, with one difference. The Crime and Safety study looks at school size rather than school district size. SSOCS (2017–2018) asked an important two-part question to surveyed schools regarding whether or not schools had crisis/safety plans that were written and for which students were drilled on the use of emergency procedures. The survey revealed that across-the-board, small schools (300–499 students) had a smaller percentage of written plans and drilled procedures when compared to large schools (500–1000+). Across all 11 crisis and drill scenarios, the percentage of small schools' inclusion of the common scenarios and drill practices was less than the large schools' percentage. The 11 scenarios are:

1 Active Shooter
2 Natural Disasters

3 Hostages
4 Bomb Threats
5 Chemical, Biological, or Radiological Threats or Incidents
6 Suicide Threat or Incident
7 Pandemic Disease
8 Post-Crisis Reunification of Students With Their Families
9 Evacuation Drill
10 Lockdown Drill
11 Shelter-in-Place Drill

The data in Table 15.4 highlight special concerns for small local educational entities, whether an individual school or district. These smaller districts and schools often have fewer community resources available and may have a smaller tax base. This reality likely accounts for the lower percentage of national standards being met in three important areas listed in Table 15.4 and the result from SSOCS reporting the lower percentage of small schools having comprehensive written crisis plans. However, district leaders in smaller districts and schools are undoubtedly as concerned about school and community disasters as are the leaders in larger districts. County-wide collaborative efforts in developing mobile and virtual resources that are paid for by foundation grants or governmental funding sources are one avenue for strengthening local plans in rural and isolated areas. One lesson learned from the COVID-19 pandemic is the huge benefit virtual technology can provide, especially in training for local school staff in crisis plan development and implementation.

A second issue that is significant for school districts as they expand the complexity of their crisis intervention plans is the increase in the rising number of children and adolescents living with mental illness and behavioral disorders. Below is a graph depicting the increase in youth who are symptomatic of mental health and behavioral disorders from 2009–2015. Paradoxically, children and teens are showing up in emergency rooms, and are not choosing psychiatric facilities which are proposed to evaluate mental, emotional, and behavioral distress and symptoms. In addition, many psychiatric hospitals will provide free emergency evaluations. It is likely that the stigma surrounding mental illness creates a barrier to choosing a psychiatric hospital over an ER that is not intended or perhaps even staffed to provide a comprehensive psychological evaluation for a patient (Meier, 2020).

The goal of initial treatment begins with hope—for the individual and the family. "I hope this will pass soon. I hope my child will be well soon. Something is not right." Schools must be equipped to help sustain this hope before *all students* will be enabled to learn and experience success in school. In the best of scenarios, recovery will follow on the heels of effective treatment. Recovery to most families means "return to normal." However, mental illness recovery often requires a lengthy journey outside of the hospital or outpatient programs. A return to school often is a student's first step towards "return to normal."

Schools and communities must seek answers to many questions soon because these recovering children and teens will be returning. The questions are important because these are all *our* children. We as adults long for and hope for them to have healthy, fulfilling lives, being loved and loving, responsible and respectful, confident and successful.

- Are school districts prepared for the post-treatment return of healthier but still vulnerable students?

- What does this mean for special education programs for students with an emotional disability?
- What does it mean for counselor to student ratios that exceed by hundreds the ASCA standard of one counselor to 250 students?
- What does it mean for the scarcity of school social workers in some states?
- What does it mean for university graduate programs that must train these mental health educational specialists?
- What can school counselors do to Stop the Stigma?

I have kept my questions in the realm of education. However, responding to the sad increase in mental illness in our youth is also a problem for government, medicine and research, private funding sources, religious groups, businesses small and large, law enforcement and emergency medical services providers, criminal justice systems, communities, neighbors, friends, and families. School counselors and others committed to improving school crisis planning are prepared to advocate for children and adolescents receiving best practice responses from the change makers in our country. School counselor leaders are valuable change makers for the futures of our youth.

Conclusion

The attention of the nation's school systems to the dramatic increase in the number and severity of events like those listed in Table 15.1 has undoubtedly resulted in school safety reaching a higher priority now than 20 years ago. School counselors are key personnel on campus to lead school staff towards greater understanding of the social, behavioral, and emotional needs of our children and adolescents. They are knowledgeable about childhood developmental stages, including the complexity of a maturing brain. We know that children and teens do not process events the same as adults, because the brain simply has not "grown up" to adult status yet. The brain is the last organ of the body to reach maturity, which occurs typically in a person's early to late twenties. It is challenging for all adults to be communicating with an adult-looking teenager and realize that the person before them seriously lacks judgment and/or refuses to see a problem that is very apparent, at least in the adult's mind. That makes *seek first to understand* a good rule to remember when students are experiencing a crisis.

This chapter has included data regarding the large increase in all kinds of crises that school counselors, teachers, principals, students, families, and communities have faced, especially in the past 5 years, 2016–2020. Another worrisome large increase we as a society are facing, is the number of children and adolescents now diagnosed with serious mental illness. The increase shows up dramatically in emergency departments of hospitals. Rather than going to a psychiatric treatment facility for an evaluation, emergency departments in medical hospitals have become the first avenue for treatment. This trend was identified in a research study looking at the number of children and adolescents going to emergency rooms for mental health and behavioral crises (Santillanes et al., 2020). The quotation that follows is from the study co-author, Michael Menchine, MD, associate professor of clinical emergency medicine and vice chair of the emergency department at the Keck School; University of Southern California Schaefer Center:

> Emergency departments are increasingly serving as a key place to initially treat children and adolescents experiencing mental health or behavioral crises. Unfortunately, we are seeing

more and more patients with the most serious crises – those who have to be admitted to the hospital – and these patients are staying longer and longer in the ED, ... But, more importantly, EDs are just not great therapeutic environments for people having these kinds of crises."

(Meier, 2020)

In 2013, I was doing research for a book I was writing on the impact of mental illness on families whose loved one is seriously mentally ill. In the book, I asked a rhetorical question about a headline from a 2012 study on survival rates of childhood leukemia. My question was, *"How long will it be before families of persons with severe mental illness can read a headline like the one below, which parents of children with leukemia are able to read?"*

Childhood Leukemia Survival Rates Improve Significantly

The 5-year survival rate for children with acute lymphoblastic leukemia (ALL) has greatly increased over time and is now about 90% overall.

(American Cancer Society, n.d.)

Almost 10 years later, I still ask the same question. However, it appears that the only thing significantly changing in mental health headlines is the even greater concern about the increase in child and adolescent mental illness.

References

ABC 13 (2020) Eyewitness News. "Dozens of Houston area campuses don't have a school nurse". Online. Available HTTP: <https://abc13.com/hisd-schools-without-nurses-covid-19-and-13-investigates-ted-oberg/6397460/>

American Cancer Society (n.d.) "Survival rates for childhood leukemias". Online. Available HTTP: <https://www.cancer.org/cancer/leukemia-in-children/detection-diagnosis-staging/survival-rates.html>

American School Counselor Association (ASCA) (2019a) *ASCA Executive Summary: Outline of Conceptual Model and Four Components*. Online. Available HTTP: <https://schoolcounselor.org/getmedia/bd376246-0b4f-413f-b3e0-1b9938f36e68/ANM-executive-summary-4th-ed.pdf>

ASCA (2019b) *The ASCA National Model: A Framework For School Counseling Programs* (4th edn), Alexandria, VA: Author.

ASCA (2022) *The ASCA Ethical Standards for School Counselors*, Alexandria, VA: Author.

Annandale, N.O., Heath, M., Kemple Reeves, A.E., and Dean, B. (2011) "Assessing cultural competency in school crisis plans", *Journal of School Violence*, 10(1): 16–33.

Centers for Disease Control and Prevention (CDC) (2016) "School Health Policies and Practices Study". Online. Available HTTP: <https://www.cdc.gov/healthyyouth/data/shpps/index.htm>

Council on Foreign Relations (CFR) (n.d.) "Major Epidemics of the Modern Era". Online. Available HTTP: <https://www.cfr.org/timeline/major-epidemics-modern-era>

Diliberti, M., Jackson, M., Correa, S., and Padget, Z. (2019) "Crime, violence, discipline, and safety in U.S. public schools: Findings from the school survey on crime and safety: 2017-18", National Center for Education Statistics. Online. Available HTTP: <https://eric.ed.gov/?id=ED596638>

Houston Public Media (2018) "Texas schools lack sufficient number of mental health professionals, experts say". Online. Available HTTP: <https://www.houstonpublicmedia.org/articles/news/2018/03/15/273686/texas-schools-lack-sufficient-number-of-mental-health-professionals-experts-say/>

Kelly, M. (2020) "American Involvement in Wars From Colonial Times to the Present". Online. Available HTTP: <https://thoughtco.com/american-involvement-wars-colonial-times-present-405976>

Mcleod, S. (2023) "Maslow's Hierarchy of Needs", Simply Psychology. Online. Available HTTP: <https://www.simplypsychology.org/maslow.html>

Meier, G. (2020) "Teens, young adults drive increase in mental health ER visits", HSC News, University of Southern California. Online. Available HTTP: <https://hscnews.usc.edu/teens-young-adults-drive-increase-in-mental-health-er-visits>

Morin, A. (2022) "Treating the Effects of Childhood Trauma", VeryWellMind. Online. Available HTTP: <https://www.verywellmind.com/what-are-the-effects-of-childhood-trauma-4147640>

National Center for Education Statistics (NCES) (n.d.) "Number of school shootings at public and private elementary and secondary schools, by type of situation associated with shooting: 2000-01 through 2018-19". Online. Available HTTP: <https://nces.ed.gov/programs/digest/d19/tables/dt19_228.13.asp>

NCES (2020) "School nurses in U.S. public schools". Online. Available HTTP: <https://nces.ed.gov/pubs2020/2020086.pdf>.

National Education Association (NEA) (n.d.) *NEA's School Crisis Guide*. Online. Available HTTP: <https://www.nea.org/resource-library/neas-school-crisis-guide>

Nelson, J. and Wines, L. (2021) *Responding to Critical Cases*, New York: Routledge.

National Center for PTSD (PTSD) (n.d.) "How Common is PTSD in Children and Teens?". Online. Available HTTP: <https://www.ptsd.va.gov/understand/common/common_children_teens.asp>

Sadkowski, M., Dennis, B., Clayden, R., ElSheikh, W., Rangarajan, S., DeJesus, J., and Samaan, Z. (2013) "The Role of the serotonergic system in suicidal behavior", *Neuropsychiatric Disease and Treatment*, 9: 1699–1716.

Santillanes, G., Axeen, S., Lam, C., and Menchine, M. (2020) "National trends in mental health-related emergency department visits by children and adults, 2009–2015", *The American Journal of Emergency Medicine*, 38: 2536–2544.

School Health Policies and Practices Study (SHPPS, 2006, 2012, 2016) Online. Available HTTP: <https://www.cdc.gov/mmwr/volumes/67/wr/mm6730a1.htm#T2_down>.

Shneidman, E. (n.d.). "About the American Association of Suicidology". Online. Available HTTP: <https://suicidology.org/about-aas/>

Texas Education Agency (TEA) (2018a) *The Texas Model for Comprehensive School Counseling Programs* (5th edn), Austin, TX: Author.

TEA (2018b) *Texas Model PDF Format: Conceptual Model and Four Service Delivery Components*. Online. Available HTTP: <https://tea.texas.gov/sites/default/files/Pub_2018_Texas-Model_5th-Edition.pdf>

Texas Constitution and Statutes (n.d.) "Education Code". Online. Available HTTP: <https://statutes.capitol.texas.gov/Docs/ED/htm/ED.33.htm>

Van Orden, K., Witte, T., Cukrowicz, K., Braithwaite, S., Selby, E., and Joiner, T. (2010) "The interpersonal theory of suicide", *Psychological Review*, 117(2): 575–600.

Wikipedia Contributors (n.d.a) "List of natural disasters in the United States". Online. Available HTTP: <https://en.wikipedia.org/wiki/List_of_natural_disasters_in_the_United_States>.

Wikipedia Contributors (n.d.b) "Terrorism in the United States". Online. Available HTTP: <https://en.wikipedia.org/wiki/Terrorism_in_the_United_States#2010%E2%80%9319>

APPENDIX A

At-Risk Protocol for Early Warning Signs in Students

Current research strongly supports early identification of serious mental illness as critical to lessening the long-term effect of these potentially life-threatening brain disorders. It is just as important to identify early signs of serious mental illness as it is to recognize and act on other serious health conditions like heart disease and cancer.

The *At-Risk Protocol for Early Warning Signs in Students* has been developed to help school counselors gather the needed information to assist students and their families in finding appropriate professional assessment, intervention, and treatment. The *At-Risk Protocol* is similar to formats of other protocols used by school counselors when assessing other serious conditions experienced by a student such as suspected child abuse or suicidal ideation.

Observations or reports of major changes in a student's academic performance, interpersonal relationships, personal appearance, and personality may be indicative of early signs of mental illness, which often first appear in adolescence and young adulthood. Research strongly supports early identification and intervention as the best course for a good outcome for the individual who experiences psychosis or other major signs of serious mental illness, including the possibility of complete recovery. This protocol is a tool for the school counselor who is aware that a student has one or more of the Vulnerability Factors, listed below, *and* is experiencing sudden and/or major changes in his or her behavior, social relationships, or academic performance. The research-based Vulnerability Factors that are associated with the possible onset of serious mental illness are:

- Family history of mental illness;
- History of Adverse Childhood Experiences (ACE) such as trauma, abuse, severe neglect, incarcerated parent, and/or family violence;
- Diagnosis of another brain disorder such as Autism Spectrum Disorder, ADHD, ODD, school phobia/anxiety.

General Instructions

Because school counselors have contact with students on a daily basis, for 10 months of the year, they are in a key position to become aware of concerns regarding a student's social and emotional development. They are also the key school professionals to be sought out by a student's parent, teacher, or friend when they become concerned about changes in a student's behavior or relationships at school, home, or in the community.

A particular student may show up on a school counselor's concern list in many ways – prior contact with the student in an individual or group counseling setting; participation in campus at-risk meetings; or a consultation with a parent or teacher. This protocol should be utilized when the school counselor has enough "soft" data from sources who know the student and personal observations to merit a decision to look more specifically into the possibility of early signs of serious mental illness and/or First Episode Psychosis. Other explanations for sudden or major changes in a student's behavior, social relationships, or academic performance should always be thoroughly explored prior to considering the possibility of the onset of symptoms of mental illness.

This *At-Risk Protocol* is research-based and was developed to help facilitate early intervention and treatment for youth whose very age and developmental stage make them more vulnerable to the onset of serious mental illness.

Limits of this Protocol

This *At-Risk Protocol* generates sensitive information and should be treated as you would any other "counselor notes" that are kept in confidential counselor files and are for the purpose of serving the best interest of the student. Parents have the right to all counselor notes, so be reminded that you may eventually provide this information to them, either because they request it or because you deem it necessary and ethical to alert them to the information. This *At-Risk Protocol* is not intended to be distributed to teachers or administrators but may be used in consultation with a supervising counselor, a school psychologist, or any other school personnel who has a legitimate interest in the information.

I I Observations or Concerns Reported by: Provide name, contact information, and date of contact.

   a Parent:

   b Teacher/School Personnel:

   c Friend of Student/Peer:

   d School Counselor

II Data/Student Records—Note **major changes** in the following areas:

	YES	NO	UNK
Grades...			
Discipline Referrals...			
Acting-out behavior...			
Withdrawn behavior...			
Self-care, personal hygiene...			
Hyper-sensitivity to sights, sounds, or sensations...			
Responds to noises as voices...			
New trouble in concentration...			
Clarity of thought and understanding of common situations			
Affective responses or expression of feelings...			
Attitude/behavior regarding trust toward others...			
Openness with peers or friends...			

III Anecdotal Data

_____

_____

IV Student Report of Possible Symptoms – Due to the frightening nature of psychotic symptoms they are rarely reported by the person experiencing them. However, if the student describes what he or <u>she is feeling or experiencing as paranoia, hallucinations, or delusions, give encouragement that he or she is in a safe place and that you will provide help.</u>

16 Data Collection and Analysis Supporting Systemic Approaches to Mental Health

Ernest Cox

Leadership Quote

Data provides validity to the myriad tasks that school counselors perform everyday.

Judy A. Nelson

Aspirational Statements

- Compelling empirical evidence demonstrates the positive impact a comprehensive school counseling program (CSCP) has on the overall academic achievement of students, their attendance and behavior as well as the overall school climate.
- Many times, administrators direct school counselors to perform other duties as assigned.
- When school counselors use data, they build awareness of the strengths in the school counseling programs while also pinpointing the areas requiring focus and growth.
- Data can evaluate and demonstrate the effectiveness of the school counseling program in measurable terms – we can determine how students are different as a result of the program.
- Data helps the school counselor show the impact the counseling programs have on student achievement, attendance, and behavior.
- Data helps evaluate, reflect, and reform future school counseling actions and allocation of time in direct school counseling services.
- Data is grounded in fact, and is measurable.
- Data supports the counseling program transformation shifting counseling services from historic to developmental (TEA, 2018).

Table 16.1 Historic and Developmental Data

Historic	Developmental
Reactive	Planned on Priorities
Crisis Counseling Only	Preventative and Crisis Counseling
Individual Guidance and Counseling	Consistent Service to All Students
Inconsistent Services to Students	Programming
Service Emphasis	Developmental and Age-Appropriate Curriculum
Information Dissemination	Goal Oriented Information Interpretation
Clerical/Administrative Task Oriented	Evaluative and Reflective
Unstructured Program	Results Driven and Shaped
Immeasurable	Data Snapshots and Measurable
Counselors Only	All Stakeholders

Created by E. Cox, 2022.

Introduction and Background

School counselors' identities, roles, and responsibilities have evolved. Spanning from the early 1900s to the late 1950s, school counselors focused on vocational guidance, mental hygiene, directive counseling, and progressive reform (Gysbers and Henderson, 2001; Savickas, 2009).

Professional school counselors' identities, roles, and responsibilities continue to expand in response to the needs of a diverse society. School counselors respond to constituents' needs while adhering to legislative mandates and providing equitable counseling services. Lapan, Gysbers, and Sun (1997) found districts, schools, and professional school counselors who fully implement a comprehensive school counseling program positively impact students. Students who attended schools with a comprehensive school counseling program, reported they feel safer, believed their education is more relevant, and were more satisfied with education quality (Lapan et al., 2001).

The Texas Model for Comprehensive School Counseling Programs (TEA, 2018) comprises four service delivery components: guidance curriculum, system support, individual planning, and responsive services. School counseling program evaluators and education practitioners are concerned with counseling service delivery and effectiveness (Murray et al., 1987).

The school counselor plans, designs, implements, and evaluates the comprehensive school counseling program, promoting and enhancing learning for all students. In Texas the school counselor provides counseling services through four counseling service delivery components:

1 Guidance Curriculum
2 Individual Planning
3 Responsive Services
4 System Support.

These service delivery components focus on the needs of all students through their academic, career, personal, and social development. Lapan et al. (1997) found more fully implemented guidance programs had positive effects on high school students' self-reporting of grades, preparations for the future, career and college resources, and perceptions of school climate. Similarly, Whiston and Quinby (2009) reported students who participated in the school counseling program interventions showed an academic improvement when compared to peers who did not receive a counseling intervention. Lapan et al. (2001) found students who attended a middle school implementing a comprehensive school counseling program reported feeling safer, had fewer interpersonal problems, and earned higher grades. Other researchers have made similar conclusions and additionally reported comprehensive school counseling programs diminished aggressive behaviors, increased prosocial behaviors, decreased classroom disturbances, enabled teachers to provide quality instruction, and yielded positive school-wide academic and behavioral outcomes (Grossman et al., 1997; Lapan et al., 1997). ASCA (2012) reported a correlation between the comprehensive school counseling program and student academic performance. Students benefited from counseling services within the school setting (Lapan et al., 1997; Sink and Stroh, 2003). Hence students benefited when school counselors implemented comprehensive school counseling programs.

A frequent struggle over the question "What do school counselors do?" has plagued the school counseling profession throughout its evolution (Beale, 2004). Historically, non-counseling duties have overwhelmed school counselors. School counselors struggled with professional identity and role clarification as indicated in the historical development of professional roles, responsibilities, and duties. Over time, and with heightened attention to the school counseling profession, school counselors and school administrators must consider what role school counselors are playing in today's schools. Do they embrace the idea of seeing their school counselor as a school change agent or advocate?

ASCA National Model: A Framework for School Counseling Programs

The comprehensive developmental school counseling program model movement increased in national recognition and prominence when the ASCA incorporated elements from the leading Comprehensive Developmental School Counseling models to develop the American School Counselor Association (2005) National Model for school counseling programs (Martin and Carey, 2012). *The ASCA National Model: A Framework for School Counseling Programs* (ASCA, 2012) "is comprehensive in scope, preventive in design, and developmental in nature." The ASCA National Model Framework (2012) outlines the components of a comprehensive school counseling program. School counselors design and deliver a comprehensive school counseling program to all students. School counselors promote student achievement. The ASCA National Model (2012) brings school counselors together with one vision and one voice, to create unity and with a focus toward improving student achievement and supporting student development.

ASCA's National Model Framework (2012) for a comprehensive school counseling program consists of four components: foundation, management, delivery, and accountability. According to the ASCA National Model, school counselors create the comprehensive school counseling program. Through the foundation, the program must include a program focus, identify student competencies delivered, and create program agreements ensuring adherence to the foundational counseling components. The counseling program foundation serves as a framework for the counselor. Next, according to the ASCA model, school counselors must design, use data, assess the program, and create action plans through the management component. After the program is designed, the school counselor serves students through counseling service delivery components. The counselor develops, identifies, and delivers services through a variety of methods including individual planning, the counseling core curriculum, and responsive services. Lastly, school counselors demonstrate the effectiveness of the school counseling program in measurable terms through the accountability component (ASCA, 2012). School counselors use program and outcome data to demonstrate the impact the school counseling program has made on students. School counselors focus their skills, time, and energy on all students through direct and indirect services in accordance with the

ASCA National Model. School counselors spend 80 percent or more of their time in direct and indirect services to students (ASCA, 2012).

ASCA promotes the comprehensive school counseling program as an integral component of the school's academic mission (2012). The comprehensive school counseling program is data-driven and based on standards for academic, career, social, and emotional student development. The comprehensive school counseling program promotes learning for all students. The ASCA National Model (2012) ensures: a. equitable access to a rigorous education for all students; b. identified knowledge and skills all students will acquire as a result of the K–12 comprehensive school counseling program; c. counseling services are delivered to all students in a systematic fashion; d. data-driven decision making; and e. counseling programs are delivered and provided by a state-credentialed school counselor. School counseling programs are a collaborative effort between school counselors, families, and other educators. A comprehensive school counseling program promotes student achievement. The school counselor designs the counseling program to support and create a diverse learning environment for all students. Comprehensive school counseling programs ensure equitable access to opportunities and rigorous curriculum for all students to participate fully in the educational process (ASCA, 2012).

School counselors develop and deliver comprehensive school counseling programs supporting and promoting student development and achievement. The ASCA National Model emphasizes the importance of implementing a planned and systematic comprehensive school counseling program. Additionally, the program must involve all students thus enhancing the learning process. ASCA states the credentialed school counselor implements the comprehensive school counseling program and is supported by appropriate resources. The ASCA National Model brings school counselors together with one vision and one voice, which creates unity and focus toward improving student achievement and supporting student development.

The Texas Model for Comprehensive School Counseling Programs

Many state departments of education have revised their state school counseling models to reflect the ASCA National Model for school counseling programs. Only a few states have developed statewide evaluation systems to gather information about program effectiveness and promote effective local program evaluation (Martin and Carey, 2012). In 1990, the Texas Counseling Association guidance advisory committee defined the counseling program in Texas public schools and established goals (Texas Education Agency (TEA; 2018)). The Texas Model for Comprehensive School Counseling Programs promulgated a process for creating and tailoring a counseling program model to meet the needs of Texas public school students. The Texas Model provides standards to enhance school counselors' roles and improve guidance and counseling programs. The Texas Model a. meets the diverse needs of students in Texas; b. acts as a resource to identify program structures, goals, and expectations enhancing the counseling program; and c. provides a framework whereby the Texas school counselor will transform the campus and district school counseling program (TEA, 2018).

The Texas Model (2018) provides a framework to ensure all students have access and benefit from comprehensive, developmental school guidance and counseling services. This guide allows educators to develop, validate, or improve their school district's guidance program. Additionally, the guide enhances efforts to increase student achievement and success. Both the Texas Education Agency (TEA) and the Texas Counseling Association (TCA) recommends the Texas Model guide for use by Texas public schools to assist districts in complying with the TEC §33.005–33.007 (TEA, 2018).

According to the TEC §33.006–33.007, "school counselors shall work with school faculty, students, parents, and community to plan, implement, and evaluate a developmental guidance and counseling program" (TEA, 2018). National expectations, as evidenced by the ASCA National Model, mirror state expectations. Texas school counselors are required to design and deliver a systematic, data-driven comprehensive school counseling program promoting student achievement. Texas Education Code §33.005 promulgates that school counselors shall design and implement a school counseling program which includes services delivered through four counseling domains: a. guidance curriculum; b. system support; c. individual planning; and d. responsive services. According to the TEA (2018), comprehensive, developmental guidance and counseling programs are vital to the achievement of excellence in education for all students. The Texas Model is an integral part of each school's total educational program. The school counselor's primary focus is to facilitate instruction by removing impediments to student learning. It is developmental by design and includes sequential activities organized and implemented by certified school counselors with the support of teachers, administrators, students, and parents. Comprehensive school counseling programs organize resources to meet the priority needs of students through the four delivery system components aforementioned. Developmentally appropriate services, delivered through guidance curriculum and individual planning address student identified needs. The responsive services component meets a student's preventive, remedial, and crisis needs. Lastly, the system support component fulfills the counseling programmatic, management, and accountability needs.

A certified Texas school counselor manages, designs, and implements the Texas Model. Texas certified school counselors have codified roles and responsibilities (TEC, n.d.: §33.007). The TEA counselor job description, developed in cooperation with Texas Counseling Association and the Texas School Counselor Association, defines the school counselor's responsibilities (TEA, 2018). The Texas Evaluation Model for Professional School Counselors (TEMPSC-II) is used to evaluate Texas school counselors. Texas Education Code codifies the Texas Model and the school counselor roles and responsibilities.

Comprehensive School Counseling Program Commonalities and Variances

Comprehensive School Counseling standards according to the ASCA National Model (ASCA, 2012) and The Texas Model have commonalities and variances. The ASCA National Model standards reinforce The Texas Model's goal of ensuring school counseling program quality and effectiveness. The comprehensive school counseling program serves all students (TEA, 2018); the ASCA National Model shares this goal. Nichter et al. (2008) found Texas school counselors are implementing the essential services determined to be most important as identified by the ASCA National Standards, even when the counselors were not aware of those standards. This may be due to the fact the ASCA National Model was developed using tenets from the Texas Model, hence the commonality identified by Nichter et al. (2008). Another commonality is both the Texas Model and ASCA models use the four service delivery components, consisting of a. guidance curriculum; b. individual planning; c. responsive services; and d. system support. Furthermore, both models promote the importance of school counselors supporting student growth by meeting the student's developmental needs in a. academic; b. career; c. personal; and d. social domains. Both the Texas Model and the ASCA National Model are comprehensive in scope, preventive in design, and developmental in nature. Lastly, commonalities include a. advocacy for appropriate school counselor roles and responsibilities; b. the importance of school counselor professional identity; and c. a focus on programmatic management and the importance of planning, designing, organizing, managing, implementing, and evaluating the comprehensive school counseling program.

Roles and Responsibilities

Many times, administrators direct school counselors to perform other tasks. Often these administrators fail to understand the contribution school counselors can make to the school (House and Hayes, 2002). The school counselor's roles, responsibilities, and tasks vary from state to state, district to district, and even school to school (House and Hayes, 2002) thus creating a challenge to support, implement, and maintain a comprehensive school counseling program.

Today's school counselors are vital members of the education team. They help all students in the areas of academic achievement, and personal, social, and career development, ensuring today's students become the productive, well-adjusted adults of tomorrow (ASCA, 2012). Students benefited from the delivery of a comprehensive school counseling program in national tests of academic knowledge and on state assessments (Sink and Stroh, 2003) and were more academically successful as measured by grade point average (Lapan et al., 1997). Similarly, elementary and middle school students who participated in school counseling curriculum and group interventions focusing on cognitive, social, and self-management skills consistently showed significantly stronger math and reading scores on state tests (Brigman and Campbell, 2003). Moreover, participation in school counseling programs empowered middle school students' grades and fourth graders' academic achievement (St. Clair, 1989).

Students in dropout prevention programs exhibited prosocial behaviors and academic gains when receiving comprehensive school counseling program services delivered by school counselors who maintained appropriate roles. A dropout prevention program for middle school students combining academic tutoring and group counseling resulted in improvements in student academic achievement, behavior, and self-esteem (Edmondson & White, 1998). A school dropout assistance program found counseling services were one of the key elements of effective dropout prevention initiatives (Kaufman, Klein, & Frase, 1999). Guidance curriculum diminished physically aggressive behavior and increased a neutral and prosocial behavior (Grossman et al., 1997). Furthermore, guidance curriculum decreased aggressive behavior, showed considerable success in impacting behaviors and related feelings of safety (Wilson et al., 2003), decreased classroom disturbances (Lapan et al., 1997), and increased prosocial behaviors (Lapan et al., 2001).

The role and function of school counselors remain a consistent concern in the school counseling profession. Aligning school counseling activities with a comprehensive school counseling practice is a way to standardize the profession (Shea, 2013). The design of comprehensive school counseling programs includes educating all students. Comprehensive school counseling programs significantly improved student behavior, attitude, and knowledge in areas designed to educate students (Schlossberg et al., 2001). Although counselors may place responsibility on their school administrators for shaping their job descriptions (Amatea and Clark, 2005), the school counselor has a responsibility to educate stakeholders on their roles, expectations, and goals.

Table 16.2 Examples of Appropriate Activities for School Counselors (ASCA, 2012)

- Planning individual student academic programs
- Interpreting cognitive, aptitude and achievement tests
- Providing counseling to students who are tardy or absent
- Providing counseling to students who have disciplinary problems
- Providing counseling to students regarding appropriate school dress
- Collaborating with teachers to present school counseling core curriculum lessons
- Analyzing grade-point averages in relationship to achievement
- Interpreting student records
- Providing teachers with suggestions for effective classroom management
- Ensuring student records are maintained as required by state and federal regulations
- Helping the school principal identify and resolve student issues, needs and problems
- Providing individual and small-group counseling services to students
- Advocating for students at individual education plan meetings, student study teams and school attendance review boards
- Analyzing disaggregated data

Note: Adapted from Campbell and Dahir (1997).

Student to Counselor Ratios

According to the US Department of Education and ASCA, the student-to-school-counselor ratio for 2013–2014 distributions ranged widely. To achieve maximum program effectiveness, ASCA recommends a school counselor-to-student ratio of one counselor to every 250 students. Additionally, ASCA recommends school counselors spend 80 percent or more of their time in direct and indirect services to students. The Texas Education Agency, the Texas Counseling Association, the Texas Association of Secondary School Principals, and the Texas Elementary Principals and Supervisors Association have recommended a maximum ratio of one counselor to every 350 students. The TEA reports the number of counselors needed to staff the program is dependent on the students' and community's needs, the goals, and the design of the local program. The ratios should be sufficiently low to meet the identified, high priority needs of the students and the school community. Additionally, TEC (n.d.: §33.002(b)) states "a school district with 500 or more students enrolled in elementary school grades shall employ a school counselor certified under the rules of the State Board for Educator Certification for each elementary school in the district." Furthermore, TEC §33.002(b) states a school district "shall employ at least one school counselor for every 500 elementary school students in the district."

The number of students in a counselor's student load who have intensified needs for responsive services dictates lower ratios. It is clear the larger the school counselor's student load, the less individual attention students receive; the smaller the student-to-counselor ratio, the increased opportunity for direct counseling services, if the district or campus staff identifies high priority needs of students who require individual assistance.

Non-Counseling Duties

The literature review includes a description of school counselor roles and responsibilities. Additionally, school counselor ratios are evaluated. School counselor role ambiguity is a continual concern despite the development and advancement of comprehensive school counseling programs. The Texas Education Code systematically defines school counselor expectations, roles, and responsibilities. Regardless, often school administrators assign school counselors numerous clerical, administrative, and non-counseling duties. These duties interfere with the time required to complete job-specific responsibilities. The American School Counseling Association (2012) defines non-counseling duties as "any activity or duty not related to the development, implementation, or evaluation of the comprehensive school counseling program." Gysbers and Henderson (2006) reported guidance and counseling departments often provide support for regular educational programs as well as other programs such as testing, discipline, and management. They found non-counseling related activities consumed 30–40 percent of a school counselor's schedules, thus decreasing the amount of time allocated for the delivery of a comprehensive school counseling program (Gysbers and Henderson, 2006).

Administrators have historically assigned school counselors non-counseling duties. These duties include data entry, clerical record keeping, new student registration, and scheduling. Additionally, school counselors have historically been assigned the coordination or administration of cognitive, aptitude, and achievement tests, signing excuses for students who are tardy or absent, performing disciplinary actions, sending students out of dress code compliance home, teaching classes when teachers are absent, and computing grade-point averages (Campbell and Dahir, 1997). Similarly, Gysbers and Henderson (2006) found that school counselors are highly engaged and associated with test coordination, distribution, and planning; duties in which the school counselor should not be involved. Beale (2004) identified one factor contributing to difficulty in program implementation is the pressure to perform non-counseling duties.

School counselors and counselor educators must take a more proactive role both in preparing themselves to assume leadership roles in the school and in reshaping the role expectations of administrators (Amatea and Clark, 2005). School counseling experts emphasize the importance of implementing and organizing a comprehensive school counseling program rather than performing ancillary services. A greater awareness of a school counselor's responsibilities is required to define, communicate, and clarify the difference between counseling and non-counseling services. Gysbers reported appropriate duties associated with comprehensive school counseling programs include classroom guidance activities and structured group experiences for all students. Therefore, school counselors must advocate for their roles. Many researchers have promoted the importance for school counselors to solidify their identity, advocate for their role, and provide direct school counseling services to students (ASCA, 2022; Clark and Stone, 2000; House and Martin, 1998; Stone and Clark, 2001).

Table 16.3 Examples of Inappropriate Activities for School Counselors (ASCA, 2012)

- Coordinating paperwork and data entry of all new students
- Coordinating cognitive, aptitude, and achievement testing programs
- Signing excuses for students who are tardy or absent for reasons other than time spent with school counselor
- Performing disciplinary actions or assigning discipline consequences
- Teaching classes when teachers are absent
- Computing grade-point averages
- Maintaining student records
- Supervising classrooms or common areas (duty)
- Keeping clerical records
- Assisting with duties in the principal's office
- Providing therapy or long-term counseling in schools to address psychological disorders
- Coordinating school wide individual education plans, student study teams and school attendance review boards
- Serving as a data entry clerk

Note: Adapted from Campbell and Dahir (1997).

Inhibitive Behavioral Factors

Inhibitive behavioral factors reflect the school counseling program leaders' self-efficacy traits, learned behaviors, and learned experiences. Participants met consensus on one theme proving inhibitive in implementing the Texas Model. School counseling program leaders reported non-counseling duties were inhibitive.

Administrators have historically assigned school counselors non-counseling duties. These duties include data entry, clerical record keeping, new student registration, and scheduling. Similarly, Gysbers and Henderson (1997) found that school counselors are highly engaged and associated with test coordination, distribution, and planning; duties in which the school counselor should not be involved. Beale (2004) supported the pressure to perform non-counseling duties contributed to difficulty in program implementation.

Counselor Roles in Program Implementation

Cox (2018) found barriers/inhibitors to implementing the CSCP that included administrator mindsets (i.e., school counselors should serve as the testing coordinator, school counselors should head 504 coordination, etc.), antiquated beliefs of counselor responsibilities (i.e., school counselor should supervise lunch or after school duty, school counselors should perform clerical responsibilities, etc.), and the lack of understanding about what counselors' roles are in schools (i.e., school counselors should coordinate the school counseling program, school counselors should deliver guidance curriculum and direct counseling services, etc.). School counseling literature (Goodloe, 1990; Gysbers and Henderson, 2006) highlight that the reluctance to change is based on familiarity of a guidance service model and an unwillingness to listen to the benefits of a comprehensive school counseling program. The school counseling program resisters may fall into several categories. These include those who: a. do not understand the school counseling program concept; b. disagree with it; c. prefer a psychological or crisis approach; d. are skeptical to the validity of the program; and e. do not believe change is possible (Gysbers and Henderson, 2006).

Leadership Program Values and Standards

When it comes to transforming the comprehensive school counseling program, and the use of data, it is important to consider the following questions:

- Why use data?
- What is the purpose of collecting data?
- What do we need the data for?
- How do we plan on using it?
- What do you want to accomplish?
- What do you hope to see?

Before we can delve into these questions it is important to review the school counseling service delivery modalities, as stated in the Texas Model.

Guidance Curriculum/Classroom Instruction

The guidance curriculum is designed to systematically provide lessons to students that facilitate growth, development, and transferable skills in the areas of educational, career, personal, and social development. The need for students to become advanced critical thinkers, efficient problem solvers, and to demonstrate appropriate behavior and dispositions offers justification for a guidance curriculum. The guidance curriculum is taught based on domains, competency indicators, and developmental stages through differentiated learning activities in the classroom, with planned lessons for various-sized groups of students. Topics are specified within the state or national model as well as in mandates from state and federal legislation.

Responsive Services

The purpose of responsive services is to support students and offer services in their time of need. PSCs might react to needs or critical situations through prevention, remedial, or crisis responses. Prevention services are designed to ensure that all students are educated and prepared to respond to plausible situations prior to a circumstance occurring. Preventive measures help to reduce or eliminate the likeliness of a scenario happening or taking shape. Remediation services, in contrast, occur once a situation has taken place. The PSCs' actions could also have a reflective component that causes PSCs to change or refine processes that are relevant to the situation. Finally, during a crisis, a PSC is expected to intercede in scenarios involving imminent danger or critical need. A crisis has processes and procedures that are pertinent and requires immediate action, documentation, and confirmation of those actions made to administrators at campus and district levels.

Individual Student Planning

The purpose of individual planning is to assist students, with focused attention, toward their personal goals. Students need opportunities to monitor and understand their own educational, career, personal, and social development, while considering individual characteristics, academic implications, specialized circumstances/services, and cultural implications. In this component, it is important that a PSC has knowledge and ability to combine district and state requirements, with student preferences, through the use of realistic and attainable goal setting processes.

Schools can systematically use a variety of resources (staff, information, services, and activities) to assist students in developing and implementing personalized plans. Through the individual planning system, students can:

- set challenging educational, career, personal, and social goals that are based on self-knowledge and information such as results on assessments or interest inventories;
- know about school, the world of work, and their society;
- make plans for achieving short-, intermediate-, and long-term goals;
- communicate the significance of their culture and family values during this process;
- select future preferences, such as pursuing a trade, technical field, career, or college options;
- analyze how their strengths and weaknesses enhance or hinder the achievement of their goals;
- assess their current progress toward their goals;
- make decisions that reflect their plans.

System Support

System support is essential to the total school counseling program. System support consists of management activities that establish, maintain, and enhance the total school counseling program. System support can be categorized in two areas: 1. Program Management Activities; and 2. Data Analysis and Accountability Services. This delivery component reaches fewer students through direct services, however through this indirect services component, a PSC will plan, organize, implement, and manage their school counseling program in order to increase the efficacy of the direct services that are provided.

System support is the foundation of the school counseling program. Without system support, the other three direct service delivery components (guidance curriculum, responsive services, and individual planning) would be ineffective. Whereas guidance curriculum, responsive services, and individual planning serve students directly, system support includes program management and program data and accountability that indirectly benefit students. This pyramid for comprehensive school counseling services provides a visual encapsulation to the service delivery components aforementioned. There are several similar models which can be reviewed and/or adapted to support the school counselor/program leader communicating to the stakeholders they work with in their setting.

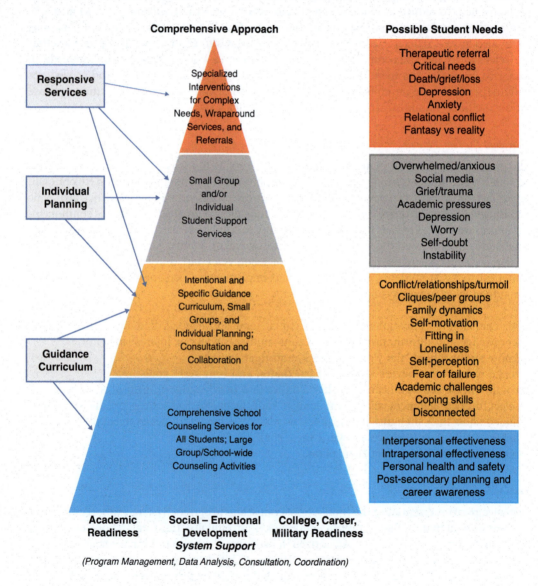

Figure 16.1 Pyramid for Comprehensive School Counseling Services. Created by E. Cox, 2022.

Leadership in Practice

When school counselors use data, they build awareness of the strengths in school counseling programs while also pinpointing the areas requiring focus and growth. With data, school counselors and school counselor leaders can evaluate and demonstrate the effectiveness of the school counseling program in measurable terms and can determine how students are different as a result of the program. Specifically, school counselors can show the impact of their programs on student achievement, attendance, and behavior, and analyze school counseling program assessments to guide future action and improve future results for all students. The story below shares an experience I had in my previous role as Director of Guidance and Counseling.

Where We Started

Historically, our school counselors provided responsive services, focusing on individual counseling and crisis counseling services on an as-needed basis. There was an uneven emphasis on services for individual students instead of focusing on the trends and needs of all students. School counselors were quasi administrators and were largely involved in administrative duties such as state assessment coordination, discipline, section 504, language proficiency coordination and, of course, other duties as assigned. The comprehensive school counseling program was nonexistent for most and unstructured for all. The department was full of advocates for students but lacked direction for the program and a way to measure and track effectiveness. The department lacked a program leader.

Program in Development

Over the past 7 years, our school counseling program has transformed its culture, beginning with the hiring of a director of School Counseling. Since the creation of that position, the district and program have taken active steps toward a program with focus, one that now provides equitable services for all students, delivered with intentionality. The school counseling program is planned, developed, implemented, analyzed, and evaluated on an ongoing basis. It is data driven, results oriented, involves all stakeholders (students, staff, and parents), and allows every student access to the services of school counselors. Over a 4-year period, the school counselors decreased non-counseling related activities from 45 percent to 11 percent and increased direct services to students.

Data and Evaluation

Reshaping the counseling program required several steps. The initial step was to evaluate the program and communicate with campus and district leadership. To determine the effectiveness of service delivery, we first focused on process data. Student outcome and perception data are imperative in a comprehensive program, but process data pinpoints what is being done, when it is happening and what needs to be changed. It provides evidence of where school counselors are allocating time within the four service components and non-school-counseling duties. Process data also describes the activities conducted and the number of students participating in an activity. The department developed a method for counselors to identify where time was being allocated and determine whether a disproportionate amount of time was being allocated to non-school-counseling duties.

Developing a Tool and Buy-in: Standardizing, Calibrating, Building Trust

Of the many data templates available, we sought to find a tool that was easy to use, tracked what we wanted and could be modified over time. Using an Excel spreadsheet, we created *The School Counselor: Counseling Program Tracking and Data Analysis Report*. It provided a method to help the school counselors and director develop, monitor, and organize the school counseling program. School counselors could use the tool to identify how time was being allocated. Based on process data (weekly, monthly, and annual) the counselor can initiate a plan of action to reallocate time to the service components requiring attention. If a counselor identifies that a disproportionate amount of time is being spent on non-school-counseling duties and/or indirect services, they may modify the data analysis template to more intentionally focus on the areas requiring change.

Before implementing the data tool, we made sure that all school counselors in our district understood the importance of using it. The process data tracking tool was (and continues to be) an "I've got your back" rather than an "I got you" tool. The department gathered and calibrated data for 2 years before publishing the findings for others to see. Initially, some of the school counselors were ambivalent and fearful of data. Some didn't see the point and felt that they were being questioned. Once they observed over time how the results were being used, however, everyone in the department came to trust the data.

Using the Data

Guidance and counseling departments often provide support for regular educational programs and testing, discipline, and management – up to 30–40 percent of school counselors' time can go to such support, according to Gysbers and Henderson's 2006 study. Obviously, this cuts the amount of time allocated for the delivery of the comprehensive school counseling program. School counselors need to build awareness about counselor responsibilities so that they can define, communicate and clarify the difference between counseling and non-counseling services.

Our first step in gathering process data, therefore, was to specifically identify where time and services were being allocated. Prior to collecting data, our school counselors spoke in feeling: "I feel that…" They communicated that they were performing certain clerical or non-counseling-related tasks but lacked evidence. But with data, things changed! Our year-one findings were not surprising, with department data indicating that over 45 percent of school counselors' time was spent in non-counseling-related functions such as state assessments, clerical duties or serving in coordinator type capacities (Section 504, ARD, LPAC or RTI). The data provided an opportunity to move from "I can feel" to "I can show."

School Counselors' Role Change

The next step was to meet with campus and district leaders and share the data. Data allocations were presented side by side with the school counselors' codified role. We provided supportive documentation and expansion in alignment with state and national definitions and discussed school counselors' roles and responsibilities in relation to non-counseling-related tasks and duties not related to the development, implementation, or evaluation of the comprehensive school counseling program. Our presentation of data and literature was met with an immediate response to change historical practice. Program leaders immediately supported the department by taking steps to remove clerical and administrative (non-counseling-related) responsibilities such as testing and other coordinator duties, reassigning these responsibilities to administrators. The role of the school counselor started to shift. Structures were put in place to begin to implement a comprehensive school counseling program that served all students, meeting their academic, personal, social, and career development needs.

New Program Focus

The district's comprehensive program is continuously developing. School counselors continue to submit monthly data that we report to campus principals, district leaders, the board of trustees, and district constituents. The program's focus uses and incorporates process, perception, and student outcome data into practice. School counselors use data in developing needs assessments; assessing stakeholders (students, staff, and parents); identifying priorities and creating calendars; implementing guidance lessons, small groups, and individual counseling services; conducting pre/post-tests; and identifying next steps.

Today, our school counselors manage the comprehensive school counseling program and use data to aid the growth and development of our students and the counseling program. Data has created an opportunity for our program to increase and sustain direct counseling services for all students. District school counselors inspire change and have a reinvigorated outlook on the innovative school counseling services they provide. What is your next step?

Brief Description of Data, Tools, and Process

The following information provides a general overview of the indirect service delivery component – System support. This delivery component includes consultation, coordination, and program management. For the purposes of our focus – we will primarily focus on data, tools, and process.

Data Analysis and Accountability Services

Data is used to evaluate and demonstrate the effectiveness of the school counseling program in measurable terms. School counselors analyze school and school counseling program data to determine how students are different as a result of the school counseling program (ASCA, 2012). School counselors use data to show the impact of the school counseling program on student achievement, attendance, and behavior. Data is used to analyze school counseling programs, to help guide future school counseling program action, and improve future results for all students. To accurately indicate the impact of the school counseling program, the school counselor should collect and analyze three different forms of data: process, perception, and student outcome or achievement data.

Process Data

- What you did for whom?
- Where did you spend your time?
- How many students did you impact?
- Can only a professional school counselor perform these functions?

School counselors use process data to evaluate and provide evidence of school counselors' allocation of time within the four service delivery components and non-counseling duties. Process data describes activities conducted in the service delivery components of the school counseling program. Additionally, process data can be used to track and indicate the number of students who have participated in a school counseling activity.

The School Counselor: Counseling Program Tracking and Data Analysis Report is provided as a template to support the school counselor in developing, monitoring, and organizing the school counseling program. School counselors may use this template to identify how they are allocating time and where they are providing services to students. Based on data results (weekly, monthly, or annually), school counselors are able to initiate a plan of action in order to reallocate time and balance the school counseling program. If school counselors identify that there is a disproportionate amount of time being allocated to non-counseling duties and/or indirect services, they may modify the data analysis template to more intentionally focus on the areas requiring change (e.g., the non-counseling duty column may be adjusted to measure the additional duties that the school counselor intends to measure).

Process Data Examples

Five small group meetings were conducted for 40 students from an eighth-grade class. Thirty percent of the school counselors' time was allocated to guidance curriculum, whereas 20 percent of the time was allocated to system support, 30 percent to responsive services, 10 percent to individual planning, and 10 percent to non-counseling duties.

Perception Data

From documenting to demonstrating. Perception data is evaluated by asking questions such as:

- What do students think they know? (knowledge)
- What do they believe? (attitude)
- What can they do or demonstrate as a result of a lesson, activity, or intervention? (skills)
- Measures competency achieved

Perception data allows school counselors to measure the knowledge and understanding of stakeholders through pre- and post-assessments based on the intervention or service provided. Perception data measures knowledge attained or attitudes and beliefs changed through the measured modification of knowledge/attitude/belief as reflected in pre- and post-assessment tools.

PERCEPTION DATA EXAMPLES

- Pre- and post-assessment data and results indicating change in knowledge/understanding
- Needs assessments (student, staff, parent, and administrator) (see Section III)
- Feedback and opinions from participants in a school-counseling-based intervention

Student Outcome Data

Proof your program has positively impacted students ability to utilize knowledge, attitudes, and skills to affect behavior in:

- Attendance rates
- Course enrollment patterns

Data Collection and Analysis 245

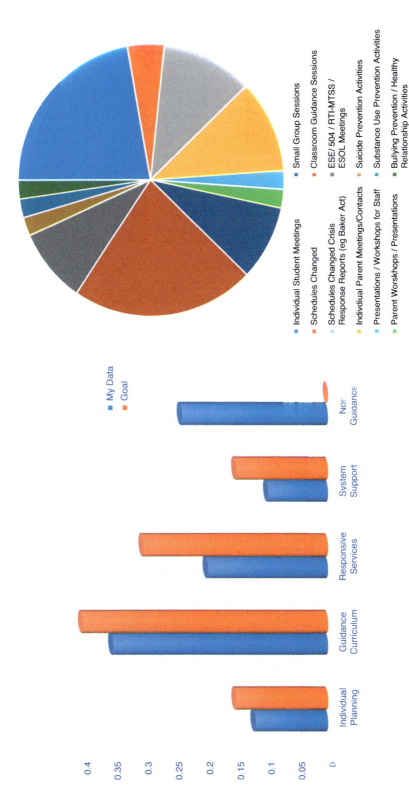

Figure 16.2 Time on Task. Created by E. Cox, 2022.

Monthly Time Analysis and Data Check-in

School_____ School Counselor_____|

A school counselor shall work with the school faculty and staff, students, parents, and the community to plan, implement, and evaluate a comprehensive school counseling program and deliver the program through **guidance curriculum, individual planning, responsive services, and system support**. Student services should align to recommended program balance distribution as recommended in the ASCA National Model.

Guidance Curriculum: _____%	Responsive Services: _____%	Individual Planning: _____%	System Support: _____%	Other Duties: _____%

Use this section to specify "Other or Non-School Counseling Duties":
Monthly Reflection on data:
Lessons gleaned and opportunities for next month:
Additional comments:

Professional school counselor(s) signature:	Date:
Principal(s) Signature:	Date:

© EC Counseling and Wellness

Figure 16.3 Monthly Time Analysis and Data Check-In. Created by E. Cox, 2022.

- Homework completion rates
- Report Card grades
- Discipline referrals and suspension rates
- Parental involvement
- Measures the impact of a lesson, activity, intervention – The "so what"
- Proof behavior has changed
- Proof of SC program effectiveness

- Hard data that shows how students are different
- Compare to previous achievement related data

The school counselor uses student outcome data to evaluate, discuss, and promote the impact the school counseling program or intervention had on student development. Outcome data examples include grade point averages, promotion and attendance rates, and discipline referrals. Based on the multitude of student outcome data measures, three categories are recommended for focus on student outcome data: achievement, attendance, and behavioral categories.

STUDENT OUTCOME DATA EXAMPLES

The following provide outcome data examples of achievement, attendance, and behavior:

- *Achievement.* Based on individual and academic support planning, a 9th grade student's GPA increased from 2.7 to 3.1 between the 6th and 18th week of school.
- *Attendance.* The 7th grade average attendance rate increased from 90.1 percent to 91.1 percent in the first quarter of school after classroom guidance lessons were implemented which addressed goal setting and motivation to achieve.
- *Behavioral.* Ms. Smith sent five of her 2nd grade students to participate in a small group that addressed interpersonal effectiveness topics. As a result, these five students had a 40 percent decrease in behavioral referrals (post-intervention).

A school counselor manages the school counseling program and uses data to aid the growth and continued development of the school counseling program. School counselors use data to identify school counseling program goals; monitor student progress; assess and evaluate programs; and demonstrate school counseling program effectiveness (Young and Kaffenberger, 2015). More specifically, ASCA (2012) asserts data assists school counselors in monitoring student progress, identifying student need (academic, behavior), identifying impediments to learning, understanding factors influencing student behavior, identifying and closing achievement gaps, assessing and evaluating services and effectiveness of activities within the school counseling program, determining services to students that need to be improved, modified, or changed, educating stakeholders about the comprehensive school counseling program, and advocating for additional resources to increase program effectiveness.

After determining the category of data that will be reviewed, school counselors efficiently use the data by disaggregating it to determine how all student groups are performing in comparison to each other (as well as in comparison to the entire student population). While not a fully inclusive list, data can be disaggregated by gender, race/ethnicity, free and reduced/socio-economic/at-risk, language of origin, special populations (Special education, Section 504, etc.), or grade level.

Now What?

The following poses questions to answer based on the data that have been collected.

- What pictures, patterns, or gaps does the data suggest?
- What problems or needs surfaced?
- What inequities exist? Are there achievement or opportunity gaps?

- Are there system changes that need to be made?
- Which programs impact students?
- Which programs meet the identified need?
- Does the data implicate some programs?
- Are there components/programs that need to be re-evaluated, eliminated, or replaced?
- How are students different because of what I've done?

The use of data in decision-making is a part of transforming the school counseling profession (Erford, 2015) and heightens the school counselor and program's accountability. It is critical to maintain perspective and priorities, all of which help to reduce decisions being made based on feelings, preferences, or historical practices (e.g. we have always done it this way; so therefore, we have no need to change our approach). In fact, the use of data tends to be more in alignment with administrative practices, and can be difficult to argue against when used as a basis to implement, revise, discontinue, or offer alternative programs and services. Data should be conceptualized, interpreted, and coalesced with research and statistics when possible.

School counselors are motivated to share data results addressing school counseling program effectiveness. They use resources available to inform stakeholders of school counseling program evaluation results as well as school counseling program plans and events through school, district, and community newsletters, presentations, and the local media.

- Use of multiple sets of data
- Time task analysis
- Reporting data to stakeholders (ex. School board, SEA, etc.)
- Stakeholder collateral to disseminate data

Reexamine Data Points

By revisiting the data elements that were reviewed when developing the school counseling program goals, the school counselor can determine if the data points are moving in a desirable direction. Plotting such data points, taken at regular intervals, onto a graph and looking for trends over time is another system to apply when evaluating the school counseling program with hard data.

EXAMPLE

The school counselor develops a needs assessment; uses the needs assessment with students, staff, and parents; gathers the assessment data; disaggregates the data; identifies the priorities; creates a weekly, monthly, and annual calendar based on priority areas; identifies possible guidance lessons; assesses knowledge through a pre-assessment; implements the guidance lesson; concludes a lesson(s); conducts post-assessments; gathers data; completes analysis and reviews results; publishes results; and finally identifies the next steps that will be taken in the future to maximize student performance.

Mental and Behavioral Health Considerations

When reviewing and analyzing data, taking into account the patterns and/or trends of mental health considerations is essential. This important data can be used to ensure the appropriate training, professional development, and direct service needs are met.

Ethical Considerations

There are many ethical considerations when a school counselor and/or school counselor leader collects and analyzes data to evaluate programming in support of comprehensive school counseling programs and student mental health.

The American School Counselor Association (ASCA, 2022) states that all students have the right to:

> Equitable access to a school counseling program that promotes academic, career and social/emotional development and improves student outcomes for all students, including students historically and currently marginalized by the education system. Equitable access to school counselors who support students from all backgrounds and circumstances and who advocate for and affirm all students regardless of but not limited to ethnic/racial identity; nationality; age; social class; economic status; abilities/disabilities; language; immigration status; sexual orientation; gender identity; gender expression; family type; religious/spiritual identity; and living situations, including emancipated minor status, wards of the state, homelessness or incarceration.

This preamble to the ASCA ethical codes highlights the importance of equitable access to school counseling programs. As described in this chapter, data collection of a CSCP allows for highlighting the access that the school community has to the school counselor.

A.3 Comprehensive School Counseling Program

School counselors:

a provide students with a culturally responsive school counseling program that promotes academic, career and social/emotional development and equitable opportunity and achievement outcomes for all students.
b collaborate with administration, teachers, staff and stakeholders for equitable school improvement goals.
c use data-collection tools adhering to standards of confidentiality as expressed in A.2.
d review and use school and student data to assess and address needs, including but not limited to data on strengths and disparities that may exist related to gender, race, ethnicity, socioeconomic status, disability and/or other relevant classifications.
e deliver research-based interventions to help close achievement, attainment, information, attendance, discipline, resource and opportunity gaps.
f collect and analyze participation, ASCA Mindsets & Behaviors and outcome data to determine the progress and effectiveness of the school counseling program.
g share data outcomes with stakeholders.

Cultural Complexities

When school counselors and school counselor leaders collect data, it is worth noting the topic of data bias. Data bias exists when individuals slant data based on gender, ethnicity, race, special populations, etc. There are many ethical considerations to consider when discussing data bias. School counselors must have a clear understanding of the unique needs of their student and school population and consider these needs when developing comprehensive school counseling programs. Data is tied to these unique needs and should be considered.

Strategic Considerations

Utilizing data in ways to highlight areas of strengths and opportunities for growth is foundational. This data can be used when walking alongside campus and district level leaders in developing district and departmental strategic plans, and district and campus improvement plans. Publishing data regularly can serve as a tool for advocating for school counselors and comprehensive school counseling programs. This Annual Report is made available to the public, posted online, and presented to the school board and provides the rationale, data, summary, and an action plan. The annual "says what we ARE doing when we aren't doing what we're NOT SUPPOSED to be doing".

Conclusion

Collecting, analyzing and evaluating the data is a starting point for school counselors and school counselor leaders. This data collection process can aid in developing a CSCP.

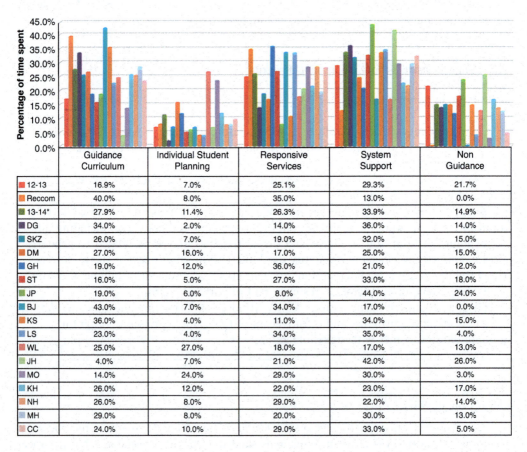

	Guidance Curriculum	Individual Student Planning	Responsive Services	System Support	Non Guidance
12-13	16.9%	7.0%	25.1%	29.3%	21.7%
Reccom	40.0%	8.0%	35.0%	13.0%	0.0%
13-14*	27.9%	11.4%	26.3%	33.9%	14.9%
DG	34.0%	2.0%	14.0%	36.0%	14.0%
SKZ	26.0%	7.0%	19.0%	32.0%	15.0%
DM	27.0%	16.0%	17.0%	25.0%	15.0%
GH	19.0%	12.0%	36.0%	21.0%	12.0%
ST	16.0%	5.0%	27.0%	33.0%	18.0%
JP	19.0%	6.0%	8.0%	44.0%	24.0%
BJ	43.0%	7.0%	34.0%	17.0%	0.0%
KS	36.0%	4.0%	11.0%	34.0%	15.0%
LS	23.0%	4.0%	34.0%	35.0%	4.0%
WL	25.0%	27.0%	18.0%	17.0%	13.0%
JH	4.0%	7.0%	21.0%	42.0%	26.0%
MO	14.0%	24.0%	29.0%	30.0%	3.0%
KH	26.0%	12.0%	22.0%	23.0%	17.0%
NH	26.0%	8.0%	29.0%	22.0%	14.0%
MH	29.0%	8.0%	20.0%	30.0%	13.0%
CC	24.0%	10.0%	29.0%	33.0%	5.0%

Figure 16.4 Services Provided by Elementary PSCs, October 2013. Created by E. Cox, 2013.

Various ways to utilize the data include, professional development where using data can guide your program and identify future professional development, taking the department to moving from "I feel" to "I can show", and processing data (data analysis) into monthly reports submitted and published. Processing and reporting out data at all levels including school counselor level, campus level, department level, senior level leadership level, cabinet, and school board level. Creating annual reports that include intentional implementation plans, an aide in supporting school counselors in counseling program buy-in, creating a culture of school counselor leader support and an "I got your back" rather than an "I got you".

The most important guiding question in data collection to analyze and support the school counseling program is to ask "how is what we are doing as school counselors (and the data being collected) going to support the students and overall school community?"

References

Note: This chapter is based on research conducted in 2018, and, therefore, the 2012 ASCA National Model is referenced throughout the chapter, rather than the updated 2019 version.

Amatea, E. and Clark, M. (2005) "Changing schools, changing counselors: a qualitative study of school administrators' conceptions of the school counselor role", *Professional School Counseling*, 9: 16–27.

American School Counselor Association (ASCA) (2012) *The ASCA National Model: A Framework for School Counseling Programs* (4th edn), Alexandria, VA: American School Counselor Association.

ASCA (2022) *ASCA Ethical Standards for School Counselors*, Alexandria, VA: Author.

Anita, Y. and Carol, K. (2015) "School counseling professional development: assessing the use of data to inform school counseling services", *Professional School Counseling*, 19(1). Online. Available HTTP: <https://doi.org/10.5330/1096-2409-19.1.46>

Beale, A.V. (2004) "Questioning whether you have a contemporary school counseling program", *The Clearing House*, 78(2): 73–76.

Brigman, G. and Campbell, C. (2003) "Helping students improve academic achievement and school success behavior", *Professional School Counseling*, 7(2): 91–98.

Campbell, C.A. and Dahir, C.A. (1997) *Sharing the Vision: The ASCA National Standards for School Counseling Programs*, Alexandria, VA: American School Counseling Association.

Carey, J.C. and Martin, I. (2015) *A Review of the Major School Counseling Policy Studies in the United States: 2000–2014*, Amherst, MA: Center for School Counseling Outcome Research and Evaluation.

Clark, M. and Stone, C. (2000) "The developmental school counselor as educational leader", in J. Wittmer (ed.) *Managing Your School Guidance Program: K-12 Developmental Strategies*, Minneapolis, MN: Educational Media Corporation, pp. 75–82.

Cox, E. (2018) "Examining school counseling program leaders' experiences in implementing the Texas Comprehensive School Counseling Model: A Delphi study". Online. Available HTTP: <https://www.proquest.com/openview/cd79806abef78f2f5d900ff50be33072/1?pq-origsite=gscholar&cbl=18750>.

Dahir, C. (2001) "The national standards for school counseling programs: development and implementation", *Professional School Counseling*, 4: 320.

Edmondson, A. (1999) "Psychological safety and learning behavior in work teams", *Administrative Science Quarterly*, 44(2): 350–383.

Edmondson, J.H. and White, J. (1998) "A tutorial and counseling program: helping students at risk of dropping out of school", *Professional School Counseling*, 1(4): 43–51.

Erford, B.T. (2015) *Transforming the School Counseling Profession*, 4th edn, Upper Saddle River, NJ: Pearson.

Goodloe, J.P. (1990) "Comprehensive guidance in Montgomery County, Maryland", in N. Gysbers and P. Henderson (eds) *Developing and Managing your School Guidance and Counseling Program*, 4th edn, Alexandria, VA: American Counseling Association.

Grossman, D.C., Neckerman, H.J., Koepsell, T.D., Liu, P.Y., Asher, K.N., Beland, K., Frey, K. and Rivara, F.P. (1997) "Effectiveness of a violence prevention curriculum among children in elementary school: a randomized controlled trial", *Journal of the American Medical Association*, 277: 1605–1611.

Gysbers, N. and Henderson, P. (1997) "Comprehensive guidance programs that work". Online. Available HTTP: <https://files.eric.ed.gov/fulltext/ED412434.pdf>

Gysbers, N. and Henderson, P. (2006) "Comprehensive guidance and counseling program evaluation: program + personnel = results", *Vistas Online*, 41: 187–190.

Gysbers, N. and Lapan, R. (2009) *Strengths-Based Career Development for School Guidance and Counseling Programs*, VA: American Counseling Association.

Heath, C. and Heath, D. (2008) *Made to Stick*, Arrow Books.

House, R.M. and Martin, P.J. (1998) "Advocating for better futures for all students: a new vision for school counselors", *Education*, 119(2): 284.

House, R. and Hayes, R. (2002) "School counselors: becoming key players in school reform", *Professional School Counseling*, 5: 249–256.

Kaufman, P., Klein, S., and Frase, M. (1999) "Dropout rates in the United States, 1997", *Statistical Analysis* Report, U.S. Department of Education.

Kaufman, P., Kwon, J., Klein, S., and Chapman, C. (2000) "Dropout rates in the United States: 1999", *Education Statistics Quarterly*, 1–75.

Lapan, R.T., Gysbers, N.C., and Sun, Y. (1997) "The impact of more fully implemented guidance programs on the school experiences of high school students: a statewide evaluation study", *Journal of Counseling & Development*, 75(4): 292–302.

Lapan, R., Gysbers, N., and Petroski, G. (2001) "Helping seventh graders be safe and successful: a statewide study of the impact of comprehensive guidance and counseling programs", *Professional School Counseling*, 79(3): 320–330.

Martin, I. and Carey, J. (2012) "Development of a logic model to guide evaluations of the ASCA National Model for school counseling programs", *The Professional Counselor*, 4: 455–466.

Murray, P.V., Levitov, L.C., Castenell, L. and Joubert, J.H. (1987) "Qualitative evaluation methods applied to a high school counseling center", *Journal of Counseling and Development*, 65: 259–265.

Nichter, M., Li, C., and Serres, S.A. (2008) "A study of ASCA National Standards in Texas schools", *International Journal of Educational Leadership Preparation*, 3: 1–8.

Savickas, M.L. (2009) "Pioneers of the vocational guidance movement: a centennial celebration", *National Career Development Association*, 57: 3.

Schlossberg, S.M., Morris, J., and Lieberman, M.G. (2001) "The effects of a counselor-led guidance intervention on students' behaviors and attitudes", *Professional School Counseling*, 4: 156–164.

Shea, M.L. (2013) *School board member and school counselor perceptions of school board knowledge, priorities, and policy*, Graduate thesis, Oregon State University. Online. Available HTTP: <https://ir.library.oregonstate.edu/concern/graduate_thesis_or_dissertations/0c483p059>

Schrader, M.K. (1989) "The image of the school counselor: whose responsibility?" *The School Counselor*, 36(3): 229–233.

Sink, C. and Stroh, H. (2003) "Raising achievement test scores of early elementary school students through comprehensive school counseling programs", *Professional School Counseling*, 6: 350–364.

St. Clair, K.L. (1989) "Middle school counseling research: a resource for school counselors", *Elementary School Guidance and Counseling*, 23: 219–226.

Stone, C. & Clark, M. (2001) "School counselors and principals: partners in support of academic achievement", *NASSP Bulletin*, 85: 46–53.

Texas Constitution and Statutes (n.d.) "Education Code". Online. Available HTTP: <https://statutes.capitol.texas.gov/Docs/ED/htm/ED.33.htm>.

Texas Education Agency (2018) *The Texas Model for Comprehensive School Counseling*, 5th edn, Austin, TX.

Whiston, S. and Quinby, R. (2009) "Review of school counseling outcome research", *Psychology in the Schools*, 46: 267–272.

Wilson, S., Lipsey, M., and Derzon, J. (2003) "The effects of school-based intervention programs on aggressive behavior: a meta-analysis", *Journal of Consulting and Clinical Psychology*, 71: 136–149.

Young, A., and Kaffenberger, C. (2015) "School counseling professional development: assessing the use of data to inform school counseling services", *Professional School Counseling*, 19(1). Online. Available HTTP: <https://doi.org/10.5330/1096-2409-19.1.46>

17 Accountability Measures for Positive Mental Health

Loree Munro

Leadership Quotes

When school counselors are accountable for their programs, they are more likely to engage in tasks that support the vision and mission of the school and are appropriate for their roles. Collecting and analyzing data, conducting program audits, and producing documents to educate school personnel, students, and parents, and the community-at-large are ways to support the effectiveness and importance of comprehensive school counseling programs.

Judy A. Nelson

Aspirational Statements

- School accountability systems are an integral and vital part of the educational landscape. They are the means by which school districts demonstrate and communicate stewardship of public trust, measure progress towards stated goals, and ensure educational equity.
- Professional school counselors are uniquely positioned to positively impact campus and district accountability and should actively engage with other school leaders in goal setting, measurement, reflection, and revision.

Introduction

In the context of education, the natural inclination is to equate accountability with school accountability systems. For our purposes, we will expand that equation to include the intersection of school counselor roles and accountability as it relates to accountability systems, federal program accountability, and the Office of Civil Rights (OCR).

School accountability is the process of measuring school performance based on the attainment of certain standards. On December 10, 2015, President Obama signed into law the Every Student Succeeds Act (ESSA). This official act replaced the No Child Left Behind Act (2001) as the most recent reauthorization of the Elementary and Secondary Education Act (1965). The ESSA offers states more autonomy over their accountability systems. In light of the new flexibility, many states transitioned from narrowly defined systems focused on student assessment and graduation rates to a system that incorporates a wider variety of school quality measures.

New accountability systems under ESSA became effective in the 2018–2019 school year. Most state plans include the following three domains: school performance rating system, school quality or student success, and student growth. Within each domain, states may measure one or more indicators. For example, the school quality/student success domain may include some variation of the following indicators: college and career readiness with or without military measure (CCR or CCMR), absenteeism/attendance, college and/or career readiness, science and/or social studies proficiency/progress, school climate/culture, English language proficiency/progress, and well-rounded education.

The American School Counselor Association (ASCA) National Model (2019) articulates student and counselor standards that align with the school accountability system measures. School counselors interact with student data and apply relevant mindsets/behaviors to facilitate and encourage student mindsets/behaviors which in turn positively impacts school accountability measures. Table 17.1 illustrates this crosswalk.

In addition to impacting school accountability system measures, counselors also engage in areas that support accountability for federal programs. State educational agencies receiving federal title funds must ensure they are compliant with the criteria for those funds. School counselors, by virtue of their training, mindsets, and implementation of a comprehensive counseling program play specific roles in Title I, Title IV, and Title VII.

Title I, Part C: Education of Migratory Children. Local Education Agencies (LEAs) utilizing funds under this title must ensure that monies are expended in advocacy and outreach activities for this vulnerable population. While facilitating the transition of all students into productive postsecondary lives is a counselor role, Title I, Part C clearly articulates this planning as it relates to migratory children. This title also supports the Migrant Education Program, whose purpose is to:

> design and support programs that help migratory students overcome the challenges of mobility, cultural and language barriers, social isolation, and other difficulties associated with a migratory lifestyle. These efforts are aimed at helping migratory students succeed in school and successfully transition to postsecondary education and/or employment.

It is incumbent on school counselors to know which of their students meet the qualification for Title I, Part C and to investigate proportionality in the various accountability measures.

Title 1, Part D: Prevention and Intervention Programs for Children and Youth who are Neglected, Delinquent, or At-Risk. Counselors interact with at-risk students on a daily basis. By collaborating on transition planning for students returning from institutionalization and providing a support system to encourage persistence through graduation, counselors assist with compliance of funding from Title 1, Part D.

Title IV, Part A: Student Support and Academic Enrichment (SSAE) Grants. By implementing drug and violence prevention programs and supporting student mental health, counselors assist with accountability for these funds.

Title VII, Part B: Education for Homeless children and Youth Program, McKinney Vento Homeless Assistance Act. Through the registration process and ongoing interaction with students, counselors gain knowledge regarding the residency status of students and assist with identifying students who may be experiencing homelessness. The McKinney Vento Act requires counselors to support the educational success, in particular college and career readiness of these students.

Table 17.1 Crosswalk of School Accountability Measures and ASCA Standards and Competencies

Accountability Measure	ASCA Counselor Mindsets (M)/Behaviors (B)	ASCA Student Mindsets (M)/Behaviors (B)
Attendance/Chronic Absenteeism	B-PE 2. Identify gaps in achievement, attendance, discipline, opportunity, and resources. B-PF 6. Demonstrate understanding of the impact of cultural, social, and environmental influences on student success and opportunities.	M 6. Positive attitude toward work and learning. B-SMS 1. Demonstrate ability to assume responsibility. B-SMS 6. Demonstrate ability to overcome barriers to learning.
English Language Proficiency/Progress		
Student Achievement	M 7. Comprehensive school counseling programs promote and enhance student academic, career, and social/emotional outcomes.	M 1. Self confidence in ability to succeed. M 5. Belief in using abilities to their fullest to achieve high-quality results and outcomes.
Student Growth	B-SS 5. Consult to support student achievement and success. B-SS 5. Consult to support student achievement and success. B-SS 6. Collaborate with families, teachers, administrators, other school staff, and education stakeholders for student achievement and success.	B-SMS 4. Demonstrate ability to delay immediate gratification for long-term rewards. B-SMS 5. Demonstrate perseverance to achieve long-and short-term goals.
College and/or Career Readiness	M 3. Every student should graduate from high school prepared for postsecondary opportunities.	M 4. Understanding that postsecondary education and life-long learning are necessary for long-term career success.
High School Graduation Rates	M 1. Every student can learn, and every student can succeed. M 3 Every student should graduate from high school prepared for postsecondary opportunities.	B-SMS 4. Demonstrate ability to delay immediate gratification for long-term rewards. B-SMS 5. Demonstrate perseverance to achieve long-and short-term goals.
School Discipline/Suspension Rate	B-PE 2. Identify gaps in achievement, attendance, discipline, opportunity and resources.	M 1. Belief in development of whole self, including a health balance of mental, social/emotional and physical well-being. B-SS 9. Demonstrate social maturity and behaviors appropriate to the situation and environment.
Student Dropout/Re-enrollment Rates	B-PE 2. Identify gaps in achievement, attendance, discipline, opportunity, and resources. B-SS 5. Consult to support student achievement and success. B-SS 6. Collaborate with families, teachers, administrators, other school staff, and education stakeholders for student achievement and success.	B-SMS 5. Demonstrate perseverance to achieve long-and short-term goals. B-SS 3. Create relationships with adults that support success.
Science Achievement/Growth; Social Studies Achievement/Growth		
Achievement Gap	B-PE 2. Identify gaps in achievement, attendance, discipline, opportunity, and resources. B-PF 6. Demonstrate understanding of the impact of cultural, social, and environmental influences on student success and opportunities.	M 1. Belief in development of whole self, including a healthy balance of mental, social/emotional, and physical well-being.
School Climate/Culture		M 3. Sense of belonging in the school environment.
Well-Rounded Education (Access/Participation)	M 2. Every student should have access to and opportunity for a high-quality education.	M 2. Sense of acceptance, respect, support, and inclusion for self and others in the school environment.

Note: Adapted from ASCA (2019b). Created by L. Munro (2023).

Accountability Measures for Positive Mental Health

Office for Civil Rights (OCR) reporting can provide a rich source of data from which counselors can draw conclusions regarding proportionality and plan and measure interventions. The mission of the OCR is to "ensure equal access to education and to promote educational excellence throughout the nation through vigorous enforcement of civil rights". This mission is supported by ASCA's Ethical Standards for School Counselors (2022) as well as the school counselor mindsets. In December 2020, the OCR received approval to require all LEAs to submit an OCR report regarding certain data elements. Certain elements have particular relevance to school counselors: discipline data (disaggregated by race, sex, 504 and EL status), harassment and bullying (number of allegations on the basis of sex, race, color or national origin, disability, sexual orientation, religion), and pathways to college and career. Counselors should interact with this data to increase their awareness of any disproportionality and to advocate for equity.

Ethical Considerations

When engaging in high-stakes areas such as school accountability systems and compliance, all educators must guard against blurring ethical lines in pursuit of more favorable outcomes. Not only do the ASCA Ethical Standards for School Counselors (2022) provide clear guidance for ethical decision-making, but they also support the counselor role in accountability. The following standards are particularly relevant:

A.3 Comprehensive Data-Informed Program

School counselors:

a Provide students with a culturally responsive school counseling program that promotes academic, career and social/emotional development and equitable opportunity and achievement outcomes for all students.
b Collaborate with administration, teachers, staff and decision makers around school-improvement goals.
c Use data-collection tools adhering to standards of confidentiality as expressed in A.2.
d Review and use school and student data to assess and address needs, including but not limited to data on strengths and disparities that may exist related to gender, race, ethnicity, socioeconomic status, disability and/or other relevant classifications.
e Deliver research-based interventions to help close achievement, attainment, information, attendance, discipline, resource and opportunity gaps.
f collect and analyze participation, ASCA Mindsets & Behaviors and outcome data to determine the progress and effectiveness of the school counseling program.
g share data outcomes with stakeholders.

When counselors consume and apply data in an ethical manner, they positively impact school accountability measures.

Cultural Complexities

We know that factors such as lack of parental education, single-parent households, and economic distress negatively impact a child's academic success. The National Center for

Educational Statistics (NCES) publishes an annual report on the Condition of Education. According to the most recent report, in 2019 roughly 9 percent of children lived in households where neither parent had a high school diploma, 34 percent lived in single-parent households, and 16 percent were living in poverty. When we dig deeper into those statistics, we find that there is a disproportionate representation of blacks and hispanics in these risk categories. For example, 22 percent of children of parents without high school completion are hispanic, compared to only 3 percent of white children. Sixty four percent of black children and 41 percent of hispanic children live in single-parent households compared to 25 percent of white children. While the percentage of children living in poverty has declined over the past decade across all races, 30 percent of black children and 23 percent of hispanic children live in poverty compared to 10 percent of white children. Counselors must be aware of factors such as those examined by NCES as well as additional factors such as Adverse Childhood Experiences (ACEs) that impact a child's ability to function optimally in general and more specifically on accountability measures.

Viewing the world through an equity lens is inherent in a school counselor's belief system and orientation. Mindsets 1, 2, 3, and 4 of the ASCA National Model (2019) specifically support this by beginning each statement with every, meaning that each student, regardless of sex, race, color or national origin, disability, sexual orientation, economic status, or religion deserves equal access to educational opportunities. Multiculturalism is a complex and evolving idea. Ratts and Greenleaf (2017) stated, "The Multicultural and Social Justice Counseling Competencies (MSJCC) sets the expectations for a new kind of school counselor leadership, including that school counselors will be competent in addressing issues of power, privilege, and oppression that is prevalent in K-12 schools" (2017: 3). An MSJCC framework challenges school counselors to consider and explore their own cultural biases, values, beliefs. Self-awareness is the first developmental domain of MSJCC. Counselors who are cognizant of, and continue to monitor, their own biases and prejudices can enter whole-heartedly into an exploration of the intersection of race, economic status, gender, sexual orientation, disability status, etc. in shaping a student's worldview. As a starting point, school counselors can explore equity issues that may be highlighted by disproportionality in their campus accountability system and OCR data. This might include measures such as academic performance, college, and career readiness, disciplinary action, harassment, and bullying.

The ASCA National Model (2019) proposed a counselor appraisal model which includes indicators around demonstrating and understanding of the impact of cultural, social, and environmental influences on student success and opportunities. Indicators with specific application to accountability include:

> b Explains how students' cultural, social and economic background may affect their academic achievement, behavior, relationships and overall performance in school.
> [...]
> d Explains the dynamics of cross-cultural communications and demonstrate the ability to communicate with persons of other cultures effectively.
> [...]
> f Understands personal limitations and biases, and articulates how they may affect the school counselor's work.

Counselor leaders can encourage school counselors to lean into equity conversations by providing forums for open discussion, professional development around equity, and time for counselors to explore the intersection of equity and accountability.

Leadership Standards and Values

School counseling standards, established by the National Board for Professional Teaching Standards (NBPTS, 2012) stated that school counselors "are comfortable and articulate in expressing data-based evidence of student needs to other educators, parent and community groups, and policy makers" (2012: 50). Interacting with accountability data should be so embedded in the school counselor's practice that communicating the data, the impact of the data, and how the school counseling program can address the data flows naturally to stakeholders at their level of understanding.

Leadership elements are woven throughout the four domains of the ASCA National Model (2019) The performance appraisal template also includes indicators which demonstrate leadership standards. The following indicators apply to a counselor's role in regard to accountability:

---

h Serves as a leader in the school and community to promote and support student success.
i Participates in the school improvement process to bring the school counseling perspective to the development of school goals.

Leadership in schools requires school counselors to respond to data derived from accountability systems. Professional school counselors' engagement with accountability indicators is supported by their mindsets, professional foundation, direct and indirect student services, and planning and assessment. By adhering to these standards, counselors can assist their campus/district achieve accountability goals. The following school counselor Mindsets and Behaviors specifically intersect with accountability measures:

M7: School counseling programs promote and enhance student academic, career and social/emotional outcomes.
B-SS 5: Consult to support student achievement and success.
B-SS 6: Collaborate with families, teachers, administrators, other school staff and education stakeholders for student achievement and success.
B-PE 2: Identify gaps in achievement, attendance, discipline, opportunity and resources.
B-PE 3: Develop annual student outcome goals based on student data.
B-PE 4: Develop and implement action plans aligned with annual student outcome goals and student data.

When one searches the keywords *school leadership*, an array of responses populate. It is not this author's intent to suggest one model over another, but to reference certain models that support school counselor leadership around accountability. Accountability Leadership and Transformational Leadership (TL) are two such models.

Ratts and Greenleaf stated: "As leaders in their schools, school counselors' emphasis on accountability ties the counseling program into other school-wide initiatives" (2018: 1). Sink (2009) uses the term Accountability Leadership in general reference to the counselor's examination and promotion of their program efficacy. However, this construct can also be applied to the school counselor's interaction with accountability measures. One of the three fundamental areas of evaluation within this leadership model is "the level of program impact on student learning, as well as on the local school and communities where the students attend and live" (Sink: 69). While program impact may not be fully captured by the accountability measures explored in this chapter, namely school accountability systems, federal program accountability, and OCR reporting, goals of improving achievement and reducing disproportionality absolutely speak to program impact. It is incumbent on school counselor leaders to provide training and opportunity for school counselors to develop accountability leadership self-efficacy. According to Sink (2009),

> School counselors and school counselor educators must do more than merely acquiesce to the rising accountability tide; rather they need to be genuinely committed to and engaged in improving student educational outcomes and the profession, rigorously testing and then jettisoning unproven practices and refining those that show positive results.
>
> (2009: 73)

Shields et al. (2018) defined Transformative Leadership (TL) as "a leadership paradigm that addresses the need for systemic, equitable change in education" (2018: 1). TL considers factors outside of the school setting that impact a student's ability to function optimally within the school setting. These factors included a child's economic reality, physical health, emotional and mental wellbeing, etc. The whole child focus aligns with school counselor mindsets and behaviors (ASCA, 2019). There are eight tenets of TL, one of which has specific application to the school counselor role in relation to accountability. Inherent in Tenet 1: A Mandate for Deep and Equitable Change, are several ideas. One idea is that of mandate, which suggests that transformation is more than a nice idea. It is an urgent necessity or requirement. The second idea is that of deep and equitable change. This word choice suggests that we are not pursuing fleeting or temporary change, but rather pervasive and permanent change. In order to effect change, school counselors must educate themselves on where transformation is needed:

> The TL school counselor would establish protocols for collecting, analyzing, and disseminating data that examine trends in student success as a means of transforming the school community into one of equity and inclusion, resulting in greater outcomes for all students.
>
> (Shields et al., 2018: 9)

Digging into accountability data can inform focus. Are some students underrepresented in advanced courses? Are certain groups of students overrepresented in disciplinary action? Are certain students less successful because they are fearful or feel marginalized? A response of "yes" to questions such as these indicates a need for systemic change.

Leadership in Practice

It is incumbent on school counselor leaders to "create the resources, culture, and support to allow all school counselors to serve as leaders" (Kneale et al., 2017: 2). Including school counselors in a vision of school accountability is a three-fold process. It begins with culture; a district and campus philosophy that counselors have unique value to add in the leadership arena. Campus and district leadership are encouraged to acquire knowledge about the American School Counselor (ASCA) School Counselor Professional Standards & Competencies (2019). This knowledge will allow leaders to leverage the Mindsets and Behaviors to achieve accountability goals. The second part of the equation is resources. Budgetary limitations in education are well known. It is therefore essential that direction is provided in the acquisition of necessary materials and resources to support the accountability goals of a school counseling program. Ideally, district resources provide for the essentials, while campus budgets provide supplemental resources specific to unique campus goals and student population. The final element is support; building counselor capacity to contribute. If we expect counselors to actively engage in the conversation, we must build their knowledge-base, competency, and self-efficacy by providing opportunity, training, and encouraging professional networking. Opportunity is reflected in the inclusion of school counselors in discussions related to school accountability and improvement. Training is reflected in the provision of information related to areas such as school accountability, federal programs, and state educational reporting systems such as the Public Education Information Management System (PEIMS) in Texas. Counselor leaders can also extend support by funding professional organization membership and encouraging networking at local, state, and national conferences. Fostering the leadership identity of school counselors can be a daunting task. Kneale et al. (2018) proposed district leadership cohorts as one model to provide the support and training necessary. Regardless of the model adopted, creating a vehicle for school counselor leadership development should be a priority for district counselor leaders.

Strategic Considerations

The inclusion of accountability as an element of a comprehensive school counseling program must be intentional. Multi-Tiered Systems of Support (MTSS) provides a framework within which all elements of a school system reside. Campus MTSS teams consist of representatives knowledgeable about academics/instruction, behavioral and mental health, social emotional learning, school policy, campus climate, and culture. These campus teams create norms and protocols and establish a data-driven model of decision making.

The MTSS process begins with collecting baseline data on every student. Teams frequently rely on accountability measures to establish a baseline for certain domains such as academic or school climate. Universal screeners are another means of establishing a baseline. An examination of campus-wide data allows a team to draw conclusions about whether systemic change is needed to drive improvement, or whether student interventions (Tier 2 and 3) are more appropriate.

Counselor leaders can model leadership standards by participating on the district leadership team (DLT) for a MTSS. As a member of the DLT, counselor leaders demonstrate the use of district accountability measures to inform district priorities as evidenced in the District Improvement Plan (DIP). School counselors, following that model, can provide leadership on their campus MTSS teams and use campus accountability data to inform campus priorities as evidenced in the Campus Improvement Plan (CIP). Let us use school safety as an example. Annually, the school counselor includes bullying prevention as part of the Tier 1 classroom guidance program. When the OCR report is prepared, it is clear that overall, there is a low incidence of bullying on the campus. However, students with a disability are disproportionately represented in incidents. Responding to that data, the school counselor may plan some Tier 2 small group intervention for victims of school bullying and add some Tier 1 guidance lessons around cultural sensitivity. If the OCR report had indicated a high incidence of bullying with no indication of disproportionality, then a systemic issue might be considered. In which case the team would explore additional schoolwide (Tier 1) strategies to address the issue. A MTSS is a powerful vehicle to drive conversation around district and campus priorities and counselors have a unique contribution to make to the MTSS team.

Conclusion

This chapter has explored the intersection of the school counselor role and accountability measures, specifically school accountability systems, federal program accountability, and OCR reporting. Implementation of a comprehensive school counseling program is predicated on the school counselor's ability to adequately assess the needs of students and create goals that address those needs. Accountability measures can provide counselors with a glimpse into student needs and inform program goals.

References

American School Counselor Association (ASCA) (2019) *The ASCA National Model: A Framework for School Counseling Programs* (4th edn), Alexandria, VA: Author.
ASCA (2019b) "ASCA Student Standards: Mindsets & Behaviors for Student Success". Online. Available HTTP: <https://www.schoolcounselor.org/getmedia/7428a787-a452-4abb-afec-d78ec77870cd/Mindsets-Behaviors.pdf>
ASCA (2022) *Ethical Standards for School Counselors*, Alexandria, VA: Author
Bemak, F. (2000) "Transforming the role of the counselor to provide leadership in educational reform through collaboration", *Professional School Counseling*, 3: 323–332.
Education Commission of the States (2018a) "50-State Comparison: States' School Accountability Systems". Online. Available HTTP: <https://www.ecs.org/50-state-comparison-states-school-accountability-systems/>
Education Commission of the States (2018b) "Comparison of State Accountability Indicators and Weights". Online. Available HTTP: <https://reports.ecs.org/comparisons/states-school-accountability-systems-02>
Kneale, M.G.M., Young, A.A., and Dollarhide, C.T. (2018) "Cultivating school counseling leaders through district leadership cohorts", *Professional School Counseling*, 21(1b). Online. Available HTTP: <https://doi.org/10.1177/2156759×X18773275>
Munoz, M.V. (2014) "Examining the relationship between school counselors' leadership styles and their counseling activities", *ETD Collection for University of Nebraska, Lincoln*, AAI3667140. Online. Available HTTP: <https://digitalcommons.unl.edu/dissertations/AAI3667140>
National Board for Professional Teaching Standards (NBPTS) (2012) *School Counseling Standards*. Online. Available HTTP: <http://nbpts.org/wp-content/uploads/ECYA-SC.pdf>
Ratts, M.J. and Greenleaf, A.T. (2018) "Multicultural and social justice counseling competencies: a leadership framework for professional school counselors", *Professional School Counseling*, 21(1b). Online. Available HTTP: <https://doi.org/10.1177/2156759×X18773582>

Shields, C.M., Dollarhide, C.T., and Young, A.A. (2017) "Transformative leadership in school counseling: an emerging paradigm for equity and excellence", *Professional School Counseling*, 21(1b). Online. Available HTTP: <https://doi.org/10.1177/2156759×X18773581>

Sink, C.A. (2009) "School counselors as accountability leaders: another call for action", *Professional School Counseling*, 13(2). Online. Available HTTP: <https://journals.sagepub.com/doi/pdf/10.1177/2156759×X0901300202>

U.S. Department of Education (2015) "Every Student Succeeds Act (ESSA)". Online. Available HTTP: <https://www.ed.gov/essa?src=rn>

U.S. Department of Education (2017) *Revised State Template for the Consolidated State Plan: The Elementary and Secondary Education Act of 1965*, as amended by the Every Student Succeeds Act. Online. Available HTTP: <https://www.ed.gov/essa?src=ft>, pp. 15–16, 19, 22–23.

U.S. Department of Education. Institute of Education Sciences, National Center for Education Statistics (2021) *Condition of Education*. Online. Available HTTP: <https://nces.ed.gov/pubsearch/pubsinfo.asp?pubid=2021144>

U.S. Department of Education, Office for Civil Rights (2023) *Civil Rights Data Collection* (CRDC). Online. Available HTTP: <https://www2.ed.gov/about/offices/list/ocr/data.html?src=rt>

Young, A.A. and Dollarhide, C.T. (2017) "Introduction to the special issue: a case for school counseling leadership", *Professional School Counseling*, 21(1b). Online. Available HTTP: <10.1177/2156759×X18772988>

18 Utilizing Budgets, Grants, Donations, and Financial Audits to Support Mental Health

Seretha J. Augustine and Judy A. Nelson

> **Leadership Quotes**
>
> Perhaps no other area of school business requires the utmost in ethical behavior than the budget.
>
> Judy A. Nelson

> **Aspirational Statement**
>
> - Funding allocation should always consider the amount available, then the needs ranging from critical first to non-essential last.

Introduction and Background

Public School Funding

Any local government or agency, which includes public schools, has to utilize their budget to support program plans for the upcoming year. When considering budgets for public schools, it is important to note that there is a big difference on how districts allocate and prioritize their funds. When discussing the operational budget for public school as it relates to counseling, we have to first look at the overall operational budget for any district. As it relates to budgeting for school districts, it is essential to understand what is important when allocating funds. Texas Education Agency (2010) states, "[i]n school districts, the adoption of a budget implies that a set of decisions have been made by school board members and school district administrators which culminate in matching a school district's resources with its needs". Every district and campus should have a budget driven by a common goal of allocating funds to accomplish a shared vision.

When managing a budget for a district or campus it is very important to be transparent and open with the process. Once you allocate the budget on the campus level, it should be aligned to district level goals and objectives, when the district looks at budget allocation it should be aligned to goals and objectives of the Board of Trustees. The combination of all budgets must reflect the vision of the district.

DOI: 10.4324/9781003219750-22

According to Ellernson (1985), "while most public and private organizations and businesses have 35 to 40 percent of their budgets tied to personnel and benefits, the comparable number in public schools is, on average, more than double, between 80 and 85 percent." This further complicates most districts from addressing budget priorities. The remaining budget is frequently affected and limited by state, local, and federal mandates. The budget provides most local educational agencies and the people that lead them the chance to explain the collection and expenditure of public funds.

Local, state, and federal funds make up the resources for the budget. It is expected that the budget is spent all year long. "Federal dollars in school budgets are also spent throughout the school year, with the rule of 'first in, first out'" (Ellernson, 1985). Districts are expected to use all of the funds for the previous year before funds for the current year can be used.

For most school districts, there should be general rules to adopting budgets. The standard practice is that the school district's Board of Trustees adopts a budget that will include the General Fund, Food Service Fund, and a Debt Service Fund. The fiscal year for adopting a budget runs from September 1st through August 31st of the following school year and the budget has to be adopted by the final day of August.

Each campus receives an allocation as a part of the district's general fund budget. This process affords campuses the opportunity for the campus to budget according to the needs of the campus. The key person to allocate resources for the campus and to cover the cost of the instructional needs of the campus is the school principal. Of course, the power to allocate the campus needs comes with the responsibility of accountability for student outcomes.

One form of allocation is a Tier 1 allocation which is at the campus level. These allocations at the campus level are based on calculations from the average daily attendance (ADA). Average daily attendance is the number of actual students in attendance on the average school day. This is the driving force of how revenue is determined and allocations are given for each campus. It is important to understand that in school finance attendance is often linked to money. The basic calculation is based on the attendance of the student from each campus. Table 18.1 is an example of how one state allocates funding per student.

Table 18.1 Example Local Allocations

Example of Local Allocations
Projected Average Daily Attendance (ADA) × Predetermined cost per student EXAMPLE: Average attendance 550 students × $6,160 per student = $3,388,000

There are other funding allotments from different sources like state compensatory, Title I, IDEA b, and other miscellaneous grants. These funds are adopted according to the population of the campus and how effective the district is with pursuing grants that will meet the needs of the district.

College and University Funding

As with school district funding, public universities receive funding from the federal, state, and local governments. Universities also might receive donations from individuals, businesses, and foundations, some of which can be substantial. According to research by Pew (2019), states and the federal government have provided considerable financial support for higher education for many decades. However, during the recession of the early 2000s, the federal government took on a greater share of that support than previously, particularly to increase the need-based Pell grants. Thus, the state funding for higher education became only about 12 percent higher than federal funding in 2015.

Although federal and state governments have similar policy goals, federal funding mainly provides financial assistance to individual students and specific research projects, while states primarily pay for the general operations of public institutions. Federal and state funding continue to provide a substantial share of public college and university budgets, at 34 percent of public schools' total revenue in 2017. Since government funding plays an essential role in higher education, policymakers often face difficult choices as they balance support for students and institutions.

Counselor education programs generally are not large programs and often do not receive the funding that business and science programs enjoy. Therefore, money for counseling programs and students might be scarce with leadership carefully designing their programs to meet the needs of as many students as possible along with professors' travel, research, and supplies. Often professors compete for more money through local, state, and federal grants.

Leadership Program Values and Standards

Public School Leadership Program Values and Standards

As school leaders, we are given certain standards to abide by according to *ASCA Ethical Standards for School Counselors* (2022). The "School Counselor Administrators and Supervisors" section shares ways that leaders can govern themselves to help support counselors in their role. Leadership standards are important to assist counselors in utilizing adequate resources to implement a comprehensive school counseling program to meet the needs of their students. Here are the school counselor administer and supervisor standards:

C. School Counselor Administrators/Supervisors

School counselor administrators/supervisors support school counselors in their charge by:

A Advocating both within and outside of their schools or districts for adequate resources to implement a comprehensive school counseling program and meet their students' needs.
B Advocating for fair and open distribution of resources among programs supervised. An allocation procedure should be developed that is nondiscriminatory, informed by data and consistently applied.
C Taking reasonable steps to ensure school and other resources are available to provide staff supervision and training.
D Providing opportunities for professional development in current research related to counseling practice and ethics.
E Taking steps to eliminate conditions or practices in their schools or organizations that may violate, discourage or interfere with compliance with the ethics and laws related to the profession.
F Monitoring school and organizational policies, regulations and procedures to ensure practices are consistent with the ASCA Ethical Standards for School Counselors.

As a leader of school counselors, the important values that make a difference in building a strong counseling team are being fair, advocating for the team, assessing the needs of the team and having an attitude of servitude to the team. Ethical leadership encompasses all of these traits. Ethical leadership consists of two elements. First, ethical leaders must act and make decisions ethically, looking at all aspects of the decision in a way that will result in a positive outcome for the people they lead. But, secondly, ethical leaders must also lead ethically – in the ways they treat people in everyday interaction, in their attitudes, in the ways they encourage, and in the directions in which they steer their organizations, institutions, or initiatives.

Ethical leadership is both visible and invisible. The visible part is in the way the leader works with and treats others, in their behavior in public, in their statements and in their actions. The invisible aspects of ethical leadership lie in the leader's character, in their decision-making process, in their mindset, in the set of values and principles on which one draws, and in their courage to make ethical decisions in tough situations.

Ethical leaders are ethical all the time, not just when someone's looking; and they are ethical over time, proving again and again that ethics are an integral part of the intellectual and philosophical framework they use to understand and relate to the world.

University Counselor Education Leadership Program Values and Standards

Counselor education programs encompass the leadership of students being trained to be counselors and counselor educators. Faculty in counselor education programs have a strong professional identity, teach courses that train students to become professionals, and model for students professional behavior, ethics, and standards. These programs are accredited by the Council for the Accreditation of Counseling and Related Educational Programs (CACREP) (2024) and are considered the gold standard for excellent counseling programs. CACREP Standards (2024) are designed to do the following: to assure the public that a program is of excellent quality, to promote a unified profession, and to ensure that graduates have a strong professional identity and have an opportunity to specialize in one or more areas. Not all programs are accredited by CACREP which often is a budgetary decision due to the expense of the application process and providing travel and lodging expenses for the visiting accreditation team. There are programs that adhere to the CACREP Standards (2024) but which are not accredited.

The CACREP Standards (2024) address the requirements for the following: the learning environment; professional counseling identity; professional practice; evaluation of the program including students, faculty, and supervisors. The specialty areas included are addiction counseling; career counseling; clinical mental health counseling; clinical rehabilitation counseling; college counseling and student affairs; marriage, couple, and family counseling; and school counseling. Standards are specified for both master's level and doctoral programs. How many programs are housed in each counseling department usually requires approval from the university administration and the state board of higher education. These additions can be time-consuming and funding must be available to implement new programs.

Leadership in Practice

Public School

School counselor leaders must meet with the business office manager to learn policies, timelines, funding streams, and so forth. at the early onset of being hired. Understanding the budgetary rules and regulations is essential to the skills of a new school counselor leader. Once the allowable funds are distributed to the district counseling department, the district leader must allocate funds to each school and to special projects of the district that are considered to be under the auspices of the counseling department. For example, some of the purchases might be district-wide testing, travel for school counselors to conferences and workshops, specialty supplies unique to counselors such as books and games, supplies for meetings and running the main counseling office, and hiring clerical help and registrars or attendance clerks. The salaries for school counselor personnel also might be allocated to the district counseling office.

District leaders in counseling might search for funds from other sources such as donations from community agencies, educational foundations, parent-teacher associations, and local businesses. Additionally, state-wide or federal grants might be available for special projects. Grants are available through, for example, U.S. Department of Education (2023), Substance Abuse and Mental Health Services Administration (2023), and state grants such as the ones in Texas (TEA, 2023).

Once funds are allocated to each school counseling department, it is incumbent on the lead counselor and/or the principal to decide how each dollar is spent. Often, school counselors are provided with a minimum budgetary allowance and are able to make requests to the district leader or the campus principal for additional funds. If the counseling budget includes personnel, the principal controls those funds. As pointed out earlier, since budgets for counseling departments are often quite scarce, the most important budgetary decisions include ethical decision-making and wise choices for how money is spent.

Universities and Colleges

Generally, money filters down from the president's office, to the deans of the various colleges or schools, and then to the chairs of the various departments. There are many federal, state, and local regulations about how money in higher education is spent. The chair of a counseling department might have an assistant whose role is to keep the books and report to the chair what money is being requested and how much is being spent. Decisions about funds generally fall to the chair who might determine how faculty travel money, scholarship funding, and miscellaneous funds are spent. Not only are the above budgetary items important, but also the day-to-day operation of the department must be funded. That might include new technology equipment, graduate assistants and funding for faculty research projects, clerical assistance and supplies, and so forth. Many counseling programs operate mental health clinics which can also incur substantial expenses, particularly if there are systems in place to record counseling sessions, to safely store those sessions, and an option to speak to students as they counsel clients (the bug-in-the-ear). Expenses such as these probably would not be included in the yearly budget, but would be a special line item request of the university administration.

Mental and Behavioral Health Considerations

Partnering with local mental health agencies is key to supporting a strong comprehensive school counseling program and can also enhance university counselor education programs. These partnerships help with funding because sometimes the services are free of charge and help bring resources and programs to students or trainees that would otherwise need funding. Most local mental health agencies are either a 403b or grant funded programs.

Creation of a community collaborative that encompasses several mental health agencies that support the mental health initiatives of a district or a university program is essential. University programs in particular need a large bank of agencies for internship sites. Since we are in the post pandemic era, the need to assist students and staff with mental health support is at an all-time high. Some creative ways to allocate funding in school districts that will help support mental health initiatives are to add additional school counselors, social service worker/specialists, and mental health support staff to directly assist students at the campus level.

Ethical Considerations

According to the ACA Code of Ethics (2014), the following applies to budgetary issues in both K–12 and higher education.

I.1 Standards and the Law

I.1.a. Knowledge. Counselors know and understand the ACA Code of Ethics and other applicable ethics codes from professional organizations or certification and licensure bodies of which they are members. Lack of knowledge or misunderstanding of an ethical responsibility is not a defense against a charge of unethical conduct.

I.1.b. Ethical Decision Making. When counselors are faced with an ethical dilemma, they use and document, as appropriate, an ethical decision making model that may include, but is not limited to, consultation; consideration of relevant ethical standards, principles, and laws; generation of potential courses of action; deliberation of risks and benefits; and selection of an objective decision based on the circumstances and welfare of all involved.

Ethical leadership is possessing the personality and skills that make other people want to follow you. The leader must act in a way that is moral and honest which makes the followers act in a way that will help achieve the common goal. Yukl (2009) summarizes the ethical leader as one who promotes honesty, and mirrors his or her actions with their values and beliefs. Leaders are challenged with considering things such as trust, honesty, and fairness.

An ethical leader models and exhibits morals and beliefs that are for the betterment of the people they are leading. This is also important in financial decision making. Ethical leaders know and do what is right and this is where people sometimes get into trouble because of their definition or understanding of what is right. People interpret that by what they have experienced, how they are raised, and the overall situational context of their surroundings. These factors will directly affect the people you are leading and the results you are trying to accomplish. This is important in dealing with finances and making decisions on how to fairly distribute your funds to needed sources.

As we look at ethical leaders and how they approach finances in public schools and universities, we must look at the model being used. Finance decision-making should focus on creating a system of funding that will provide the needed resources to determine a child's access to the best educational opportunity in public schools and excellent training at universities. When determining where to allocate funds we must consider two ethical issues: 1. Does it encourage behaviors that we do not want to see among our students and faculty? 2. Does the funding align with the mission and vision of the campus, district, department, and university?

When we are tasked with handling funding and finances we must consider our code of ethics, internal policies, and practices and how we view finances to better support our goals. Given the added focus on distribution of finances in a fair way we must look for ways to incorporate the important factors needed to make an ethical decision. A good way to approach it is to consider the situation and circumstances, identify if there are any ethical issues involved, and look at an established procedure to fairly distribute funds.

Cultural Complexities

According to Section 3 of CACREP (2024):

> Ethical behavior, diversity, equity, inclusion, and critical thinking are integral to counselor preparation and should be infused throughout the curriculum. Diversity refers to all aspects of intersectional and cultural identity. Counselor preparation programs address culturally sustaining content and strategies across the eight foundational curriculum areas.
>
> (CACREP, 2024: 14)

In the section under Foundational Counseling Curriculum, 11 standards relevant to social and cultural diversity are required knowledge of all entry-level counselor education graduates. Counselor education programs must document where each of the standards is taught in the curriculum.

Multicultural considerations have to be examined when managing a budget in both school districts and university programs. The goal is to avoid biased management decisions when allocating funds for respective programs. Understanding and respecting the differences in people, as well as understanding the complexity of diverse people, is a vital trait for any leader to have to avoid funding biases. It is important to understand that the different cultural groups will have different expectations for their leaders. These expectations will ultimately affect the behaviors of employees and their leaders. The goal is to ensure that these expectations do not affect the allocation of funds to the appropriate programs that are needed.

With the dramatic change in the demographic composition of our student populations, it is imperative that we look at our demographics when we are making decisions about finances. As we decide on the programs needed for our students, we must look at who our students are and their cultural background to make a decision to best meet the needs of the students. We cannot budget based on a uniform system but on the basis of differential budgeting where we are looking at all aspects of the students' backgrounds. Soliciting the input from educators and faculty who understand this is important so that the allocation of funds to meet those needs are taken into consideration.

Strategic Considerations

School District Budgets

As a leader for all school counselors in a district, budgeting is very important. Making a detailed plan ahead of time to understand where you would like to distribute your funds is essential. Understanding where to allocate funds and deciding on what areas to prioritize is important in budgeting and funding usage. The overall goal in budgeting should be to ensure that it is used as a valuable tool for planning and the evaluation processes. The budgeting tool should explain educational goals and programs in the form of a financial resource plan.

Assisting and giving resources to help assist counselors in making good sound budgeting decisions is most important so that the program goals are accomplished. One example of assisting is to have a budgeting planning day where counselors can come together and collaborate on ideas to utilize their budget in an efficient way. Sharing best practices on how to create ideas and programs is a great tool so that counselors can present to their campuses to solicit more funding or monies from the local campus budget. If there is a plan based on needs of the campus, then the likelihood of getting the funding is higher than not having a plan.

When determining budgetary allocations, the plan should be to meet student educational needs and goals for student success. The school creates a campus improvement plan that outlines what is needed on the campus based on the needs assessment, the counseling department is a part of this plan. There are several methods used to allocate school counselor funding for departments. One method is based on percentage distribution based on student enrollment. This is where funds are distributed based on your student enrollment and attendance. Once the amount is determined then the monies are given to the campus level to help with counseling needs. Another method is to prepare a projected plan that is needed for the upcoming year. If approved, then the department is issued the projected amount or even more.

According to some school districts, department allocations are usually based on prior year allocation which may include any increases or decreases that may have occurred during the year which will give you a good estimate of how to adjust your budget. One district states that department managers should consider factors like: goals and objectives identified in the DIP, past expenditures from the department based on function and object codes, analyzing your staff needs, and ideas based on campus improvement plan (Galena Park Independent School District, 2021).

A good practice would be to solicit funding from different resources for training and professional development. Most leaders are given a general local budget that can be used to conduct training and provide professional development for counselors districtwide. Training and professional development is extremely important for continued growth for counselors. Another source of funding for training and professional development is to ask the campus principals to help support funding for their counselors to attend training and professional development. One common practice is to ask all principals to pay for their counselors to be a part of a professional association as well as allow them to attend at least one conference a year.

Districts that get Title One funding could get support from federal funds to help support training for your campus counselors. Asking those departments that have federal funds to help support the training for counselors since they support all populations which is a good source of funding. From past experience, most are willing to help support training and professional development.

Guest speakers and consultants are utilized to bring good sound professional development to help support different programs counselors want for their students. Guest speakers and consultants are essential to meeting the needs of the goals of the counseling plan. Both may help improve student academic and social learning by bringing expertise, and exposure to external services and programs. When seeking guest speakers and/or consultants, it is important to get referrals or some type of review of the services provided. This will give you an idea of what to expect from the services you are requesting. Often vetting the vendor is required and is a process which can be overwhelming to some prospective candidates. However, the process is necessary to ensure the district/department is vetting all possible vendors and getting the best potential candidate with the best quality of services.

Some districts require the preparation of a proposal to justify funding requests. Researching and getting background information to get a clear explanation for the request of funding is essential. The proposal should include the following: the purpose for the funding, steps needed to achieve the purpose, how the funding will be used – what resources will be purchased, timeline for the need of the funds, and what will be the outcome from the use of the funds.

The goal for assessing the needs of counselors is to compile a wishlist with every counselor to determine what they feel they need. The list could be supplies, guidance curriculum suggestions, counseling programs, guest speakers, and training suggestions. This list should be completed at the beginning and end of the year. Once received, a good rule of thumb would be to have individual conversations to get a better understanding of how those items or programs will be used. If there is reasonableness to the need then determine an estimated dollar amount. At that point reviewing the actual budget and setting an estimated budget amount could be distributed to counselors if approved.

Grant usage is important in any area of education. Oftentimes, counselors do not translate the importance of usage of grant funding or how to pursue grants that help their programs. When counselors understand how to look for grants that would be beneficial to their programs they provide a multitude of services to their students. Because districts are given federal funds there are many benefits to receiving grants.

Good leaders should share best practices on how grant funding could be utilized and how to actively seek grants that will support their counseling programs. Most districts have funding through their educational foundation department that has many opportunities for employees to write grants to get awarded funding through the foundation. The key is to understand what you need for your students and seek ways to prepare to get grant funding to assist.

University Budgets

Leaders in counselor education programs make decisions about programs and policies that determine how money is spent and must take into account many factors. For example, tenured faculty might believe that they should have the lion's share of the budget because they are seasoned researchers and are published in journals. On the other hand, new faculty need opportunities and the ability to begin their journey toward tenure and advancement in the field, and they need funding also. Additionally, state and federal rules and regulations about funding will determine how certain funds can be utilized.

Sometimes competing budget requests can put the department head in a difficult position which is why departmental budget policies should be in place rather than a helter skelter way of divvying up money. These policies are best discussed and written by the entire faculty or a budget committee, so that they seem fair and so that faculty understand how much money is available and which line items are non-negotiable such as money needed for orientation and graduation. Special events, speakers, and new programs must be included in the budget also. Again, faculty input is important so that everyone feels that they understand the budget and know where money is being spent.

Grant writing is very important in higher education, and professors compete vigorously for funding from the government and from individuals and foundations. Many universities have courses on grant writing, so that professors can learn how best to be competitive in grant awards. Universities also often have entire departments dedicated to locating grants currently being offered and assisting professors in the writing and submission of grant applications. The United States Department of Education, the Substance Abuse and Mental

Health Services Administration, and Health and Human Services are three federal agencies that provide grant funding that are relevant to the counseling field. When federal grants are announced, phone consultations and technological help are offered, but it is up to grant writers to find out when these assists are offered. Grant writers must submit a good case for why grant money should be allocated to their university and their program in order to be competitive. Federal grants are complex and time-consuming, but they can often bring millions of extra dollars to a university.

Conclusion

School and university budgets are complex and often require specially trained personnel to manage them. Individuals, departments, schools, and universities need money and depend on state and federal funding to run their programs, operate their facilities, pay their employees, and provide as much as possible for those who are served. Often leaders are competing with each other for funding and find themselves spending a great deal of time trying to convince those who hold the purse strings that their needs are urgent. School counselor leaders, directors, and administrators must be savvy about budgeting in order to avoid depleting funds before the end of the financial cycle. Additionally, transparency about the budget is critical to maintaining trustworthiness and fairness when it comes to dividing funds among individuals, committees, and departments.

References

American School Counselor Association (2022) *ASCA Ethical Standards for School Counselors*, Alexandria, VA: Author.

Council of the Accreditation of Counseling and Related Educational Programs (CACREP) (2024) "2024 CACREP Standards". Online. Available HTTP: <https://www.cacrep.org/wp-content/uploads/2022/10/Draft-4-2024-CACREP-Standards.pdf>

Galena Park Independent School District (2021) *Galena Park Independent School District Fiscal Manual 2021*, Houston, TX: Author.

Ellerson, N. (1985) "School budget 101", *American Association of School Administrators*. Online. Available HTTP: <https://docplayer.net/5387270-School-budgets-101-prepared-by-noelle-ellerson-policy-analyst-american-association-of-school-administrators-nellerson-aasa.html>

Pew (2019) "Two Decades of Change in Federal and State Higher Education Funding: Recent trends across levels of government". Online. Available HTTP: <pewtrusts.org/en/research-and-analysis/issue-briefs/2019/10/two-decades-of-change-in-federal-and-state-higher-education-funding>

Substance Abuse and Mental Health Services Administration (2023) "Grants". Online. Available HTTP: <https://www.samhsa.gov/grants>

Texas Education Agency (TEA) (2010) Texas Education Agency (2010) "2010 Comprehensive Annual Report on Texas Public Schools". Online. Available HTTP: <https://tea.texas.gov/sites/default/files/Comp_Annual_2010.pdf>

TEA (2023) "Grants Administration". Online. Available HTTP: <https://tea.texas.gov/finance-and-grants/grants/grants-administration>

U.S. Department of Education (2023) "Apply for a Grant". Online. Available HTTP: <https://www2.ed.gov/fund/grant/apply/grantapps/index.html?src=ft>

Yukl, G. (2009) "Leadership and organizational learning: An evaluative essay", *Leadership Quarterly*, 20: 49–53.

Young, A. (2013) "Building-level leadership", *ASCA School Counselor*. Online. Available HTTP: <https://www.schoolcounselor.org/getmedia/b17aaa18-60f0-42f8-ad1e-52552e0959b7/Building-Level.pdf20-23>

19 Partnerships that Streamline Mental Health Services in Schools

Carlete Metoyer

Leadership Quote

Great strides in education are never accomplished alone, but rather with the support of research at institutions of higher education, businesses, agencies and nonprofits, volunteers from the community-at-large, and, of course, students, their families, and school personnel.

Judy A. Nelson

Aspirational Statements

- Strategic partnerships enhance the richness of school counseling programs by increasing professional capacity and broadening access to resources.
- School counselor leaders should view partnerships from a multifaceted perspective and use general business principles to cultivate enriched experiences for students.

Introduction and Background

School counselors create comprehensive school counseling programs by defining, managing, delivering, and assessing each program component individually and collectively. Oftentimes, the comprehensive plan is implemented with limited resources: time, energy (human capital), and funding.

Time

Counselors must find time to accomplish the comprehensive plan against time constraints and priorities of the campus and school district, which can include non-counseling responsibilities. According to the American School Counseling Association (ASCA) (2021a), 39 percent of school counselors reported being assigned inappropriate duties relative to the scope of the profession, 29 percent reported challenges finding time to engage in professional development, and 27 percent reported difficulty finding time to connect with students during the school day (pre-COVID).

DOI: 10.4324/9781003219750-23

Energy (Human Capital)

Counselor/students ratio recommendations have been established for a number of years at the national level and some at the state level. However, ratios continue to exceed the recommendations, leading counselors to find creative ways to address student academic and mental health needs without sacrificing quality. According to ASCA (2021a), 51 percent of school counselors reported managing high caseloads as a daily challenge.

Funding

Every year, school districts are challenged to improve student outcomes with shrinking budgets. Some school counselors have reported not having a programming budget to facilitate the necessary programming for student success. The following chapter will address methods to access funding for programming.

What Are Partnerships?

Partnerships enable schools and school counselors to address these limited resources. School–family–community partnerships are:

> collaborative initiatives and relationships between school personnel, families, and community members who function as equal and mutual partners in the planning, coordinating, and implementing of programs at home, at school, and in the community to help increase students' academic, social/emotional, and college-career outcomes for students and their families.
>
> (Bryan and Henry, 2012)

Partnerships can include collaboration with universities, businesses, faith-based organizations, as well as mental health and social service agencies.

The ASCA (2021b) supports the school counselor's role in developing partnerships: school counselors work with students, their families, school staff and community members in the implementation of a school counseling program in establishing school and community partnerships that:

- promote student academic, career and social/emotional development;
- inform the school community about relevant community resources;
- actively pursue collaboration with family members and community stakeholders;
- remove barriers to the successful implementation of school–family–community partnerships (e.g., mistrust and miscommunication between parties, resistance to the concept and practice, transportation and childcare issues, accessible meeting times).

School counselors serve as advocates, leaders, facilitators, initiators, evaluators, and collaborators to create, enrich, and assess the effect of these partnerships on student success within the school counseling program.

Effective partnerships can positively influence the school climate and increase student outcomes in academic development, social/emotional development as well as college-career planning. The table below shows the indirect and the direct impact of partnerships:

Table 19.1 Impact of Partnerships

Indirect Impact	Direct Impact
• Creates a robust school counselor applicant pipeline • Enhances program effectiveness • Increases opportunities for professional growth and training	• Increases academic achievement • Fosters resilience in students • Reduces risks for students
Positively Impacts the School Climate and Culture	

Created by C. Metoyer, 2022.

Effective partnerships can be the key to accessing support, skills, new networks and additional programming. Using a formal partnership agreement (e.g., contractual agreements and/or memorandum of understanding) helps to outline clear expectations, allows the work to continue beyond staff changes, and creates equity in the power structure, and decision making between partners. This chapter will discuss implementation strategies, implications, and considerations for selecting appropriate partnerships and measures to assess partnership effectiveness.

Leadership Program Values and Standards

The Council for the Accreditation of Counseling and Related Educational Programs (CACREP) (2024) outlines specific standards and competencies for partnerships between school districts and graduate programs for internships and practicum completion in Section 4: Professional Practice:

> **ENTRY-LEVEL PROFESSIONAL PRACTICE**
>
> A The counselor education program provides on-going support to help students find field experience sites that are sufficient to provide the quality, quantity, and variety of expected experiences to prepare students for their roles and responsibilities as professional counselors within their specialized practice areas.
> B Students are covered by individual professional counseling liability insurance while enrolled in practicum and internship.
> C Supervision of practicum and internship students includes secure audio/video recordings and/or live supervision of students' interactions with clients that are in compliance with applicable institutional, state, federal, and international privacy requirements for all program delivery types.
> D Students have the opportunity to become familiar with a variety of professional activities and resources, including technology, during their practicum and internship.
> E Formative and summative evaluations of the student's counseling performance and ability to integrate and apply knowledge are conducted as part of the student's practicum and internship.
> F Students have regular, systematic opportunities to evaluate their experience with the practicum and internship placement process.
> G Students have regular, systematic opportunities to evaluate practicum and internship sites and supervisors.

H Programs provide a fieldwork handbook to all students and site supervisors, in all program delivery types, detailing requirements, expectations, policies and procedures including:

1 CACREP standards and definitions related to supervised practicum and internship,
2 supervision agreement,
3 evaluation procedures and requirements, and
4 policy for student retention, remediation, and dismissal from the program.

I In addition to the development of individual counseling skills, during either the practicum or internship, students must lead or co-lead a counseling or psychoeducational group.
J The counselor education program provides orientation to site supervisors regarding program requirements and expectations.
K During entry-level professional practice experiences, the counselor education program engages in consultation with the site to monitor student learning.
L Professional development opportunities are provided by the counselor education program to site supervisors for all program delivery types.
M Written supervision agreements:

1 define the roles and responsibilities of the faculty supervisor, site supervisor, and student during practicum and internship,
2 include emergency procedures, and
3 detail the format and frequency of consultation between the program and the site to monitor student learning.

SUPERVISOR QUALIFICATIONS

N Counselor education program core or affiliate faculty members serving as individual/triadic or group practicum/internship supervisors for students in entry-level programs have:

1 relevant training for in-person and/or distance counseling supervision,
2 active certifications and/or licenses required for practice preferably in counseling, or a related profession, and
3 proficiency in the use of technology utilized for supervision.

O Doctoral students serving as individual/triadic or group practicum/internship supervisors for students in entry-level programs must:

1 have completed entry-level counseling degree requirements consistent with CACREP standards,
2 have completed or are receiving preparation in counseling supervision, including instruction in in-person and/or distance supervision, and
3 be under supervision on a regular schedule that averages one hour a week from a qualified counselor education program faculty supervisor.

P Site supervisors have:

1 a minimum of a master's degree, preferably in counseling, or a related profession,

2 active certifications and/or licenses required for practice preferably in counseling, or a related profession,
3 a minimum of two years post-master's professional experience in the specialized practice area in which the student is enrolled,
4 proficiency in the use of technology utilized for supervision,
5 knowledge of the program's expectations, requirements, and evaluation procedures for students, and
6 relevant training for in-person and/or distance counseling supervision.

PRACTICUM

Q Students complete supervised counseling practicum experiences that total a minimum of 100 hours over a full academic term that is a minimum of 8 weeks consistent with the institution's academic calendar.

R Practicum students complete at least 40 hours of direct service with actual clients that contributes to the development of counseling skills.

PRACTICUM SUPERVISION

S Throughout the duration of practicum, each student receives individual and/or triadic supervision on a regular schedule that averages one hour a week and is provided by at least one of the following:

1 a counselor education program core or affiliate faculty member, or
2 a doctoral student supervisor who is under the supervision of a counselor education program faculty member, or
3 a site supervisor who is working in consultation on a regular schedule with a counselor education program faculty member in accordance with the supervision agreement.

T Throughout the duration of practicum, each student receives group supervision on a regular schedule that averages 1 1/2 hours per week and is provided by at least one of the following:

1 a counselor education program core or affiliate faculty member, or
2 a doctoral student supervisor who is under the supervision of a counselor education program faculty member.

INTERNSHIP

U After successful completion of the practicum, students complete 600 hours of supervised counseling internship in roles and settings with actual clients relevant to their specialized practice area.

V Internship students complete at least 240 hours of direct service with actual clients.

INTERNSHIP SUPERVISION

W Throughout the duration of internship, each student receives individual and/or triadic supervision on a regular schedule that averages one hour a week and is provided by at least one of the following:

1 a counselor education program core or affiliate faculty member, or
2 a doctoral student supervisor who is under the supervision of a counselor education program faculty member, or
3 a site supervisor who is working in consultation on a regular schedule with a counselor education program faculty member in accordance with the supervision agreement.

X Throughout the duration of internship, each student receives group supervision on a regular schedule that averages 1 1/2 hours per week and is provided by at least one of the following:

1 a counselor education program core or affiliate faculty member, or
2 a doctoral student supervisor who is under the supervision of a counselor education program faculty member.

Leadership in Practice

The ideal school–parent–community partnership uses a systematic approach, understanding the value of supporting the whole child. Therefore, schools and school counselors should identify potential partners that can address both in school and out of school challenges that impede student success.

Below are steps to take to identify where a partnership may be useful and how to engage:

1 **Review needs assessment data (student, staff, community).** Needs assessments, which are included in the comprehensive school counseling plan, assist school counselors in determining the health and impact of the program. They can also provide vital information about gaps in services or support. The needs assessment may also help school counselors generate a list of potential partners as students, staff, parents, and community may make recommendations to address gaps. Focus groups or thought exchanges can also be useful in clarifying needs assessment data and generating ideas for possible partnerships. Using needs assessment data to determine where a partnership is needed will ensure that partnerships

address the end-user (students, families, school, communities) and serve as a future data collection point to determine the impact of the partnership.

2 **Complete an analysis** to determine the areas the current program or school counselors can address the needs identified in the assessment. This will reduce the potential for overlapping services, causing underutilization. In the same manner businesses use the SWOT (Strengths, Weaknesses, Opportunities, Threats) analysis model, school counselors can use a similar version:

- Strengths
- Challenges
- Opportunities
- Vulnerabilities

It may be helpful to capture analysis data from the school counselor, the school counseling team, and the district school counseling department. The results may reveal areas where support can be shifted before starting to engage with partnerships.

3 **Identify key stakeholders** by asking who should have a voice in the decision making. Stakeholders not only inform the decision making, but can also serve as allies to increase buy-in and participation. To identify key stakeholders, identify all areas where the partnership may have an impact or require engagement. Potential key stakeholders can include:

- Student representative
- School counselors
- Teacher representative
- Administrators
- Parent representative
- Community representative

Depending on the nature of the partnership, additional stakeholders may be included for wrap-around support:

- Information Technology
- Legal Services
- Communications
- Transportation/Logistics
- Food Services
- Health Services

4 **Create success criteria** for both partnership identification, selection, and evaluation. The success criteria should align with the school and school district's mission, vision, and focus. To create success criteria, complete the following statement: "We will know we are successful if we ..." Using success criteria will also serve as a guide for the formal agreement and assist in identifying potential barriers to entry early. The established success criteria combined with the Heath and Heath (2013) Decision Making Model can be used to guide the identification and research process:

- Widen Your Options
- Reality-Test Your Assumptions
- Attain Distance Before Deciding
- Prepare to be Wrong

Connect with your current partners and stakeholders during the search as they may be the link to accessing new individuals and organizations.

5 **Interview and engage potential partners** from the perspective of the end-user (students, families, staff, community). Great organizations exist; however, this does not mean all great organizations are ideal partners. Use the information from your needs assessment, analysis, and success criteria to determine if potential partners address the identified needs, enhance the overall program by strengthening identified weaknesses, create a new opportunity, and fill the gap of a vulnerability. Involve your key stakeholders in the interviews, site visits and/or product demonstrations to gain a multifaceted perspective. Include questions about the organization's mission, vision, and values. Misaligned values can eventually become a detriment to the partnership.
6 **Establish a formal agreement** through vendorship, a contractual agreement and/or a memorandum of understanding (MOU). A formal agreement legitimizes the partnership and will enable the work to continue even when staff changes occur. The document should outline the specific roles and responsibilities of the partnership, stipulations for data collection and sharing, as well as partnership evaluation. The agreement should also include a projected timeline, benchmarks for progress monitoring, and detail how partnership outcomes will be evaluated.
7 **Evaluate the health of the partnership** using process, perception, and outcome data. Is the partnership addressing the identified need(s) from the assessment? Is the partnership increasing the strengths of the program identified in the analysis?

Mental and Behavioral Health Considerations

As Chapter 1 notes, schools have become de facto mental health centers for students while also continuing to address academic development as well as college-career planning. Partnerships with mental health service providers can aid in timely prevention and intervention of mental health challenges and crises. To adequately address student needs, ASCA Professional Standards and Competencies (2019) outlines steps school counselors should take to connect students and parents with community mental health providers:

B-SS 4. Make referrals to appropriate school and community resources

a Maintain a list of current referral resources, consistent with school and district policies, for students, staff and families to effectively address academic, career and social/emotional issues
b Communicate the limits of school counseling and the continuum of mental health services
c Articulate why diagnoses and long-term therapy are outside the scope of school counseling

(2019: 5)

In addition to the steps outlined in Leadership in Practice, special consideration should be given to potential partnerships with community mental health providers:

- **Location Access** – Will students and parents be able to access the location using various means of transportation? Does the mental health provider have the ability to set up an office on campus or in a centralized area of the district?
- **Hours of Operation** – Does the mental health provider offer flexible scheduling to align with school or parent/guardian work schedules?
- **Services Offered** – Do the services address the identified student needs? What is the process to connect the student with services not offered by the mental health provider?
- **Cost** – Will families be responsible for the cost, whether using their private insurance or paying out of pocket? Will the district provide cost-sharing through grants and other funding sources?
- **Coordination of Care** – How will the mental health provider engage with the school counselor to support successful outcomes? What information will be required from the school and what information will be shared back to the school from the mental health provider?
- **Site Visits** – Will school leaders have opportunities for site visits? Observing the care environment is important to understanding how outcome success is achieved as well as maintaining the school counselor's referral credibility. When visiting, ask "is this a place I would send my student to receive care?"
- **Legal Considerations** – What items need to be addressed in the data collection/data sharing agreement? Does the partnership adhere to FERPA and HIPAA laws?

Ethical Considerations

As previously mentioned, misaligned values can be a detriment to a successful partnership. The same is true regarding each organization's ethical guidelines. Therefore, the partnership will benefit from reviewing each organization's ethical guidelines and identifying scope of practice, professional discretion and as well as limits. ASCA (2022) outlines ethical practice guidelines to engage in partnerships for school counselors in section A.6 Appropriate Collaboration, Advocacy and Referrals for Counseling. Any identified areas of potential conflict should be addressed early in the partnership development phase. Early identification may also help both organizations avoid potential legal issues. Figure 19.1 shows a process map to address ethical issues.

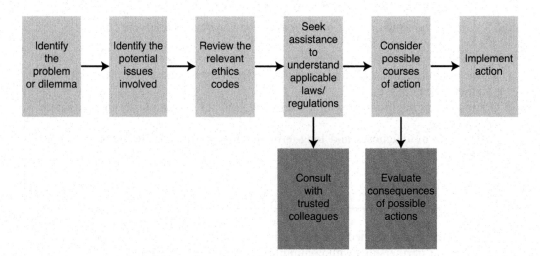

Figure 19.1 Addressing Ethical Issues. Created by C. Metoyer, 2022.

Cultural Complexities

Equally important to the success of a partnership are multicultural considerations as they can have ethical implications. School counselors recognize the importance of creating culturally diverse programs for students. ASCA (2019) *Professional Standards and Competencies* advise school counselors to:

B-PF 6. Demonstrate understanding of the impact of cultural, social and environmental influences on student success and opportunities

a Demonstrate basic knowledge and respect of differences in customs, communications, traditions, values, and other traits among students based on race, religion, ethnicity, nationality, sexual orientation, gender identity, physical or intellectual ability, and other factors.
b Explain how students' cultural, social and economic background may affect their academic achievement, behavior, relationships and overall performance in school.
c Maintain and communicate high expectations for every student, regardless of cultural, social or economic background.
d Explain the dynamics of cross-cultural communications and demonstrate the ability to communicate with persons of other cultures effectively.
e Collaborate with administrators, teachers and other staff in the school and district to ensure culturally responsive curricula and student-centered instruction.
f Understand personal limitations and biases, and articulate how they may affect the school counselor's work.

School counselors should seek out potential partners who also give high priority to cultural competence. The above standards can also be used to guide and inform partnership development. As part of step 5: Identify, Research, Interview outlined in Leadership in Practice, consider including a cultural awareness evaluation. Scorecard elements can include:

- **Cultural Awareness** – an understanding of the various cultures served by the school
- **Cultural Responsiveness** – including programming and offering that address different languages, customs, and beliefs
- **Cultural Representation** – materials, technology, partners reflect the diversity of the organization.

Strategic Considerations

Thoughtful planning and consideration of the development process increases the likelihood of reaching the partnership's success outcomes. The sample timeline from Bryan and Henry (2012), Dougherty (2013), Heath and Heath (2013), and Walsh (2019) shown in Figure 19.2 illustrates how to pace development tasks:

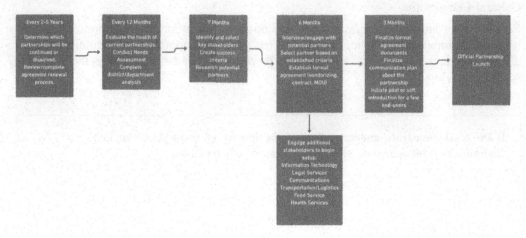

Figure 19.2 Partnership Timelines. Created by C. Metoyer, 2022.

Conclusion

The practices outlined above are based on general business principles, therefore state agencies and higher education institutions can use them as well when considering a partnership. The key is to take a multifaceted perspective in identifying the student needs, analyzing current program and personnel strengths, and selecting partners aligned to the mission, vision, values, and focus of the district, school, and comprehensive school counseling plan.

References

American School Counselor Association (ASCA) (2019) *ASCA School Counselor Professional Standards & Competencies*. Alexandria, VA: Author.

ASCA (2021a) *ASCA Research Report: State of the Profession 2020*. Online. Available HTTP: <https://www.schoolcounselor.org/getmedia/bb23299b-678d-4bce-8863-cfcb55f7df87/2020-State-of-the-Profession.pdf>

ASCA (2021b) "The School Counselor and School-Family-Community Partnerships". Online. Available HTTP: <https://www.schoolcounselor.org/Standards-Positions/Position-Statements/ASCA-Position-Statements/The-School-Counselor-and-School-Family-Community-P>

ASCA (2022) *ASCA Ethical Standards for School Counselors*, Alexandria, VA: Author.

Bryan, J. and Henry, L. (2012) "A model for building school–family–community partnerships: principles and process", *Journal of Counseling & Development*, 90(4): 408–420.

Council of the Accreditation of Counseling and Related Educational Programs (CACREP) (2024) "2024 CACREP Standards". Online. Available HTTP: <https://www.cacrep.org/wp-content/uploads/2022/10/Draft-4-2024-CACREP-Standards.pdf>

Dougherty, A.M. (2013) *Psychological Consultation and Collaboration in School and Community Settings*, Boston, MA: Cengage Learning.

Heath, C. and Heath, D. (2013) *Decisive: How to Make Better Choices in Life and Work*, New York: Random House.

Walsh, M. (2019) *Practice Brief: How to Work with Community Partners*. Boston College Center for Optimized Student Support. Online. Available HTTP: <https://www.bc.edu/content/dam/bc1/schools/lsoe/sites/coss/Practicebriefs/How%20to%20work%20with%20community%20partners%20NEW%20FORMAT%204.2.19.pdf>

Section V

Professional Advocacy to Ensure Mental Health Services for All Students

School counselors are professionally trained to conduct themselves ethically and to use the unique expertise of their training to contribute to the well-being and academic success of students. As such in Section V, it is discussed how school counselors advocate for mental health practices in programs and schools, understand complex personal and professional ethics that embody mental health, and learn about some unstated rules of what leaders overall should know to facilitate optimal mental health. Administrative leaders are thoroughly trained in ethical and legal considerations and understand how issues of mental health can impede the rendering of a proper education for all students.

There is sometimes an underpinning and subtle top-down lens, from which administrative leaders operate toward school counselors, that can stifle and impede professional progress in serving students and families. How is this mindset even possible (or ethical) when these educational leaders, with professional credentials, hold master and doctorate-level degrees within their respective disciplines? How can anyone believe they are superior to the other? It behooves all school leadership (inclusive of school counselors) to operate collaboratively on a plane of parallelism, to understand there are many competencies in their credentials that overlap, and respectfully acknowledge that neither has been trained like the other, which ultimately should elicit a professional respect that engenders collaboration and a choice to accomplish more together than apart.

Lisa A. Wines

As we read more in the news about children and teens who are in trouble, who are depressed, who contemplate suicide, and so on, we realize that the school counselor's services are in great demand. Students, parents, and staff rely on the school counselor to adhere to a set of standards that guarantees integrity, sound decision-making, satisfactory working relationships, and well-planned interventions for individuals and groups.

Judy A. Nelson

A school administrator views the role of a professional school counselor in the way(s) that they experienced a school counselor when they were in the classroom. Their roles have greatly evolved. Today, the role of a professional school counselor is more expansive than ever and the graduate school requirements have increased and are more focused on mental and behavioral health. A professional school counselor and administrative leader MUST operate ethically on behalf of all students and part of this is operating within their scope of practice.

Natalie Fikac

DOI: 10.4324/9781003219750-24

Section V

Professional Advocacy to
Ensure Mental Health
Services for All Students

20 School Counselors Advocating for Mental Health Practices

Lesley Casarez

> **Leadership Quote**
>
> There is no greater accomplishment in school counseling advocacy than to model advocacy for students and families, then watch as they begin to advocate for themselves.
>
> Judy A. Nelson

> **Aspirational Statement**
>
> - School counselors advocate for students, the profession, and systemic change within their schools, their districts, their state, and beyond.
> - Professional organizations provide the resources and the knowledge for school counselors to advocate on behalf of their students and the profession.

Introduction and Background

School counselors are in a unique position as advocates for students, the profession, and their role. Through professional associations, school counselors gain the knowledge and resources to be able to advocate for effective programs that will enhance the mental health of students in schools. Historically, there are particular barriers to implementation of effective comprehensive school counseling programs. These barriers continue to persist, and advocating to remove these barriers allows for students to be more successful in school and beyond. Realizing the importance of how to implement effective comprehensive school counseling programs, how to advocate for students, for the role of the school counselor, and for the profession is the focus of this chapter.

Professional Associations

Counseling is one of the few professions in which specialty areas emerged first in response to the variety of human needs and were later conceptualized as belonging to the common professional home of counseling. This unusual sequence of events also had an impact on the professional associations that represent the profession. From the early 1950s to the 1970s,

DOI: 10.4324/9781003219750-25

certain specializations made significant strides, including school counseling. One critical significance of these specialty areas is that practitioners typically identify first with their specialty area of practice, and secondarily with the profession of counseling (Leahy et al., 2015).

The first professional association to represent counselors was the American Personnel and Guidance Association (APGA) founded in 1952, which changed to the American Association for Counseling and Development (AACD) in 1983, and eventually became the American Counseling Association (ACA) in 1992. This organization is the largest professional association of counselors in the world with 18 chartered divisions and 56 chartered branches in the United States, Europe, and Latin America (ACA, 2021a). The divisions provide leadership, resources, and information that is unique to specialized areas and/or principles of counseling, while the branches are specific to the location. The ACA Center for Policy, Practice, and Research provides professional support, tools, and content to meet the needs of ACA school counselor members. ACA provides webinars, podcasts, practice briefs, articles, opportunities to earn continuing education credits, tip-sheets, issue briefs, and more (ACA, 2021b).

The American School Counselor Association (ASCA):

> [s]upports school counselors' efforts to help students focus on academic, career and social/emotional development so they achieve success in school and are prepared to lead fulfilling lives as responsible members of society. ASCA provides professional development, publications and other resources, research and advocacy to school counselors around the globe.
>
> (ASCA, 2020)

The ASCA has granted division charters to 48 states and Guam. Membership of ASCA is not required to join a state or territory association.

Depending on the state in which an individual lives, there may be multiple school counseling associations in which to join. These associations may be affiliated with ACA or ASCA.

History of School Counseling Services and Barriers to Implementation

Counseling Services, Ratios, and Programs

In order to understand the importance of advocacy in school counseling, it is important to first understand the history of school counseling services and the barriers to implementing a comprehensive school counseling program (CSCP). School counseling has evolved from providing individualized vocational and occupational information to high school students, to focusing on CSCP frameworks, such as the ASCA National Model (ASCA, 2019) and some state frameworks, such as the Texas Model for Comprehensive School Counseling Programs (Texas Education Agency, 2018) and the West Virginia Department of Education Comprehensive Developmental School Counseling Model (2014). Additionally, school counselors have had to respond to a myriad of mental health crises as these scenarios appear to be growing more prevalent in school settings.

Although implementation of a CSCP may be the most efficacious way to influence student outcomes, this increasing school counselor professional role is increasingly nuanced, complex, and multifaceted to meet the needs of students (Goodman-Scott et al., 2018). There have historically been two barriers faced by school counselors: unmanageable ratios and the number of non-counseling duties that reduce time spent on direct student services.

These can lead to compassion fatigue, stress, emotional disengagement, and burnout (Goodman-Scott et al., 2018).

Foxx et al. (2017) stated that although ratios of school counselors to students may not meet the ideal, they must be reduced for school counselors to be effective in their role, as traditionally the most successful guidance programs are associated with lower student-to-counselor ratios. Large caseloads tend to lead to school counselors who have an inability to address the needs of all students and who become overwhelmed with providing services to students (Moyer, 2011). Smaller student-to-counselor ratios in one particular study were significantly associated with higher graduation rates and lower disciplinary incidents (Lapan et al., 2012a). Research has shown that interactions with a school counselor are paramount to a student's postsecondary success.

A study by the National Association for College Admission Counseling (NACAC) revealed that students who receive one-on-one guidance from a school counselor are 3.2 times more likely to attend college and 6.8 times more likely to apply for financial aid than their peers who do not receive such guidance (Velez, 2016). Lower ratios also improve the overall school climate. One of the strongest studies to date on the role of school counselor ratios and discipline, Carrell and Carrell (2006) found that lower ratios decreased recurrence of disciplinary problems and disciplinary incidents in the first place. These effects were shown to be the strongest for minority and low-income students. Whitson et al. (2010) highlighted how school counseling interventions significantly reduce student behavioral problems.

The American School Counselor Association notes that school counselors should "spend 80 percent or more of their time in direct and indirect services to students" (ASCA, 2017). ASCA defines indirect student services as services in support of students and involves interactions with stakeholders other than the student, such as parents, administrators, or teachers. Direct services are those that occur face-to-face with students and involve facilitating the curriculum and individual or group counseling.

Non-Counseling Duties

Student-to-counselor ratios are valuable sources of data to discern school counselors' ability to fulfill their professional responsibilities. However, some elements that are not readily apparent by merely looking at student to counselor ratios are the actual duties and activities school counselors engage in and the number of non-counseling duties and additional assignments school counselors in small districts are often delegated. The Texas Model for Comprehensive School Counseling Programs (2018) points out that, "Non-counseling duties take valuable time from implementing a school counseling program that meets the needs of all students" (2018: 117). The ASCA Ethical Standards for School Counselors (2022) does not include non-counseling duties as part of a school counselor's duties and emphasizes that all activities provided by the school counselor should correlate with the total school counseling program's mission and goals.

Although fair-share duties delegated to school counselors should be welcomed, all assigned and expected duties should be equitably distributed, reasonable, and should not interfere with a school counselor's ability to provide direct counseling services that students require (Texas Education Agency, 2018). In some cases, school administrators lack knowledge regarding appropriate school counselor duties, which results in them assigning non-counseling activities such as "scheduling, monitoring duties, test coordination, substitute teaching, providing classroom coverage, and data entry that remove counselors from providing direct, face-to-face counseling services to students" (Levin-Epstein, 2018). In smaller school districts the challenge may also be a lack of personnel to cover all needs. Additionally, administrators might not be knowledgeable about the training of school counselors which includes mental health assessment and interventions.

The school counselor position is one in which there are frequent expectations to perform tasks unrelated to professional school counseling, and little importance is given to defined roles (Baggerly and Osborn, 2006). "School counselors often feel pulled in many directions and are at risk for high levels of stress, exhaustion, and overall burnout in their daily work" (Moyer, 2011: 4). Moyer's 2011 study showed that as school counselors' time on non-counseling activities increased, so did their feelings of exhaustion, incompetence, and negativity towards their work environment.

Gysbers and Henderson (2012) placed non-counseling duties as typically fitting into four categories: student supervision (monitoring assemblies, cafeteria duty, bus duty), instruction (substituting for absent teachers, tutoring), clerical (maintaining permanent records, monitoring attendance, calculating grade point averages), and administrative (coordinating school-wide testing program, developing master schedules, covering for the principal). Baggerly and Osborn (2006) pointed out that school counselors often express concern over non-counseling tasks that take time away from their ability to counsel students and that these inappropriate tasks significantly affect their job satisfaction.

School counselors are expected to deliver comprehensive school counselor programs that promote student achievement in academic, social, emotional, and career competencies, as outlined in the *ASCA National Model* (2019). Compelling empirical evidence demonstrates the positive impact a comprehensive school counseling program has on the overall academic achievement of students, their attendance and behavior as well as the overall school climate (Carey and Dimmitt, 2012; Lapan et al., 2012b; Wilkerson et al., 2013). However, when school counselors are unable to deliver the comprehensive school counseling program, or come up against barriers to do so, the next step they must take is to advocate on behalf of the program and the profession.

Advocacy

History of Advocacy

The American School Counselor Association (ASCA) defines an advocate as a person who promotes the well-being of students, parents/guardians and the school counseling profession. School counselors advocate to close the gaps of school success for all students. At its core, advocacy is a means of systemic change. As systemic change agents, school counselors work to either replicate systems that enhance opportunities or eradicate systems that inhibit opportunities (ASCA, 2019). Advocacy includes multiple school counseling roles, and, therefore, it is logical to conclude that everything school counselors do is advocacy (Trusty and Brown, 2005).

Historically, advocacy can be traced back to the early 1900s with Frank Parson's work related to vocational guidance in underserved communities, along with Clifford Beer's efforts in client mental health advocacy. In 1992, the publication of the Multicultural Counseling Competencies (Sue et al., 1992) by the ACA identified advocacy efforts at both individual and systems levels to address disparities and discrimination. In the late 1990s, the ACA began codifying advocacy and highlighting the importance of it, both for the profession and for the work that counselors do for their clients. In 2003, the ACA Governing Council endorsed a comprehensive set of Advocacy Competencies (Lewis et al., 2003), which were updated in 2018 (Toporek and Daniels, 2018). These competencies guide counselors' activities when engaging in advocacy work and address actions across three levels of intervention: the individual client or student; the school, community, or organization; and the public arena.

The ACA focuses on two types of advocacy: 1. issue advocacy, and 2. legislative advocacy. Issue advocacy promotes a particular position on an issue that is usually supported by interest groups rather than candidates. Legislative advocacy involves using methods and procedures to support or discourage the passage of legislation. The ACA encourages members and supporters to contact their legislators to communicate a stance on legislation and ask for their representatives' support or opposition for the legislation. The participation of professional counselors in advocacy is critical because of their expertise in the counseling profession. As experts in the field, professional counselors can effectively explain how bills or state licensure board regulations would affect them and those they serve (ACA, n.d.).

School counselors advocate for the development of programs to support students, but also advocate for their role within their district and to legislative bodies. It is imperative to advocate for awareness and understanding of school counseling standards among educational leaders and policymakers and identify how these support student success. Additionally, ethical standards are utilized as the basis for policies addressing school counseling practices or expectations to ensure school, district, and state leaders have a clear understanding of ethical standards that school counselors are expected to follow (Young and Miller-Kneale, 2013).

Role of Legislators in Advocacy

Legislators have numerous issues and bills to consider for their support, which means they must know about a wide range of issues. These issues may not receive attention until it is time for a vote. The information on each legislator is typically available online and allows the public to read their biographies, research their district(s), committee assignments, how many terms they have served, what kind of voting record they have, and their position on certain issues. These pages will often contain links to sign up for email lists maintained by the legislators' offices to obtain information. Many legislators also have active social media accounts that can be followed for up-to-date information.

When it comes to the role of legislators in advocacy, school counselors should find a champion in the legislature who will support the efforts and issues that school counselors face. Although school counselors may want to start with their own legislators, it is okay to look for others if their own elected representatives aren't in the majority party or on the appropriate committee(s). It is important to learn about the committee that the bill was, or will be, referred to, as well as the members and chair of the committee. These are the legislators who will have the most influence about what happens (ACA, n.d.).

Leadership Program Values and Standards

Standards and Competencies

At the practitioner level, the National Association for College Admission Counseling (NACAC) highlights the need for school counselors to serve as leaders "through demonstration of advocacy and leadership in advancing the concerns of students" (2000: 7). Similarly, the American School Counselor Association (ASCA) acknowledges the importance of leadership through implementation of a comprehensive school counseling program and following the *ASCA School Counselor Professional Standards & Competencies* (ASCA, 2019). Some of the standards and competencies directly related to advocacy and leadership include:

- **Mindset (M) 6.** School counselors are leaders in the school, district, state, and nation.
- **Behavior-Professional Foundation (B-PF) 7.** Demonstrate leadership through the development and implementation of a school counseling program.

    a Identify sources of power and formal and informal leadership.
    b Identify and demonstrate professional and personal qualities and skills of effective leaders.
    c Apply a model of leadership to a school counseling program.
    f Use leadership skills to facilitate positive change for the school counseling program.
    h Serve as a leader in the school and community to promote and support student success.

- **Behavior-Professional Foundation (B-PF) 8.** Demonstrate advocacy for a school counseling program.

    a Model school counselor advocacy competencies to promote school counseling program development and student success.
    b Advocate responsibly for school board policy and local, state, and federal statutory requirements in students' best interests.

- **Behavior-Direct and Indirect Student Services (B-SS) 6.** Collaborate with families, teachers, administrators, other school staff, and education stakeholders for student achievement and success.

    a Partner with others to advocate for student achievement and educational equity and opportunities.

- **Behavior-Planning and Assessment (B-PA) 7.** Establish agreement with the principal and other administrators about the school counseling program.

    e Advocate for the appropriate use of school counselor time based on national recommendations and student needs.

- **Behavior-Planning and Assessment (B-PA) 9.** Use appropriate school counselor performance appraisal process.

    a Explain and advocate for appropriate school counselor performance appraisal process based on school counselor standards and implementation of the school counseling program.

Leadership in Practice

Dispositions, Knowledge, and Skills

To be effective advocates, school counselors must have the advocacy dispositions, knowledge, and skills necessary to be useful in their efforts. According to Trusty and Brown (2005), knowledge of the following basic parameters are required for effective advocacy: a. school policies and procedures; b. local and state political and school-governance structures; c. special education laws (Individuals with Disabilities Education Act, or IDEA) and procedures; d. Section 504 of the Rehabilitation Act of 1973 and the functions of local-school 504 committees; e. Child Protective Services or Youth and Family Services laws and procedures; f. particular state family codes (laws regarding families and children); and g. student assistance program and child study team processes and procedures.

Various skills are also needed to be an effective advocate. As school counselors already know about building and maintaining relationships, they have an advantage. Communication skills, collaboration skills, problem-assessment skills, problem-solving skills, organizational skills, and self-care skills are those needed in advocacy endeavors (Trusty and Brown, 2005). Communication, both verbal and written, will be needed to educate and persuade on various topics. Collaboration and developing positive relationships is paramount to effective advocacy. Problem assessment is typically one of the first steps in advocacy models so that advocacy problems can be assessed and advocacy actions can be taken based on two major criteria: a. the reason for advocacy is compelling, and b. it is likely that a viable solution can be attained (Eriksen, 1997). Once these problems are assessed and defined, then problem-solving skills are used in developing detailed action plans. For advocacy to be successful, school counselors need organizational skills for a. collecting, analyzing, and presenting data; b. planning and organizing actions on multiple fronts; and c. managing the advocacy process (Trusty and Brown, 2005). Finally, self-care skills are needed, particularly when advocacy efforts are not successful. When considerable time and energy is devoted to an advocacy effort and fails to produce change, burnout can result.

How to Talk to Legislators

There are various ways to contact members of Congress, state representatives, and regulators to discuss issues. When time is of the essence, such as when a vote is upcoming, phone calls tend to be the most effective. In addition to phone calls, elected officials may also prefer to receive electronic communications from constituents. Many legislators have online contact forms on their official websites to enable constituents to share policy opinions and questions. Postal mail to legislators may be significantly delayed due to security procedures in place which screen incoming mail (ACA, n.d.).

Calling an elective official is an easy way to communicate with them and requires very little effort on the part of the advocate. However, the call will most likely be answered by a staff member and not the legislator themselves. When calling, school counselors should identify themselves as constituents if they are one and ask to speak with the legislative aide assigned to the issue that they are calling about. When speaking with the aide, identify the legislation and your position (whether you support or oppose). Be prepared to provide reasoning for your support or opposition and ask for the legislator's position on the bill (ACA, n.d.).

Writing to legislators is a personal and effective method to engage and educate about an issue. There are several guides to help with what should go into written communication with legislators. The following key information is provided by ACA (n.d.):

- Introduce yourself and include personal information, such as your counseling specialty and the types of clients you treat.
- After introducing yourself, begin with the purpose for writing your email or letter.
- Identify any specific legislation relevant to your correspondence. Make sure that you correctly reference the legislation to the correct body of Congress.
  - House bills should be written as "H.R. ___"
  - Senate bills are "S. ___"
- To eliminate any risk of confusion of one issue with another, you should only address one issue per e-mail or letter.

- Include any personal information or narrative about the importance of the issue to you and your clients. Ask the member to support or oppose the targeted legislation.
- Regardless of the topic or your opinion of the legislator, always be courteous.

Finally, requesting an in-person meeting with your legislator is a valuable advocacy effort. It is important to plan your visit when the legislature is in session. This is the time that legislators are most likely to be on Capitol Hill or at the state capitol, rather than in their districts. If you schedule a meeting during a recess period, it is likely that you will meet with a staff member. As schedules fill quickly, try to schedule the meeting at least 1 month in advance. If the legislator is unavailable, try to arrange to meet with the staff member who directly handles the issue that you wish to discuss. When you arrive, at least 5 minutes prior to the meeting, be prepared to discuss your issue and your position. Highlight important details, such as statistics about how the issue will affect the legislator's district and constituents. When you finish, be sure to send a thank you letter, either by mail or email to thank them for meeting with you and for their commitment (ACA, n.d.).

Know Legislation that Impacts School Counselors

In order to keep up with legislation that impacts school counselors, it is necessary to be engaged in associations that track and follow important legislation. Many of the associations that were mentioned at the beginning of this chapter offer advocacy resources and updates that are sent to members during legislative sessions. For example, ACA's Advocacy Resources website offers a legislative agenda, an advocacy toolkit, a government affairs and public policy glossary, and an advocacy social media guide (https://www.counseling.org/government-affairs/advocacy-tips-tools). There are also resources for current national issues and many issues that states are facing.

The National Association for College Admission Counseling provides a Monthly Advocacy Checklist (https://www.nacacnet.org/advocacy/take-action/) that has been adapted below to fit the needs of school counselors:

Table 20.1 Advocacy Calendar

January	• Check your Secretary of State's[1] website for important voting dates, including registration deadlines, and mark your calendar. Register to vote if you haven't already done so, or double-check to ensure you are registered.[2] Learn more about the student voting requirements in your state.[3]
February	• Meet with your members of Congress[4] in their district office during Presidents' Day district work period.
	• Because most state legislatures[5] are in full swing, many associations hold state-level advocacy days this time of year. Attend yours, if available. If your state does not host an advocacy day, consider setting up a meeting with your state elected officials to share more information about school counselors.
March	• Check the Education Commission of the States' State Education Policy Tracker[6] for any relevant legislation in your state and contact your representative(s) to share your support or concerns.
April	• It's the beginning of appropriations[7] season on Capitol Hill. Call your members of Congress and encourage them to support increased education funding.
	• Meet with your members of Congress[8] in their district offices during spring district work period.

(Continued)

Table 20.1 (Continued)

May	• It's graduation season! Write your members of Congress to share a story about a student you've known or worked with this year who benefitted from access to quality school counseling.
June	• Consider inviting elected officials – local and federal – to your school or campus for a visit in the new school year. Invite them to attend a college application night, host a financial aid night, or simply visit campus to speak to students.
July	• Most states' legislative sessions have adjourned. Reach out to your state elected officials and offer to meet with them to discuss potential legislation for the next session. • See if there are any mailing lists that you can sign up for on your association webpages. These may allow you to receive updates on federal education policy and other relevant issues throughout the year.
August	• Visit your members of Congress while they are home for August district work period. • Happy new school year! Encourage any students you work with who are eligible to vote to register[9] if they have not already done so.
September	• Congress must pass all appropriations[10] bills by Sept. 30 to fund the next fiscal year. Call your members of Congress and remind them to prioritize increased education funding.
October	• October means one thing in the college admission world: FAFSA[11] is open! As you work with students who complete the FAFSA, consider sharing stories with Congress about how FAFSA simplification and increased funding for need-based financial aid[12] would benefit your students. • Several states require[13] voters to register up to 30 days in advance of Election Day. Complete your registration,[14] if necessary, or double-check that you are registered.[15]
November	• VOTE! • Before the semester ends, reach out to one of your colleagues and encourage them to get engaged with advocacy opportunities in the new year.
December	• Get a jump on the new Congressional and state legislative sessions! Reach out to your newly elected or re-elected representatives and encourage them to support school counseling legislative priorities in the upcoming session.

Source: Permission granted by NACAC (https://www.nacacnet.org/advocacy/take-action/).

Notes
1. https://www.nass.org/membership
2. https://www.vote.org/am-i-registered-to-vote/
3. https://www.campusvoteproject.org/state-student-voting-guides
4. https://whoismyrepresentative.com/
5. https://www.congress.gov/state-legislature-websites
6. https://www.ecs.org/state-education-policy-tracking/
7. https://www.crfb.org/papers/appropriations-101
8. https://whoismyrepresentative.com/
9. https://vote.gov/
10. https://www.crfb.org/papers/appropriations-101
11. https://studentaid.gov/h/apply-for-aid/fafsa
12. https://www.nacacnet.org/advocacy--ethics/initiatives/need-based-financial-aid/
13. https://www.usa.gov/state-election-office
14. https://vote.gov/
15. https://www.vote.org/am-i-registered-to-vote/

It is also important to check with state associations to see if you can get on any mailing lists for legislative alerts at the state level. Depending on the state in which you are a practicing school counselor, legislative sessions may occur on a yearly or more infrequent basis. Other associations may be available at a regional or more local level as well.

Be Active in Professional Associations

While being a member in associations is generally the best way to receive information on legislation that will be impacting you as a school counselor, it is also important to be more than a passive member. Many of these professional associations are non-profit organizations and depend on the commitment of members to keep them running strong. The work of each individual helps shape the information that goes into committees, which in turn goes to board members, and then is pushed back out to membership to share with others. When you would like to have more of a voice, it is important to be more involved in these associations.

Mental and Behavioral Health Considerations

Ultimately, advocacy for the appropriate role of the school counselor leads to benefits for mental and behavioral health of students. Several studies have shown the effectiveness of school counselors on mental and behavioral health, shown as follows. When focusing on certain mental health aspects, such as student self-efficacy, the presence of a school counselor and the implementation of programs can make a difference for students. Bardhoshi et al. (2018) examined counseling intervention on student self-efficacy development. School counselors who focus on interventions that enhance students' internal beliefs regarding their ability to succeed can serve as an essential foundation for both academic and life success. Additionally, the study by Lemberger et al. (2018) supports the type of social and emotional learning, as well as cognitive learning outcomes possible when school counselors are able to deliver direct counseling services within a classroom or small group setting.

Looking at how school counselors can positively influence behavioral health, research also supports the value of schoolwide positive behavioral support programs and the role a counselor plays in the success of these programs (Curtis et al., 2010). Additionally, Lapan et al. (2012a) found that high school students who received more access to their school counselor through lower student-to-school-counselor ratios, and received related college and career counseling services, were more likely to graduate and less likely to have behavioral problems. Finally, Amatea et al. (2010) discovered how a family-focused intervention implemented by school counselors decreased problem behavior by small children. Simply having a stronger presence of school counselors in elementary schools can reduce misbehavior and improve boys' academic achievement (Carrell and Hoekstra, 2014).

Ethical Considerations

In addition to these standards and competencies, school counselors have an ethical imperative to lead and advocate for "providing equitable educational access and success" and demonstrating "their belief that all students have the ability to learn by advocating for an education system that provides optimal learning for all students (ASCA, 2022). These ASCA Ethical Standards for School Counselors (2022) also include that school counselors:

> **A.4.b** Provide and advocate for all students' pre-K–postsecondary career awareness, exploration, and postsecondary planning and decision-making to support students' right to choose from the wide array of career and postsecondary options, including but not limited to college/university, career and technical school, military or workforce.
>
> **A.10.b** Actively work to establish a safe, equitable, affirming school environment in which all members of the school community demonstrate respect, inclusion and acceptance.

> **A.10.f** Advocate for the equitable right and access to free, appropriate public education for all youth in which students are not stigmatized or isolated based on race, gender identity, gender expression, sexual orientation, language, immigration status, juvenile justice/court involvement, housing, socioeconomic status, ability, foster care, transportation, special education, mental health and/or any other exceptionality or special need.
>
> **A.13.b** Advocate for the ethical use of student data and records and inform administration of inappropriate or harmful practices.
>
> **A.15.a** Advocate for equal access to technology for all students.
>
> **B.2.c** Advocate for a school counseling program free of non-school-counseling assignments identified by "The ASCA National Model: A Framework for School Counseling Programs" as inappropriate to the school counselor's role.
>
> **B.2.d** Exercise leadership to create systemic change to create a safe and supportive environment and equitable outcomes for all students.
>
> **B.2.h** Advocate for administrators to place in school counseling positions certified school counselors who are competent, qualified, and hold a master's degree or higher in school counseling from an accredited program.
>
> **B.2.i** Advocate for equitable school counseling program policies and practices for all students and stakeholders.
>
> **B.2.k** Affirm the abilities of and advocate for the learning needs of all students. School counselors support the provision of appropriate accommodations and accessibility.

Cultural Complexities

In addition to helping students with academic, behavioral, career, and emotional concerns, school counselors also advocate for social justice for students and communities. Social justice advocacy can be defined as supporting a person or particular policy in ensuring social justice. Social justice contains two parts. One part is making sure that everyone in society has equal access to opportunities, rights, and freedoms. The second part is helping disadvantaged people in society (Gonzalez, 2021).

This aspect of advocacy is also an ethical imperative, as indicated in the *ASCA Ethical Standards for School Counselors* (2022):

> **A.10.h** Actively advocate for systemic and other changes needed for equitable participation and outcomes in educational programs when disproportionality exists regarding enrollment in such programs by race, gender identity, gender expression, sexual orientation, language, immigration status, juvenile justice/court involvement, housing, socioeconomic status, ability, foster care, transportation, special education, mental health and/or any other exceptionality or special need.

By advocating for social justice, school counselors can help reverse individual and community biases and prejudices. They can take a stand against both intentional and unintentional oppression and discrimination of minority groups and anyone who is being treated unfairly (Gonzalez, 2021). The ASCA and ACA also offer position statements on relevant current events and important topics to inform school counseling practice and justify inclusion of social justice throughout a comprehensive school counseling program. School counselors are expected to serve and affirm all students and to speak up when any marginalized student is being harmed and denied access to equitable education. This is the right thing to do for students, and when school counselors can point to ethical standards and position statements that show research and additional information on why these issues are important, it shows others how these issues may be affecting students and what can be done.

Strategic Considerations

Although there are various issues that affect school counselors on a national level, there are also some considerations that should be taken into consideration on a state and local level.

Certification and Licensure

According to ASCA, school counselors are either certified or licensed and credentialed by the state where they are employed. Typically, this licensure or certification requires documented school counseling education and coursework from an accredited college or university, completion of a practicum or internship in a K–12 school setting, and passage of a state or national comprehensive exam. State requirements vary from state to state and may change or be updated frequently. The state education department in each state is the best place to check for current licensure or certification requirements.

Case Loads

Although the American School Counselor Association (ASCA) recommends a student-to-school-counselor ratio of 250:1, the state and national averages are often much higher. The national average student-to-school-counselor ratio in 2019–2020 was 424:1 (ASCA, n.d.). The highest state was Arizona, with an average of 848:1, and the lowest was Vermont with 201:1. Even more startling, nearly one in five students, or about 8 million children, do not have access to a school counselor at all, and nearly 3 million of those students do not even have access to other school support staff, such as a school psychologist or social workers (Education Trust, 2019).

Political Considerations or Politicking in Districts of Bureaucracy in Schools

Effective systemic change requires political acumen, an important skill for school counselors to master (Stone and Zirkel, 2010). Negotiating the politics with administrators at the school district level can at times be daunting work, but adhering to ethical standards requires that school counselors use their interpersonal skills to demonstrate respect for the position of authority that has been entrusted to school administrators (Stone and Zirkel, 2010).

Many of the same knowledge and dispositions that were discussed earlier in this chapter regarding advocacy can be utilized within a district. As mentioned, school counselors are often tasked with duties outside the realm of their responsibilities because many administrators do not know what the appropriate duties of a school counselor entail. Advocacy within a district many times simply comes down to educating others on the appropriate and inappropriate roles and duties of a school counselor. Utilizing resources from professional associations, national and potentially state laws or policies, and data from personal time spent on duties will help show administration what school counselors should and should not be doing.

One of the best ways to advocate for appropriate duties and responsibilities of a school counselor is to sit down with the school administrator at the beginning of the school year to jointly complete a principal–school counselor agreement. This written document helps guide the conversation between the principal and school counselor about the school counseling program goals, how the school counselor will work towards spending their time in service to students, and what type of professional development activities they will attend throughout the school year. This agreement and the conversations that take place during the meeting to complete it can help administrators understand what school counselors should be doing and what the administrators can do to support the school counselor to be successful in providing students the social-emotional, mental, and behavioral health services, as well as the academic and career development they need.

Rules and Regulations

School counselors encounter a range of legal issues on a daily basis. These issues include confidentiality, working with student harmful behavior, dual relationships, technology, and more. In addition, there are state laws and statutes that school counselors must be aware of in order to know what they are able and unable to do in certain situations. For example, what is the age at which a minor is no longer considered a minor in your state? Does your state require you to report child abuse?

Local school policies, rules, and regulations also dictate what school counselors may and may not do in certain situations. In all of these situations, school counselors must know what the laws, statutes, policies, rules, and regulations are, how they may conflict with ethical standards, and which ones will take precedence. When advocating on issues in particular, it is important to know what is already in place and how any new policies or regulations will affect those.

Conclusion

School counselors effect change on many levels: with students, with their role, and with the profession. To make this change happen, advocacy and leadership are key. Certain responsibilities, knowledge, and skills as a leader and an advocate help make these more effective and more easily accomplished. This chapter has provided an overview of the history of counseling associations, history of advocacy, barriers to implementation of comprehensive school counseling programs, role of legislators in advocacy, leadership values, leadership in practice, multicultural considerations, and strategic considerations.

References

Amatea, E.S., Thompson, I.A., Rankin-Clemons, L., and Ettinger, M.L. (2010) "Becoming partners: a school-based intervention for families of young children who are disruptive", *Journal of School Counseling*, 8(36): 1–31.

American Counseling Association (ACA) (n.d.). *American Counseling Association Advocacy Toolkit*. Online. Available HTTP: <https://www.counseling.org/docs/default-source/government-affairs/2020-advocacy-toolkit.pdf?sfvrsn=f9815e2c_4>

ACA (2021a) "About ACA". Online. Available HTTP: <https://www.counseling.org/about-us/about-aca>

ACA (2021b) "Your school counselor connection". Online. Available HTTP: <https://www.counseling.org/membership/aca-and-you/school-counselors/school-counselor>

American School Counselor Association (ASCA) (n.d.) *Student-to-school-counselor ratio 2019–2020*. https://www.schoolcounselor.org/getmedia/cd689f6a-252a-4e0a-ac8b-39b9b66d700d/ratios-19-20.pdf

ASCA (2017) *ASCA School Counselor Professional Standards and Competencies*. Online. Available HTTP: <https://www.schoolcounselor.org/getmedia/a8d59c2c-51de-4ec3-a565-a3235f3b93c3/SC-Competencies.pdf>

ASCA (2019) *The ASCA National Model: A Framework for School Counseling Programs* (3rd edn), Alexandria, VA: Author

ASCA (2020) "About ASCA". Online. Available HTTP: <https://www.schoolcounselor.org/About-ASCA>

ASCA (2022) *ASCA Ethical Standards for School Counselors*, Alexandria, VA: Author.

Baggerly, J. and Osborn, D. (2006) "School counselors' career satisfaction and commitment: correlates and predictors", *Professional School Counseling*, 9(3): 197–205.

Bardhoshi, G., Duncan, K., and Erford, B. (2018) "Effect of a specialized classroom counseling intervention on increasing self-efficacy among first-grade rural students", *Professional School Counseling*, 21(1): 12–25.

Carey, J. and Dimmitt, C. (2012) "School counseling and student outcomes: summary of six statewide studies", *Professional School Counseling*, 16(2): 146–153.

Carrell, S.E. and Carrell, S.A. (2006) "Do lower student to counselor ratios reduce school disciplinary problems?", *Contributions to Economic Analysis & Policy*, 5: 1–24.

Carrell, S.E. and Hoekstra, M. (2014) "Are school counselors an effective educational input?", *Economic Letters*, 125: 66–69.

Curtis, R. Van Horne, J.W., Robertson, R., and Karvonen, M. (2010) "Outcomes of a school-wide positive behavioral support program", *Professional School Counseling*, 13(3): 159–164.

Education Trust (2019) *School Counselors Matter*. Online. Available HTTP: <https://www.schoolcounselor.org/getmedia/b079d17d-6265-4166-a120-3b1f56077649/School-Counselors-Matter.pdf>

Eriksen, K. (1997) *Making an Impact: A Handbook on Counselor Advocacy*, New York: Taylor & Francis.

Foxx, S.P., Baker, S.B., and Gerler, E.R. (2017) *School Counseling for the 21st Century* (6th edn), New York: Routledge.

Gonzalez, K. (2021) "Counselor's Role as a Social Justice Advocate". Online (May 13). Available HTTP: <https://study.com/academy/lesson/counselors-role-as-a-social-justice-advocate.html>

Goodman-Scott, E., Sink, C.A., Burgess, M., and Cholewa, B.E. (2018) "An ecological view of school counselor ratios and student academic outcomes", *Journal of Counseling & Development*, 96: 388–398.

Gysbers, N.C. and Henderson, P. (2012) *Developing and Managing your School Guidance and Counseling Program* (5th edn), Alexandria, VA: American Counseling Association.

Lapan, R.T., Whitcomb, S.A., and Aleman, N.M. (2012a) "Connecticut professional school counselors: college and career counseling services and smaller ratios benefit students", *Professional School Counseling*, 16(2): 117–124.

Lapan, R.T., Gysbers, N.C., Stanley, B., and Pierce, M.E. (2012b) "Missouri professional school counselors: ratios matter, especially in high-poverty schools", *Professional School Counseling*, 16(2): 108–116.

Leahy, M.J., Rak, E., and Zanskas, S.A. (2015) "A brief history of counseling and specialty areas of practice", in I. Marini and M. Stebnicki (eds) *The Professional Counselor's Desk Reference* (2nd edn), New York: Springer, pp. 3–8.

Lemberger, M., Carbonneau, K., Selig, J., and Bowers, H. (2018) "The role of social-emotional mediators on middle school students' academic growth as fostered by an evidence-based intervention", *Journal of Counseling and Development*, 96(1): 27–40.

Levin-Epstein, M. (2018) "Exploring the dynamics of an evolving relationship", *Principal Leadership*, 19. Online. Available HTTP: <https://www.nassp.org/publication/principal-leadership/volume-19-2018-2019/principal-leadership-december-2018/school-counselors-and-principals/>

Lewis, J.A., Arnold, M.S., House, R., and Toporek, R.L. (2003) *American Counseling Association Advocacy Competencies*. Online. Available HTTP: <https://www.counseling.org/docs/default-source/competencies/aca-advocacy-competencies-updated-may-2020.pdf?sfvrsn=f410212c_4>

Moyer, M. (2011) "Effects of non-guidance activities, supervision, and student-to-counselor ratios on school counselor burnout", *Journal of School Counseling*, 9(5): 1–31.

National Association for College and Admission Counseling (NACAC) (2000) *Statement on Counselor Competencies*. Online. Available HTTP: <https://www.nacacnet.org/globalassets/documents/advocacy-and-ethics/cepp/counselorcompetencies.pdf>

NACAC and ASCA (2017) *State-by-State Student-to-Counselor Ratio Report 10 Year Trends*, Alexandria, VA: Authors.

Stone, C.B. and Zirkel, P.A. (2010) "School counselor advocacy: when law and ethics may collide", *Professional School Counseling*, 13(4): 244–247.

Sue, D.W., Arredondo, P., and McDavis, R.J. (1992) "Multicultural counseling competencies and standards: a call to the profession", *Journal of Multicultural Counseling and Development*, 20(2): 64–88.

Texas Education Agency (2018) *The Texas Model for Comprehensive School Counseling Programs* (5th edn), Austin, TX: Texas Counseling Association.

Toporek, R.L. and Daniels, J. (2018) *ACA Advocacy Competencies*. Online. Available HTTP: <https://www.counseling.org/docs/default-source/competencies/aca-advocacy-competencies-updated-may-2020.pdf?sfvrsn=f410212c_4>

Trusty, J. and Brown, D. (2005) "Advocacy competencies for professional school counselors", *Professional School Counseling*, 8(3): 259–265.

Velez, E.D. (2020) "How can high school counseling shape students' postsecondary attendance? Exploring the relationship between high school counseling context and students' subsequent postsecondary enrollment", *National Association for College Admission Counseling*. Online. Available HTTP: <https://files.eric.ed.gov/fulltext/ED608301.pdf>

West Virginia Board of Education (2014) *West Virginia Comprehensive Developmental School Counseling Model*. Online. Available HTTP: <https://wvde.us/student-support-well-being/wv-school-counselors/>

Whitson, S.C., Tai, W.L., Rahardja, D., and Eder, K. (2010) "School counseling outcome: a meta analytic examination of interventions", *Journal of Counseling & Development*, 89: 37–55.

Wilkerson, K., Perusse, R., and Hughes, A. (2013) "Comprehensive school counseling programs and student achievement outcomes: a comparative analysis of RAMP versus non-RAMP schools", *Professional School Counseling*, 16(3): 172–184.

Young, A. and Miller-Kneale, M. (2013) *School Counselor Leadership*, Alexandria, VA: American School Counselor Association.

21 Administrative Leaders and School Counselors Advocating for Supporting Mental Health in Their Programs

Summer Martin

Leadership Quote

When a partnership exists to support a specific initiative, energy is created and accomplishments abound. School counselors and administrators must band together for the mental health of students; society is banking on it!

Judy A. Nelson

Aspirational Statement

Professional school counselors can impact student success through advocacy on several levels:

- **Individual student advocacy:** School counselors advocate for individual student success through listening to students' needs and working to break down barriers for students.
- **Campus level student advocacy:** School counselors advocate for marginalized (and other student groups) by closing achievement through data-driven methods to impact student success.
- **Counseling program advocacy:** School counselors advocate for a comprehensive school counseling program by following the ACA and ASCA standards and collaborating with stakeholders, which results in positive student outcomes.
- **Counseling profession advocacy:** School counselors advocate for the counseling profession through collaboration with other school counseling professionals to reach goals that impact the future of the profession.

Introduction and Background

If you were to ask school counselors to summarize their job in one word, many would answer *advocate*, which covers not only individual students, but the whole of the profession of school counseling. The American School Counselor Association's (ASCA) Ethical Standards (2022) defines a professional school counselor advocate as "a person who speaks, writes or acts to promote the well-being of students, parents/guardians and the school counseling profession. School counselors advocate to close the information, opportunity, intervention, and attainment gaps for all students" (2022: 9). Additionally, the American Counseling Association (ACA) Code of Ethics (2014) describes advocacy as the "promotion of the well-being of individuals, groups, and the counseling profession within systems and organizations. Advocacy seeks to remove barriers and obstacles that inhibit access, growth, and development" (2014: 20).

Through advocacy, the overall achievement of students increases in the areas of academic achievement, social-emotional learning, and college and career readiness (ASCA, 2019b). School counselors advocate on many levels: individual student advocacy, campus level student advocacy, counseling program advocacy, and counseling profession advocacy. The ASCA (2022) summarizes these levels:

> School counselors are advocates, leaders, collaborators and consultants who create systemic change by providing equitable educational access and success by connecting their school counseling programs to the district's mission and improvement plans. School counselors demonstrate their belief that all students have the ability to learn by advocating for an education system that provides optimal learning environments for all students.
>
> (2022: 1)

The cornerstone of any counseling relationship is empathic listening. Truly, this is cornerstone of *any* relationship. School counselors are uniquely trained in the art of empathic listening or understanding someone from their viewpoint. As Covey (1989) states, empathic listening allows you to "see the world the way they see the world, you understand their paradigm, you understand how they feel" (1989: 240). Generally, when we listen, we are primarily waiting to respond to the other person. School counselors use all senses to engage in empathic listening: watching facial expressions, body language, listening for feelings and emotions, and listening to the actual words being spoken as well. For school counselors, school counselor directors, and other school counseling professionals to advocate at the four levels of advocacy, we must first seek to understand the problem by using the first skill we learned as school counselors. Then, we must find solutions together by seeking to be understood.

Advocating for student success requires a special set of skills and knowledge that are implicit within a school counselor's repertoire of counseling skills. A main trait of professional school counselors is empathy, which helps school counselors understand students' needs from their perspective. This trait is foundational in relationship building, another key characteristic of effective school counselors (Trusty and Brown, 2005). Trusty and Brown (2005) also state that "advocacy must be balanced with diplomacy and relationships because if collaborative relationships suffer due to advocacy, then advocacy is less likely to be successful in the future" (2005: 263). School counselors naturally have the disposition for relationships through the internal trait of empathy and must use this skill in acting with diplomacy for advocacy success.

When applying diplomacy to an advocacy lens, school counselors must follow a counseling session style of advocacy by listening first to understand the position from others' point of view, be it a student who is in an inequitable situation or the actors instilling the inequitable situation on the student. By treating advocacy as a counseling session, a school counselor will be able to gather information, and create a positive, solution-focused plan, all while building relationships with stakeholders and allowing other positions to be understood in the process.

School counselors need an additional skill for successful advocacy which is understanding the micropolitics of the campus or situation as well as understanding the micropolitical literacy. Micropolitics describes the power structures within a school, and micropolitical literacy is the ability to navigate the micropolitical environment (Ball, 1987; Kelchtermans and Ballet, 2002a, 2002b; Oehrtman and Dollarhide, 2021). School counselors must understand the relationships and structures of a school to effectively advocate for students and a comprehensive school counseling program. Each level of micropolitics requires different knowledge, skills, and relationships to advocate appropriately and influence stakeholders to create a comprehensive school counseling program resulting in systemic change for all students.

Trusty and Brown (2005) noted that advocacy happens on multiple levels such as advocating for particular students or groups of students along with advocating for better school counseling programs, better schools and community resources, as well as professional advocacy at the local, state, and national levels. A common theme in the literature about advocacy (ASCA, 2019b; Dimmitt and Wilkerson, 2012; Salina et al., 2013; Wilkerson et al., 2013) is taking action to meet the needs of all students through a comprehensive school counseling program.

Trusty and Brown (2005) developed three competency domains professional school counselors need to develop to fully exhibit the role of advocate for all levels: advocacy disposition, advocacy knowledge, and advocacy skills. Included in advocacy disposition is the general idea of altruism directed at all students' well-being, family support/empowerment, social advocacy efforts to eliminate inequities for student groups, and an ethical disposition which allows school counselors to advocate for students while reviewing and adhering to ethics and laws. The knowledge domain comprises knowledge of resources, knowledge of parameters, knowledge of dispute resolution mechanisms, knowledge of advocacy models, and knowledge of systems change. Skills needed for advocacy include communication skills, collaboration skills, problem-assessment skills, problem-solving skills, organizational skills, and self-care skills.

The ASCA National Model (2019b) previously included themes of leadership, systemic change, collaboration, and advocacy; however, as all are integral in a comprehensive school counseling program, they are considered *woven* throughout a school counselor's work with individual students, student groups, and professional advocacy (2019b: 19). This suggests that school counselors must understand the ecosystem of each level of advocacy (McMahon et al., 2014) and the micropolitics that go with each of these ecosystems (Ball, 1987; Oehrtman and Dollarhide, 2021). The way school counseling was provided to students in the past no longer works – all students simply do not fit the model once outlined by traditional schooling. School counselors must and have adapted to serve students through advocacy efforts (McMahon et al., 2014). Systemic change occurs when school counselors use leadership and collaboration to enact advocacy.

Additionally, research demonstrates that by providing a comprehensive school counseling program, school counselors can impact student outcomes in multiple ways. This is in effect inherent advocacy for all students on a campus or in a district/organization. Studies (Carey and Dimmitt, 2012; Carrell and Hoekstra, 2014; Cholewa et al., 2015) indicate that critical school-wide student outcomes in academics, attendance, and behavior are impacted by schools with comprehensive school counseling programs as well as describe how school counselors are the most influential school personnel to help first-generation college students think about postsecondary education. Additional studies (Davis et al., 2013; Dimmitt and Wilkerson, 2012) also illustrate how school counselors directly impact advanced course choices and performance on Advanced Placement tests for underserved students, along with positive academic outcomes and connections to school. School counselors delivering a comprehensive school counseling program at all levels, specifically at low performing schools, show higher academic achievement than those without a comprehensive school counseling program (Salina et al., 2013; Wilkerson et al., 2013). Advocacy as a theme woven within the National Model (ASCA, 2019b) leads school counselors to naturally provide advocacy to all students through a comprehensive school counseling program.

Leadership Program Values and Standards

There are many values and standards applicable to advocacy in school counseling. Some of these standards are shared among principals and school counselors. The professional standards of a school counselor lend themselves to an attitude of advocacy for all areas of school counseling. Competencies and standards from ACA, CACREP, and ASCA provide values for school counselors leading to overall student achievement in the areas of academic achievement, social emotional learning, and college, and career readiness.

American Counseling Association

The American Counseling Association (ACA) developed Advocacy Competencies (Lewis et al., 2003) separate from the ACA Code of Ethics (2014) due to the need to specify how counselors can systemically break down barriers for clients. This work began with the original publishing of the Advocacy Competencies and has been updated recently (ACA, 2018). The Advocacy Competencies lays out advocacy as a central *pillar* in its strategic initiatives. Added to the dimensions of advocacy are six domains: client empowerment, client advocacy, community collaboration, systems advocacy, collective action, and social/political advocacy, as shown in Table 21.1.

The first domain, Client Empowerment, focuses on the counselor working collaboratively with the client to identify barriers and how to address the barriers, whereas Client/Student Advocacy is when the counselor advocates on behalf of an individual client or student. Sometimes this involves breaking down systemic barriers within the counselor's own system (ACA, 2018).

In the next domain, Community Collaboration, the counselor is collaborating with the community to recognize and address systemic barriers and develop an action plan, where Systems Advocacy is the counselor advocating on behalf of the community or group. This type of advocacy may be especially important as the counselor can see the whole picture of the potential barriers to success and can *rally the troops* to break down these barriers. Additionally, the counselor may have increased access to the actors involved in the advocacy situation where the clients do not have the same level of access (ACA, 2018; Ratts et al., 2007).

The last set of domains speaks to strategies needed to advocate for policy level type of changes. Collective Action denotes advocacy with groups to impact public perception or policy, while Social/Political Advocacy designates strategies the counselor takes on behalf of a group to impact perception or public policy (ACA, 2018; Ratts et al., 2007).

The ACA Competencies (2018) mirror the levels of advocacy described by ASCA and other researchers (Colbert et al., 2006; Oehrtman and Dollarhide, 2021; Ratts et al., 2007;

Table 21.1 Shared School Leadership Advocacy Standards and Skills among Superintendents, Principals, and School Counselors

Advocacy Standards and Skills	Colleagues, Co-Worker, and Employee Advocacy	Community and Public Advocacy	District Culture Advocacy	Campus Culture or Climate Advocacy	Student and Family Advocacy	Advocacy with Depth and Breadth at Macrocosm and Microcosm Levels
		In Tandem Systemic Integration of Standards and Stakeholders				
Facilitating, Supporting, Coaching, and Influencing	• Offer on-going supervision, conferences, and feedback • Promote professional growth opportunities and advancement in leadership roles • Use creative critical thinking and problem solving tools	• Remain informed on federal, state, and local policy relevant to field of education and counseling	• Move toward process of change initiatives • Recognize problems as opportunities • Encourage dynamic thinking	• Set initiatives and goals • Foster a spirit of collegiality with enhancement	• Access to needed in-district services • To address whole person out-of-district services • Act with integrity and champion for students and families	
Use of Verbal, Written, Non-Verbal, and Technological Communication	• Begin all forms of communication by leading with compassion and strengths • Practice honest and transparent communication • Effective articulation	• Use and adjust communication skills based on audience, initiative, and goals • Understanding of truths and realistic • Know the communication strategy for the public • Proactive communication that promotes district and campus vision	• Express policy and procedures • Effectively and systematically gather input from stakeholders • Use technology, telecommunications, and information systems to enrich curriculum, learning, and safety	• Create statements of position that support campus vision	• Utilize diverse language, appropriate to their culture of origin or a particular audience, to foster strong communication skills • Foster strong written and verbal communication	
Empowering and Inspiring	• Strong work relationships that are positive, non-competitive, and professionally enhancing	• Take responsive action to improve practices	• Use theory of motivation and change	• Change systemically, interpersonally, and intrapersonally	• Direct dialogic and therapeutic services • Elimination of systemic oppression	
Modeling and Promoting	• Maintain personal, physical, and emotional wellness • Engage in fair and equitable practices • Elimination or reduction of bias and discriminatory practice	• Invite public and community figures to engage in shadowing experiences that convey intricacies of leadership roles	• Use and integration of technology • Operate with highest standard of ethics • The investment of human capital	• Set high expectations that promote learning and intellectual stimulation • Encourage awareness and appreciation of diversity and gender appreciation	• SEL and engaged development of all learners • Special programs for students in need of specialized, flexible programs and services	

Allying, Collaborating, and Consulting	• Demonstrate highest standard of conduct, ethical principles, and integrity both internally and externally • Treat all with respect • Recognize partnerships and the limitations of operating in silos	• Establish partnerships with community entities or agencies	• Ensure time and capacity is available • Use learning communities • Coordinate collaborative processes to ensure appropriate scope, sequence, content, and alignment	• Allocating appropriate funding for campus utilization	• Use of local, state, and federal
			• Implementation and modification of campus vision and plans • Implement group processes that define roles, assign functions, delegate effectively, and determine accountability		• Ensure integral inclusion • Host timely student conferences
Identifying and Recognizing	• Yourself as an educational leader • The need for consensus building and conflict management	• The need for partnerships for various programs and services	• Review multiple data sets relevant to district culture • Institute a comprehensive school program using student assessment and interpretation of data	• The need for rigorous educational and SEL curriculum • Collecting data, particularly reflective of innovative thinking and inclusive culture	• Authenticity of their life • Strengths and resources • Need for mental health services • External barriers or factors
Intervening, Allocating, and Responding	• Resources that support school priorities and goals	• Contact outside resource for a particular issue	• Implement policy and procedures	• Resources in the most effective and equitable manner	• To students need for effective educators and learning opportunities • Create necessary special programs and specialized services
Developing, Creating, and Modifying	• Efforts to create transformational change are within the individual (internal) and in the environment (external) • Adjust systemic processes and procedures in which promote and improve individuals in threat	• Draft proposals that connect schools with outside agencies	• Plan of safety, strategic operation, and work-flow	• Promote an environment for learning • Comprehensive school programming where campus priorities, goals, and targets • Use various data sets for shared vision	• Action planning • Change processes to improve students' learning and the climate for learning

(Continued)

Table 21.1 (Continued)

Advocacy Standards and Skills	Colleagues, Co-Worker, and Employee Advocacy	Community and Public Advocacy	District Culture Advocacy	Campus Culture or Climate Advocacy	Student and Family Advocacy	Advocacy with Depth and Breadth at Macrocosm and Microcosm Levels
Researching, Assessing, and Best-Practicing			• Use formal and informal techniques to research and/or assess school climate • Use research-based theory and techniques for classroom management, discipline, and school safety • Encourage an ongoing study of best practices and relevant research	• Monitoring guidance curriculum and instruction through observation and evaluation processes	• Stakeholders should use research and best-practice to inform their diversified approach, making it tailor-made for each student and family	
Reflecting, Managing, and Evaluating	• Practice and implement a form of reflective practice • Manage vested persons using specific techniques and group processes to assess goal attainment		• Plan and manage student programs to fulfill developmental, social, cultural, athletic, and scholastic needs	• Multiple data points with all stakeholders to evaluate progress toward goals and monitor program and service effectiveness	• Looking at past events or performance as a base-line for reflection • Understanding that students and their families, case-by-case require managing and evaluating to ensure programs and services are effective	
Informing, Training, Providing, and Disseminating	• Implement use of all educators' codes of ethics	• Offer public and community town-halls or forums that enhance understanding of specific events or vision	• Promote high-quality educational, extracurricular, and SEL instruction based on best-practices • Facilitate the development of a learning organization for improvement curriculum for content and counseling • Institute a comprehensive school program using student assessment to report state and national data results	• Use the outcomes of a campus climate survey and other forms of data to change the culture of staff and students	• Intra and interpersonal advocacy	

In Tandem System Integration of Cultural, Ethical, Educational, Social, Political, Economic, Developmental, Psychological, Emotional, and Behavioral Functioning of All Stakeholders

Note: Permission granted by L. Wines, 2022.

Trusty and Brown, 2005) and provide beneficial examples of knowledge, skills, and behaviors that all school counselors must possess in order to be an effective advocate for each individual or group, regardless of advocacy dimension or domain needed.

Council for Accreditation of Counseling and Related Educational Programs

The Council for Accreditation of Counseling and Related Educational Programs, or CACREP (2024), developed standards for counselor education programs with requirements for program faculty, administrators, and other agency personnel. Included in the CACREP standards are specifics for the contextual dimensions of the school counseling specialty. Several university-based standards require advocacy training for counselors, including:

> 6 School counselor roles as leaders, advocates, and systems change agents in P-12 schools
> 7 qualities and styles of effective leadership in schools
> 8 advocacy for school counseling roles
> 10 school counselor consultation with families, PK-12 and post-secondary school personnel, community agencies, and other referral sources
> 11 skills to critically examine the connections between social, familial, emotional, and behavior problems and academic achievement
> 19 strategies to promote equity in student achievement and access to postsecondary education opportunities

The CACREP's 2024 standards are the base level for school counselors' training in advocacy. To develop full school counselor advocates, school counselor training programs must understand their roles and responsibilities to individual students, groups of students, the campus school counseling program, and the school counseling profession.

School counselor preparation programs provide many courses in counseling students and working towards academic, social/emotional, and college/career readiness; however, it is not always made clear the school counselor's role as advocate in these courses. Specifically stating what the level or dimension of advocacy is when training school counselors on the knowledge and skills of school counseling would greatly enhance the understanding of advocacy for the school counseling profession (Haskins and Singh, 2016; Osborne et al., 1998; Singh et al., 2010). Additionally, reviewing the situation and the plan of action from an advocacy perspective would not only help the school counselors see how to help students in their success, but would also help them intrinsically and innately break down systemic barriers which impede students' success (Haskins and Singh, 2016; Osborne et al., 1998; Singh et al., 2010).

American School Counselor Association

The ASCA's School Counselor Professional Standards & Competencies (2019a) describes mindsets and behaviors for all school counselors with specific mindsets associated with advocacy for students and the school counseling profession:

> M 1. Every student can learn, and every student can succeed.
> M 2. Every student should have access to and opportunity for a high quality education.
> M 3. Every student should graduate from high school prepared for postsecondary opportunities.

These first three mindsets speak to the first and second areas of advocacy, individual student advocacy and campus level student advocacy. School counselors ensure that each student has access and opportunity to achieve at the highest level through individual planning. This advocacy includes working with the student and parent to ensure that all students have knowledge of opportunities available to them to be prepared for a successful future. Through a regular review of data and the implementation of student outcome goals, school counselors can ensure that all students on their campus receive needed services to achieve at the highest level.

> M 4. Every student should have access to a comprehensive school counseling program.

This mindset speaks to the third area of advocacy, the campus counseling program advocacy. By advocating for a comprehensive program, the school counselor ensures that all students have equitable access to opportunities available to them.

> M 5. Effective school counseling is a collaborative process involving school counselors, students, families, teachers, administrators, other school staff, and education stakeholders.
> M 6. School counselors are leaders in the school, district, state and nation.
> M 7. Comprehensive school counseling programs promote and enhance student academic, career, and social/emotional outcomes.

These last three mindsets speak to the last area of advocacy, the school counseling profession advocacy. School counselors are the *heart* of the school, which does not leave them out of leadership – school counselors have specific knowledge about all stakeholders involved in a school, making them uniquely qualified to offer a different perspective on what is needed at each level of advocacy, specifically the school counseling profession. By advocating for the school counseling profession, school counselors provide all students opportunities to succeed.

School counselors demonstrate the mindsets through the behaviors associated with a comprehensive school counseling program. The categories of ASCA's professional behaviors (2019a) include professional foundation, direct and indirect student services, and planning and assessment.

> B-PF 5. Use ASCA Mindsets & Behaviors for student success to inform the implementation of a comprehensive school counseling program.
> B-PF 7. Demonstrate leadership through the development and implementation of a comprehensive school counseling program.
> B-PF 8. Demonstrate advocacy in a comprehensive school counseling program.
> B-PF 9. Create systemic change through the implementation of a comprehensive school counseling program.
> B-SS 1. Design and implement instructions aligned to ASCA Mindsets & Behaviors for Student Success in large-group, classroom, small-group and individual settings.
> B-PA 2. Identify gaps in achievement, attendance, discipline, opportunity and resources
> B-PA 4. Develop and implement action plans aligned with annual student outcome goals and student data
> B-PA 7. Establish agreement with the principal and other administrators about the school counseling program
> B-PA 8. Establish and convene an advisory council for the comprehensive school counseling program.

These professional behaviors allow school counselors to demonstrate behaviors linked to advocacy through the development of a comprehensive school counseling program along with advocating for the school counseling profession, which leads to overall systemic change for schools and for students. As mentioned previously, school counseling training programs must explicitly address these competencies in courses to clearly help pre-service counselors understand the need for each of these competencies along with how they link to advocacy for student success. ASCA (2019b) clearly states specific activities (e.g., advisory councils) which provide ways for school counselors to naturally be advocates for their students.

Leadership in Practice

School counselors must use their considerable skills and knowledge of relationship-building through empathic listening to start making systemic changes at each level of advocacy. Using the model of the advocacy process laid out by Trusty and Brown (2005), we can apply specific actions for school counselors in each of the areas of advocacy:

1 Develop advocacy dispositions.
2 Develop advocacy relationships and advocacy knowledge.
3 Define the advocacy problem.
4 Develop action plans.
5 Implement action plans.
6 Make an evaluation.
7 Celebrate or regroup.

Individual Student Advocacy

In working with students individually, school counselors listen empathically to their problems and work to help the students seek their own student-driven solutions. A student may need assistance in this endeavor and may find barriers to solutions that lead to student success. As a school counselor begins to develop this relationship with the student, he or she needs to rely on their personal identity as an advocate along with identifying the ethical and legal implications of the situation. In this step, the school counselor begins to visualize the needed actions to solve the problem and how the school counselor can use their strengths in advocating for the student. The school counselor also needs to review the ethical and legal standards for school counselors before enacting any plan. This may involve collaborating with other school counselors, directors, mentors, or experts at the state or national level.

After a school counselor identifies a barrier to success, he or she must identify the actors in the situation along with the desired outcome. School counselors must also determine who needs to advocate on the student's behalf – is the student developmentally ready and prepared to attempt the advocacy on his or her own behalf? Or does the school counselor need to work with the actors in the situation because the student is not developmentally ready or prepared for this delicate conversation? An additional consideration is to evaluate the micropolitical (Oehrtman and Dollarhide, 2021) landscape of the situation. Consider the actors and situation and from whom the counselor will need support.

To breathe life into the advocacy steps, application to a simple situation (which many counselors have confronted) with solution-focused questions and activities (Bannink, 2006) will help with visualization of how to enact these steps personally. Additionally, to demonstrate solidarity in advocacy efforts, the term *we* is used in place of *school counselors*. Pronouns for the school counselor advocacy actor are attached to the situations for the reader's ease as well.

A student is struggling with mental health concerns that are requiring him to miss class for scheduled therapy appointments. The appointments occur on the same day, at the same time weekly, which means he misses the same class weekly. The student's teacher has not been flexible with deadlines for assignments. This is the beginning of an individual student advocacy situation. Before we as school counselors move forward, we must accept the role of advocate for this student, and internally answer the questions, "What does this look like for me?", along with, "What barriers will I face?", and "What are the ethical and legal implications of advocacy for this situation?" When the student comes to us concerned about his grade in the course, together with the student we can develop a plan of action for the situation, but is the student in a position to work with the teacher first, or should we advocate on the student's behalf? We must look at the developmental stage of the student, what has already occurred in the situation between the student and teacher, and what interactions have included the parents or guardians. When meeting with the student, we will want to include solution-focused (Bannink, 2006) counseling strategies to help assess the situation and answer the question of who should be advocating for the student. Approaching the situation with the student and asking questions to elicit exceptions like, "What have you tried?" and "When was the last time you handled a situation like this?" will help the school counselor gather details as well. As the client is the student, remembering to make sure we express empathy and understanding through questions like "How have you managed to make it so far?" while reflecting on the student's strength through the difficult time will enhance the relationship and provide hope for the student.

To find solutions, we must develop relationships with stakeholders in the school and any other potential stakeholders outside the school. Of course, this takes time. A new counselor may have his or her first interaction with an actor in an advocacy setting and not have a foundational relationship with said actor, which can sometimes hinder the relationship building process. Many authors (Oehrtman and Dollarhide, 2021; Singh et al., 2010; Trusty and Brown, 2005) suggest building advocacy relationships with stakeholders. While this is important, building genuine relationships with all stakeholders will allow the school counselor to first understand the individual person, what is important to him or her, and how to interact with the person.

To continue the previous example, after speaking with the student about the course concern, we work together with the student to get all the details regarding the situation, discuss the impact this is having on the student both academically and emotionally, and determine how to go about solving the problem. The student does not feel confident enough to discuss the mental health issues with his teacher, so the decision is made to have the school counselor speak to the teacher about the situation.

Let's break the situation down between a school counselor with knowledge of this teacher and a new school counselor. A school counselor who has a relationship with the teacher can make an appointment to see the teacher in the teacher's classroom. Each advocate's personality is different and will address the situation differently; however, with the relationship built, a brief conversation about personal life and *catching up* is appropriate and may even be necessary. Then, the school counselor should first seek to understand the teacher's beliefs and concerns about the student and the situation. It is also important to listen with empathy and treat the conversation as a counseling conversation, asking more questions than speaking. Through this approach, the school counselor will be able to see the teacher's perspective and begin to develop an advocacy plan. Solution-focused style questions (Bannink, 2006) are appropriate for the conversation and will help both the school counselor feel comfortable in the manner of questioning, and the teacher to feel comfortable in a non-judgmental, open professional conversation. Questions that elicit more information ("Tell me more about …", "What would you like to see …", "What could it look like …", "What is one thing that could be done differently?") are more likely to help the school counselor develop a picture of how to create an educational compromise with the teacher and protect the student's mental health and the goal of being mentally healthy.

Conversely, a new school counselor does not necessarily have the background relationship to have a congenial visit with the teacher; however, using solution-focused (Bannink, 2006) style questions can help the school counselor find out more about the teacher and his or her *reason* behind teaching. Learning about the stakeholder and his or her passion along with what is important to him or her helps build genuine relationships. Questions like "How long have you been teaching?" "What makes you love _____ (subject or grade level)?" Including questions that elicit the positive such as, "What have you enjoyed about this school year?", along with offering personal support with, "What can I do for you?" shows the stakeholder the conversation is not just about getting advocacy needs met.

Now that the school counselor has determined the what and who in the advocacy situation, the school counselor must determine the plan of action based on the knowledge and data gathered. During this step, the school counselor may need to consult additional resources in the school, district, or community. Sometimes, outside-the-box thinking (this can be defined as something that has never been done before) is needed. Many times, school counselors present outside-the-box ideas, and the school counselor is met with pushback. When asked to explain, a common response is "This is how we have always done it." Many times organizations have not examined their processes and how they could be perpetuating systemic inequality.

Additionally, a common response is "if it isn't broken, why fix it?" When it comes to systems impacting people, the idea of a majority of the clients being able to work within the system does not, in fact, mean that the system isn't broken, because if it doesn't work for all clients, then it is, in fact, broken. School counselor advocates can listen to the pushback and propose ideas that are both ethical and legal while breaking down these barriers. The school counselor can anticipate responses to the plan by reviewing the situation with both positive and negative outcomes, which allows the school counselor to not only see systemic change in action but also the difficulties he or she may face. Role-playing responses with colleagues helps prepare the school counselor mentally, allows him or her to have the words and phrases for an empathetic rebuttal, and allows for new attempts at solving the problem. Being able to respond to statements about fairness for others or a procedure fraught with barriers for students will allow the school counselor to rebut with solution-focused (Bannink, 2006) questions like, "What else has been tried?" "What is one thing we could do differently?" and will help the respondent join the school counselor in outside-the-box thinking reducing an attitude of uncooperativeness or defensive attitude.

To continue our example, we meet with the teacher and through the solution-focused (Bannink, 2006) style conversation, we create an acceptable plan of action with the teacher that allows the teacher to maintain instructional integrity and fairness in grading while allowing the student to attend his mental health appointments. This was achieved by discussing what the teacher felt was important for the course and the school counselor explaining (while protecting confidentiality) the issue with the student. The next step in our plan is to set a time for the school counselor, teacher, student, and his or her parents to meet and review the plan.

This plan is put into action and to evaluate its effectiveness, we make continued follow-up visits with both the student and the teacher. Follow-up is an important step in ensuring that school counselors are creating systemic change for students. If we do not continue to work through situations or provide solutions, then school counselors become part of perpetuating systemic inequalities, or simply not assisting students in their endeavors to be successful at the highest possible level.

The above is a simple example with a positive advocacy outcome. This will not always be the case and the school counselor may have to regroup and attempt a different solution to the problem. The school counselor may also need to include other stakeholders – not as *respondents* to the situation, but as *collaborators* of new ideas to solve the problem. In the celebrating or regrouping step, support for all participants is important, which includes the school counselor. Checking in on the mental health status of the actors in the situation is an additional way to continue the role of advocate by the school counselor. We may also need support from a colleague, director, mentor, or others to join in celebrating the joys of success or empathize with the struggles of systemic change for students.

Campus Level Student Advocacy

School counselors advocating for a comprehensive school counseling program will routinely review data to identify systemic barriers to success for groups of students. To continue to illustrate the advocacy steps the following is an example as applied to a situation involving campus level student advocacy.

We have reviewed the attendance and discipline data for the school and realize that the number of Black, Indigenous, and Persons of Color (BIPOC) students with discipline referrals is disproportionate to the number of discipline referrals for non-BIPOC students. This situation is different from the individual student advocacy situation as there are many more actors involved, different resources needed, and the solution will not simply be between one teacher and one student.

The first advocacy step in this situation is recognizing the advocacy disposition and personal advocacy identity of the school counselor and how this might look different based on the situation. Again, starting with, "What does this look like for me?", along with, "What barriers will I face?", and "What are the ethical and legal implications of advocacy for this situation?" are the first questions to answer.

The campus may not be challenging equity issues, may have just begun the work of equity, or may be blind to the need. An internal evaluation of where the campus is will allow us to assess what disposition will be needed for advocacy work on behalf of the BIPOC students. We need to start visualizing the who, what, when, and how of the action plan, infusing our strengths into the situation while reviewing the ethical and legal implications of the situation. Then, we will need to evaluate the relationships needed to advocate for the students. The question of "From whom do I need to elicit assistance?" is a starting question to ask internally, and then evaluate the relationship with that person or persons. Reviewing the micropolitical landscape and the micropolitical literacy (Oehrtman and Dollarhide, 2021) needed at the campus and district will help prepare us for areas of challenge in finding a solution. All of this goes into defining the advocacy problem and developing the action plan. Regardless of the challenges we are facing, using Solution-Focused (Bannink, 2006) counseling to understand the opposing viewpoints allows us to then share the viewpoint of the students and to be understood by the actors in the advocacy situation.

Next we create a multi-level action plan. In order to address the immediate needs of the students, we will create a group for these students to address their feelings about behavior and create solutions for these students while learning about inequities these students are facing. As part of the immediate action plan, we will work with the teachers on PBIS strategies for the classroom and a review of the SEL morning meetings. To address the overall understanding of other student groups on campus, we also research restorative practices professional development for the campus to implement in the following semester. We will also review this solution in the counseling advisory committee to help stakeholders understand the problem and elicit feedback and support for the solution.

In reviewing the plan with the principal, there is pushback on the idea of meetings with the teachers to review PBIS and SEL lessons along with the restorative practices and professional development for the campus. The principal is concerned that the teachers will become defensive about their classroom management strategies and not listen to the strategies suggested. Additionally, the principal is concerned about the cost of a campus-wide professional development not provided by the district and that by forcing it on all teachers implementation would not be done with fidelity. We should use good counseling skills and flexibility during these difficult conversations to elicit more information and discern what ideas the principal has to start making these changes.

Together with the principal, we decide the best course of action is to work with the students in the group setting, and when meeting with the teachers, we will meet individually with each teacher and elicit information and feedback through a conversation about the student's behavior. With the school counselor acting as an "information gatherer", seeking to understand his or her position versus someone who is attempting to correct a teacher's behavior, the teacher is more likely to listen to ideas for change in the areas of PBIS and SEL strategies. We also decide to find a few teachers who are interested in restorative practices and will help begin a grassroots effort to spread the learning across the campus. This will also fall within the principal's budget limitations. We enact the re-envisioned plan and slowly begin to see changes and have a plan of action for the future to continue to impact a group of students on campus.

In this example, the school counselor has to reinvent the action plan based on additional actors influencing decisions on the campus and for the students. By involving additional actors in the action plan, additional advocacy support is garnered for the situation. In the end, the school counselor has to regroup and work towards a solution for a situation that meets the needs of the students, but does not undermine the micropolitics of the campus (Kelchtermans and Ballet, 2002a, 2002b, Oehrtman and Dollarhide, 2021). The school counselor can celebrate the forward trajectory of equity at the campus and for these students.

Campus Program Advocacy

A common theme in the literature about advocacy (ASCA, 2019b; Haskins and Singh, 2016; Oehrtman and Dollarhide, 2021; Singh et al., 2010) is taking action to meet the needs of all students through a comprehensive school counseling program. The development of the ASCA National Model (2019b) over the past 16 years has taken the school counseling profession from a profession with a myriad of job duties to a consistent program demonstrating systemic change and student achievement due to the work of school counselors. Each campus customizes and personalizes the program based on the needs of the students at the campus to impact all students. District directors can be specifically impactful in helping school counselors create and manage programs that impact student achievement through their leadership of program management.

Counseling program advocacy is different from the other two levels of counselor advocacy as it is specific to the actions taken daily by the counselor; in other words, this is advocacy for the counselor's job duties as it relates to student achievement. By running a truly comprehensive program, school counselors can show how students are better due to the efforts of the work of the counselor and the counseling program (Carey and Dimmitt, 2012; Carrell and Hoekstra, 2014; Cholewa et al., 2015; Davis et al., 2013; Dimmitt and Wilkerson, 2012; Midgett et al., 2018; Salina et al., 2013; Wilkerson et al., 2013).

This area of advocacy can be considerably more difficult than the other areas as it can be seen as a *tug-of-war* between the school counselor advocating for a comprehensive program and an administrator advocating for how he or she wants the campus to *run*. In other words, the administrator prefers to be in control of the duties of all employees on campus to make the campus day-to-day activities run smoothly, which can at times directly interfere with a comprehensive school counseling program. The steps for advocacy are of utmost importance in this situation.

To minimize the *tug-of-war* on individual campuses, a best practice to help clarify roles is to ensure that the school counselor(s) and administrator(s) participate in the Annual Administrative Conference (ASCA, 2019b). This activity allows the school counselor to present data on the previously stated area of campus student advocacy and the plan of action. The plan of action is presented in goal format with the intention of assisting the campus in closing the achievement gap in an area of need at the campus. School counselors gather data from the campus improvement plan, and in the meeting can explain to the administrator how the comprehensive school counseling program is assisting the campus in meeting the campus wide goals, not setting arbitrary goals. This meeting also allows the school counselor(s) and administrator(s) to agree on how the school counselor will spend his or her time meeting these (and other) goals, which all goes back to student achievement. When approached in collaboration, advocating for the counseling program does not feel adversarial when benefits to student achievement are shown. The Annual Administrative Conference should be held within the first 2 months of school to help set the tone and plan for the year.

At the district level, directors can assist this activity by modeling by example. District directors can create an Annual Administrative Conference to review the plan for the counseling program across the district and present it to the director's supervisor. By reaching an agreement at the district level, central office support will *trickle down* to the campus administration and become an expectation of all school counselors in the district. Directors can also assist by reviewing the plan of action for each school counselor and campus. The director can help counselors avoid pitfalls and help them anticipate pushback and role-play how to handle the situation. Assisting in goal development and data gathering techniques will allow school counselors to have confidence in their goals and plan, and help ensure the goals are implemented throughout the school year across the district.

In addition to the Annual Administrative Conference, each campus should have a Counseling Advisory Council. This advisory council helps garner feedback from stakeholders and helps spread the goals of the campus counseling program. By including stakeholders from the campus (teachers, administrators, students, etc.), community members (parents, clergy, business leaders), and the district (central office members, school board trustee, etc.), resources can be provided from each member of the advisory council to promote a comprehensive school counseling program. Advisory council meetings should start with an explanation of a comprehensive school counseling program, campus counseling program goals, and feedback. The more stakeholders who understand what a school counselor does and the benefits of a comprehensive school counseling program, the more advocates you elicit for student achievement through the counseling program.

At the district level, directors of counseling programs can assist the development of advisory councils by helping school counselors create agendas, review the campus goals, and assist in planning meetings. By holding a district level counseling advisory council, directors can model by example and receive feedback from stakeholders on the district counseling program along with barriers to student achievement. This can also include participating on the district's School Health Advisory Council. The director can share data-driven evidence of student needs or evidence of student achievement in all areas through the work of the school counselor.

When the school district leaders or campus leaders act as barriers to student achievement through non-support of a comprehensive school counseling program, the members of the advisory council can act as advocates for the program by speaking to the leaders to help change the understanding of the role of the school counselor and what is needed to achieve and maintain a comprehensive program.

To continue a deeper understanding of the advocacy role, we will provide an example for counseling program advocacy.

An elementary school counselor returns from summer break and begins to review campus improvement plan data and sets data-driven goals for student groups on campus. In the back-to-school meetings with the administrators, he is told that he must do daily lunch duty; however, others do not. While he doesn't mind fair share duties, he had planned to hold *lunch bunch* groups to meet his student achievement goals. He continues to create the Annual Administrative Conference document and plans to meet with his administrator to review the program before school begins, hopefully solving this problem before students arrive.

In this situation, he must first ask, "What does this look like for me?", along with, "What barriers will I face?", and "What are the ethical and legal implications of advocacy for this situation?" In thinking about the pushback he may receive while holding the Annual Administrative Conference, he elicits feedback from his district director, colleagues, and mentors who help him devise alternative solutions. In this example, a smoothly running school is of utmost importance to the principal. Coming to the meeting with additional solutions shows a willingness to understand the principal's perspective and the ability to be flexible, all with the goal of both actors reaching their goals. When eliciting feedback from colleagues, he also gains a better perspective of the micropolitical landscape of the school and his micropolitical literacy improves.

The school counselor meets with the principal and together, they review the Annual Administrative Conference. The principal understands the point of view of the school counselor, but still needs someone to monitor the students in the lunchroom. Not swayed against meeting the goals for student achievement, the school counselor presents the alternative solutions he created based on feedback from his colleagues. The school counselor listens to the perspective of the principal and uses solution-focused questioning to find out more about the situation and goals of the principal. The principal and school counselor were eventually able to come to an agreement about lunch duty. When the counselor does not have *lunch bunch* groups, he will monitor the lunchroom, but will rotate with the librarian and additional aides in case of crisis situations. While it was not the original goal, the school counselor is able to meet his goals of student achievement and is a participant in the principal's goal of a smoothly functioning school. It is important for the school counselor to be part of the solution for the principal, not as someone who does not function as part of the team in the running of the school. A school counselor who is seen as separate from the campus goals and campus functionality is a school counselor who does not have the support of his or her principal, and thus there is a lack of understanding of the role of the counselor. In the advocacy steps, anticipating pushback and coming to the meeting with additional ideas allows the school counselor to evaluate the plan, regroup, and present a new action plan while in the meeting with the principal.

In the end, the school counselor can celebrate that he is going to be able to work towards his goals for student achievement with the support of the principal, and his relationship with the principal is not harmed. It will be important for the school counselor to implement his action plan with fidelity and then present his data from his goals at the end of the year. Goals without follow-up will not elicit more support from the administration; however, by showing the benefits of the *lunch bunch* groups, the principal will see the benefits to student achievement and will (most likely) be an advocate for a comprehensive school counseling program as time goes on.

Counseling Profession Advocacy

Like the advocacy level of counseling program advocacy, advocating for the counseling profession is also advocacy for the role of the school counselor. As school counselors collaborate to determine the challenges to the role of the school counselor (at all levels of governance) in the district, region, or state, action plans can be created.

The disposition of a school counselor advocating to broader levels of stakeholders requires a different knowledge of the micropolitical landscape and a different level of micropolitical literacy (Kelchtermans and Ballet, 2002a, 2002b; Oehrtman and Dollarhide, 2021). Advocacy at the regional and state levels requires knowledge of the political actors who make decisions for the area. Collaborating with professionals who understand their perspectives will allow school counselors to develop relationships with these politicians and begin to share the struggles associated with the issue at hand. Difficulties will arise when attempting to come to a common understanding of the advocacy problem and a collected idea of how to solve the problem. Creating multiple solutions to the issue will allow the school counselors to regroup when needed. There are other groups advocating for needs that will require precious resources, and the politicians may see a bigger benefit to solving a different problem. Thus this advocacy process may involve many *regroupings* before the counselors are able to celebrate movement towards the goal.

In the final example, school counselors in a large state begin to realize that many in the profession are not able to meet with students in direct student services 80 percent of the time as recommended by ASCA (2019b). Many administrators and districts believe the school counselor is part of the administrative team, and as issues arise in the running of the campus, the school counselor can step in and do whatever *duty* is needed, even if it is not in the scope of the school counselor's role (e.g., threat assessments, assigning discipline, etc.). The state organization for school counselors gathers data and works with their lobbyist to begin conversation with legislators to create a law for school counselors to be in direct contact with students 80 percent of the time. The lobbyist assists the school counselors in understanding the legislators' perspective and their goals in the upcoming session. The state organization receives support from some of the legislators and begins moving forward with proposing a bill. The bill is scheduled to be heard on the legislative floor when the organization finds out that an administrative group opposes the bill, is lobbying the legislators to vote against it, and will be speaking out at the hearing. The state organization regroups and ensures that school counselors will attend the state hearing to testify on behalf of the bill. The state group also reaches out to the administrative group to understand their opposition to the bill and suggests a compromise. Unfortunately, the administrative group does not budge. They do not want a specific campus role legislated, which would take away the freedom for administrators to have local control over their entire campus. As the school counselor explained, school counselors following their role would only enhance student achievement, and we would not be separate from the rest of the school, rather we would continue to be the *heart* of the school. Regardless of the points, the group is still opposed to the bill.

At the hearing, the opposition did state their perspective on local control, but the voice of the school counselor advocating for the mental health needs of students, the goals for student achievement and the systemic change that happens because of the work of the school counselors outweighed the idea of local control and the bill was passed.

This is a real-life example from a state's legislative session which happened recently. For this, the school counselor must first ask, "If not me, then who?" when it comes to making systemic changes for the school counseling profession. The state organization is composed of volunteer school counselors who share the goal of supporting other school counselors. It is imperative that state organizations hear the voice of the school counselor and are staffed by civic minded individuals who will join the cause and work together to impact the state of the profession and in turn impact student achievement holistically.

Mental and Behavioral Health Considerations

Schools today function as the main provider of most resources for students. When a student comes to school without food, the school provides food for the student. When a student comes to school without a coat in the wintertime, the school finds a resource to provide clothing for the student. If a student's home burns down, the school works on helping the family get back on their feet. Generally, the person who is the source of the resources for the student is the school counselor. Furthermore, not only does a school counselor help provide for basic needs of students, the school counselor is the person working with a student on behavioral skills for classroom issues, social, emotional and mental health needs on a day-to-day basis. Interventions created for students after the first appearance of personal situations require specific training embedded within a school counselor's continuing education.

In order to see the students holistically and work with them on the root of issues impacting student success, it is imperative that school counselors are able to fulfill the role of a school counselor inscribed by the ACA and ASCA (ACA, 2014; ASCA, 2022; ASCA, 2019a, ASCA, 2019b). School counselors are the only members on campus specifically trained in mental health who work with all students; therefore, school counselors must be able to work with students on mental health issues and advocate on their behalf when a mental health or behavioral situation is impairing their ability to succeed.

School counselors know that we must "Maslow before we can Bloom." In other words, we must meet the needs of students on a basic level and an emotional level before they will be able to function academically or behaviorally. Maslow posited a hierarchy of needs (Maslow, 1943) that one must achieve for self-actualization which has allowed school personnel to see how basic needs and mental health needs must come before beginning Bloom's Taxonomy of Educational Objectives (also referred to by educators as "Bloom's Taxonomy") (Bloom, 1956) in the classroom.

A review of the recent literature (Carrell and Hoekstra, 2014; Goodman-Scott, 2013; Harrington et al., 2012; Reback, 2010; Rose and Steen, 2014; Steen et al., 2014; Whiston and Quinby, 2009) provides evidence that a comprehensive school counseling program not only impacts student achievement but also impacts students in multiple other ways, including social-emotional development. Research has found that expanded school counseling services can impact student learning, behavior, and mental health. Additionally, reducing school counselor ratios has a greater impact on student achievement and behavioral outcomes than does reducing class sizes. School counselors enacting PBIS and school-wide behavior support systems impact behavior and learning outcomes while group counseling teaches students important life skills for improved behavior and mental health, all of which impacts learning positively.

As advocates, school counselors can use examples from recent research literature to build an action plan for an individual student advocacy situation or a campus student group advocacy situation. The specific activities presented in the literature can assist school counselors in creating and implementing the advocacy action plans, backed with research-driven strategies. For the counseling program advocacy and counseling profession advocacy levels, school counselors can use the review of literature to show the benefits of comprehensive school counseling programs in multiple areas of school counselors' domains and can help advocate for the school counseling profession. This recent research literature also helps us advocate for students with other educational professionals to help them understand how mental health is ultimately tied to academic achievement.

When advocating for an individual student or a campus student group, the school counselor must consider the mental health state of the student or students and how best to include the mental health considerations in the action plan. The school counselor will need to first listen empathically to the student or students to understand their perspective and confidentially ensure that mental health is being considered in the advocacy action plan. Working with other educational professionals to understand how mental health is tied to academic achievement can be difficult as each individual has his or her own understanding of mental health and its impact on daily activities and achievement. When working with other educational professionals in an advocacy setting, it is important to remember to first seek to understand their understanding of the impacts of mental health on daily activities and achievement. By starting with an understanding of the other person's perspective, the school counselor will be able to adjust the discussion to help the other actor understand the mental health implications on daily activities and achievement.

School counselors must continue to advocate for a comprehensive school counseling program, for the school counseling profession, and the school counselor's role in mental health and its ties to achievement by implementing data-driven programs which show the school counselor's role in student improvement and success in multiple ways – academically, socially, mentally, and behaviorally. The more others see how academic achievement and mental and behavioral concerns are intertwined, the more advocates school counselors will have from the campus level to the state and national level.

Ethical Considerations

Ethics and advocacy go hand-in-hand for school counselors according to both ACA (2014) and ASCA (2022) as school counselors are obligated to enact the code of ethics, which calls for individual student advocacy, campus level student advocacy, campus program advocacy, and counseling profession advocacy. "Counseling is a professional relationship that empowers diverse individuals, families, and groups to accomplish mental health, education, and career goals" (ACA, 2014: 3). Additionally, "counselors are expected to advocate to promote changes at the individual, group, institutional, and societal levels that improve the quality of life for individuals and groups and remove potential barriers" (ACA, 2014: 8).

School counselors have an obligation to provide effective counseling services and interventions in response to student needs individually and as a campus as well as collaborate with school stakeholders to close achievement gaps. School counselors are also obligated to provide a data-driven comprehensive school counseling program where the school counselor provides college and career awareness and exploration which support the student's right to choose a postsecondary path.

Section A) Responsibility to Students (ASCA, 2022), A.10. requires that school counselors take specific actions to support and advocate for underserved and at-risk populations by advocating for a school environment which is safe for all, and when it is not, school counselors "support students from all backgrounds and circumstances" (ASCA, 2022: 1). Individual student advocacy and campus level student advocacy address the ethical requirements to support all students.

The ASCA Ethical Code (2022) goes on to state that school counselors must develop relationships across all stakeholder groups and advocate for a comprehensive school counseling program and collaborate with others to help remove barriers that may impede the effectiveness of the school counseling program.

Furthermore, counseling directors have an ethical responsibility to advocate for district resources to assist school counselors in providing a comprehensive school counseling program designed to meet the needs of students from gathered and analyzed data.

Overall, as school counselors advocate for students at each advocacy level, the ethical codes for both ACA (2014) and ASCA (2022) support the school counselor in removing barriers to achievement in all areas; however, school counselors should review their ethical decision making as part of the first advocacy step (develop advocacy dispositions, Trusty and Brown, 2005) through the use of the Solutions to Ethical Problems in Schools (STEPS) Model (Stone, 2009):

1 Define the problem emotionally and intellectually
2 Apply the ASCA Ethical standards for School Counselors and the law
3 Consider the students' chronological and developmental levels
4 Consider the setting, parental rights and minors' rights

5 Apply the ethical principles of beneficence, autonomy, non-maleficence, loyalty and justice
6 Determine potential courses of action and their consequences
7 Evaluate the selected action
8 Consult
9 Implement the course of action

By combining the STEPS (Stone, 2009) model with the Advocacy Process for Professional School Counselors (Trusty and Brown, 2005), school counselors are first seeking understanding of school counselor obligations and will then understand that their advocacy efforts are supported not only by the ethical codes, but by strategic steps created to provide ethical and advocacy solutions to break down barriers to student achievement.

Cultural Complexities

Many times, school counselors are advocating for students in various minority groups, therefore considerations must be taken into account for this advocacy. First, school counselors must take time to truly reflect on their implicit biases and where they might be "blind" to systemic barriers for students. By individually spending time to analyze their true beliefs and areas of growth, school counselors can ensure equity in advocacy for all students. Sue et al. (1992) point out that "the worldview of the counselor and client is ultimately linked to the historical and current experiences of racism and oppression in the United States" (1992: 481). For this reason, school counselors must acknowledge the differences, personally address them, and seek training in this area (Sue and Sue, 1990) to be true school counselor advocates.

When working with individual students or student groups, we must first truly listen to understand – especially someone else's point of view in a group we may or may not belong to. If we are not a member of the oppressed group, it is imperative that we reflect and summarize in collaboration with the individual or group in the situation so as not to minimize or dismiss the issue. Additionally, it may be within our power as someone who is not a member of the oppressed group to act on their behalf because we have access to the actors and decision makers who can collaborate with us to make needed changes (Oehrtman and Dollarhide, 2021). Conversely, we may be within the oppressed group's identification and may be able to bridge the gap between the individual students or group and the actors and decision makers who can collaborate with us to make needed changes.

As school counselors are ethically bound to help all students, so are other stakeholders on campuses or districts/organizations; however, this does not mean that they are aware of or addressing their implicit bias. Therefore, those who have not addressed their own biases may prove challenging in the advocacy process. Additional measures and explanations may be needed to help the actor understand the situation and its implications on students and their success. During this time, rifts could arise between the school counselor and others involved in the situation. It is important to remember to continue to build and rebuild relationships during the advocacy process when needed as it will be necessary to work with the actor(s) to resolve this issue until equity is achieved. This can be disheartening to those working towards student success through advocacy efforts, but we must not give up. Students need school counselors to listen and advocate daily as we are the catalyst for systemic change and better and brighter futures for our students. We must remember the advocacy step of regrouping and continuing to build and rebuild relationships, while enacting our new action plan. We must remember that a minor change is progress and multiple minor changes will add up to a large-scale change, which results in equity for students.

Strategic Considerations

We have provided an explanation of *how to* address each level of school counselor advocacy; however, without an understanding of the political strategy needed to implement the action steps, the school counselor (especially new counselors) will face adversity when trying to break down systemic barriers for students.

At the base of any understanding of the micropolitical landscape (Oehrtman and Dollarhide, 2021) of a campus or an organization is the main tenet of "Seek first to understand, then to be understood" (Covey, 1989). As new school counselors, we do not understand the power structure of the organization and need to be reflective and inquisitive with the actors in the organization to learn more about the power structure by taking "the time to listen to the desires of the other professional(s), synthesizing and reflecting what it is they value, and then highlight how what the school counselor is championing also appeals to those values" (Oehrtman and Dollarhide, 2021: 4). Veteran school counselors have developed relationships with the actors on their campuses/within their organizations over time which has impacted (positively or negatively) their ability to advocate for students. Being an active listener to all stakeholders is imperative to build positive relationships with actors in the organization or on the campus.

The ASCA National Model (2019b) is set up, naturally, for school counselors to build relationships with those of influence on their campus or within their district all while reflecting on important data to assist in breaking down systemic barriers for students. By implementing a comprehensive school counseling program, school counselors will be able advocate for students through their work in completing a comprehensive school counseling program.

For example, we must first find out what we need to focus on for the program by reviewing the previous year's (and additional years if needed) data to create student outcome goals. Through this data review, systemic barriers can be identified and action plans created. Additionally, we may want to gather perception data to find out what our stakeholders know and believe about the school counseling program. This data, provided through surveys to students, parents, and staff members, will allow us to reflect on the school counseling program's impact and where additional time and resources may need to be spent on building strategic relationships with actors on the campus or within the district/organization. Between campus outcome data and perception data, school counselors can eventually utilize this information to assist and direct decisions for the school to positively impact student success in all areas (Oehrtman and Dollarhide, 2021).

As with any relationship, compromise is also needed. While we will review the data to make informed decisions on what our student outcome goals should be (which should generally match the campus or district goals), sometimes the goals may differ from that of the campus or district. In this case, we should assess our shared goals and proactively work towards a collaborative effort to reach these goals. This does not mean we should abandon any goal that breaks down barriers for students; however, it means that we may have to spend more time with others in seeking to be understood. This also means we may have to recognize when a level of *give and take* is needed. School counselors who are social justice advocates must first seek to understand and then be understood in certain situations as a narrow focus without and understanding of the micropolitical landscape, actors, and power structure of the campus or district/organization can lead to being ignored or the feeling of being ignored by leadership if we are not willing to compromise.

As part of the ASCA National Model (2019b), school counselors develop their student outcome goals and work with administration on a plan for the year in the Annual

Administrative Conference. Again, this activity provided through the National Model (2019b), lends itself directly to advocacy and collaboration. Through this meeting, school counselors review the plan of action for the year, review data and goals, and agree on the school counselor's role for the year. This is a perfect opportunity for seeking to understand, then to be understood (Covey, 1989) while collaborating with supervisors and building a relationship.

Additionally, school counselors are called to create an Advisory Council to collaborate with stakeholders on the school counseling program. This council provides needed feedback on the perception and understanding of the school counseling program while learning about the systemic barriers school counselors are breaking down through the student outcome goals. This addresses multiple levels of school counselor advocacy all in one ASCA National Model (2019b) activity. By sharing the needs of students, the school counselors, and the school counseling program, the opportunity for solutions to come from the advisory council abounds. Consequently, many advocacy goals can be reached through the advisory council. It is imperative that school counselors provide ending year data for the council to help make informed decisions about the future of the program and the needs at all levels: individual students, student groups, the school counseling program, and even in the school counseling profession.

Finally, school counselors must review data and outcomes from the school counseling program at the end of each school year in order to demonstrate how the school counseling program is beneficial to all students. It is imperative that the school counselor takes the time to present the end of year student outcome data with all stakeholders – this includes teachers, parents, administrators, advisory council members, and school board members. Generally, school counselors are loath to brag, but taking the time to share student successes through the school counseling program enhances our ability to advocate for students, increases our credibility (Covey, 1989) and in the end, the students are more successful – which is the ultimate goal.

Through advocating for a comprehensive school counseling program, other important data can be gathered and reviewed. For example, as we see how our efforts are impacting more students and leading to measured success, we can advocate for additional school counselors as needed based on our student-to-school counselor ratio. By having the evidentiary backing, advocating for our needs will most likely be understood by those making allocation decisions.

All of this takes time to develop. As I was told by my counseling mentor, "How do you eat an elephant? One bite at a time." New school counselors and veteran school counselors alike should first begin with a reflection on the campus or district/organization and its obvious needs. Perhaps the school counselor is at a new campus, the campus has new campus administration, the district has new administration, or the school counseling program needs revitalization. Start with one advocacy activity (especially those described by the ASCA National Model, 2019b) for the first year. Work on building relationships with the stakeholders, and be certain to share outcomes with all stakeholders. Then, expand the program with an additional advocacy activity the following year. Over time, school counselor advocates will develop a comprehensive school counseling program that breaks down systemic barriers for all students.

Conclusion

By seeking first to understand and then to be understood, we are finding a "balance between courage and consideration. Seeking to understand requires consideration; seeking to be understood takes courage" (Covey, 1989: 255). Being a school counselor advocate takes courage to break down barriers for students, but it must first be met with consideration for the micropolitical landscape and micropolitical literacy (Kelchtermans and Ballet, 2002a, 2002b; Oehrtman and Dollarhide, 2021) on the campus or in the district. School counselors can impact all students academically, socially/emotionally, and in college/career readiness through implementing a comprehensive school counseling program. By implementing a comprehensive school counseling program, school counselors are innately able to advocate for the needs of their students, their campus, the school counseling program on the campus, and even the school counseling profession. In conjunction with a comprehensive school counseling program, school counselors can become confident advocates by following the advocacy actions of: developing an advocacy disposition, developing advocacy relationships and advocacy knowledge, defining the advocacy problem, developing action plans, implementing action plans, making evaluations of the advocacy efforts, and celebrating or regrouping. Taken at each level, the comprehensive school counseling program with the advocacy activities at the individual student level, the student group level, the school counseling program level, and the school counseling profession level, school counselors have the opportunity to make impactful changes and lead all students to the highest level of success possible.

References

American Counseling Association (ACA) (2014) *ACA Code of Ethics*, Alexandria, VA: Author.
ACA (2018) *Advocacy Competencies*, Alexandria, VA: Author.
American School Counselor Association (ASCA) (2019a) *ASCA School Counselor Professional Standards & Competencies*, Alexandria, VA: Author.
ASCA (2019b) *The ASCA National Model: A Framework for School Counseling Programs* (4th edn), Alexandria, VA: Author.
ASCA (2022) *ASCA Ethical Standards for School Counselors*, Alexandria, VA: Author.
Ball, S.J. (1987) *The Micro-Politics of the School: Towards a Theory of School Organization*, London: Routledge.
Bannink, F. (2006) *1001 Solution-Focused Questions*, New York, NY: W.W. Norton & Company.
Bloom, B. (1956) *Taxonomy of Educational Objectives*, London: Longman.
Carey, J. and Dimmitt, C. (2012) "School counseling and student outcomes: summary of six statewide studies", *Professional School Counseling*, 16(2): 146–153.
Carrell, S.E. and Hoekstra, M. (2014) "Are school counselors an effective educational input?", *Economic Letters*, 125: 66–69.
Cholewa, B., Burkhardt, C., and Hull, M. (2015) "Are school counseling impacting underrepresented students' thinking about postsecondary education? A nationally representative study", *Professional School Counseling*, 19(1): 144–154.
Colbert, R.D., Perusse, R., Bouknight, T., and Ballard, D. (2006) "Developing school counselor advocacy competencies within a leadership role in education reform", in G.R. Waltz and J.C. Bleuer (eds), *VISTAS Counselor Professional and Career Development, 2006*, Alexandria, VA: American Counseling Association, pp. 149–152.
Council for Accreditation of Counseling and Related Educational Programs (CACREP) (2024) *2024 CACREP Standards*, Alexandria, VA: Author.
Covey, S. (1989) *The 7 Habits of Highly Effective People*, New York: Simon & Schuster.
Davis, P., Davis, M.P., & Mobley, J.A. (2013) "The school counselor's role in addressing the Advanced Placement equity and excellence gap for African American students", *Professional School Counseling*, 17(1): 32–39.

Dimmitt, C. and Wilkerson, B. (2012) "Comprehensive school counseling in Rhode Island: access to services and student outcomes", *Professional School Counseling*, 16(2): 125–135.

Goodman-Scott, E. (2013) "Maximizing school counselors' efforts by implementing school-wide positive behavioral interventions and supports: a case study from the field", *Professional School Counseling*, 17(1): 111–119.

Harrington, C.J., Martin, I., and Hoffman, D. (2012) "A state-wide evaluation of the outcomes of the implementation of ASCA National Model school counseling programs in rural and suburban Nebraska high schools", *Professional School Counseling*, 16(2): 100–107.

Haskins, N.H. and Singh, A.A. (2016) "Advocacy competency of school counselors: an exploratory factor analysis", *Professional School Counseling*, 20(1): 149–158.

Kelchtermans, G. and Ballet, K. (2002a) "Micropolitical literacy: reconstructing a neglected dimension in teacher development", *International Journal of Educational Research*, 37(8): 755–767.

Kelchtermans, G. and Ballet, K. (2002b) "The micropolitics of teacher induction. A narrative-biographical study on teacher socialization", *Teacher and Teacher Education*, 18(1): 105–120.

Lewis, J.A., Arnold, M.S., House, R., and Toporek, R.L. (2003) "ACA Advocacy Competencies", Reprinted in R.L. Toporek, J. Lewis, and H.C. Crethar, "Promoting systemic change through the Advocacy Competencies", in the Special Section on Advocacy Competencies, *Journal of Counseling and Development*, 87: 260–268.

Maslow, A. (1943) "A theory of human motivation", *Psychological Review*, 50(4): 370–396.

McMahon, H.G., Mason, E.C.M., Daluga-Guenther, N., and Ruiz, A. (2014) "An ecological model of professional school counseling", *Journal of Counseling and Development*, 92: 459–471.

Midgett, A., Doumas, D., and Johnson, A. (2018) "Establishing school counselors as leaders in bullying curriculum delivery: evaluation of a brief, schoolwide bystander intervention", *Professional School Counseling*, 21(1): 1–9.

Oehrtman, J.P. and Dollarhide, C.T. (2021) "Advocacy without adversity: developing an understanding of micropolitical theory to promote a comprehensive school counseling program", *Professional School Counseling*, 25(1): 1–9.

Osborne, J.L., Collison, B.B., House, R.M., Gray, L.A., Firth, J., and LeCompte, M.L. (1998) "Developing a social advocacy model for counselor education", *Counselor Education and Supervision*, 37(3): 190–202.

Ratts, M.J., DeKruyf, L., and Chen-Hayes, S.F. (2007) "The ACA Advocacy Competencies: a social justice framework for professional school counselors", *Professional School Counseling*, 11(2): 90–97.

Rebak, R. (2010) "Schools' mental health services and young children's emotions, behavior, and learning", *Journal of Policy Analysis and Management*, 29(4): 698–727.

Rose, J. and Steen, S. (2014) "The Achieving Success Everyday group counseling model: fostering resiliency in middle school students", *Professional School Counseling*, 18(1): 28–37.

Salina, C., Girtz, S., Eppinga, J., Martinez, D., Blumer Kilian, D., Lozano, E., Martinez, A., Crowe, D., De La Barrera, M., Mendez, M., and Shines, T. (2013) "All hands on deck: a comprehensive, results-driven counseling model", *Professional School Counseling*, 17(1): 63–75.

Singh, A.A., Urbano, A., Haston, M., and McMahan, E. (2010) "School counselors' strategies for social justice change: a grounded theory of what works in the real world", *Professional School Counseling*, 13(3): 135–145.

Steen, S. Henfield, M.S., and Booker, B. (2014) "The Achieving Success Everyday group counseling model: implications for professional school counselors", *Journal of Specialists in Group Work*, 39(1): 29–46.

Stone, C. (2009) *School Counseling Principles: Ethics and Law* (2nd edn), Alexandria, VA: American School Counselor Association.

Sue, D.W. and Sue, D. (1990) *Counseling the Culturally Different: Theory and Practice*, New York: Wiley.

Sue, D.W., Arredondo, P., and McDavis, R.J. (1992) "Multicultural counseling competencies and standards: a call to the profession", *Journal of Counseling and Development*, 70(4): 477–486.

Trusty, J. and Brown, D. (2005) "Advocacy competencies for professional school counselors", *Professional School Counseling*, 8: 259–265.

Whiston, S.C. and Quinby, R.F. (2009) "Review of school counseling outcome research", *Psychology in the Schools*, 46(3): 267–272.

Wilkerson, K., Perusse, R., and Hughes, A. (2013) "Comprehensive school counseling programs and student achievement outcomes: a comparative analysis of RAMP versus non-RAMP schools", *Professional School Counseling*, 16(3): 172–184.

Index

Page numbers in italics refer to figures. Page numbers in bold refer to tables.

4 Essential Roles of Leadership Model 199, 203

AACD *see* American Association for Counseling and Development (AACD)
AAQEP *see* Association for Advancing Quality Education Programs (AAQEP)
AAS *see* American Association of Suicidology (AAS)
ACA *see* American Counseling Association (ACA)
academic performance, significance of 86
accountability measures, for positive mental health 254–257; cultural complexities in 257–259; ethical considerations in 257; leadership in practice and 261; leadership standards and values and 259–260; strategic considerations in 261–262
ACES *see* Adverse Childhood Experiences (ACES)
ADDRESSING model 11–12
ADL *see* average daily allowance (ADL)
administrator leadership model, with counselor attributes 7, *8*
administrators/supervisors 63–64, 131, 266
Adobe Connect 75
Advance Student Phase 105, *106*
Adverse Childhood Experiences (ACES) 217
Advisory Council 317, 324
advocacy 21, 34, 37, 40–42, 66, 67–68; ACA on 303, 305–309; activeness in professional associations 296; ASCA on 288–291, 296–298, 303, 309–311; CACREP and 309; calendar **294–295**; caseloads and 298; certification and licensure and 298; counselor 149; cultural complexities and 297–298; cultural complexities and 322; directors and 159; disposition 304, 314, 318; dispositions, knowledge, and skills and 292–293; ethical considerations and 296–297, 321–322; history of 290–291; knowledge 304; leadership in practice and 311–319; legislation knowledge about impacting counselors 294–295; legislators role in 291; mental and behavioral health considerations and 296, 319–321; political considerations and politicking and bureaucracy and 298–299; professional associations and 287–288; rules and regulations and 299; school counseling services history and implementation barriers and 288–290; skills 304; standards and competencies and 291–292; strategic considerations and 323–324; talking to legislators and 293–294
Amatea, E. S. 296
American Academy of Pediatrics 207
American Association for Counseling and Development (AACD) 288
American Association of State Licensing Boards 77
American Association of Suicidology (AAS) 215
American Cancer Society 225
American Counseling Association (ACA) 27, 41, 76, 77, 290–291, 321; on advocacy 303, 305–309; Advocacy Competencies 305; Advocacy Resources Website 294; Center for Policy, Practice, and Research 288; Code of Ethics 22, 23, 24, 42, 116, 269, 303; Governing Council 290; Multicultural Counseling Competencies 290; recommendations of 35
American Personnel and Guidance Association (APGA) 288
American School Counseling Association 5, 237
American School Counselor Association (ASCA) 34, 35, 60, 76, 157, 172, 199–201, 247, 274, 275, 319; on advocacy 288–291, 296–298, 303, 309–311; Aspects 35; Code of Ethics 12, 321; on equitable access to school counseling programs 249; Ethical Standards for School Counselors 8, 24–25, 26, 27, 37, 38, 39–40, 51, 52, 62–66,

86, 130, 132, 137, 148, 150, 191, 202, 218–219, 257, 266, 289, 296, 297, 302; guidance curriculum in 18; on mental health needs 80; Model Framework 40; National Model 17–18, 32, 41, 48, 64, 65, 135, 196–197, 208, 232–233, 234, 255, 258, 259, 288, 290, 304, 305, 316, 323–324; National Model Framework for School Counseling Programs 154; on professional development 121; Professional Standards and Competencies 281, 283; sample interview questions by 174; School Counseling Leadership Specialist Training 73; School Counselor Professional Standards & Competencies 64, 260, 291, 309–310; Standards for School Counselor Preparation Programs 86; standards for training programs 73–74; on time metric usage 136

American School Counselor Ethical Standards 22

Annual Administrative Conference 316–318, 323–324

APGA *see* American Personnel and Guidance Association (APGA)

application 89

application fee 89

appropriate activities, for school counselors **236**

ASCA *see* American School Counselor Association (ASCA)

Aspiring School Counselor Academy 132

aspiring school counselor institutes 141

assessments, performing 147

asset map *see* resource map

Association for Advancing Quality Education Programs (AAQEP) 86

At-Risk Protocol for Early Warning Signs in Students 218, 227–228

attunement, definition of 134

authentic experiences, providing 140–141

autonomy xxv, 6, 27, 93, 145, 254

average daily allowance (ADL) 265

award-winning school counseling programs, criteria for **122–126**

Baggerly, J. 290
Baker, S. B. 155
Bardhoshi, G. 296
Beale, A. V. 164, 237, 238
Beer, C. 290
Beginning Student Phase 104, 105
Beland, A. 36
beneficence 28
Bernard, J. 154
Bernier, C. 49
best practices, significance of 208
best school counseling 183–184; becoming unstruck and 187–188; cultural complexities and 191; ethical considerations and 190–191; heart-centered leadership and 184; mental and behavioral health considerations and 190; modeling meetings and 188–189; professional learning and 186–187; recognition and praise and 189–190; right people hiring and 185–186; servant leadership and 184–185; strategic considerations and 191–192; tough conversations and 187

bias: avoiding 220; types of 177–178, 179
Blackboard Collaborate 75
Blackboard Safe Assign program 98
Blake, M. K. 33
Borto, J. 48, 49
Bost, W. A. 164
boundaried leaders 148
brain development, and fear and stress 48
Brown, B. 61, 127
Brown, D. 34, 52, 292, 303, 304, 311
Bryan, J. 283
budgets, grants, donations, and financial audits: college and university funding and 265–266; cultural complexities and 270–270; ethical considerations and 269–270; mental and behavioral health considerations and 268–269; in public school 267–268; public school funding and 264–265; public school leadership program values and standards and 266–267; school district budgets and 270–272; in universities and colleges 268; university budgets and 272–273; university counselor education leadership program values and standards and 267

bullying, avoiding 220

burnout: significance of xxv, 23, 34, 62, 127, 140, 162, 289, 293; stress and 135, 137, 290

CAC *see* Counseling Advisory Committee (CAC)
CACREP *see* Council for Accreditation of Counseling and Related Educational Programs (CACREP)
CAEP *see* Council for the Accreditation of Educator Preparation (CAEP)
C.A.F.E. supervision model 156
campus: leaders on 181; student advocacy on 302, 310; principals 271; program advocacy 316–318
Campus Improvement Plan (CIP) 262
Carey, J. 34
Carrell, S. A. 289
Carrell, S. E. 289
CDC *see* Center for Disease Control (CDC)
Center for Disease Control (CDC) 17, 203
certified school counselor (CSC) 25

CEUs *see* continuing education units (CEUs)
Chandler, J. W. 33
change, importance of 195
character, as critical C **50**
character and disposition 145–147; diversity, equity, and inclusion for 150–151; ethical considerations in 150; leadership in practice for 148–149; leadership program values and standards for 148; mental and behavioral health considerations for 149–150; strategic considerations in 151
child abuse, avoiding 220
childhood trauma 217–218
Children's Protective Services (CPS) 218
CIP *see* Campus Improvement Plan (CIP)
circle facilitators 47–48
CIS *see* Communities in Schools (CIS)
Claus, R. E. 37
Clayton, I. 49, 50
client advocacy/empowerment 305
Close, G. 163
cohort model 188
collaboration 29, 36, 37, 40, 161, 186, 210, 312, 314, 318
collaborative leaders 170
collective action 17, 29, 57, 61, 158, 305
college and university funding 265–266, 268
College Board 176
Columbine High School Shooting (1999) 206, 207
Communities in Schools (CIS) 211
community: collaboration 305; partnerships, need for 181
compassion 7, 31, 163
compassion fatigue 62, 162, 190, 289
competence, as critical C **50**
comprehensive data-informed program 202, 257
comprehensive school counseling program (CSCP); cultural complexities in 165; ethical considerations in 164; importance of 17–18, 21, 63, 153–156, 191, 230, 238, 249, 288; leadership in practice and 159–162; leadership program values and 156–159; mental and behavioral health considerations and 162–164; strategic considerations in 166
comprehensive school counseling services, pyramid for *240*
Comprehensive School Mental Health System (CSMHS) 13, 14
confidence, as critical C **50**
confidentiality 62, 109
connections, as critical C **50**
Constantine, M.G. 139
consultant competency 24
consultations, on ethical obligations 22
continuing education units (CEUs) 77
continuous quality improvement (CQI) cycle 127

contracted social workers, for home support 210–211
contributions, as critical C **50**
control, as critical C **50**
coping, as critical C **50**
Cottone, R. R. 37
Cotton-Royal, L. 34
Council for Accreditation of Counseling and Related Educational Programs (CACREP) 41, 65, 71, 77, 139, 270; advocacy and 309; in mission and core values 72; on professional practice 276–279; Standards 72–73, 267
Council for the Accreditation of Educator Preparation (CAEP) 86
counseling: profession advocacy 302, 310, 318–319; program advocacy 302, 317–318
Counseling Advisory Committee (CAC) 176
counselor–principal relationships 161
Counselors Reinforcing Excellence for Students in Texas (CREST); award 156, 189; chart 127
course development counseling 70–71; certification and licensure requirements for 76–77; continuing education units (CEUs) for 77; course design types and 75–76; course syllabus as training and instructional strategy and 74–75; cultural complexities in 82; ethical considerations in 81–82; leadership as added component to school counselor curriculum and 74; leadership values and standards and 71–74; mental health consciousness and 78–80; mental health needs preparation for students and 80–81; portability and standardized certification and licensure for 77; program handbook as leadership tool and 74; strategic considerations in 83
Course Hero website 98
courtesy interviews, avoiding 178–179
Covey, S. 196, 303
COVID-19 pandemic 36, 40–41
Cox, E. 238
CPS *see* Children's Protective Services (CPS)
CQI *see* continuous quality improvement (CQI) cycle
CREST *see* Counselors Reinforcing Excellence for Students in Texas (CREST)
crisis: experience of 16; response 16–17, 239
crisis planning 205–206; childhood trauma and 217–218; cultural complexities and 220–222; ethical considerations and 218–220; evidence of need for 206; intervention measures 212–215; joint impact of stressors on families and schools and 206–207; leadership and best practices and 208; local school district

values and 207–208; postvention measures 215–217; prevention measures 210–212; school counselor leadership as advocates for campus programs and 209–210; school counselor leadership in practice and 208; strategic considerations and 222–224; Texas Model as codified in statute and 209
critical Cs 49–51, **50**
critical self-analysis, for student development 107–108
Crowe, A. 140
CSC *see* certified school counselor (CSC)
CSCP *see* comprehensive school counseling program (CSCP)
CSMHS *see* Comprehensive School Mental Health System (CSMHS)
Culminating-Format Sanctions **97**, 115
culture/cultural: awareness 165, 283; competence 64, 139, 165, 221–222; representation 283; responsiveness 283
curiosity, sense of 29

Dare to Lead (Brown) 61, 127
data: bias 249–250; -centered approach, to comprehensive school counseling programs 160; in decision-making 248
data collection and analysis 230–232; ASCA National Model and 232–233; comprehensive school counseling program commonalities and variances and 234–235; counselor role in program implementation and 238; cultural complexities in 249–250; data analysis and accountability services and 243; data points re-examination and 248; data usage and 242; ethical considerations in 249; guidance curriculum classroom instruction and 238–239; historic and developmental data and **231**; individual student planning and 239; inhibitive behavioral factors and 238; new program focus and 243; non-counseling duties and 236–237; perception data and 244; process data and 243–244; responsive services and 239; role change of counselor and 242–243; roles and responsibilities and 235; strategic considerations in 250; student outcome data and 244, 246–247; student to counselor ratios and 236; system support and 239–240; Texas Model for Comprehensive School Counseling Programs and 233–234; tool development and 242
Davis, R. J. 71
Davis, T. E. 28

decision-making model, ethical 27–29; foundational principles of 27–28; steps in 28–29
DEI *see* diversity, equity, and inclusion-related (DEI) interview questions
Developing and Managing Your School Counselor Program (Gysbers and Henderson) 202
Dickinson ISD 170
Dimmitt, C. 34
DIP *see* District Improvement Plan (DIP)
directors/administrators/supervisors 63–64, 191; importance of 157; role of 157–159
direct student services 289
discrimination, avoiding 220
dispositional performance, significance of 86
distributed leadership xxv
district administration 39
District Improvement Plan (DIP) 261, 271
district leaders, in counseling 268
district leadership team (DLT) 261
diversity, equity, and inclusion-related (DEI) interview questions: guidelines of quality responses and 179–180; samples of 180
DLT *see* district leadership team (DLT)
documentation of therapy services 90
doer, counselor as 162
Dollarhide, C. T. 32, 161
Dorn, E. 42
Doughterty, A. M. 283
dropout prevention program 235
Duckworth, A. 140
due process 91, 101

Education for Homeless Children and Youth Program 255
Education Trust 165
Education Week Research Center 40
Ellerson, N. 265
ELL *see* English Language Learners (ELL)
emotional intelligence 147
empathy: leaders with 148; listening with 303, 311, 313, 320; sense of 29, 31, 48, 50, 52, 146, 151, 162
empowerment, of students 166–167
English Language Learners (ELL) 220–221
Enhancing the Principal School Counselor Relationship toolkit 176
environmental scan *see* resource map
equality 91, 101, 151
equifinality 91, 101
equitable access, right to 249, 310
equity 11, 12, 26, 52, 64, 191, 276, 322; accountability measures and 257, 258–260; character and disposition and 148, 150–151; directors and 160, 165; interview and placement and 174,

179–180; positive mental health promotion and 40–42; school counselors-in-training and 91, 101, 108
Erford, B. T. 32
ESSA *see* Every Student Succeeds Act (ESSA)
ethics: decision making and 269; leadership and 267, 269
Every Student Succeeds Act (ESSA) 254–255
explicit bias 178

face-to face sessions 76, 77
Family Educational Rights and Privacy Act (FERPA, 1974) 39
fear and stress, and brain development 48
FERPA *see* Family Educational Rights and Privacy Act (FERPA, 1974)
fidelity 28
flipped course 76
focus groups 279
Forester-Miller, H. 28
formal agreement, establishing 281
Foxx, S. P. 289
Franklin Covey 198–199
Freeman, S. J. 39
Freudenberger, H.J. 162
Fullan, M. 167
Furlonger, B. 71

gatekeeping as protection for public, for student development 108
Gehris, J. S. 54
Gerler, E. R. 155
Ginsburg, K. 49, 50
golden circle concept 197–198
Goodman-Scott, E. 135, 157
Goodwin, B. 166
GPA *see* grade point average (GPA)
grade point average (GPA) 89
graduate record exam (GRE) 89
grant: funding, for mental health services 19; writing 272–273
Greenleaf, A. T. 258, 260
Greenleaf, R. 184
GRE *see* graduate record exam (GRE)
grit, importance of 140
guest speakers and consultants 271
guidance curriculum 239
Gysbers, N. 202, 231, 237, 238, 290

harassment, avoiding 220
harm, avoiding 23, 219
Harris, P.N. 61
Harvard Business Review 179
Harvard Graduate School of Education 36
Hatch, T. 62, 160
hate incidents, avoiding 220
Hayes, R.L. 155, 158

Health and Human Services 273
Health Insurance Portability and Accountability Act (HIPAA, 1996) 39
heart-ccentered leadership 184
Heath, C. 283
Heath, D. 283
Heath and Heath Decision Making Model 280–281
Hecht-Weber, K. 156
Henderson, P. 202, 237, 238, 290
Henry, L. 283
HIPAA *see* Health Insurance Portability and Accountability Act (HIPAA, 1996)
hope, sense of 48
Hopkins, B. 48
House, R.M. 155, 158
human capital 164
humor, sense of 147
Hurricane Katrina 214
Hurt, J. 135
hybrid course, as course design 76

idealized influence 6
impairment signs, tackling 23
implicit bias 178
inappropriate activities, for school counselors **237**
inclusion/inclusivity 12, 40, 41, 64, 72, 132, 150–151, 179–180, 191, 203, 270
indirect student services 289
individualized consideration 6, 17
informed consent, in formal consultation 24
inspirational motivation 6
institutional bias 177–178
intellectual simulation 6
intern site supervisors 131, 137
Interpersonal Theory of Suicide, The 216
interview and placement 169; counselors and administrators divide dispelling and 170–171; counselors as leaders during 171–172; diversity, equity, and inclusion-related (DEI) 179–181; ethical considerations and 177–179; interview process model and 172–176; mental and behavioral health considerations and 177; pitfalls to avoid during 178–179; strategic considerations and 181
interview process 90, 172; applicant presentation during 175; best candidate selection during 176; diverse representation for interview committee during 175–176; evaluation criteria determination during 174; interview questions creation during 174–175; job description review during 172–173; qualifications relating to job during 173; scoring rubric creation during 175
intrapersonal development, significance of 86

issue advocacy 291

Jablow, M. 49, 50
Jackson-Cherry, L. R. 32
Janson, C. 161
Jean-Pierre, J. 47
Jones, L. M. 166
justice 28

Kaltura Virtual Classroom 75
Kehoe, M. 47
Kneale, M. G. M. 261
Kneale, M. M. 41
Kokoro Development Model: access stage of 102, 104; chisel stage of 104–105; mold stage of 104; refine stage of 105–106; stage review for *103*
Kokoroian student 101

Lapan, R. 231
Lapan, R. T. 296
Lawson, G. 162, 163
Layperson Helper Phase 102
leadership, in mental health services: as change agent, in school counselor role 17–18; partnerships and supports for 18–19; in practice 19–21; procedures and protocols for 19
leadership, significance of 41
Leadership Traits Every Counselor Should Have (Wake Forest) 146
Leadership WISE Academy 68
lead meetings 188
LEA *see* local education agency (LEA)
legal and advocate representation, for student development 109
legislative advocacy 291
Lemberger, M. 296
Lenertz, M. 47
letter: of interest 89; of practical response 90; of recommendation 89
licensed professional counselor (LPC) 25
listening, importance of 146
Literary-Format Sanctions **96–97**, 115
LMHA *see* local mental health authority (LMHA)
local education agency (LEA) 26, 255
local mental health authority (LMHA) 132
logistical leaders 148
Long, B. 41
Lopez-Perry, C. 159
Lowery, K. 33
LPC *see* licensed professional counselor (LPC)
Luke, M. 154

Madanagopal, D. 102

mainstream and unacculturated, for student development 109–110
major plagiarism, definition of 99
marginalized populations 66
Maslow's Hierarchy of Human Needs 214–215, 320
McCormick, K. 140
McKinney Vento Homeless Assistance Act 255
McLothlin, J. M. 164
Meier, G. 225
Mellin, E. A. 37
Menchine, M. 224
mental health in schools 16–17; comprehensive school counseling program and 21; cultural complexities in 29; ethical considerations in 22–29; leadership values and program standards and 17–21; school counselors and 21–22; stakeholders in 21; strategic considerations in 29
Mental Health Technology Transfer Centers (MHTTCs) 132, 205
mentoring: importance of 127; of school counselors 139–140
MHTTCs *see* Mental Health Technology Transfer Centers (MHTTCs)
micro-learning 187
micropolitics 304, 312
Migrant Education Program 255
Militello, M. 161
Miller, L.G. 164
Milsom, A. 140
minor plagiarism, definition of 99
monthly time analysis and data check-in *246*
Morin, A. 217
MSJCC *see* Multicultural and Social Justice Counseling Competencies (MSJCC)
MTSS *see* Multi-tiered System of Support
Mulhern, C. 165
Mullen, P. R. 140
Multicultural and Social Justice Counseling Competencies (MSJCC) 258
multiculturalism/multicultural 11, 12, 270; competence 64, 139; proficiency 82
Multi-tiered System of Support (MTSS) 13, 132, 156, 261, 262

NACAC *see* National Association for College Admission Counseling (NACAC)
Nagoski, A. 162
Nagoski, E. 162
NAMI *see* National Alliance for Mental Illness (NAMI)
National Alliance for Mental Illness (NAMI) 205
National Association for College Admission Counseling (NACAC) 289, 291, 294
National Association of Social Workers 210

National Board for Professional Teaching Standards (NBPT) 5, 47, 259
National Center for Educational Statistics (NCES) 257–258
National Center for School Mental Health (NCSMH) 13–14
National Education Association (NEA) 205
National Institute of Mental Health (NIMH) 17
National School Board Association (NSBA) 4
National Scientific Council on the Developing Child 48
natural disasters intervention 214
NBPT see National Board for Professional Teaching Standards (NBPT)
NCES see National Center for Educational Statistics (NCES)
NCSMH see National Center for School Mental Health (NCSMH)
NEA see National Education Association (NEA)
NEA's School Crisis Guide 205
needs assessment 13, 279
Neff, K. 163
Nelson, J. 146, 153
Nelson, J. A. 16, 46, 59, 169, 230, 254, 274
Nguyen, H.O. 52
Nichter, M. 234
NIMH see National Institute of Mental Health (NIMH)
Nisenbaum, M. 210
non-counseling duties 289–290
non-discrimination 22
nonmaleficence 28
Normore, A. 52
Northouse, P. 6, 17
NSBA see National School Board Association (NSBA)

Obama, B. 254
Ockerman, M. S. 156, 159
OCR see Office for Civil Rights (OCR)
Office for Civil Rights (OCR) 257, 262
Online Counselor Education (Sheperis and Davis) 71
online courses 75–76
organizational awareness 159
Osborn, D. 290

parent involvement programs 211
Parris-Drummond, S. 47
Parson, F. 290
Participatory-Format Sanctions **95**, 115
partnerships, significance of 18–19
partnerships, streamlining mental health services 274; cultural complexities and 283; energy (human capital) in 275; ethical considerations and 282; funding and 275; impact of **276**; leadership in practice and 279–281; leadership program values and standards and 276–279; mental and behavioral health considerations and 281–282; strategic considerations and 283; time factor in 274; timelines and *284*
peers, positive relationship with 49
PEIMS see Public Education Information Management System (PEIMS)
personal crisis intervention 212
Pew 265
physiological needs, importance of 214
Piaget, J. 102
Pianta, R. 159
plagiarism: issues, and academic dishonesty 98–99; major and minor, definitions of 99
portability 77
positive mental health, promotion of 31–32; behavioral health considerations and 36–37; crisis management and 32; cultural complexities in 39–41; ethical considerations in 37–39; leadership program values and standards and 33–34; in practice 34–36; school counselor role and 32; strategic considerations in 41–42
Post-Traumatic Stress Disorder (PTSD) 217, 218
postvention measures 215–216; documented suicide risk factors and 216; suicide survivors and those with other risks 216–217
potential, coaching of 199–200
preferred provider model 4
Preferred Provider School Counseling Model (NSBA) 4–5
Prevention and Intervention Programs for Children and Youth 255
prevention services 239
principal–school counselor agreement 299
process data: examples of 244; importance of 243–244; tracking tool 242
professional development 121–127; cultural complexities and 132; definition of 121; ethical considerations for 130–131; leadership program values and standards for 127–129; mental and behavioral health considerations for 129–130; strategic considerations for 132
professional distance 39
professional learning 186–187
professional school counselor advocate 302–303
professional school counselors (PSCs) 47–51, 239
Profile of a Leader (Dickinson ISD) 170
programs, managing 195; counselors building program capacity and 198–200; counselors as advocating and 197–198; cultural complexities and 202–203; ethical considerations and 201–202; leadership importance and 197; leadership program

values and standards and 196–197; mental and behavioral health considerations and 200–201; strategic considerations and 203; success measurement and 200
program values 4
PSCs *see* professional school counselors (PSCs)
PTSD *see* Post-Traumatic Stress Disorder (PTSD)
Publication Manual of the American Psychological Association 74
Public Education Information Management System (PEIMS) 261
publicity 28
public school: funding 264–265, 267–268; leadership program, values and standards 266–267
punitive approach 88

quality 91
Quinby, R. 231

Rabindran, R. 102
RAMP *see* Recognized ASCA Model Program (RAMP)
Rath, A. 36
Ratts, M.J. 258, 260
Recognized ASCA Model Program (RAMP) **122**, 156
Reese, D. M. 41
referral and incident form 113
relationship building, importance of 146–147
remediation plan 99–100; format 99–100; sanctioning and 111; for school counselors in training within clinical settings 115–118; university counseling department 119
remediation services 239
resiliency 48–50, 54; critical Cs and 49–51; in youth 49
resource map 13
Responding to Critical Cases in School Counseling (Nelson and Wines) 214
responsibility: to parents and guardians 25, 26, 67; to school 10–11, 67; to self 25, 26, 130; to students 10, 12–13, 25–26, 27, 51–52
responsive services and data collection 239
restorative practices (RP) 46; behavioral health needs addressal of 48; cultural complexities and 52; ethical considerations and 51–52; history and origin of 46–47; leadership in practice and 47–48; leadership program values and standards and 47; mental health addressal of 48–51; strategic considerations and 52–53; tiers of support by 52
right people, hiring 185–186
risk assessments, use of 10

role-playing responses 314
Rønnestad, M. 102, 104, 105, 106
Roseberry, D. B. 47
RP *see* restorative practices (RP)
Rubenstein, B. 36
Rutledge 41

Safe Assign Score 98–99
safety needs, importance of 214–215
Saginak, K. A. 32
same-race counselor 165
SAMHSA *see* Substance Abuse and Mental Health Services Administration (SAMHSA)
Savitz-Romer, M. 32, 33, 34, 36
School Counselor (magazine) 35
School Counselor: Counseling, The Program Tracking and Data Analysis Report 242, 244
School Counselor and Student Mental Health, The (ASCA) 200
School Counselors as Practitioners (Wines and Nelson) 75
school district budgets 270–272
school–parent community partnership 279
School Survey on Crime and Safety (SSOCS) 222, 223
scoring rubric, creation of 175
self-awareness 23, 48, 149, 159, 177, 258
self-care 293; deficits possibility in 149; practices, need for 137; significance of 177
self-compassion 23, 163
self-discipline 48
self-preservation 62
self-reflection 48, 64, 136
self-worth 163
Sensi Mindset 101
servant leadership 7, 17, 61, 184–185
Sheasley, C. 36
Sheperis, C. 71
Shields, C. M. 260
Shneidman, E. 215
SHPPS 222
Simon, C. 41
Sinek, S. 197, 198
Sink, C. A. 260
site supervision and mentorship 134–135; ethical considerations in 137–139; leadership in practice for 136; leadership program values and standards and 135; mental and behavioral health considerations in 136–137; standards for 139; strategic considerations in 139–141
Skovholt, T. 102, 104, 105, 106
Smith, L. 47
social and emotional learning (SEL) 156
social justice advocacy 297–298

social/political advocacy 305
solution-focused counseling 313, 314, 315
Solutions to Ethical Problems in Schools (STEPS) 37, 321–322, 148; solutions to *38*; steps in 37
SSAE *see* Student Support and Academic Enrichment (SSAE) Grants
SSOCS *see* School Survey on Crime and Safety (SSOCS)
Staff Wellness Program 211–212
stakeholders, identification of 280
Start With Why (Sinek) 197–198
STEPS *see* Solutions to Ethical Problems in Schools (STEPS)
Stone, C. 37
strategic counselor 147
strategy, execution of 199
Strear, M. M. 59
student advocacy: campus level 302, 314–316; individual 302, 311–314
student development 85–86; academic and dispositional progress as mental health indicators for 107; in admission process 89–90; case identification for 110; case study and sanctions for 100–101; character and personality modification challenges for 110; committee meetings for 110; committee member role in 87; confidentiality and disclosure for 109; critical self-analysis for 107–108; dual roles and relationships for 108–109; educational shift from external processes to internal exploration and modification for 107; faculty roles in data collection, tracking, and review process for 111; gatekeeping as protection for public and 108; leadership program values and standards and 86–87; legal and advocate representation for 109; mainstream and unacculturated for 109–110; mental health training for 106–107; novice, experienced, and senior professional phase of 106; plagiarism issues and academic dishonesty and 98–99; policy and stated guidelines violations and 108; policy manual template for 113–114; process role for 87–88; remediation plan and sanctioning 111; remediation plan format for 99–100; review stages for 101–106; sanction letter for 114–115; student appeals and grievance for 111; student hearing for 110; student referral and incident reporting and 90–93; student sanctions and 93–98; student services referral for 111; supporting 9, 24, 25, 51–52, 66
student hearing protocol 120
student infraction and incident types 92–93, **92**
Student Support and Academic Enrichment (SSAE) Grants 255
student-to-counselor ratios 289, 298
Substance Abuse and Mental Health Services Administration (SAMHSA) 5, 268, 272–273
success criteria, creation of 280
Sue, D. W. 322
suicide 4, 16, 17
Sun, Y. 231
Superintendent's Student Leadership Conference 206
supportive adult, notion of 49
SWOT analysis 280
systemic change 40–42, 64, 260, 261, 311, 316, 319; advocacy and 290, 304; through ASCA National model 65; effective 298
systems advocacy 305
system support 239–240

TBRI *see* Trust Based Relational Intervention (TBRI)
TCA *see* Texas Counseling Association (TCA)
TEA *see* Texas Education Agency (TEA)
TEC *see* Texas Education Code (TEC)
Technological-Format Sanctions **96**, 115
TEMPSC *see* Texas Evaluation Model for Professional School Counselors (TEMPSC)
Terry, M. 52
Texas Counseling Association (TCA) 233–234
Texas Education Agency (TEA) 130, 155–156, 209, 233, 236, 264, 288
Texas Education Code (TEC) 154, 164, 170, 209, 233–234, 236
Texas Evaluation Model for Professional School Counselors (TEMPSC) 155, 234
Texas Legislative Session, Senate Bill 179 170
Texas Model for Comprehensive School Counseling Programs 18, 154, 155, 157, 170, 208, 209, 231, 233–234, 288, 289
Texas School Counselor Association 156
Theory of Cognitive Development 106; Concrete Operational Stage 105; Formal Operational Stage 105; Preoperational Stage 104; Sensorimotor Stage 102
thought exchanges 279
time on task *245*
TL *see* Transformative Leadership (TL)
tough conversations 187
transactional leadership 7
transformational leaders xxv, 17; data support by 60; guidance of 63; individualized support of 60; as servant leaders 61; shared vision of 60; support and communication of 61; systemic training of 60

transformational leadership 6–7; conceptual framework for 59–60; cultural complexities of 64–68; ethical considerations of 62–64; mental and behavioral health considerations of 62; in practice 62; program values and standards 61; strategic considerations of 68; types of 6
Transformative Leadership (TL) 260
trauma informed space, facilitating 49
trust: building of 47, 155, 161; significance of 149, 199
Trust Based Relational Intervention (TBRI) 184
Trusty, J. 34, 292, 303, 304, 311
tunnel vision 177
Turn-It-In program 98
typical school-based counseling 4

unconscious bias 179
unexpected large crisis intervention 213–214
United States Department of Health and Human Services 3
universality 28
university: budgets 272–273; counselor education leadership program, values and standards 267
University of Washington Human Resources website 177
US Department of Education 35–36, 268, 272

Venart, N. 162, 163
Veterans Administration 217–218
video submission 90
virtual/distance school counseling, guidelines on 38
vision, creation of 199

Wake Forest 146
Walsh, M. 283
Warner School of Education 36
wellness days 62
Whiston, S. 231
Whitson, S. C. 289
whole-child approach, to student wellness and learning 154
WizIQ 75
work groups 189
wraparound approach 128
Written-Format Sanctions **94**, 114

year-at-a-glance program 199
Young, A. 5, 41, 162, 171–172
Youth Behavior Risk Survey Assessment 4
Youth Services Program 210
Youth Services Specialists (YSS) 211
YSS *see* Youth Services Specialists (YSS)
Yukl, G. 269

Zacarian, D. 166